NEW DIRECTIONS
IN BIBLICAL THEOLOGY

# SUPPLEMENTS TO
# NOVUM TESTAMENTUM

EDITORIAL BOARD

C.K. Barrett, Durham - P. Borgen, Trondheim
J.K. Elliott, Leeds - H.J. de Jonge, Leiden
M.J.J. Menken, Heerlen - J. Smit Sibinga, Amsterdam

*Executive Editors*

A.J. Malherbe, New Haven
D.P. Moessner, Atlanta

VOLUME LXXVI

Poul Nepper-Christensen

Jacob Jervell   Kirsten Nielsen   Judith M. Lieu

Mogens Müller   Hans Hübner   Aage Pilgaard

A.J.M. Wedderburn   Otfried Hofius   Helge Kjær Nielsen

Karl Kertelge   Hans Weder   Johannes Nissen

Sigfred Pedersen

# NEW DIRECTIONS IN BIBLICAL THEOLOGY

*Papers of the Aarhus Conference, 16-19 September 1992*

EDITED BY

SIGFRED PEDERSEN

E.J. BRILL
LEIDEN · NEW YORK · KÖLN
1994

The paper in this book meets the guidelines for permanence and durability of the Committee on Production Guidelines for Book Longevity of the Council on Library Resources

**Library of Congress Cataloging-in-Publication Data**

New directions in biblical theology : papers of the Aarhus Conference, 16-19 September 1992 / edited by Sigfred Pedersen.
    p.  cm. — (Supplements to Novum Testamentum, ISSN 0167-9732 ; v. 76)
  Includes bibliographical references and indexes.
  ISBN 9004101209 (alk. paper)
  1. Bible—Theology—Congresses.    I. Pedersen, Sigfred, 1932–
II. Series.
BS543.N48    1994
230—dc20                                            94-28789
                                                                                    CIP

**Die Deutsche Bibliothek - CIP-Einheitsaufnahme**

**New directions in biblical theology** : papers of the Aarhus conference, 16 - 19 September 1992 / ed. by Sigfred Pedersen. – Leiden ; New York ; Köln : Brill, 1994
  (Supplements to Novum testamentum; Vol. 76)
  ISBN 90–04–10120–9
NE: Pedersen, Sigfred [Hrsg.]; Novum testamentum / Supplements

ISSN  0167-9732
ISBN  90 04 10120 9

© *Copyright 1994 by E.J. Brill, Leiden, The Netherlands*

*All rights reserved. No part of this publication may be reproduced, translated, stored in a retrieval system, or transmitted in any form or by any means, electronic, mechanical, photocopying, recording or otherwise, without prior written permission from the publisher.*

*Authorization to photocopy items for internal or personal use is granted by E.J. Brill provided that the appropriate fees are paid directly to The Copyright Clearance Center, 222 Rosewood Drive, Suite 910 Danvers MA 01923, USA. Fees are subject to change.*

PRINTED IN THE NETHERLANDS

Dedicated to

Poul Nepper-Christensen

TABLE OF CONTENTS

PREFACE . . . . . . . . . . . . . . . . . . . . . . . . . . .   ix
ABBREVIATIONS . . . . . . . . . . . . . . . . . . . . . .   xi
INTRODUCTION . . . . . . . . . . . . . . . . . . . . . .   1

1. *Hans Hübner*: Offenbarungen und Offenbarung. Philosophische und theologische Erwägungen zum Verhältnis von Altem und Neuem Testament . . . .   10

2. *A. J. M. Wedderburn*: Paul and "Biblical Theology"   24

3. *Karl Kertelge*: Biblische Theologie im Römerbrief .   47

4. *Mogens Müller*: Salvation-History in the Gospel of Matthew. An Example of Biblical Theology. . . . .   58

5. *Jacob Jervell*: The Lucan Interpretation of Jesus as Biblical Theology. . . . . . . . . . . . . . . . . . . . .   77

6. *Judith M. Lieu*: Biblical Theology and the Johannine Literature . . . . . . . . . . . . . . . . . . . . . . . .   93

7. *Otfried Hofius*: Biblische Theologie im Lichte des Hebräerbriefes . . . . . . . . . . . . . . . . . . . . .   108

8. *Kirsten Nielsen*: Old Testament Metaphors in the New Testament . . . . . . . . . . . . . . . . .   126

9. *Hans Weder*: Die Weisheit in menschlicher Gestalt. Weisheitstheologie im Johannesprolog als Paradigma einer Biblischen Theologie . . . . . . . . . . . . .   143

10. *Aage Pilgaard*: Apokalyptik als bibeltheologisches Thema. Dargestellt an Dan 9 und Mk 13 . . . . .   180

11. *Helge Kjær Nielsen*: Diakonia als bibeltheologisches
    Thema .......................... 201

12. *Johannes Nissen*: Jesus, the People of God, and the Poor.
    The Social Embodiment of Biblical Faith ..... 220

13. *Sigfred Pedersen*: The Concept of God as Theme of
    Biblical Theology ................... 243

INDEX OF AUTHORS ..................... 267
INDEX OF PASSAGES .................... 272

PREFACE

The theological faculty of the University of Aarhus was able to celebrate its 50th anniversary in 1992. Whereas the theological faculty in Copenhagen can trace its beginnings back to the founding of the University of Copenhagen in 1479, and hence is among the older group of theological faculties round about Europe, the theological faculty in Aarhus, which is the only other theological faculty in Denmark, is among the younger.

Having spent some quiet but, in professional terms, solid developmental years, the Aarhus faculty has undergone an extraordinary evolution in recent decades, so that today it includes research and teaching in all of the theological disciplines, in addition to which are to be counted independently affiliated institutes for the study of religions and for semitic philology. In the year of the university's jubilee the official number of immatriculated students was 1259.

Under the inspiration of the earlier dean, Viggo Mortensen, the jubilee was observed with a broad spectrum of scientific conferences / symposia at both the national and the international levels. The Institute for New Testament arranged two conferences. One of these was a joint nordic affair which took place in close association with the very day of the jubilee, February 4, 1992; it was under the direction of Søren Giversen (Århus), in collaboration with Peder Borgen (Trondheim), Lars Hartman (Uppsala), and Karl-Gustav Sandelin (Åbo). Here scholars concerned themselves with the relationship of the New Testament to its hellenistic environment.

The other New Testament jubilee conference was held on a more broad European level in the autumn semester, more precisely in the days 16th-20th of September, under the direction of Helge Kjær Nielsen. The topic was the attempts made in recent years to construct a biblical theology, understood as the relationship between the two principal parts of the Christian canon, on the terms of contemporary scholarship.

The organisers of the conference were pleased that a number of prominent New Testament scholars accepted the invitation to present their views at the conference; likewise, a significant number of both foreign and Danish participants took part in the discussions.

We should like on this occasion to express our thanks to E.J. Brill in Leiden, as represented by editor Hans van der Meij for his willingness to publish the lectures presented at the conference in article form. It is especially satisfactory that the publication of this study has been able to appear in the series *Supplements to Novum Testamentum*, from whose editorial board we had the pleasure of a visit from David P. Moessner,

Atlanta, in November of 1993. It is our hope that this publication will be able to stimulate the discussion surrounding a central Biblical topic both as an historical and a presently relevant topic.

This work is dedicated to Poul Nepper-Christensen, who tried in the course of his long association with our institute to keep us focused on the tradition leading back to the founder of the institute, Johannes Munck, so that the scientific study of the New Testament texts in Århus may always be part of the endeavour of an international community.

Finally, we should like to thank those members of the staff who were specifically engaged in preparing this manuscript for printing: Tut Amnéus and Gerd Margrethe Askøe. We should also like to thank the Faculty Board for its financial assistance.

New Year 1994,

Helge Kjær Nielsen                                         Sigfred Pedersen

# ABBREVIATIONS

| | |
|---|---|
| AASF | Annales academiae scientiarum Fennicae |
| AB | The Anchor Bible |
| AJut.TS | Acta Jutlandica. Theology Series |
| AnBib | Analecta Biblica |
| ANRW | Aufstieg und Niedergang der römischen Welt |
| ASNU | Acta Seminarii Neotestamentici Upsaliensis |
| ASTI | Annual of the Swedish Theological Institute |
| ATD | Das Alte Testament Deutsch |
| AThANT | Abhandlungen zur Theologie des Alten und Neuen Testaments |
| AThD | Acta Theologica Danica |
| BBB | Bonner Biblische Beiträge |
| BETL | Bibliotheca ephemeridum theologicarum lovaniensium |
| BEvTh | Beiträge zur evangelischen Theologie |
| BFChTh | Beiträge zur Förderung christlicher Theologie |
| BGBE | Beiträge zur Geschichte der biblischen Exegese |
| BHTh | Beiträge zur historischen Theologie |
| BibB | Biblische Beiträge |
| BiKi | Bibel und Kirche |
| Bill | H.L. Strack-P. Billerbeck |
| BThSt | Bibel-theologische Studien |
| BKAT | Biblischer Kommentar: Altes Testament |
| BU | Biblische Untersuchungen |
| BWANT | Beiträge zur Wissenschaft vom Alten und Neuen Testament |
| BZ | Biblische Zeitschrift |
| BZNW | Beihefte zur Zeitschrift für die neutestamentliche Wissenschaft |
| CBQ | Catholic Biblical Quarterly |
| ConB.NTS | Coniectanea Biblica. New Testament Series |
| DKNT | Dansk kommentar til Det nye Testamente |
| DTT | Dansk teologisk Tidsskrift |
| EdF | Erträge der Forschung |
| EHS.T | Europäische Hochschulschriften. Theologie |
| EKK | Evangelisch-Katholischer Kommentar |
| EPRO | Études préliminaires aux religions orientales l'empire romain |
| EvQ | Evangelical Quarterly |

| | |
|---|---|
| EvTh | Evangelische Theologie |
| EWNT | Exegetisches Wörterbuch zum Neuen Testament |
| FB | Forschung zur Bibel |
| FOTL | The Forms of the Old Testament Literature |
| FRLANT | Forschungen zur Religion und Literatur des Alten und Neuen Testaments |
| FrThSt | Frankfurter theologische Studien |
| GAT | Grundrisse zum Alten Testament |
| GNT | Grundrisse zum Neuen Testament |
| GSL | Geistliche Schriftlesung |
| HBT | Horizons in Biblical Theology |
| HNT | Handbuch zum Neuen Testament |
| HThK | Herders theologischer Kommentar zum Neuen Testament |
| HThR | The Harvard Theological Review |
| HUCA | Hebrew Union College Annual |
| ICC | International Critical Commentary |
| Int | Interpretation |
| IOSOT | The International Organization for the Study of the Old Testament |
| JBL | Journal of Biblical Literature |
| JBTh | Jahrbuch für Biblische Theologie |
| JeC | Judaica et Christiana |
| JSNT.SS | Journal for the Study of the New Testament. Supplement Series |
| JSOT | Journal for the Study of the Old Testament |
| JThS | The Journal of Theological Studies |
| KD | Kirchliche Dogmatik, K.Barth |
| KeK | Kritisch-exegetischer Kommentar über das Neue Testament |
| KT | Kaiser Traktate |
| KuD | Kerygma und Dogma |
| LB | Linguistica Biblica |
| LD | Lectio divina |
| LW | Lutheran World |
| MThSt | Marburger theologische Studien |
| NLC | New London Commentary |
| NovTest.S | Novum Testamentum. Supplements |
| NTA | Neutestamentliche Abhandlungen |
| NTOA | Novum Testamentum et Orbis Antiquus |
| NTS | New Testament Studies |
| OTL | Old Testament Library |
| ÖTK | Ökumenischer Taschenbuchkommentar zum Neuen Testament |
| PFES | Publications of the Finnish Exegetical Society |
| QD | Quaestiones disputatae |

| | |
|---|---|
| REJ | Revue des études juives |
| SBL.DS | Society of Biblical Literature. Dissertation Series |
| SBS | Stuttgarter Bibelstudien |
| SBT | Studies in Biblical Theology |
| SEÅ | Svensk Exegetisk Årsbok |
| SJLA | Studies in Judaism in Late Antiquity |
| SJOT | Scandinavian Journal for the Old Testament |
| SN | Studia neotestamentica |
| SNTA | Studiorum Novi Testamenti auxilia |
| SNTS.MS | Society for New Testament Studies. Monograph Series |
| SPIB | Scripta pontificii instituti biblici |
| StJ | Studia Judaica |
| StNT | Studien zum Neuen Testament |
| StTh | Studia Theologica |
| StUNT | Studien zur Umwelt des Neuen Testaments |
| TDNT | Theological Dictionary of the New Testament |
| ThB | Theologische Bücherei |
| ThD | Theology digest |
| ThExH | Theologische Existenz heute |
| ThLZ | Theologische Literaturzeitung |
| ThQ | Theologische Quartalschrift |
| ThSt (B) | Theologische Studien, ed. K.Barth |
| ThWAT | Theologisches Wörterbuch zum Alten Testament |
| ThWNT | Theologisches Wörterbuch zum Neuen Testament |
| TRE | Theologische Realenzyklopädie |
| TThZ | Trierer theologische Zeitschrift |
| TU | Texte und Untersuchungen zur Geschichte der altchristlichen Literatur |
| TynBul | Tyndale Bulletin |
| VF | Verkündigung und Forschung |
| WBC | Word Biblical Commentary |
| WdF | Wege der Forschung |
| VigChr | Vigiliae Christianae |
| WMANT | Wissenschaftliche Monographien zum Alten und Neuen Testament |
| WUNT | Wissenschaftliche Untersuchungen zum Neuen Testament |
| ZAW | Zeitschrift für die alttestamentliche Wissenschaft |
| ZBK | Zürcher Bibelkommentare |
| ZNW | Zeitschrift für die neutestamentliche Wissenschaft |
| ZThK | Zeitschrift für Theologie und Kirche |

# INTRODUCTION

The theme of "Biblical theology", as defined by the reciprocal relationship between the collections of Old and New Testament writings, has been associated in the modern context with the development of historical-critical research.

During the century of Reformation, as an expression of the inheritance from the rhetorical traditions of antiquity the relationship between the two main parts of the Christian canon was understood on the basis of the concept of biological organism, which is to say that the Old and New Testaments were regarded as an intimately-functioning unity which had room for both similarities and differences as well as both a periphery and a centre. This applies, for example, to the important two-volume study by the Croatian Matthias Flacius, *Clavis scripturae sacrae*, which appeared in Basel in 1567. Being a unity of both the Old and New Testaments, the Scriptures are, on Flacius' view, identifiable in their totality with the word of God and hence with the reliable and sufficient sources for the truth concerning God and his salvation of man.[1]

The Dutch jurist and philologist, Hugo Grotius, had also pointed in his influential work, *De veritate religionis christianae* (Paris, 1627), to the correspondence between the Old Testament prophecies and their fulfilment in the New Testament (taken together with the miracle narratives) as a confirmation of the truth of Christianity. However, in the course of the further development of his understanding of Scripture, Grotius ended by concluding that the inspired prophets and apostles had composed their works entirely on their own human authority, and were accordingly constrained by their respective specific historical backgrounds (*Annotata ad Vetus Testamentum*, Paris 1644). The consequence of this analysis was necessarily a significant weakening of the christological relationship linking the Old to the New Testament. Thus Isaiah 7 speaks only of the *prophet's* son, just as Isaiah 53 is not to be under-

---

[1] The central sections of this hermeneutically pioneering work have been published: Matthias Flacius Illyricus, *De ratione cognoscendi sacras literas*. Lateinisch-deutsch Parallelausgabe... von L. Geldsetzer, Düsseldorf, 1968. Note further R. Keller, *Der Schlüssel zur Schrift. Die Lehre vom Wort Gottes bei Matthias Flacius Illyricus*, Hannover, 1984.

stood, according to Grotius, as referring to Jesus as the Christ, but to the prophet Jeremiah.²

Although the German orientalist and deist Hermann Samuel Reimarus had presented in 1731 (under nascent criticism from some quarters) a lecture MSS (Hamburg) containing an argument to support the orthodox view of Scripture,³ he nevertheless worked in the immediately succeeding years and until shortly before his death in 1768, under English influence (A. Collins),⁴ on a strongly critical account of the Biblical narrative as related in the OT to accentuate its distance from the Jesus tradition of the Gospels.⁵ Prominent historians of scholarship would prefer to claim that modern Biblical scholarship had already made its main theoretical breakthrough in the previous century, when the French Catholic Richard Simon had begun to interpret the Old and New Testaments as two mutually independent collections of tradition.⁶

At the beginning of the present century, the eminent church historian, Adolf von Harnack, writing, above all, as a Protestant theologian, was forced to deny to the Old Testament any significant relevance in connexion with Christianity.⁷ According to Rudolf Bultmann, the most influential New Testament scholar in this century, from a theological point of view Jesus' proclamation belongs within the framework of early Judaism as the religio-historical presupposition of Christianity, exactly as does the Old Testament.⁸

---

² See further details in E. Hirsch, *Geschichte der neuern evangelischen Theologie*, Vol. 1, Gütersloh, 1949, 225-36; H. Graf Reventlow, "Humanistic Exegesis: The Famous Hugo Grotius", in B. Uffenheimer and H. Graf Reventlow (eds.), *Creative Biblical Exegesis* (SJOT.SS 59), Sheffield 1988, 175-191.
³ Hermann Samuel Reimarus, *Vindicatio dictorum Veteris Testamenti in Novo allegatorum 1731*, ed. P. Stemmer, Göttingen, 1983. See further P. Stemmer, *Weissagung und Kritik*, Göttingen, 1983, esp. 59-91; 147-171 ("Die Einheit von Altem und Neuem Testament ist aufgehoben", 67).
⁴ See H. Graf Reventlow, "Das Arsenal der Bibelkritik des Reimarus", in: *Hermann Samuel Reimarus (1694-1768) ein 'bekannter Unbekannter' der Auferklärung in Hamburg*, Göttingen, 1973, 44-65.
⁵ H.S. Reimarus, *Apologie oder Schutzschrift für die vernünftigen Verehrer Gottes*, I-II (ed. G. Alexander), Frankfurt am Main 1972. Note further H. Graf Reventlow, "Die Auffassung vom Alten Testament bei Hermann Samuel Reimarus und Gotthold Ephraim Lessing", *EvTh* 25 (1965), 429-448.
⁶ H.-J. Kraus, *Geschichte der historisch-kritischen Erforschung des Alten Testaments*, 3. Aufl., Neukirchen-Vluyn 1982, 65-70; H. Graf Reventlow, "Richard Simon und seine Bedeutung für die kritische Erforschung der Bibel", in: G. Schwaiger (ed.), *Historische Kritik in der Theologie*, Göttingen 1980, 11-36.
⁷ A. von Harnack summarises his historical survey as follows: "...Aus geschichtskritischen und religiösen Grunden folgte von hier aus mit zwingender Notwendigkeit und Evidenz...dass jede Art der Gleichstellung des AT mit dem NT und jede Autorität desselben im Christentum unstatthaft ist...Marcion hat Recht bekommen, wenn auch teilweise mit anderer Begründung" (*Marcion: Das Evangelium vom fremden Gott*, 2. Aufl., Leipzig, 1924, 222).
⁸ For a differentiated evaluation, see P.-G. Müller, "Altes Testament, Israel und das Judentum in der Theologie Rudolf Bultmanns", in P.-G. Müller and W. Stenger (eds.), *Kontinuität und Einheit* (= FS F. Mussner), Freiburg-Basel-Wien, 1981, 439-472; H. Hübner, "Rudolf Bultmann und das Alte Testament", *KuD* 30 (1984), 250-272.

The ever-sharpening precision of the essential distinction between Jewish and Christian has, in recent years, been included among the reasons behind the Christian deprecation of Jewish faith and conduct of life which culminated in the systematic attempt in this century to exterminate the Jews and Judaism from Europe.

There are thus several pressing reasons for seeking to develop a "Biblical theology" that answers to the requirements of modern Biblical research.

As suggested, the question as to the relationship between Judaism and Christianity since the Western European Holocaust is urgent, but also extremely delicate.[9] Some seek to develop a "Biblical theology" in conjunction with their insistence on a cohesive understanding of salvation which has been dominant throughout long and central periods of the history of the Christian church, with its centre in the interpretation of the death of Jesus as a vicariously atoning death.[10] We have also seen occasional attempts to develop a "Biblical theology" as a theology of creation, with all the perspectives for a contemporary dialogue with other views of life that might be implicit in such an approach.[11] Finally, there is also reason to examine the possibilities contained in the study of "Biblical theology" for progress for NT scholarship in general.[12]

In the introductory article in the present work, *Hans Hübner* moves in the direction of an elementary delimitation of what is implied by the Biblical concept of revelation. The Biblical axiom for the encounter between God and man is that the transcendental God speaks or reveals

---

[9] See, among others, P. von der Osten-Sacken, "Der Wille zur Erneuerung des christlich-jüdischen Verhältnisses in seiner Bedeutung für biblische Exegese und Theologie", *JBTh* 6 (1991), 243-67 (with a clarification of the need to include the rabbinical tradition as an independent interpretation of the common Bible as part of any Biblical theology).

[10] The many-sided attempts of the leading figure of the "new" Tübingen-school, P. Stuhlmacher, to develop a "Biblical theology" whose centre is soteriology has recently received its most intense expression in his *Biblische Theologie des Neuen Testaments*, Bd. 1, Göttingen, 1992 (definition: "Die Biblische Theologie des (Alten und) Neuen Testaments wird konstituiert durch das kerygmatische Zeugnis von dem einen Gott, der die Welt geschaffen, Israel zu seinem Eigentumsvolk erwählt und in der Sendung Jesu als Christus für das Heil von Juden und Heiden genug getan hat", 38).

[11] U. Luck, *Welterfahrung und Glaube als Grundproblem biblischer Theologie* (ThExH 191), München, 1976 ("Die verbindende Einheit der biblischen Überlieferung Alten und Neuen Testaments ist die Auseinandersetzung mit der spezifischen Erfahrung, die der Mensch als Mensch in der Welt macht", 15). In addition to this, H. Klein has suggested the following theme for Biblical theology: "Leben - neues Leben" ("Leben - neues Leben - Möglichkeiten und Grenzen einer gesamtbiblischen Theologie des Alten und Neuen Testaments", in: O. Merk (ed.), *Schriftauslegung als theologische Aufklärung*, Gütersloh, 1984, 76-93.

[12] M. Weinrich notes that, "Die unüberschaubare Fülle exegetischer Literatur kann nicht darüber hinwegtäuschen, dass die entscheidenden Grundlagenprobleme der Exegese bisher kaum eine befriedigende Lösung gefunden haben" ("Grenzen der Erinnerung. Historischer Kritik und Dogmatik im Horizont Biblischer Theologie", in: H.G. Geyer et al. (eds.), *Wenn nicht jetzt, wann dann?* (= FS H.-J. Kraus), Neukirchen-Vluyn, 1983, 328).

himself, while it is the immanent man who hears or sees this God (Gen 12.1-3; John 1.14; 14.9). The reflection as to the distance between God and man which is provoked by this leads to a profound awareness of sin, and religious experience receives God's forgiveness of sin as its soteriological content (Isa 6.5-7; 1 Cor 9.1; Rom 3.25).

In other words, "revelation" means "to be open"; and it is reciprocal openness which, from the Biblical point of view, constitutes the relationship between God and man. "Nur verstandene Offenbarung ist Offenbarung Gottes als Offensein Gottes für den Menschen und Offensein des Menschen für den offenbarenden bzw. sich offenbarenden Gott". Revelation is namely a variety of personal address as "ein den Menschen betreffendes Geschehen". At the same time, what is decisive is that man's "encounter" with the God who makes men righteous has as its personal, present content ($\dot{\eta}$ δόξα τοῦ θεοῦ) the restoration of the broken fellowship. Or, to use a theological rewriting of Gal 2.20, "Christus als Gottes Doxa ist Gottes ständige Epiphanie für unser Dasein".

This repeated Pauline use of one of the most frequently-used Biblical expressions for the presence of the transcendent God in the immanent world of man accentuates the question as to both the tradition-historical and theological nature of Paul's christological interpretation of the Biblical tradition. *A.J.M. Wedderburn* straightforwardly acknowledges that, as a designation for a theology that attempts constructively to include both Biblical traditions in its thought, "Biblical theology" is synonymous with a strongly selective and extremely controversial use of both of them. He accordingly sees the exegetical-theological task to consist in delineating, through the analysis of selected texts, the contours of a contemporary faith in God which seeks to be, if not identical with, then at least to some extent related to the belief in God in both Israel and the early church.

The element of continuity in both traditions is namely not the content of God's respective promises, but rather the *faith* in them, which is man's reaction — with Abraham as the Biblical-theological paradigm, interpreted on the basis of the experience of the resurrection in the early church (Rom 4). In this continuity of faith there is a continuity of the understanding of God as the one who intervenes in the same fashion, present, past, and future. Thus the concept of "Biblical theology" signifies a confession of faith that the God who manifested himself in Jesus Christ was the same one who manifested himself in the Old Testament.

*Karl Kertelge* develops this line of thought further by emphasizing that, for Paul, "Biblical theology" is not some sort of appendix, as is often the case in modern Biblical scholarship, but rather a deeply integrated part of his theological reflection. Being himself an apostolically legitimated interpreter, Paul attempts the bold leap to transfer the Biblical text, which was originally proclaimed to the chosen people of Israel, to all of those who believe in the God who awakened Christ from the dead (Rom 4.23-25; 15.4).

Thus in a contemporary context, "Biblical theology" undertaken from a Pauline viewpoint possesses ecumenical relevance.

The depth of the christological interpretation of the common Biblical tradition leads *Mogens Müller* to the assertion that the Jewish Bible simply became a different book in the interpretation of it practised in the Christian congregations. However, this fact did not prevent the Biblical writings from, as "prehistory", serving as the hermeneutical "code" which endows the interpreting Jesus-narrative with its salvation-historical character. This schismatic type of hermeneutical integration is evidenced in the Gospel of Matthew by, among other things, the reflective quotations in which the fulfilments interpret the predictions via a reductive emptying of them of their original statements.

According to Müller, the salvation-historical background for this is the idea of the new covenant (attached to Jesus' last meal as the covenant-constituting anticipation of his ensuing death) to replace the old covenant as "the hidden substructure". This means that in his periodic account of the jesuanic salvation history, Matthew expresses at one and the same time both revelation-theological continuity with the ethnic Israel, to which the historical activity of Jesus was primarily directed, and ecclesiological identity with the Israel of faith, the christological foundation of which embraces all the peoples of the earth (Matt 10; 28.20).

How does the evangelist Luke understands his Biblical-theological task, and how does he solve it? To *Jacob Jervell*, it is essential that we discern the special character of the Lucan position vis à vis the early church. Luke works as an independent historian with the duty to interpret the Biblical writings in all their still-actual validity, which is to say that his "sources" emerge in their entirety as nothing less than the word of God. Luke is thus a fundamentalist! For him, it is the Scriptures that confirm the jesuanic history, and not the other way about. In other words, for Luke history writing is synonymous with scriptural theology.

This notion has implicit theological consequences. Luke is dealing with the one and only people of God, the people of the history of Israel, and that history includes the history of the church. To Luke it is therefore nonsense that the history of Israel has come to an end. If this were the case, there would be no church. Naturally, this fact is of decisive importance for Lucan christology. Luke employs the supra-ordinate

Palestinian-Jewish title ὁ χριστός primarily in order to designate Jesus' scripturally-attested relation to Israel as the people of God. He is the anointed one of Israel, the son of Israel — as a positive and still-relevant present.

The contrast with the Gospel of John is accordingly palpable. On the view of *Judith M. Lieu*, we do not in this connexion have to do with an actual soteriological conception in a Biblical-theological sense here, not in the prologue, nor even in John 4.22. "Indeed to speak of Salvation History in John is to mislead for the past has no content, of growth or even of preparation, except Jesus". The author then analyses the "wave effect", that is, the integration of scriptural exegesis into the tradition history of Johannine literature and its impact on that literature in the cases of two widely ramified traditions of "Biblical theology": the "hardening" statement in Isa 6.9-10 and the Cain tradition in Gen 4.

The dualistically-influenced use of these traditions, as signalled by, for example, John 8.44, raises some questions as to the legitimacy and expediency of a "Biblical theology" based on John: how could a "Biblical theology" conducted on this basis avoid an insurmountable barrier to a dialogue with Judaism?

The nature of the integration between the Old and the New Testaments is perhaps most pointedly expressed in the Letter to the Hebrews. *Otfried Hofius* demonstrates how the author indicates already in the exordium of the letter that we have to do with anything but two revelations of equal worth pertaining to one and the same God. As the pre-existent son, Jesus is in an entirely unique sense the equal of God, and hence is not only the one who mediates God's revelation, as the prophets did; rather, he is himself the word of God addressed to man: "found worthy to deserve a much greater glory" (ἡ δόξα, Heb 3.3). In consequence of this, the revelation of the Son serves to display the revelation to the fathers in all its temporariness and inadequacy (10.1).

In other words, the tension between continuity and discontinuity within the Biblical-theological view of Scripture had reached its breaking point already towards the end of the first Christian century. The christological interpretation of Ps 2.7-8; 45.7-8 and 110.1,4 serves to delineate a Son-figure who is equal to God, which is quite foreign to the original contents of these texts (cf. M. Müller). The same applies to the soteriological statements in the Letter to the Hebrews with respect to the Biblical conceptions of atonement as associated with the levitical priesthood, with their centre in the high-priestly functions attaching to the Great Day of Atonement (Ps 110.4; Jer 31.31-34; Ps 40.7-9).

It may be possible for "Biblical theology" to be a critical theology, but on the premises of historical-critical scholarship rather than those of the Letter to the Hebrews.

In what might be termed the second main section of the present study the discussion of the supra-ordinate theme of "Biblical theology" has been attached to the analysis of a number of pervasive basic themes.

*Kirsten Nielsen* treats an issue that is quite new in this connexion, namely the fact — of great importance in conjunction with "Biblical theology" — that the "reuse" of a given tradition is invariably synonymous with the "reinterpretation" of it. As is illustrated by several of the preceding treatments, the quotation of a concrete Biblical statement, even in a formally virtually identical form, by no means rules out its receiving a new content in its new historical context (cf. O. Hofius; J.M. Lieu). This intertextual fact applies generally, but is accentuated in connexion with metaphors, the interpretation of which is to an even higher degree dependent on context.

How comprehensively is the hermeneutically determining context to be understood? Does the interpretation of prophetic texts raise special issues — such as the prophetic interpretation of the Old Testament by the New Testament authors? Is it possible for us on the basis of our postmodern conceptions to speak in any sense of a responsible exegesis with respect to intertextuality? The discussion of this is centred around two pairs of metaphors which are central for a "Biblical theology": shepherd-lamb (Rev 7.14,17) and father-son (Matt 4.1-11).

*Hans Weder* warns against imposing too narrow a Biblical-theological frame of reference, one which might exclude modern experience of the world. Weder's warning is grounded in the theology of creation through a Biblical-theological analysis of the prologue to the Gospel of John. Here the Christian congregation's fundamental experience of the fact that grace and truth, as expressions of God's glory ($\dot{\eta}$ δόξα τοῦ θεοῦ) are associated with the incarnate Logos, rather than with the Law of Moses (Joh 1.14,16), is explained with the aid of the Israelite-Jewish Wisdom tradition. As the pre-existent Logos, Jesus Christ is related through this by his nature to God (1.1-2), by mediation to the Creation (1.3-5), and universally to all mankind (1.9-12).

This does not mean that "the light" and hence "the life" are associated with Christ alone. But it does mean that there is no light and thus no life that has not been touched and so determined by Christ. What is positive in a Biblical-theological sense about the Wisdom tradition is that it makes sure of the universality of the revelation in Christ by attaching it to the Creation as an experience of God. Thus there is no knowledge of the world that is not theologically relevant. Nor is there any theological insight which does not have meaning for the world. Or, to use Hans Weder's own words, "Die Interpretationsleistung der Weisheit ist es...die exklusive Wahrheit des Christus auszulegen in die Weiten der Welterfahrung, sie preiszugeben an die Evidenz der Erfahrung".

There is yet another circle of theological tradition which possesses what is to some extent its own peculiar literary form which, to a limited, but significant extent, is common to both OT and NT; this is, of course, apocalyptic. *Aage Pilgaard* notes that, the nucleus of apocalyptic is the way God's will is interpreted as manifested in history in its last epoch, when the present world order is led to its close and the evil, unfortunate time is definitively replaced by a good and blessed time.

In Dan 9 we find this kind of interpretation of time in the form of a new-interpretative continuation of the tradition about the 70 weeks of years in the prophet Jeremiah. There is already present in Daniel a tension in terms of contents between tradition and new interpretation: an open-ended statement by God has become a shadowy word of God, one which requires a special, heavenly interpretation. In other words, the divine word is an expression of both transcendence and immanence; and it is here that the apocalyptic tradition enters as a hermeneutical key (Dan 9.24-27). The danielic interpretation of history is an important presupposition for Mark 13; in both contexts, the expectations about the final salvation als solely associated with God's transcendent intervention. But a christologically-motivated difference is the fact that the Markian expectation is not dependent in some way on the temple, but rather, to the universal proclamation of the Gospel.

There is another circle of theological problems, and it is, moreover, one which has been up to the present largely unnoticed in the modern "Biblical theology" discussion, which runs connectively through both OT and NT. This is the "vertically" grounded consciousness of the "horizontal" obligation to care for one's neighbour. *Helge Kjær Nielsen* points out that the service of one's neighbour is not only grounded christologically (for which reason it is not solely a concern of the NT), but also in terms of theology of creation. Hence the common conception of creation gives rise to both people's individual responsibility and to their reciprocal obligation.

The general assumption that the decisive difference from a Biblical-theological point of view resides ethically in the concept of "mercy" is simply not true. It is therefore striking that the OT places so much importance on the care for the stranger, which it does, among other things, with reference to Israel's experiences during the sojourn in Egypt.

However, the true context would rather seem to lie in the understanding of the messianic salvation and new creation.

The point of departure for *Johannes Nissen's* contribution is that the believing community plays a decisive role in the course of the on-going process of transmission and interpretation which is reflected in the Bible (cf. M. Müller). Indeed, the very concept of "congregation" turns out to be constitutive of Biblical history. It is not a question of God and the individual man, but of God and humanity, as is illustrated by such collective designations as "Israel", "the people of God", or "the body of Christ". This process may accordingly not be adequately analysed without the inclusion of sociological interpretations, both historical and contemporary.

Jesus understood his task as a reforming renewal of Israel as a whole by means of a radical continuation of ethical prophetism. The disciples who accepted this proclamation became, after Easter, according to Paul, the body of Christ. The group-formation in this instance was not of a popularly exclusive, but of a universally inclusive character, and its Biblical-theological consequence was a new social structure, as well as a new reading of the Biblical texts.

The book concludes with an account of primary aspects of the conception of God within the Biblical tradition. The idea of God is, in part, the fundamental concept on to which the various Biblical-theological streams converge, and in part it is the basic conception against which the various messianic ideas about the immanent presence of the transcendent God can be seen as prismatic spectra.

The concept of God is, then, the locus, in a Biblical-theological sense, in which the tradition-historical and hermeneutical continuity and discontinuity between both OT and NT is most clearly and powerfully expressed. What they have in common is the confession of the one and the same God, who has bound himself to man as creator and saviour-god (Exod 3.6,7; 4.22; Joh 4.22-24). What is schismatically controversial about the concept of God, with all its implicit anthropological consequences, consists in the respective fundamental events by means of which the conception of God has received its determinative content, namely, on the one hand, the liberation from Egypt and, on the other, God's awakening of the crucified Jesus from the dead as the Messiah, the Son of God.

Sigfred Pedersen

CHAPTER ONE

OFFENBARUNGEN UND OFFENBARUNG

*Philosophische und theologische Erwägungen zum Verhältnis von Altem und Neuem Testament*

Hans Hübner, Göttingen

Angesichts des weitgesteckten Themas muß es heute in so manchen Punkten bei Andeutungen bleiben; ich bin auch genötigt, zentrale Sachverhalte etwas zu simplifizieren. Andererseits möchte ich aber - und die eben genannte Simplifizierung ist eben der Preis dafür - ein gewisses *Gesamtbild* vor Ihnen entwerfen, eine Gesamtperspektive, in die dann notwendig offenbleibende Detailfragen eingeordnet werden können. Eine Gesamtperspektive bleibt etwas Unfertiges - da tröstet uns St. Paulus mit seinen Worten "Stückwerk ist unser Wissen" (1 Kor 13.9) - , aber sie läßt uns, zumindest in einer gewissen Vorläufigkeit, wichtige *Zusammenhänge* erkennen und verstehen.

*I. Was ist Offenbarung? - Erste Hinführung*

Über Offenbarungen und Offenbarung soll es heute gehen, und zwar im größeren Rahmen des Themas "Biblische Theologie", also des Themas "Theologie des Alten und des Neuen Testaments". Vielleicht ist Ihre Erwartungshaltung angesichts dieser Themenstellung die, daß Sie den Plural "Offenbarungen" als Angabe dessen verstehen, was zum Alten Testament zu sagen ist, und den Singular "Offenbarung", was zum Neuen Testament zu sagen ist. Nun ist an diesem Vorverständnis schon ein Körnchen Wahrheit, wenn man die Geschichte des Alten Bundes als eine Abfolge von Offenbarungen Gottes sieht, aber nur eine neutestamentliche Offenbarung Gottes annimmt, nämlich die Offenbarung Gottes in Jesus Christus. Das Problem ist jedoch komplizierter.

Die Frage ist, was wir denn überhaupt unter Offenbarung verstehen. Ich verzichte zunächst auf eine genauere Begriffsbestimmung. Vergegenwärtigen wir uns statt dessen erst einmal einige Szenen des Alten Testaments! Wir kennen Gen 12: Jahwäh spricht zu Abraham: "Geh weg aus deinem Vaterland! Ich werde dich zu einem großen Volk machen. Du sollst ein Segen sein." Ganz unbefangen ist hier davon die Rede, daß

Gott redet und daß der Mensch hört. Kein schlechtes theologisches Gewissen, daß eine solche verbale Kommunikation zwischen Gott und Mensch doch etwas Unerhörtes sei! Wir können hier sogar ein Reden Gottes zur Kenntnis nehmen, das wir mit dem theologisch schwergewichtigen Begriff "Verheißung" umschreiben können. Der von uns mit dem theologischen Begriff "Transzendenz" bestimmte Gott spricht in unsere Immanenz hinein. Und das klappt sogar! Der immanente Mensch versteht des transzendenten Gottes Reden! Doch es bleibt nicht beim Reden und Hören. Das Sehen kommt hinzu. Schon wenige Verse danach (V. 7) lesen wir: "Und Jahwäh ließ sich von Abraham sehen, *wajjerâh*, und sprach: 'Deinen Nachkommen gebe ich das Land.'" Wiederum also die bereits genannte Unbefangenheit der Darstellung: Der in sichtbarer Weise dem Abraham begegnende Gott verheißt Nachkommenschaft. Man mag sagen, hier werde noch ganz mythisch von Gott geredet. Schön und gut! Das läßt sich nicht leugnen.

Nur bleibt, daß hier bereits eine Grundkategorie der Begegnung zwischen Gott und Mensch ausgesagt wird, die bis ins Neue Testament theologisch konstitutiv bleibt. Es bleibt dabei, daß im Alten und Neuen Testament Gott spricht und der Mensch hört. Es bleibt dabei, daß noch in einer der jüngsten Schriften des Neuen Testaments, dem Joh, die Rede davon sein wird, daß Gott sichtbar wird. So heißt es Joh 1.14: "Wir haben seine Herrlichkeit, seine göttliche δόξα, gesehen". Und wer nach Joh 14.9 Jesus gesehen hat, hat auch den Vater gesehen. Wer das nicht begreift, wird von dem getadelt, der die Inkarnation der göttlichen δόξα ist.

Zurück zum Alten Testament! Schauen wir nun auf eine Stelle, die auch ihre neutestamentliche Nachgeschichte hat, nämlich die Tempelvision des Propheten Jesaja, Jes 6. Er sieht sich verloren, weil er, ein Mann mit unreinen Lippen und mitten in einem Volke mit unreinen Lippen lebend, den König, Jahwäh Zebaoth, gesehen hat. Nicht der Tatbestand, fähig zu sein, Gott zu sehen, ist für ihn das Bestürzende; schlimmer ist, als Sünder mitten unter Sündern in unmittelbarer Begegnung mit Gott zu stehen und so das Leben verwirkt zu haben. Hier verbindet sich - und das ist für das Verständnis von Jes 6 entscheidend - *religiöse Erfahrung mit theologischer Reflexion*. Die religiöse Erfahrung ist die der unmittelbaren Begegnung mit Gott. Die theologische Reflexion hingegen bedenkt die Differenz zwischen dem heiligen Gott und dem unheiligen Menschen. Wo der Mensch in statu peccati mit dem alle Sünde verdammenden Gott zusammentrifft, da ist der Mensch erledigt.

Die theologische Reflexion bedenkt also den Menschen in seinem durch die Sünde verursachten unendlichen Abstand von Gott. Jesaja bleibt am Leben, freilich nur durch einen Gnadenakt Gottes. Weil Gott die Schuld Jesajas getilgt, seine Sünden gesühnt hat (V. 6-7), bleibt dieser am Leben. Zur neutestamentlichen Nachgeschichte von Jes 6: Nach 1 Kor 9.1 sagt Paulus, er habe den Herrn gesehen, 'Ιησοῦν τὸν κύριον ἡμῶν ἑόρακα. Auch das Damaskusgeschehen, auf das der Apostel hier anspielt und das er mit den Worten von Jes 6 formuliert, ist nur möglich aufgrund der Sühne, die Gott selbst verwirklicht (Röm 3.25).

Bleiben wir beim Jes-Buch, doch diesmal im Tritojesaja-Teil! Nach Jes 60.1-3 wird der Stadt Jerusalem verheißen, daß die Herrlichkeit Jahwähs, der *kebôd JHWH*, über ihr aufgeht. Während Dunkel die übrigen Völker bedeckt, geht leuchtend über ihr Jahwäh auf, wird der *Kabod Jahwähs* über ihr sichtbar, *jerā-æh*. Wird aber der *Kabod Jahwähs* über Jerusalem sichtbar, so wird Jahwäh selbst in dieser seiner Manifestation über ihn sichtbar. Doch wird Gottes Sichtbarkeit am Ende der Tage - wir sind hier mittem im apokalyptischen Sprachspiel - nicht nur Jerusalem zuteil; vielmehr werden nach Jes 66.18 alle Völker Gottes *Kabod* sehen!

## II. Was ist Offenbarung? - Begriffserklärung

Wir könnten in diesem Zusammenhang noch eine ganze Reihe verwandter Texte bedenken. Da aber Wesentliches bereits deutlich wurde, möge es mit den wenigen genannten Stellen sein Bewenden haben. Sie alle sagen das aus, was wir unter dem Begriff "Offenbarung" fassen können. Wir müssen jedoch noch hinzufügen, daß es im Alten Testament für Offenbarung kein spezielles Begriffswort gibt. Mit recht unterschiedlicher Terminologie wird das Offenbarwerden Gottes ausgesagt, mit unterschiedlichen Termini, die alle ihren ursprünglichen Sinn im Bereich des Profanen, im Bereich des Alltäglichen haben.

Wir sind zwar noch nicht mit der Palette der heranzuziehenden biblischen Aussagen zum Ende gelangt; es wird aber Zeit, daß wir erst einmal im Anschluß an die bereits vorgeführten alttestamentlichen Stellen tiefer über Gottes Offenbarung nachdenken sollten. Erlauben Sie, daß ich als Deutscher vom deutschen Wort "Offenbarung" ausgehe. Ich darf es aber um so mehr tun, als es auch für die Sprache des gastgebenden Landes, für das Dänische, zutrifft. In ihm heißt Offenbarung åbenbaring. Mit Offenbarung bzw. åbenbaring ist ja der Hinweis auf ein Offen-Sein gegeben. Der Weg zwischen dem offenbarenden Gott und dem diese Offenbarung empfangenden Menschen ist offen. Gott offenbart, genauer noch: Gott offenbart sich. Gott beseitigt alle Hindernisse zwischen sich und dem Menschen, so daß der für den Menschen offene Gott dem für Gott offenen Menschen begegnen kann. Somit besteht Offenheit zwischen Gott und Mensch. Damit die Offenbarung Gottes beim Menschen ankommt, muß dieser aber fähig sein, sie zu empfangen. Damit sind wir jedoch bei einer anthropologischen Überlegung.

Ich möchte sie hier *phänomenologisch* mit Ihnen zusammen durchdenken. Es sei mir erlaubt, an dieser Stelle ein wenig Anleihe bei der Existenzialphilosophie Martin Heideggers zu machen.[1] Um von vornherein Mißverständnisse abzuwehren: Es geht dabei nicht um eine individualistische Engführung theologischer Gedanken. Übrigens wäre damit auch Heidegger völlig mißverstanden. Das geläufige Klischee vom individualistischen Existenzialismus Heideggers ist nämlich wurzelhaft falsch. Es ist zwar sehr verbreitet und scheint fast unausrottbar; doch wer es vertritt, zeigt nur, daß er Heidegger nicht wirklich zur Kenntnis genommen hat. Worum es mir hier geht, ist, einige Strukturen des *menschlichen Daseins* aufzuzeigen. In dieser Hinsicht ist der phänomenologische Ansatz für unsere theologischen Überlegungen äußerst hilfreich. Und nur um dieser Absicht willen greife ich auf die Phänomenologie zurück.

Der Mensch ist, phänomenologisch gesehen, nie ohne seine jeweilige Welt. Kann man das menschliche Dasein mit Heidegger als In-der-Welt-sein aufweisen, so ist der Mensch jeweils offen für seine Welt. Er ist immer schon bei ihr, ist als Wesen der *Intentionalität* immer schon verstehend bei ihr. Natürlich kann - kein Phänomenologe würde es bestreiten - dieses Verstehen der je eigenen Welt zu einem argen Mißverstehen pervertieren, zu einem Irrweg von Täuschungen und Selbsttäuschungen. Aber eben als ein grundsätzlich intentionales Wesen kann der Mensch nicht anders als mit seinen fünf Sinnen und seinem Denken offen für die ihm offenstehende Welt zu sein. Das Offensein der Welt für den Menschen und das Offensein des Menschen für die Welt können verzerrt sein, können bis zur Unsinnigkeit verstellt sein. Aber irgendwie bleibt es beim gegenseitigen Offensein von Mensch und Welt. Von diesem Axiom gehe ich aus.

Was aber bedeutet das nun für unsere Frage nach der Offenbarung Gottes? Es bedeutet ganz einfach, daß der Mensch, will und soll sie wirklich Offen-barung Gottes sein, verstehend für sie offen ist. Sie muß also, phänomenologisch gesprochen, für ihn so offen sein, daß er sie in seiner Intentionalität verstehend erfaßt. Konkret: Er muß sie hörend erfassen können. Vielleicht auch: Er muß sie sehend erfassen können. Vor allem aber: Wenn er sie, in welcher Weise auch immer, verstehend ergreift, dann ist er als Denkender bei diesem Ergreifen der Offenbarung.

Als lutherischer Theologe nenne ich in diesem Zusammenhang den vielleicht größten katholischen Theologen unseres Jahrhunderts, nämlich Karl Rahner. Er hat 1941 eine der wichtigsten fundamentaltheologischen

---

[1] M. Heidegger, *Sein und Zeit*, Tübingen 1986$^{16}$ (= 1927$^{1}$).

Schriften unseres Jahrhunderts verfaßt; der Titel: *Hörer des Wortes*.[2] Dem Wortcharakter der Offenbarung entspricht es, wenn Rahner ausdrücklich erklärt: "Gott kann nur das offenbaren, was der Mensch hören kann".[3] Lassen wir im Augenblick noch unbeantwortet, ob Offenbarung nach dem Neuen Testament nur als Wortoffenbarung möglich ist. Insofern Offenbarung jedenfalls Wortcharakter hat - und Wortoffenbarung gibt es ja alt- und neutestamentlich - , gilt dieser Satz. Denn wenn Gott sich im Wort offenbaren will und wenn diese Wortoffenbarung den Menschen erreichen soll, also beim Menschen ankommen soll, dann muß der Mensch sie hören können. Das heißt aber: Dann muß der Mensch sie hörend verstehen können. Nur verstandene Offenbarung ist Offenbarung als Offensein Gottes für den Menschen und Offensein des Menschen für den offenbarenden bzw. sich offenbarenden Gott.

Der Satz "Nur verstandene Offenbarung ist Offenbarung Gottes" bedarf aber der klärenden Interpretation. Zunächst einmal besagt er nicht, daß verstandene Offenbarung auch der verstandene Gott ist. Einen verstandenen Gott gibt es nicht! Wenn Gott, mit Karl Rahner gesprochen, nur das offenbaren kann, was der Mensch hören kann, so *muß Offenbarung etwas mit dem zu tun haben, was des Menschen ist*. Es muß sich irgendwie um das Sein des Menschen handeln. Schauen wir unter diesem Aspekt noch einmal auf die alttestamentlichen Beispiele von eben! In allen kommt nämlich zur Sprache, was den Menschen betrifft. Ich formuliere zugespitzter: *Was den Menschen betroffen macht*.

Bei Abraham ging es um Landbesitz und Nachkommenschaft. Überflüssig zu sagen, daß beides für einen Menschen in der damaligen soziologischen Situation von existentieller Bedeutsamkeit war. Der Gott, der ihm erschienen war, war ihm als Garant dieser so lebensnotwendigen Bedingungen erschienen. Ohne Land wären seine Tiere dem Tode preisgegeben und folglich auch er samt seiner Familie! Ohne Nachkommenschaft wäre sein eigenes Leben sinnlos. Gott war somit der Garant des Lebens und des Lebenssinnes.

Jesajas Betroffenheit ging noch tiefer. Der Prophet wußte etwas von Sünde, wußte etwas davon, daß der Mensch aufgrund seiner Sünde, aufgrund seiner Schuld vor Gott und somit auch vor sich selbst nicht mehr bestehen kann. Er wußte, daß Sünde nicht nur das ist, was der Mensch eben auch hat, sondern daß Sünde den Menschen zum Sünder macht. Er wußte, daß der Sünder sein eigenes Ich vergiftet, sich selbst negiert, sich selbst vor der höchsten Instanz, vor Gott nämlich, um seine

---

[2] K. Rahner, *Hörer des Wortes. Zur Grundlegung einer Religionsphilosophie*, München 1941, 3. Aufl. neu bearbeitet von J.B. Metz, München 1985; Zitate nach dieser Aufl.
[3] K. Rahner, 142; Hervorhebung durch mich.

Rechtfertigung bringt und sich so als Nichtgerechtfertigter aufreibt. Jesaja wußte, daß der Mensch als Sünder seine Sünde ist. Sünde hat man nicht, Sünde ist man. *Der Sünder ist seine Sünde.* Die Sünde ist das Sein des Menschen. Wenn Gott aber dann dem Menschen vergibt, so ist das ein Geschehen, in welchem der Mensch neu geschaffen ist, in welchem er ein *neues Geschöpf* geworden ist. Gottes vergebendes Wort nimmt also dem Menschen nicht nur irgendetwas ab, was ihm zu tragen zu schwer geworden ist. Nein, wo Gott Sünde vergibt, da ist der Mensch zu einem anderen, zu einem neuen Menschen geworden, da geschieht Gen 1 und 2 von neuem. Seine sündige Existenz zu beseitigen vermag niemals der Mensch selbst. Sündenvergebung ist göttliche Tat, denn Sündenvergebung kann nur als Neuschöpfung verstanden werden. Jesaja wußte, was der Mensch ist, weil er wußte, was Sünde ist. Und zugleich wußte er, was der neue Mensch ist, weil er wußte, was Vergebung der Sünden ist.

Daß Sündenvergebung wesenhaft mit dem Wort zu tun hatte, versteht sich nach den letzten Ausführungen von selbst. Und daß dieses Wort der Vergebung als Offenbarung Gottes ein durchaus verstehbares Wort ist, bedarf wohl keiner Begründung. Rahners Aussage "Gott kann nur das offenbaren, was der Mensch hören kann" dürfte sich also an unseren letzten Überlegungen bewahrheiten. Es ist schon bezeichnend, daß diese Überlegungen in die Nähe dessen kommen, was Rudolf Bultmann in seinem 1929 publizierten Aufsatz "Der Begriff der Offenbarung im Neuen Testament"[4] dargelegt hat. Beide Theologen, Karl Rahner und Rudolf Bultmann, kommen in bestimmter Hinsicht von Martin Heidegger her. Rahner war in Freiburg sein Schüler, Bultmann in Marburg sein Kollege.

Zum Offenbarungsverständnis Bultmanns also: Er versteht Offenbarung nicht als Wissensmitteilung, sondern als ein den Menschen betreffendes Geschehen.[5] Offenbarung, wie sie im Neuen Testament verstanden ist, kann nicht als eine einfache Mitteilung, sondern nur als *Anrede* verstanden werden.[6] Wird die Gottesgerechtigkeit offenbart, so wird sie uns in der begegnenden Anrede zugesprochen. "Die reformatorische Auslegung hat recht: die Gerechtigkeit wird uns 'imputiert' als 'iustitia aliena'".[7] Hat Bultmann vieren seiner Aufsatzbände den Titel gegeben "Glauben und Verstehen", so ist das programmatisch gemeint und für uns deutlich genug: Es gibt nur ein *verstehendes Glauben* und im Blick auf Gottes Offenbarung in Jesus Christus nur ein *glaubendes Verstehen*.

---

[4] Jetzt in: R. Bultmann, *Glauben und Verstehen* III, Tübingen 1965³, 1-34.
[5] Ibid., 4.
[6] Ibid., 7.
[7] Ibid., 31.

Gibt es Grenzen des phänomenologischen Aufweises für die Frage nach der Offenbarung Gottes? Daß der schuldbeladene Mensch sich nicht selber von seiner Schuld befreien kann, mag vielleicht phänomenologisch noch aufweisbar sein. Die Grenze des phänomenologisch Aufweisbaren ist aber sicherlich da überschritten, wo der theologische Satz ausgesagt ist, daß Gott die Sünde vergeben hat. Daß der Mensch, dem die Sünde vergeben ist, der befreite Mensch ist, der Mensch ist, dem wieder ein Zukunft offensteht - auch das mag phänomenologisch noch deduzierbar sein. Aber eben daß Gott den Menschen von seiner sündhaften Vergangenheit, also von seinem sündhaften Ich befreit hat, genau das ist ein phänomenologisch nicht mehr zu verantwortender Satz. Soviel dürfte nun die bisherige Darlegung deutlich gemacht haben: Dadurch, daß der Mensch als dasjenige Wesen vorgestellt werden kann, dessen Daseinsstruktur als In-der-Welt-sein die Ansprechbarkeit impliziert, gerade dadurch läßt sich zeigen, was das Offenbarungswort für ihn bedeuten kann. So banal es zunächst vielleicht klingen mag, so tiefsinnig ist es im Grunde: *Der Mensch, der in existentiell betroffen machender Weise angesprochen ist, ist nicht mehr der Mensch, der er zuvor war.* Gilt dies schon im alltäglichen Leben - und das weiß ja wohl jeder von uns - , so gilt dies um so mehr vom Menschen, der sich durch die Offenbarung Gottes angesprochen weiß. Das beste alttestamentliche Beispiel ist Nathans bekanntes Wort an David: "Du bist der Mann!" Was existenzielle Wahrheit ist, hat ja der Däne Søren Kierkegaard deutlich genug gezeigt.

Mit unseren Überlegungen über die Grenzen des phänomenologischen Aufweises ist erneut der Wahrheitsgehalt eines Gedankens von Karl Rahner aufgewiesen: Der Satz, daß Gott nur das nur das offenbaren kann, was der Mensch hören kann, besagt keinesfalls eine "vorgängige Begrenzung möglicher Gegenstände einer Offenbarung".[8] Der faktische Inhalt der Offenbarung ist nicht aus der Immanenz deduzierbar. Subjekt der Offenbarung ist Gott, ist einzig Gott. Inhalt der Offenbarung kann keinesfalls sein, worauf der Mensch von sich allein kommen könnte. Was Vergebung und Beseitigung der Sünde meint, kann der Mensch aus sich heraus verstehen. Daß Vergebung und Beseitigung der Sünde durch Gott erfolgt ist, kann nur offenbarendes Wort Gottes sein, das dem Menschen zugesprochen wird. Und auch wie Gott dies tut, kann nur Aussage eines Offenbarungswortes Gottes sein.

---

[8] K. Rahners, 142; zu Rahners fundamentaltheologischem Ansatz s. H. Hübner, *Biblische Theologie des Neuen Testaments I: Prolegomena*, Göttingen 1990, 208-239.

## III. Wortoffenbarung und Personoffenbarung Gottes

Die nächste Frage, die sich stellt, ist - es wurde bereits angedeutet - , ob Offenbarung *nur* Wortoffenbarung ist. Vielleicht erwartet man von einem Lutheraner, daß er darauf ein eindeutiges Ja sagt. Nun, als lutherischer Theologe sage ich auch zunächst, daß Offenbarung im eben dargelegten Sinne *essentiell* Wortoffenbarung ist. Es wäre aber eine erheblich Verengung des Offenbarungsbegriffs, wollte man im fraglos konstitutiven Wortelement der Offenbarung das Ganze der Offenbarung sehen.

Schauen wir zunächst wieder auf das Alte Testament! Da ist, wie wir gesehen haben, die Rede vom Sehen Gottes. Jahwäh ließ sich von Abraham und anderen sehen. Aber das Entscheidende war doch, daß dieses Sehen Gottes nicht das Eigentliche des Offenbarungsaktes darstellt. Daß Jahwäh sich von den Patriarchen sehen ließ, geschah ja um des von ihm gesprochenen Wortes, um der von ihm gegebenen Verheißung willen. Dieses Sehen war gerade nicht wesenhaft für das Offenbarwerden Gottes. Anders schon war es in Jes 6. Hier lag der Akzent wirklich auf dem Sehen, und zwar im Zusammenhang mit dem Wissen um die Sünde vor Gott, aber auch um den Akt der Vergebung durch Gott. Der Mensch durfte, weil Gott ihn dazu fähig machte, diesen auch sehen.

Der tragende theologische Gedanke war, daß das Sehen-Können Ausdruck der *wiedererlangten Gemeinschaft mit Gott* ist. Dieser offenbart sich als der, der den Menschen erneut in seine göttliche Gemeinschaft hineinnimmt. Ohne das Moment der Vergebungsbedürftigkeit finden wir den Topos des Sehens Gottes in Ex 24.9-11, wo Mose mit seinem Gefolge nach dem Bundesschluß auf dem Sinai auf den Berg hinaufsteigt und wo sie den Gott Israels sehen, um dann zu essen und zu trinken. Dieser hochmythologische Text bringt die Gemeinschaft mit Gott in beeindruckend anschaulicher Weise zum Ausdruck.

Auf die neutestamentliche Wirkungsgeschichte der alttestamentlichen Aussagen vom Sehen Gottes wurde auch schon hingewiesen. Heben wir in diesem Zusammenhang hervor, daß dabei das Sehen der *Doxa* Christi und somit das Sehen der *Doxa* Gottes der entscheidende Aspekt ist. Es ist aber gerade diese *Doxa*, die auch vom Menschen selbst ausgesagt wird. Schauen wir dabei zunächst auf Paulus! Ich wähle drei Stellen aus, die das Offenbarungsgeschehen in der theologischen Sicht des Apostels verdeutlichen: Röm 1.16-17, Röm 3.21 und 2 Kor 3.18. Zwar spricht erst die dritte Stelle von der *Doxa*; doch geben uns die beiden zuerst genannten Stellen den erforderlichen theologischen Horizont, in den das in 2 Kor 3.18 Gesagte eingefügt werden kann.

Röm 1.16-17 ist bekanntlich jenes Pauluswort, dem Martin Luther seine reformatorische Erkenntnis verdankt. Die exegetische Situation ist aber heute die, daß es zwischen katholischen und evangelischen Theologen über diesen so zentralen Text des Paulus so gut wie keinen Dissens gibt. Wir dürfen darüber hinaus noch sagen, daß wir heute diese Worte des Paulus in einem wohl noch tieferen Sinne verstehen können als damals Martin Luther. Der Apostel sagt, daß das Evangelium eine Kraft Gottes sei, δύναμις θεοῦ, und zwar für jeden Glaubenden zum eschatologischen Heil, εἰς σωτηρίαν. Wer vom Evangelium spricht, spricht von der Macht der Wortes. Wer jedoch das Evangelium spricht, spricht mit dieser Macht. Warum? Paulus begründet es in V. 17: Weil die Gerechtigkeit Gottes in ihm offenbart wird. Der griechische Text ist aufschlußreich: δικαιοσύνη γὰρ θεοῦ ἐν αὐτῷ ἀποκαλύπτεται, wobei das geradezu unendliche Vermögen des Glaubens durch die Redefigur ἐκ πίστεως εἰς πίστιν zum Ausdruck kommt. *Offenbarung geschieht* also in der Verkündigung, *in der Verkündigung des Evangeliums*. Offenbarung ist nach Röm 1.16-17 kein punktuelles Geschehen im Verlaufe der Weltgeschichte.

Nun meint freilich das je neue Offenbarwerden der Gerechtigkeit Gottes nicht, daß im Wort des Evangliums diese Gerechtigkeit mitgeteilt würde und das intellektuelle Verstehen der Botschaft den Menschen in seinem Selbstverständnis änderte. Das wäre viel zu wenig! Das wäre viel zu flach! Viel zu oberflächlich! Alles hängt allerdings am Verständnis des Begriffs "Gerechtigkeit Gottes, δικαιοσύνη θεοῦ". Ist sie - mit Ernst Käsemann[9]- nicht nur Gabe Gottes, sondern darüber hinaus auch Macht Gottes, ist somit im Evangelium der den Menschen rechtfertigende Gott präsent, ist also das verkündete Evangelium die machtvolle Repräsentation und Manifestation Gottes, so ist das ἀποκαλύπτεται der Akt des Offenbarwerdens Gottes selbst. Wenn Rudolf Bultmann die Verkündigung als das je neu eschatologische Ereignis sieht[10], so ist er in diesem Punkte - man mag sonst kritisch über ihn sagen, was man will - in der Wolle gefärbter Lutheraner. Halten wir fest: *Wo das Evangelium als die Manifestation des rechtfertigenden Gottes verkündet wird, da wird jeweils Gott selbst präsent.* Verkündigung ist Vergegenwärtigung Gottes, mehr noch: ist der Vorgang, in welchem Gott selbst sich vergegenwärtigt. In der mündlichen Wortoffenbarung geschieht zugleich die Personoffenbarung Gottes. Da aber der Glaube hinzukommt und so der glaubende Mensch in seiner Geschichtlichkeit konstitutiv zum Offenbarungsgeschehen hinzugehört, sind Gott und Mensch in eben dieser Geschichtlichkeit zusammengekommen. Phänomenologisch läßt sich sagen, daß der

---

[9] E. Käsemann, "Gottesgerechtigkeit bei Paulus" in: ders., *Exegetische Versuche und Besinnungen* II, Göttingen 1970³, 181-193.
[10] R. Bultmann, *Theologie des Neuen Testaments*, Tübingen 1984⁹, § 34. Das Wort, die Kirche, die Sakramente.

Mensch als hörendes Wesen versteht, was Gott sagt. Jenseits aller Phänomenologie muß aber sofort hinzugefügt werden, daß die *repraesentatio Dei phänomenologisch nicht mehr erfaßbar ist*. Daß Gott zum In-der-Welt-sein des Glaubenden gehört, ist kein phänomenologisch aussagbarer Satz, so sehr menschliches Dasein phänomenologisch grundsätzlich ein In-der-Welt-sein ist.

Schauen wir nun auf Röm 3.21! Auch hier ist von der Gerechtigkeit Gottes die Rede, auch hier von ihrem Offenbarwerden, von ihrem Erscheinen. Aber hier geht es nicht um die kerygmatische Dimension der Gerechtigkeit Gottes. Hören wir den griechischen Text: νυνὶ δὲ χωρὶς νόμου δικαιοσύνη θεοῦ πεφανέρωται. Entscheidend ist das Verb πεφανέρωται, eine Perfektform. Es geht also um ein Geschehen der Vergangenheit, das seine Auswirkungen bis in die Gegenwart zeitigt. Gemeint ist, daß in Jesus Christus, in der Inkarnation des Gottessohnes, die Gerechtigkeit Gottes erschienen ist. Hier also ist nun das Ereignis der Offenbarung Gottes im damaligen geschichtlichen Auftreten Jesu Christi gesehen. Hier also ist Offenbarung als einmaliges Geschehen in der Vergangenheit gemeint - freilich als ein Geschehen, daß seine Heilswirkung in alle Zukunft hinein haben wird.

Das eigentliche theologische Problem besteht nun darin, wie das *einmalige* Offenbarungsgeschehen in der Inkarnation und im Kreuzes- und Auferstehungsereignis mit dem *ständigen* Offenbarungsgeschehen im verkündeten Evangelium, das im Glauben gehört wird, zusammenkommt. Die Extremlösungen zeichnen sich ab: 1. Alles ist bereits im Kreuz und in der Auferstehung Christi geschehen; des Menschen Rechtfertigung ist bereits am Kreuz erfolgt - also die klassische Lösung Karl Barths.[11] 2. Die radikale kerygmatische Lösung, die alles nur im Glauben geschehen sieht. Beide Extremlösungen sind falsch, weil zu kurz gedacht.

Die Lösung, die theologisch allein verantwortbar ist, muß sowohl die *Geschichtlichkeit* des Wirkens Gottes in der geschichtlichen Existenz Christi als auch die *Geschichtlichkeit* der jeweils glaubenden Existenz ernst nehmen. Karfreitag und Ostern einerseits und die Existenz des Glaubenden andererseits müssen als jeweils geschichtliches Geschehen verstanden werden. Zugespitzt: Gott ist in Christus Geschichte geworden, damit die geschichtlich existierenden Menschen Anteil an seinem geschichtlichen Erlösungswerk erhalten. Die unlösbare innere Verbindung von ἀποκαλύπτεται in Röm 1.17 und πεφανέρωται in Röm 3.21 ist der theologische Schlüssel zum Verständnis dessen, wie Paulus Offenbarung versteht.

---

[11] K. Barth, *Kirchliche Dogmatik* IV/1, Zürich 1986⁵, passim.

Der dritte und letzte der hier zu bedenkenden Texte ist 2 Kor 3.18, einer der schwierigsten Paulustexte, zugleich auch einer der gefährlichsten. Die deutsche Einheitsübersetzung gibt ihn wie folgt wieder: "Wir alle spiegeln mit enthülltem Angesicht die Herrlichkeit des Herrn wider und werden so in sein eigenes Bild verwandelt, von Herrlichkeit zu Herrlichkeit, durch den Geist des Herrn." Jetzt also sind wir bei der Sichtung relevanter Paulusaussagen zu einer solchen gekommen, die von der *Doxa* spricht. Die übliche Übersetzung des hebräischen *kābôd* und griechischem δόξα mit "Herrlichkeit" ist äußerst schwach. Es gibt aber kein dieser Realität entsprechendes deutsches Wort. Denn *Doxa* ist etwas, was zur göttlichen Transzendenz gehört, was - vielleicht genauer formuliert - zur Epiphanie, zur Manifestation des göttlichen Wesens gehört. Gott in seiner Epiphanie - so zeigt es gerade das Sinaigeschehen Ex 19 in beeindruckender Weise - ist geradezu seine *Doxa*, ist geradezu sein *Kabod*. Und nun wird ausgerechnet dieses Gottes spezifisches Wesen wiedergebende Prädikat den Menschen zugesprochen, den glaubenden Christen zugesprochen! Wer 2 Kor 3.18 unbefangen liest, wird zunächst einmal den Eindruck haben, daß hier die Grenze zwischen Gott und Mensch verwischt wird.

Sehen wir auf den griechischen Urtext! Da heißt es zunächst τὴν δόξαν κυρίου κατοπτριζόμενοι, wir spiegeln, wenn wir mit enthülltem Angesicht die *Doxa* schauen, diese wider. Diese Aussage ist theologisch noch einigermaßen erträglich. Aber dann! τὴν αὐτὴν εἰκόνα μεταμορφούμεθα ἀπὸ δόξης εἰς δόξαν. Das heißt doch, daß wir in einen Prozeß hineingenommen werden, in dem wir mehr und mehr in die göttliche *Doxa* umgestaltet werden. Werden wir vergottet? Haben diejenigen Kirchenväter recht, die von der Vergottung des Menschen gesprochen haben, etwa im Sinne des Irenäus von Lyon: "Gott ist Mensch geworden, damit wir Gott werden"? Wo bleibt da unsere nüchterne evangelische Worttheologie, die das ganze Heilsgeschehen im Vorgang der Rechtfertigung, der Gerechtsprechung *sola fide* et *sola gratia* erblickt? Wenn irgendwo, dann ist hier theologische Grundlagenarbeit erforderlich! Daß an dieser Stelle auch die konfessionelle Problematik mitspielt, bedarf keiner Begründung!

*IV. Vergottung?*

Das Wort "Vergottung" ist in der Tat ein Reizwort. Nehmen wir aber in diesem Zusammenhang zunächst einmal zur Kenntnis, daß Paulus in Röm 3.23 von der Sünde aller Menschen spricht und dem dadurch erfolgten Verlust der *Doxa* Gottes. Danach war der paradiesische Adam der Mensch der *Doxa* - übrigens eine Auffassung, die nicht spezifisch paulinisch ist, sondern im damaligen Judentum mehrfach begegnet. Ich nenne hier nur die apokryphe Schrift *Vita Adae et Evae* 20-21, wo Eva zur Schlange sagt:

> Und zur selben Stunde wurden mir die Augen aufgetan, und ich erkannte, daß ich entblößt war von der Gerechtigkeit, mit der ich bekleidet gewesen. Da weinte ich und sprach: Warum hast du mir das angetan, daß ich entfremdet war von meiner *Doxa*, mit der ich bekleidet war!

Und dann Adam zu Eva:

> Du böses Weib, was hast du angerichtet! Entfremdet hast du mich von der *Doxa* Gottes!

Hier aber stehen *Doxa* und Gerechtigkeit in paralleler Aussage. Die dem Menschen von Gott geschenkte *Doxa* hat also irgendetwas mit Gottes Gerechtigkeit zu tun. Vielleicht ist es noch bedeutsamer, daß Eva davon spricht, sie sei mit der *Doxa* bekleidet gewesen. Sie war also von der *Doxa* Gottes umgeben. Dann ist aber mit dieser Stelle ausgesagt, daß sich Adam und Eva im Paradiese als der Stätte aufgehalten hatten, an der, indem Gottes *Doxa* sie engstens umgab, Gott selbst zu ihrer paradiesischen Welt gehörte. Ihr In-der-Welt-sein war also ein *In-der-Welt--Gottes-sein*. Und nach dem Verlust der *Doxa* ist ihr In-der-Welt-Gottessein ein *In-der-Welt-der-Gottlosigkeit-sein*, wobei Gottlosigkeit zunächst einmal nicht im religiös-ethischen Sinne, sondern im ganz wörtlichen Sinne zu verstehen ist: Das Sein ohne Gott und somit das total nihilistische Sein. Das Leben ist nun ein nihil, ein Nichts!

Dürfen wir Vit Ad 20-21 in dieser Weise deuten, so legt es sich nahe, zumindest den Versuch zu unternehmen, Röm 3.23 im gleichen Sinne zu interpretieren. Dann bedeutet diese Stelle im Lichte auch von Röm 1.18-3.9, daß die Gottlosigkeit gemäß der eben vorgetragenen Deutung in der Sicht des Paulus Hand in Hand geht mit der Gottlosigkeit im Sinne schlimmster Sündhaftigkeit. Interpretieren wir nun von hier aus 2 Kor 3.18, dann bedeutet die Verwandlung von *Doxa* zu *Doxa*, daß das In-Gott-Sein eine ständige Intensivierung erfährt. Da aber Christus als Gottes Bild (εἰκών) und *Doxa* existiert, ist unsere gottgewirkte Begabung mit der wachsenden *Doxa* als In-Christus-Sein zu interpretieren, als εἶναι ἐν Χριστῷ.

Machen wir uns klar, daß sich der Mensch grundsätzlich in einem bestimmten Raum befindet. Auch Räumlichkeit ist ein grundlegendes Existenzial des Menschen. Theologisch qualifiziert bedeutet unsere Räumlichkeit, daß wir uns im Raum der Gottesgegenwart aufhalten: Wir existieren in Christus und vice versa existiert Christus in uns (Gal 2.20). Christus als Gottes *Doxa* ist dann Gottes ständige Epiphanie für unser Dasein.

Dies ist noch *pneumatologisch* zu beleuchten. 2 Kor 3.18 ist ja bekanntlich Abschluß des theologisch so zentralen Kapitels 2 Kor 3, wo es programmatisch um den Geist des Kyrios geht. Nach Röm 8 ist christliche Existenz grundlegend Existenz im Geiste Gottes, der in uns wohnt. Es ist der Geist Gottes und zugleich der Geist Christi. Zugespitzt formuliert: Zusammen mit Gott und Christus besitzen wir denselben göttlichen Geist! Was für Gott und Christus wesenhaft gilt, gilt für uns geschenkweise. Unsere *Doxa*-Existenz ist also dadurch ermöglicht, daß wir nicht mehr κατὰ σάρκα leben, sondern aufgrund des in uns wohnenden Geistes κατὰ πνεῦμα.

Eingangs war davon die Rede, daß es im Alten Testament um Offenbarungen Gottes gehe (Plural), im Neuen Testament aber um die eine Offenbarung Gottes in Jesus Christus. Unsere Überlegungen dürften aber gezeigt haben, daß dies eine zumindest simplifizierende Sicht ist, so sehr auch ein Wahrheitskern in ihr steckt. Auch im Neuen Testament ist Offenbarung Gottes kein punktuelles, kein einmaliges Geschehen innerhalb der Weltgeschichte. Es geht vielmehr im Neuen Testament zentral um die *wesenhafte Zusammengehörigkeit* des einmaligen geschichtlichen Offenbarungsgeschehens in Jesus Christus mit dem je neuen Offenbarwerden Gottes in seinem rechtfertigenden Wort. Soteriologie und kerygmatische Theologie sind untrennbar. Soteriologie ohne kerygmatische Dimension negiert die Geschichtlichkeit des glaubenden Menschens, kerygmatische Theologie ohne Verankerung im geschichtlichen Heilsgeschehen von Karfreitag und Bußtag ist existenzialistische Paralyse der Theologie. Das rettende Kreuz Christi ist immer zugleich das geglaubte rettende Kreuz Christi. Die *theologia crucis* ist immer nur die *theologia verbi crucis*.[12] Wortgeschehen ist aber immer zugleich Geschehen im Geiste Gottes. Glaubensexistenz ist nämlich Existenz im Geiste Gottes. Denn der Glaube hat seine pneumatologische Dimension. Wo jedoch der Geist Gottes das Dasein des Menschen bestimmt, wo also das glaubende Dasein das εἶναι κατὰ πνεῦμα ist, Röm 8, da ist das Wortgeschehen der Rechtfertigung im Sein-in-Christus zur Vollendung gekommen. So hat das Wortgeschehen grundsätzlich seine *ontologische* Seite. Nicht umsonst spricht Martin Heidegger von der Sprache als vom "Haus des Seins".[13] Wer durch das freisprechende Wort Gottes gerechtfertigt ist, der ist in Christus, im Geiste, der existiert in Christus, im

---

[12] S. H. Hübner, *Biblische Theologie des Neuen Testaments* II: Die Theologie des Paulus und ihre neutestamentliche Wirkungsgeschichte, Göttingen 1993, 112-139.
[13] M. Heidegger, *Unterwegs zur Sprache*, Pfullingen 1971[4], 166.

Geiste. Damit ist der Mensch ins Offenbarungsgeschehen Gottes hineingenommen. Der Fundamentaltheologe Max Seckler hat zwischen epiphanischem Offenbarungsverständnis, instruktionstheoretischem Offenbarungsverständnis und Offenbarung als Selbstmitteilung Gottes unterschieden.[14] Der Ansatz ist richtig; man wird aber zwischen dem epiphanischen Offenbarungsverständnis und der Offenbarung als Selbstmitteilung Gottes keinen allzu großen Unterschied machen können. Seine Unterscheidung dürfte verdeutlichen, was wir miteinander überlegt haben.

Daß unsere Überlegungen sich gerade an der paulinischen Theologie verifizieren lassen, haben wir gesehen. Ein Paulusschüler, der Vf. des Kol, hat diesen Gedanken weitergetrieben, wie wir in Kol 3.4 lesen: "Wenn Christus, unser Leben, (am Ende der Tage) offenbar wird, $\varphi\alpha\nu\epsilon\rho\omega\vartheta\hat{\eta}$, dann werden auch wir mit ihm in der *Doxa* offenbar werden, $\varphi\alpha\nu\epsilon\rho\omega\vartheta\acute{\eta}\sigma\epsilon\sigma\vartheta\epsilon\ \grave{\epsilon}\nu\ \delta\acute{o}\xi\eta$. "Für Christus und für die Christen ist also eschatologisch das gleiche ausgesagt, nämlich das in der *Doxa* Gottes Offenbarwerden. Das Reflektieren des $\varphi\alpha\nu\epsilon\rho\omega\vartheta\hat{\eta}\nu\alpha\iota$ bleibt für uns eine wichtige theologische Aufgabe.

---

[14] M. Seckler, "Der Begriff der Offenbarung", in: *Handbuch der Fundamentaltheologie* 2: Traktat Offenbarung (Hg. von W. Kern u.a.), Freiburg/Basel/Wien 1985, 60-70.

CHAPTER TWO

PAUL AND "BIBLICAL THEOLOGY"·

A. J. M. Wedderburn, Durham, now München

*I. Paul and "Biblical Theology"*

The not inconsiderable task of this paper is to bring two entities into relationship with one another, and to discuss the light which the one sheds on the other. The first of these entities, the apostle Paul, is a controversial figure, controversial to his contemporaries, controversial still today, and particularly controversial, too, in relation to that aspect of his life and thought which most concerns us here, his relation to his Jewish heritage which is implicit in the reference here to "biblical theology". For at this very point his fellow Jews considered him to have betrayed their ancestral traditions and his own; there is no reason to dispute the accuracy of the suspicions voiced concerning Paul in Acts 21.21, that he taught "apostasy from Moses".[1]

The other entity, it will be noted, "biblical theology", has been placed in inverted commas, as a warning sign, not least in order to highlight the lack of agreement over what is meant by the phrase. It is elusive in its meaning. For a start, it should be noted that the reason for our interest in the topic today is a very different one to that of our predecessors. Originally the demand for a "biblical theology" arose in contrast to systematic or dogmatic theology, a demand particularly inspired by Johann Philipp Gabler; the resultant pursuit of that goal in two parts, in separate theologies of the Old Testament and the New, from the time of Georg Lorenz Baur onwards, led to a new problem, the discovery of a theology that is "biblical" in the sense of embracing both parts of the Christian Bible. Unlike an earlier generation we no longer seek a theology that is "biblical" as opposed to "dogmatic", but we seek one that is "biblical" as opposed to being confined to either the Old or the New Testament.[2]

---

· I am deeply grateful to my colleague Dr R. W. L. Moberly for his help with, and comments on, this essay; those familiar with his views will, however, see that he is in no way to be held responsible for the views of this paper.

[1] Cf. H. Räisänen, "Der Bruch des Paulus mit Israels Bund", in T. Veijola (ed.), *The Law in the Bible and in Its Environment* (PFES 51; Helsinki/Göttingen, 1990), 156-72, here 163-4, 169.

[2] Indeed it may be combined with a search for a "dogmatics that will correct and guide" exegesis (P. Stuhlmacher, *Schriftauslegung auf dem Wege zur biblischen Theologie* [Göttingen, 1975], 113).

However, there is a further ambiguity inherent in the phrase: as G. Ebeling observed, as he too placed the phrase within inverted commas, it could mean "the theology contained in the Bible" or a "theology which is according to the Bible, according to scripture".[3] In turn, neither of these is clearly defined: should the former be re-phrased as "the theologies contained in the Bible", lest we assume that one unified and coherent system of thought is found in its pages?[4] Or are we looking for a single, central "core" theology to be found within and amongst the welter of differing ideas in both Testaments, a single unifying thread interwoven with a tangled mass of others which we, through our selection of that one thread, implicitly relegate to a subordinate position?[5] But, then, with which scriptures does the "thread" accord? All or just some, the Bible in all its totality, the canons of both Testaments, or certain parts or certain themes within its various parts? And is that part of "the scriptures" which is not our New Testament to be limited to our Old Testament or should it also include, for example, the wider range of writings contained in the Septuagint? For why should Christians be bound by the decisions reached after the fall of Jerusalem, when Jesus and the earliest Christians knew of, and drew upon the resources of, a wider and more fluidly defined corpus of writings?[6]

It is small wonder, then, that both in the earlier history of "biblical theology" and among its more recent exponents there has been a wide variety of aims and approaches.

So Hans Frei[7] notes how various different trends in scholarship laid claim to the name "biblical theology": (1) "biblical" (as opposed to

---

[3] "Was heißt 'Biblische Theologie'?", *Wort und Glaube,* 1 (3rd ed.; Tübingen, 1967), 69–89, here 69 (a revised version of "The Meaning of 'Biblical Theology'", which appeared in English in *JThS* 6 [1955], 210-25 and elsewhere). I do not see how C. H. H. Scobie, "The Challenge of Biblical Theology", *TynBul* 42 (1991), 31-61, can claim that for Ebeling "Biblical theology is to be understood as 'the theology contained in the Bible ...', not 'the theology that accords with the Bible'", when Ebeling holds that the Bible contains no theology in the strict sense, but calls for a theological explication which is the continuing task of Old and New Testament theology (86); "biblical theology" in turn must give an account of the varied witness of both Testaments (88).

[4] Cf. H. Boers, *What Is New Testament Theology? The Rise of Criticism and the Problem of a Theology of the New Testament* (Philadelphia, 1979), who, following the philosopher A. N. Whitehead, adopts as a definition of "theology" the following: "A coherent, logical, necessary system of general ideas in terms of which every element of our experience concerning matters relating to God can be interpreted" (13). As a result he finds no "theology" contained in the New Testament (14), let alone in both Testaments.

[5] Cf. J. D. G. Dunn, *Unity and Diversity in the New Testament: An Inquiry into the Character of Earliest Christianity* ( London, 1977; 2nd ed. 1990), e.g. 30. But, although Dunn uses the idea of a "core" kerygma with regard to the New Testament he does not claim to find a "core" running through both Testaments, nor is he so ready to recognize that discovery of this "core" pushes other elements to the periphery.

[6] Cf. H. Hübner, *Biblische Theologie des Neuen Testaments,* 1: *Prolegomena* (Göttingen, 1990), 63.

[7] *The Eclipse of Biblical Narrative: a Study in Eighteenth and Nineteenth Century Hermeneutics* (New Haven/London, 1974), 165-9. Cf. also Ebeling, *Wort,* 74-82, on the development of the concept and the different uses of the term (esp. 82).

systematic or dogmatic) theology worked out historically the variegated contents of the Bible (*wahre biblische Theologie*), and inductive generalizations enabled one then to formulate permanent and normative (and no longer time-conditioned) concepts as the basis for abiding theological claims (*reine biblische Theologie*; so Gabler); (2) analysing the concepts of the Bible and organizing its doctrines into a coherent whole, partly logical and partly historical, so as to show the correctness of traditional Protestant doctrines (Zachariä); (3) finding the unity of the Bible in the single sacred history described in it and in its inspiration that made it bring grace to the faithful (Cocceius, Bengel).

In more modern times Henning Graf Reventlow[8] detects three different models for a "biblical theology": (1) "a coherent description of Israel's tradition history, of early Judaism and primitive Christianity"; (2) isolating a particular concept or central idea or a collection of these as a link between both Testaments or their centre; (3) starting from the idea of a world order.

Unfortunately, we cannot just leave the term fluid without plunging the following discussion into considerable confusion and uncertainty. Ebeling's alternatives, mentioned above, are, in my view, not entirely satisfactory, for I do not think that "biblical theology" in a viable sense can be either "*the* theology contained in the Bible" or a "theology which is according to the Bible" *in toto*. A more hopeful approach is to see "biblical theology" as a discipline, a mode of theological thought, which seeks to take both Testaments into account and to build upon insights reflected in both; at the same time, we shall see, it has to react both positively and critically to different elements in both Testaments, responding with (still critical) enthusiasm to some, rejecting others.

It is a constructive process, which seeks to build out of a selection of the materials contained in both parts of the Christian Bible a contemporary exposition of faith in God which can be shown to be in some measure of continuity with, but is not identical to, the central thrust of the faith of Israel and the earliest Church; it tries to view these two as one movement of faith, however wavering a movement that may be. It seeks to make sense of the tangled web of often conflicting witness to God and to trace within the vicissitudes of the history within which that witness was borne a coherent experience of, and insight into, the nature and reality of God.

---

[8] *Problems of Biblical Theology in the Twentieth Century* (London, 1986; ET of EdF 203; Darmstadt, 1983), 148–78.

## II. Paul, Israel and the Law

Paul, I have already mentioned, is and was a controversial figure. Moreover, his views on the subject of his Jewish heritage and on the relation of his new faith and message to that heritage are beset with ambiguities and ambivalence. That should not altogether surprise us if we recall who Paul was and how he came to faith in Christ. For Heikki Räisänen provides us with what is to my mind the best explanation of at least part of the ambivalence in Paul's statements on the Jewish Law: Paul as a Jew inherited a reverence for the Jewish Law as God's revelation;[9] yet, through his participation in the mission of the Hellenists whom he had once persecuted, Paul the Christian had grown accustomed to their "somewhat relaxed attitude to the observance of the ritual Torah", perhaps even neglecting to demand circumcision of those who joined them.[10] This at least enables us to understand one aspect of Paul's dilemma with regard to the Law and his Jewish heritage, and to try to do justice to his conflicting statements on the Law.

To this, however, we should perhaps add another tension within Paul's experience: on the one hand there is Paul's bitterness and disappointment at the rejection of the gospel by the bulk of his fellow Jews, which had caused him personal suffering (2 Cor 11.24) and had led him to speak as if he washed his hands of them (cf., e.g., 1 Thess 2.14-16)—a dimension of his experience which Johannes Munck in particular emphasized as part of the background to Rom 9-11[11] —and, on the other hand, there is his trust in God's faithfulness and his conviction that God had called Israel. If there are, as we shall see, tensions within Rom 9-11 then these tensions are in large measure due to these two aspects of Paul's experience.

---

[9] J. D. G. Dunn, *The Partings of the Ways between Christianity and Judaism and Their Significance for the Character of Christianity* (London/Philadelphia, 1991), 140, accuses Räisänen of seeing Paul as "totally alienated from his ancestral faith, from Judaism". That is one-sided, for the essence of Räisänen's position is that he sees Paul as "vacillating", torn in two directions; he may over the years of work with the Hellenist Jewish Christians have become "internally alienated from the *ritual aspects* of the law" (*Paul and the Law* [WUNT 29; Tübingen, 1983] 258, my italics), but he still regarded the Law as divine (e.g. 266) and still regarded himself as a true Jew (e.g. 200).

[10] *Paul and the Law*, p. 254, his italics. This still seems to me possible despite the reluctance of M. Hengel, *The Pre-Christian Paul* (London/Philadelphia, 1991), 81, to go thus far; for one thing he does not consider the issue of circumcision, an especial stumbling block to Gentiles; for another, the question need not be of "mission" so much as of receiving interested Gentiles into fellowship (see my *Paul and Jesus: Collected Essays* [JSNT.S 37; Sheffield, 1989], 136 n. 48. And I do not see that such a position is excluded by the fact that it anticipates later developments, for how certain are we how early these developments started? Some earlier foreshadowing of these later developments would also make it easier to understand how the latter eventually took place. Whatever we do, we need to find an adequate reason for the vehemence of the outbreak of persecution.

[11] J. Munck, *Christus und Israel: eine Auslegung von Röm 9-11* (AJut.TS 7; Kopenhagen, 1956), 42-6.

In addition to these two tensions within Paul's experience we shall also find a third one within Paul's Jewish heritage, in the Old Testament itself, in the form of a basic ambivalence which allows those writings to be understood, as Gunneweg puts it, as either law or gospel.[12] That tension will be particularly important to bear in mind when we come to look at a passage like Rom 10.5-8.

A particularly useful starting-point for charting our way through these troubled exegetical waters is a recent paper by Ulrich Luz on "Paulinische Theologie als Biblische Theologie",[13] which I shall use as a way into the discussion of this question. For Paul's theology can, Luz notes, very naturally be described as a "biblical theology" in the sense that he quite manifestly appeals to the Old Testament in support of his views, though, as Philipp Vielhauer observed,[14] surprisingly little as a basis for his Christology. This would support the contention of Werner Kramer that Paul was no Christological innovator, but rather showed his creativity in the way that he applied Christological traditions passed on to him by his fellow Christians.[15] Paul shared with his fellow-Christians the conviction that those writings bore witness to Christ. However, they could only do that, Luz rightly argues, by their reading the Old Testament selectively, and very often also by reading it in a different way to their fellow Jews. For to the latter, as they read the Old Testament without the light of Christ, the scriptures were veiled (2 Cor 3).

Paul used the Old Testament selectively. Not all its writings bore witness to Christ, or, as Luz puts it, not all of them give expression to the gospel. Some parts of the Old Testament are passed over in total silence or receive relatively little attention.[16] That is perhaps not surprising if, as Hans Hübner remarks, it is a "fact that *only a part* of

---

[12] A. H. J. Gunneweg, *Vom Verstehen des Alten Testaments: Eine Hermeneutik* (GAT 5; 2nd ed.; Göttingen, 1988), 110-20; cf. also on the ambivalence of the Old Testament, e.g., 104, 174.

[13] In M. Klopfenstein, U. Luz (ed.), *Mitte der Schrift: Ein jüdisch-christliches Gespräch* (JeC 11; Bern, 1987), 119-47.

[14] "Paulus und das Alte Testament", in *Oikodome* (ThB 65; München, 1979), here 206.

[15] *Christos, Kyrios, Gottessohn: Untersuchungen zu Gebrauch und Bedeutung der christologischen Bezeichnungen bei Paulus und den vorpaulinischen Gemeinden* (AThANT 44; Zürich/Stuttgart, 1963), esp. 193.

[16] Cf. also D.-A. Koch, *Die Schrift als Zeuge des Evangeliums: Untersuchungen zur Verwendung und zum Verständnis der Schrift bei Paulus* (Tübingen, 1985), 45-8, and "'...bezeugt durch das Gesetz und die Propheten'. Zur Funktion der Schrift bei Paulus", in H. J. Schmid, J. Mehlhausen (ed.), *Sola Scriptura: Das reformatorische Schriftprinzip in der säkularen Welt* (Gütersloh, 1991), 169-79, esp. 170-2.

the Old Testament is theologically relevant for *the whole* of the New Testament".[17]

For within the writings of the Old Testament, too, there is, in Paul's view, according to Luz, a dialectic between law and promise.[18] The Law tends for Paul to be relegated to something episodic in the history of God's dealings with humanity, an interlude inaugurated at Sinai; foreign to Paul is the idea that the Law was God's pre-existent wisdom (that rôle, we may add, he and other early Christians tended to claim for Christ); foreign, too, is the idea that it was God's plan of creation. If it has a continuing function, it is to "show humanity the depth of its sin and, as the enduring rival of the gospel", to enable us to grasp the greatness of the gospel's saving power (p. 134). Here, however, we need to ask whether Luz has not leaned too heavily towards a reading of Paul's view of the Law that is based more on Galatians,[19] and therefore attributes to him a greater unity of view than his writings in fact display.

One partner or pole in this dialectic, "promise", is for Paul a term that is catapulted from relative obscurity into considerable prominence as a key term in his thought. What is important for Paul is, however, not so much the content of the promise as the way in which it is given; it is an analogy to the gospel, pointing to Christ and thus, in common with the gospel, revealing God's faithfulness. Its epitome, its paradigm Paul finds in the promise to Abraham. This is for him *"the* promise".[20] There is thus an analogy of structure between the new and the now superseded old order.

And yet we have to note at this point that, although there is indeed here a continuity, an analogy, it is a continuity which Paul traces through the response to God of a human being, Abraham. In contrast to those who have seen a continuity between old and new in terms of God's saving actions, we need to stress that the continuity of which Paul speaks

---

[17] *Biblische Theologie*, 18 (italics his); cf. also 29, 65). In that case it becomes problematic if it is demanded of a "biblical theology" that it "do full justice to the Old Testament" and "do justice to the biblical material in its totality" (Scobie, "Challenge", 55, 57). Or does the "justice" that is to be done to the Old Testament include the possibility that a large part of its contents are to be rejected as outmoded and superseded by the gospel, left on the sidelines of history by the onward march of God's purposes more adequately realized in Christ? Does the "justice" that is to be done allow room for the recognition also that the witness of the Old Testament is a varied one and contains in some measure conflicting elements (cf. Hübner, 237)?

[18] This dialectic, or antithesis, is, according to C. Dietzfelbinger, *Paulus und das Alte Testament: Die Hermeneutik des Paulus, untersucht an seiner Deutung der Gestalt Abrahams* (ThExH NF 95; München, 1961), 39–45, that which prevents Israel's history from being identified with *Heilsgeschichte simpliciter*. Similarly Vielhauer, "Paulus", 222, argues that Paul, unlike Matthew or Luke, saw that not all of the Old Testament, but only that in it which was ἐπαγγελία, was a witness that legitimated the Christian message.

[19] Yet, to be fair, Luz also cites Rom 7.7–24 in support of his contention.

[20] Although he does refer to "promises" in the plural in Rom 9.4; 2 Cor 1.20.

here is between the human response of Abraham and the human response of Christians—his faith and theirs. Of course that faith is seen as a response to something, to God's gracious action in making promises to Abraham and to God's gracious action in Christ. Yet this character of God is expressed in terms of the faith of the one who trusts God to have this character (πιστεύοντι, 4.5; ἐπίστευσεν, 4.17). Whether or not God is in fact like that, both Abraham and Christians believed God was like that and responded and acted accordingly and in analogous ways. In other words, we come again to the fact that, as Ebeling observed, what we find in the words of the Bible is not, properly speaking, "theology" but "something that happens to human beings".[21] Or, to quote one of Luz's earlier works, "Paul constantly and energetically relates his theological thinking to the human experience of reality."[22]

At the same time, however, we may add that that response is similar because in both cases it is expected that God will act similarly. So Abraham's faith has the character which it has because it is directed towards a creator God who calls things which do not exist into being. But before God is identified as the God who is able to do that Paul identifies God as the one who makes the dead alive (Rom 4.17). Here Paul is clearly reading back into the story of Abraham the Christian experience of the God of resurrection power, so that Abraham's faith is seen as a faith in a God who is able to do that sort of thing. At the same time, Paul can also read forward from that same Christ-event to make the confident affirmation that the sort of God who did not spare Christ, God's own Son, but gave him up for our sakes, will surely in the future grant us everything with him (Rom 8.32). Christ becomes, as it were, a "hermeneutical middle" of history for the understanding of the past and for expectation for the future. Yet this is not a continuity of God's "mighty acts" but a continuity of human confidence in a God who consistently desires to do certain things and is able to do them. Moreover what this faith responds to in the case of Abraham is not so much an act of God but a word of God, a promise (Rom 4.17-21; cf. Gal 3.8). If that is so then we can most appropriately speak of a continuity in response to what was perceived to be God's word.

It is also true that, if we are to speak of "types" and "typology", as many do in handling this topic, it is again human beings and their actions which are so described by Paul: it is Adam who is a "type" of the coming one; and it is the experiences of the Israelites in the wilderness

---

[21] "'Biblische Theologie'", 85.
[22] U. Luz, *Das Geschichtsverständnis des Paulus* (BEvTh 49; München, 1968), 383.

that occur τυπικῶς (1 Cor 10.11).[23] In other words, the continuity that is observed is again observed and described "from ground-level", as it were: the actions of a person or persons at one point of time foreshadow those which are actually performed by another at a later point of time, or foreshadow those which future persons, in a similar situation, might perform (1 Cor 10.11).[24]

To return to Luz's essay: he argues that the dialectic between "law" and "promise" which he discovers in Paul corresponds to the two "poles" which G. Scholem discovered in the Old Testament, God's revelation as tradition or Torah over against the hope for the "inauguration of a new dimension of redemption or messianism".[25] The Old Testament as a whole holds together God's foundational act on Sinai where Israel received the Torah as an abiding sign of its election and a commission to it, and also the conviction that the God who was revealed in Exod 3.14 is the living God who is never limited and so always offers new hope.

It corresponds, too, to the view of W. Zimmerli that God's self-disclosure was expounded in the Old Testament in very different ways, despite their constant reference to one another and interweaving with one another: tradition could take precedence over the messianic hope of a new saving action of Yahweh or *vice versa*.[26] The first, the dominant strand in the Old Testament writings, retained its vitality by constantly expounding the inherited tradition anew, establishing it and applying it afresh. Over against it are many voices, particularly those of the prophetic writings that announce with ever increasing clarity what is basically a new saving action, thus relativizing the former saving action to a "historical intermezzo" (p. 145). Corresponding to all these different voices there are also, we should note, a whole plethora of different possible ways of interpreting the Old Testament: Haenchen vividly and

---

[23] Yet Koch, *Schrift*, 216-20, is disinclined to accord the name of "typology" to the second instance; according to his preferred definition of "typology" Paul only uses two examples, Adam–Christ and the covenant of death/condemnation–the covenant of the Spirit/righteousness. My inclination is to use "typology", if one uses the expression at all, in a way that reflects Paul's own usage of such terminology.

[24] For this important qualification cf. I. Dugandzic, *Das "Ja" Gottes in Christus: Eine Studie zur Bedeutung des Alten Testaments für das Christusverständnis des Paulus* (FB 26; Würzburg, 1977), 247.

[25] "Paulinische Theologie", 143, quoting G. Scholem, "Die Krise der Tradition im jüdischen Messianismus", in his *Judaica*, 3 (2nd ed.; Frankfurt, 1977), esp. 153-7, and "Zum Verständnis der messianischen Idee im Judentum", in *Über einige Grundbegriffe des Judentums* (Frankfurt, 1970), esp. 123-42.

[26] Luz refers to Zimmerli's "Verheißung und Erfüllung", in C. Westermann (ed.), *Probleme alttestamentlicher Hermeneutik* (ThB 11; München, 1960), here 88; "Das Gesetz im Alten Testament", in *Gottes Offenbarung* (ThB 19; München, 1963), here 270-3; "Die Bedeutung der großen Schriftprophetie für das alttestamentliche Reden von Gott", in *Studien zur alttestamentlichen Theologie und Prophetie* (ThB 51; München, 1974), 55-72; and, more recently, "Biblische Theologie", in *TRE* 6 (Berlin/New York, 1980), here 447; *Grundriß der alttestamentlichen Theologie* (Theologische Wissenschaft 3; Stuttgart, etc., 1972), 147-207. Cf. too H. G. Reventlow, *Problems*, 151.

fittingly compares it to a room with not just one door for access to it, but many;[27] Jews of different persuasions utilized many of these approaches to their text and Christians too were subsequently to interpret these same texts in a variety of ways.

Nor did Paul always read the Old Testament in the same way as his fellow Jews. Indeed his exegesis was often diametrically opposed to that of his contemporaries, a sort of *Protestexegese*. Not that he appealed to some esoteric exegetical method; Luz insists that Paul addressed his appeal to unbelieving Israel on the basis of the Old Testament in the conviction that it "speaks openly and plainly" so that he could hope to win Israel over by it (p. 124), and in his interpretation he believed that he was remaining faithful to the meaning of the texts. Nor did he differ from them in believing that the Old Testament spoke to the present, but where he did part company was in affirming that they spoke to those gripped by God's saving action in Christ, i.e. to Gentile Christians as well as Jewish. It is also clear that he saw them as speaking still to those Jews who had not yet felt, or responded to, that saving appeal.

### III. Romans 9-11

As a prime example of his concern for Israel, if not a direct appeal to it, Romans 9-11 is perhaps better fitted than any other passage in Paul's writings to show the apostle's perception of the relationship of his new faith to his Jewish heritage.[28] Moreover, the fact that he writes these chapters, not in the heat of controversy and argument as in Galatians, but with the calmer and more circumspect bearing of the apologist defending his message against the charge that it impugns God's character,[29] makes it the more necessary that he should attend to the sort of issues which concern us here and thus makes it the more probable that we should see here his considered view on these matters.[30] It moreover shows Paul's answer to this problem in all its complexity. For the passage is marked by a number of tensions, some would even say contradictions or U-turns, in Paul's thought that point to the difficulty which this relationship posed

---

[27] "Das alte 'Neue Testament' und das neue 'Alte Testament'", in *Die Bibel und wir: Gesammelte Aufsätze*, 2 (Tübingen, 1968), 13-27, here 26.

[28] For Reventlow, *Problems*, 94, "to some degree Rom. 9-11 is the touchstone for deciding between two alternative understandings of Pauline theology: that in terms of existentialist theology and that in terms of salvation history"—unless, of course, one reinterprets salvation history existentially and existentialist theology in terms of a history of salvation.

[29] For a justification of this assessment of Romans cf. my *The Reasons for Romans* (Studies of the New Testament and Its World; Edinburgh, 1988).

[30] Cf. H. Hübner, "Biblische Theologie und Theologie des Neuen Testaments. Eine programmatische Skizze", *KuD* 27 (1981), 2-19, here 15: "Paul's discussion of Israel in Romans is one of the high points in the theological treatment of Israel in the New Testament."

for him.[31] So, for instance, he begins with a delimitation of those designated by the term "Israel": the term applies only to the children of the promise, not those of the flesh (9.8). Yet by the end of the passage he is talking again of that Israel, part of which has been hardened (11.25) and all of which will be saved (11.26). Even if he consistently upholds the faithfulness of God throughout the passage (9.6; 11.29), yet he seems to change his tack in his handling of the questions of who will benefit from that faithfulness, and whether any have so chosen and acted that they have put themselves beyond the scope of God's promises. It is true that he does not state unequivocally in chap. 9 that God has doomed some people, particularly the majority of the Jews, to final destruction, but, as Hübner notes, the reader who followed Paul's argument up to 9.29 "must be convinced that the majority of the Jews are irretrievably lost in the final judgement".[32]

At the same time, however, the final outcome of Paul's argument in chap. 11 is far more positive, far more hopeful, in its convictions about Israel, and in its expectations for it, than were the apostle's utterances in passages like 1 Thess 2.14-16 or Gal 3-4.[33] Thus, if we are to have any hope of finding in Paul some light to shed upon the vexed problem of any positive relationship of the New Testament to the Old, it must be here rather than with his earlier, far more negative statements on the subject that we must begin.

Now in this passage we can see how Paul stresses both the continuity of his Christian faith with his Jewish heritage and, at the same time, the discontinuity; few passages show better "the remarkable mingling of

---

[31] Cf. here esp. H. Räisänen, "Römer 9-11: Analyse eines geistigen Ringens", *ANRW* II.25.4 (Berlin/New York, 1987), 2891-939, and "Paul, God, and Israel: Romans 9-11 in Recent Research", in J. Neusner, P. Borgen, E. S. Frerichs, R. Horsley (ed.), *The Social World of Formative Christianity and Judaism. Essays in Tribute to Howard Clark Kee* (Philadelphia, 1988), 178-202. For others, e.g. Hübner and Wilckens, the tensions are part of a "dramatic" shaping of the argument of these three chapters, in which Paul leaves his readers thinking that he has said his last word on the matter of Israel's fate, only to speak yet another word. And yet Hübner grants that the distinction between two different senses of "Israel" in chap. 9 cannot be harmonized with the view that all "Israel" will be saved: "as far as the rules of our logic are concerned we cannot but grant that there is a contradiction here" (*Gottes Ich und Israel: Zum Schriftgebrauch des Paulus in Römer 9-11* [FRLANT 136; Göttingen, 1984], 122). How one evaluates these tensions will thus in large measure turn on the question how far one thinks Paul knew the end of his argument and his route to it before he embarked on it at the start of chap. 9. To my mind the twists and turns of the argument look more like the work of one who is thinking his position through as he goes rather than one who knows his position before he starts. To Hübner these are not due to Paul's carelessness in argument, but the sort of *aporia* which great thinkers are prepared to allow to remain in their thought. But for N. Walter, "Zur Interpretation von Römer 9-11", *ZThK* 81 (1984), 172-95, here 176, "one can deduce from the three stages of the argument that this solution [in 11.11-36] did not yet occur to him as he started out in 9.1-5 and then wrote down 9.6-29"; rather it only occurred to him as he wrote, and as he realized the unsatisfactory nature of the first two stages of the argument.
[32] *Gottes Ich*, 57.
[33] Cf Hübner, *Gottes Ich*, 127-35.

continuity and discontinuity" to which Hübner refers.[34] From the start Paul acknowledges the heritage that is Israel's; the only question is to which "Israel" it belongs. To it belongs the status of God's children, it enjoys God's glory, with it God's covenants are made, and for it the Law was given; it has the privilege of worshipping God, and God's promises have been given to it. From this chosen people has come the Messiah, Christ (9.4-5). God's calling and God's gifts are irrevocable (11.29) and Paul is led by this to assert that "all Israel will be saved" (11.26) and, as we have seen, it is hard in this context to limit that to "Israel" in the narrower sense, the children of the promise as opposed to those of the flesh.

To that extent Paul seems to issue an unqualified endorsement of all that he had inherited as a Jew: these things are the Jews' heritage and that heritage cannot be taken away from them. At the same time how this will be achieved is a "mystery" (11.25), and it seems likeliest that by this Paul refers to insights gleaned from a Spirit-led exegesis of the Old Testament;[35] that in turn reminds us how much Paul's understanding and use of the Old Testament is guided by Christ and by the Spirit of Christ as 2 Cor 3.16-17 shows, a veil lies on Israel's heart as it reads the scriptures, but when it turns to the Lord who is the Spirit, as Paul has done, that veil is removed.

Fundamental here, however, is the conviction that the God in whom Paul puts his faith is Israel's God, the same God whom he sought to serve as an ardent Pharisee, however perverse he may later have deemed his service to be. This prevents him from cutting loose from his Jewish heritage, just as it should prevent modern scholars, even those most sceptical about the possibility or legitimacy of a "biblical theology", from cutting loose their exposition of the New Testament theology entirely from the Old Testament. For the writers of the various theologies contained in the New Testament all in varying degrees demonstrated that their message was in some kind of continuity with that of the Old Testament.[36] For Paul, like the author of Hebrews, passes a negative verdict on the old covenant while at the same time using for his argument the documents of that old covenant, the Old Testament scriptures.[37] Moreover, at the very least, as Hübner puts it, "the continuity of Old and New Testament is ... God".[38] Yet that in turn raises, as he recognizes,

---

[34] *Biblische Theologie*, 95.
[35] Cf. Hübner, *Gottes Ich*, 121; cf. also his *Biblische Theologie*, 95.
[36] Cf. Dunn, *Unity*, chap. 5.
[37] So Hübner, *Biblische Theologie*, 97.
[38] *Gottes Ich*, 123-4.

the question whether there is also a continuity in the belief in, or perception of, that one God.[39]

However, there is also nonetheless a discontinuity between Israel's faith and Paul's Christian faith. This cannot be explained as due simply to Israel's failure to perceive what their faith and their inheritance truly were; it is not just that they misunderstood what God had offered them and wanted of them, and so went astray. For Paul seems to make it clear that the Old Testament did plainly offer them life through faithful keeping of the commandments of the Law: there is "a righteousness based on the Law" and the Law does hold out the promise of life to those who keep its commandments (Rom 10.5, quoting Lev 18.5).[40]

That surely means that there are different voices to be heard within the Old Testament, pointing hearers in different directions. That at least seems to be the most obvious interpretation of the use made of the Old Testament in Rom 10.5-8. For these verses, with their opening antithesis of "the righteousness based on the Law" and "the righteousness based on faith",[41] do not, on the surface at least, seem to be speaking of "the impossibility and therefore also the end of righteousness by the Law".[42] For the Law is still there, still speaking, we must assume, with a siren-voice that lures one to seek salvation through faithful obedience to its commands. It is only those whose ears are open to the other righteousness who can hear in the scriptures their witness to that other righteousness.

It would seem to be the consequence of this that, for Paul, there could be no Christian faith, no Christian theology, that was at the same time a "biblical theology" in the sense of one that represented the variegated perspectives of the Bible *in their entirety*. For Christian faith must, by its very nature, listen to and appropriate those voices within the Old

---

[39] That is a distinction that emerges more clearly in his *Gottes Ich*, 35, but seems somewhat more blurred in his *Biblische Theologie*, 35, when he moves from the question of the "identity" of Yahweh and the Father of Jesus Christ to that of "differences in the understanding of God" in the two Testaments.

[40] However, A. Lindemann, "Die Gerechtigkeit aus dem Gesetz: Erwägungen zur Auslegung und zur Textgeschichte von Röm 10,5", *ZNW* 73 (1982), 231-50, esp. 241, is inclined to regard ἐν αὐτοῖς (preferring the reading of N-A[26] and *GNT*[3]) as referring to the circumstances of the life promised: Paul refers to the "Einbindung des Menschen in den Lebenshorizont der Werke (oder der Gebote)" (cf. Rom 6.2). This is not understood by Paul as a rival promise of the eschatological gift of life. Cf. J. D. G. Dunn, "'Righteousness from the Law' and 'Righteousness from Faith': Paul's Interpretation of Scripture in Romans 10:1-11", in G. F. Hawthorne, O. Betz (ed.), *Tradition and Interpretation in the New Testament: Essays in Honor of E. Earle Ellis for His 60th Birthday* (Grand Rapids/Tübingen, 1987), 216-28, here 219.

[41] Not all, of course, interpret these antithetically; see, e.g. C. E. B. Cranfield, *A Critical and Exegetical Commentary on the Epistle to the Romans*, 2 (ICC; Edinburgh, 1979), 521-2, who, following Barth, interprets v. 5 Christologically. Cf., however, J. D. G. Dunn, *Romans 9-16* (WBC 38B; Dallas, 1988), 602, and "'Righteousness'", esp. 218-19; J. S. Vos, "Die hermeneutische Antinomie bei Paulus (Galater 3.11-12; Römer 10.5-10)", *NTS* 38 (1992), 254-70, here 267-70.

[42] Dugandzic, *"Ja" Gottes*, 63.

Testament which bear witness to Christ. Now there is of course room for debate as to which voices do that and how, but Paul seems here to recognize some that do so and some that do not. His very selectivity in his use of the Old Testament attests his recognition that not all parts of it speak alike or point in the same direction.

It is another matter, too, whether Paul's way of hearing these voices was one which his Jewish contemporaries, let alone the original writers and hearers of the scriptures, would have recognized at all.[43] The possibility of that is perhaps not something that would have greatly troubled Paul; after all, he recognized in 2 Cor 3.15 that up to his day a veil had lain on the hearts of Israel when Moses was read to them. Certainly the drastic way in which Paul adapts Deut 30.12-14 in Rom 10.6-8 has often been commented upon; indeed it can be regarded as giving the text a thrust that is diametrically opposed to its original sense.[44] That he does so should be a warning to us that the "biblical theology" which we discover by taking the New Testament, and especially Paul, as our starting-point in interpreting the Old Testament will yield a theology which the Old Testament exegete will have to disown as an exegesis of the Old Testament in its own right.[45]

In the previous verse before the antithesis of Rom 10.5 and 10.6-8, in 10.4, Paul had made a statement which could and should prove a vital key to his understanding of the relationship between Israel's faith and the Christian faith; unfortunately, however, it is at the same time a statement which at the crucial point is beset by a considerable measure of ambiguity: Christ is the τέλος of the Law.[46] For some the word τέλος means "end" in the sense of "termination" and that interpretation then lays all the stress upon the discontinuity between the old and the new.

---

[43] So Haenchen remarks that the Old Testament understood in its original sense would never have found a place in the Christian canon ("Alte 'Neue Testament'", 18). Put more pointedly still, the Old Testament understood on its own terms would simply dismiss Jesus as accursed (Deut 21.23 quoted in Gal 3.13; cf. E. Gräßer, "Offene Fragen im Umkreis einer Biblischen Theologie", *ZThK* 77 [1980], 200-221, here 215).

[44] Cf. Vielhauer, "Paulus", 215; Koch, *Schrift*, 129-132, 351; also E. Käsemann, *An die Römer* (HNT 8a; 2nd ed.; Tübingen, 1974), 273. Hübner, *Gottes Ich* , 68, notes how in 9.33 Paul also transforms a promise into a threat in Isa 28.16 by his insertion of λίθον προσκόμματος καὶ πέτραν σκανδάλου from Isa 8.14, and on Rom 11.8 remarks that "once again Paul saw himself as justified and authorized so to modify a text of scripture that it said what Paul needed as a scriptural proof"-"only scripture read by faith and interpreted by faith provides the warrant for faith" (104).

[45] That holds good however much one may see a preparation for Paul's handling of the text in Jewish exegesis of that age, in its attempts to understand Deut 30.11-14 as having "a more transcendent referent" (Dunn, "'Righteousness'", 220; Dunn, however, recognizes that Baruch and Philo "see that more universal ideal to be focused in the law", 224).

[46] Hübner, *Gottes Ich*, 94, seems to wish to take εἰς δικαιοσύνην with νόμου and speaks of a νόμος εἰς δικαιοσύνην - a "Gesetz auf Gerechtigkeit und Leben hin"; but νόμου and εἰς δικαιοσύνην are separated in Paul's text by Χριστός and that surely means that the production of righteousness is the result or purpose of *the ending of* the Law and not that of the Law itself.

Yet we also have to note that there are good reasons for giving the word τέλος a sense such as "goal" which allows a far greater measure of continuity.

Badenas has made out a strong case for the primacy of ideas of direction, purpose, and completion in the semantic field of the word, both in classical and in biblical Greek; this is particularly the case when it is used with a dependent genitive, and above all the four statements in the New Testament which are most closely parallel in structure to Rom 10.4, namely Rom 6.21 and 22, 1 Tim 1.5, and 1 Pet 1.9, all clearly show this.[47] J. S. Vos, too, tellingly compares Philo *Deus imm* 61, 67, where Philo speaks of the divine Lawgiver's τέλος in the giving of the Law; he thus argues for τέλος in the sense of *voluntas, sententia* here.[48]

In addition it should be noted how much the context speaks of goals and the pursuit of goals and the achievement or non-achievement of goals.[49] While the Gentiles did not pursue (διώκοντα) the goal of righteousness they nevertheless gained it, on the basis of faith, whereas Israel, which was pursuing a "Law of righteousness",[50] failed to attain to the Law (9.30-31).[51] They were zealous in God's service but their zeal lacked discernment; because of that they attempted to establish their own righteousness (10.2-3).

And yet in the last analysis τέλος in the sense of "goal" does not rule out the sense of "termination" either.[52] For Siegert is right here to

---

[47] R. Badenas, *Christ the End of the Law: Romans 10.4 in Pauline Perspective* (JSNT.SS 10; Sheffield, 1985), chap. 2.

[48] "Antinomie", 264-5, 268.

[49] Cf. J. A. Fitzmyer, *Paul and His Theology: A Brief Sketch* (2nd ed.; Englewood Cliffs, NJ, 1987), 80.

[50] Hübner, *Gottes Ich*, 62, notes how rarely commentators attend to the sharpness of the dilemma posed by the translation of νόμος δικαιοσύνης: is it a "Law which is misused to attain righteousness" or, more positively, a "Law whose inner intention according to God's will is righteousness"? In the light of the parallels with Isa 51 in the context he prefers the latter, agreeing with Cranfield, *Romans*, 2, 508.

[51] This argument is, of course, less compelling if one sees in 10.1 the beginning of a new section of Paul's argument as does, e.g., M. Rese, "Israels Unwissen und Ungehorsam und die Verkündigung des Glaubens durch Paulus in Römer 10", in D.-A. Koch, G. Sellin, A. Lindemann (ed.), *Jesu Rede von Gott und ihre Nachgeschichte im frühen Christentum: Beiträge zur Verkündigung Jesu und zum Kerygma der Kirche* (FS W. Marxsen; Gütersloh, 1989), 252-66, here 255. But whether ἀδελφοί is any clearer a signal of a new start than the τί οὖν ἐροῦμεν of 9.30 is questionable. But here too, as in the rest of Romans, one should note how Paul's mode of argument in Romans is not to develop it in clearly defined sections but to have "bridge" passages which link the preceding and the following together (cf. N. A. Dahl, "The Missionary Theology in the Letter to the Romans", in *Studies in Paul: Theology for the Early Christian Mission* [Minneapolis, 1977], 70-94, here 79). So 9.30-3 may round off the argument of chap. 9, as Rese argues, *and* introduce the theme of chap. 10 (cf. Rese, 256).

[52] And so I do not see that the arguments which Dugandzic, *"Ja" Gottes*, 66-8, brings to bear against the sense of "goal" apply here: I do not wish to restrict ϑεοῦ in the phrase δικαιοσύνη ϑεοῦ to describing a quality of God (although this would be better described as a possessive genitive rather than a subjective, *pace* Dugandzic, 67), nor do I wish to deny the antithesis in vv. 5 and 6. It is a considerable weakness of Dugandzic's account that he treats 10.4-13 as a unit, severing 10.4's connection with 9.30ff., and the argument of these verses does seem to support the meaning "goal" (see above). The γάρ of 10.5 need not mean that *only* v. 5 provides the basis of 10.4. Rather v. 5 together with the contrasted vv. 6-8

complain that it is wrong to pose "end" and "goal" as alternatives "as long as one means [by 'goal'] a goal that has been reached".[53] For with the reaching of a goal the pursuit of that goal is over; once one breaks the finishing tape the race has been run. But the presence of this nuance of meaning in τέλος as "goal" means that the pursuit and the striving that preceded it are not necessarily devalued: the race was worth running even if Israel missed the way and failed to cross the finishing line.

This may perhaps help to explain the curious fact that in 9.31 Israel are said to fail to attain, not righteousness, but the Law, as if reaching or attaining the Law were indeed something that was worth doing. Were the pursuit of the "Law of righteousness" something wholly negative then their failure should have been seen as a blessing, or at least a blessing in disguise. Of that there is, however, no hint.

One has to do justice to the fact that, even for those who insist solely upon the meaning "end" *qua* "termination" here, the usability of the Law and its validity for his arguments does not end with the coming of Christ, for Paul continues to make his case by appeal to the Law as well as speaking of the Christian's life in the Spirit as a fulfilment of the "righteous requirement of the Law" (Rom 8.4). This paradox of the superseding of the Law, at least as regards our salvation, coupled with continuing appeal to the Law is found in a concise form also in 3.21: God's righteousness has been revealed apart from the Law but at the same time is attested by that Law and by the prophets.[54] Nor is that surprising, for, as Hübner has shown, Paul "hears the very voice of God speaking to him from the scripture".[55] Even in Galatians, where Paul so sharply criticizes part of the scriptures, the Mosaic Law, the scriptures, including the Pentateuch, still contain God's voice of promise, for it was in them that Abraham was told what God had promised him (3.8).

So, if we keep the analogy of a race and I am well aware of the pitfalls of beguiling analogies then the race that Israel was trying to run was not one on a single, clearly laid out track, but more like some cross-

---

explain v. 4. That both righteousnesses are found in the Law, including that of the righteousness based on faith, means that the salvation that Christ brings is indeed that towards which the Law has pointed (cf. 3.21), but in so pointing it points to that which will supersede it as a way of salvation by "doing" what it demands; with the *"near"* word of Christ there is no need for another righteousness and indeed, since it is the word of *Christ*, to choose any other path would be disobedient folly.

[53] F. Siegert, *Argumentation bei Paulus gezeigt an Röm 9-11* (WUNT 34; Tübingen, 1985), 149: these are not alternatives for "Christ is the *end* of the Law (as a means of human striving after righteousness) in that he anticipates its *purpose* and incarnated it in his person"; cf. also U. Wilckens, *Der Brief an die Römer*, 2: *Röm 6-11* (EKK 6.2; Zürich, etc./Neukirchen-Vluyn, 1980), 222-3 (although there is little in the context to justify his assertion that Christ is the "end" of the Law in that he ends its function of cursing sinners).

[54] Cf. Koch, "'... bezeugt'", 169.

[55] "Biblische Theologie", 16; cf. also his *Gottes Ich*.

country or orienteering course where it was all too possible to miss the way and end up at the wrong place. I am also conscious, however, that this suggestion raises questions about the competence and fairness of the course marshal, in this instance God. That is, however, an issue which Paul does not confront in that form here.

Yet perhaps Paul should have raised the question of the fairness or, to use his term, the righteousness of God's dealings if he saw that the Law actually contained instructions that encouraged Israel in its mistaken course (10.5). Had he faced up to this issue, he might merely have taken the line that God is God and God can therefore do what God chooses; it is not for us to question the correctness of God's actions. That is, after all the line that he adopts when dealing with the question of God's treatment of the likes of Pharaoh (9.16-23): God's actions are likened to those of a potter with lumps of clay, however incongruous that may seem when speaking of the God of Jesus Christ whose boundless love Paul has just described in such lyrical terms at the close of chap. 8. Or he might have waxed lyrical again and might have praised the gracious but ultimately inscrutable ways of God as in 11.33-36. The latter is, of course, more uplifting, but the problem remains: why did God give Israel potentially and actually ambiguous instructions? Is one not, then, better to treat with extreme caution (the somewhat anthropomorphic) talk of God "giving" these instructions and, again, to think more in terms of human attempts to trace out ways of living that were in keeping with the perceived nature of the God who was believed to be the ultimate reality in our world?[56]

## IV. "Biblical Theology"?

Luz's conclusion was that "seen from Paul's perspective there can be no other theology than one which expounds the gospel of Jesus Christ and is therefore biblical theology".[57] Taken by itself that statement could all too easily be misunderstood. There can, of course, be other theologies, and Paul knew of them amongst his fellow Jews; there was, however, *for Christians* only one way of talking about God, and this was for him the

---

[56] Cf. Räisänen as quoted below (at n. 76). I have used the term "Old Testament" for convenience throughout, although aware of protests at the possible connotations of the phrase, particularly the possible negative implications of "Old". Yet I also feel uneasy that "Testament" or even "dispensation" implies a testator, a dispenser, who is responsible for making two different arrangements with humanity; this could easily distort matters, for what we have, at least in the first instance, are different stages in, or modes of, human perception of God, with correspondingly different ways of living according to the perceived will of God; we would be best to start by talking of these different *human* perceptions, even if we later want to go on to speak also of varying receptivity to God's self-disclosure.
[57] "Paulinische Theologie", 141.

true way, and this way took as its starting-point the gospel of Christ. This way of talking of God, this theology, is at the same time biblical theology in the sense that it appeals not just to Christian traditions, be they oral or written; it appeals to Jewish traditions too or at least to some of them. And a biblical theology is also in a sense a peculiarly Christian enterprise if the adjective "biblical" refers to the Bible in the sense of the corpus of writings of both the Old and the New Testament; it is *Christians* and not Jews who would want to base their theology on this *two*fold foundation.[58]

So when the editors of the *Theologische Realenzyklopädie* came to the article on "Biblische Theologie"[59] they divided the article into two halves, Old Testament (W. Zimmerli) and New Testament (O. Merk). Although occasionally Zimmerli in the first of these mentions those Old Testament scholars who have seen the Old Testament as incomplete in itself and waiting for its fulfilment in the future, he sets his face resolutely against that approach, finding in the Old Testament a coherent collection of writings centred around the theme which R. Smend sums up as "Yahweh the God of Israel and Israel the people of Yahweh".[60] In the light of that it seems to me questionable whether the study of the Old Testament, without that of the New, would cease to be a theological discipline.[61] It would not yield the same theology, but could nonetheless be a theological enterprise.

Merk, besides chronicling the rise of the separate discipline of New Testament theology, also pays more attention to those scholars who have sought to bring together the thought of both Testaments in a "biblical theology", but in the last analysis finds these attempts unsatisfactory from a New Testament perspective as well: not only do they neglect the diversity within the New Testament by speaking of a single *Endstufe* of the *Traditionsprozeß*, but they distort the nature of the New Testament; here he quotes with approval from Adolf Schlatter:

---

[58] Scobie, "Challenge", 53-4; yet he obscures this issue by immediately veering off into a discussion of Old Testament theology.

It is true, however, that it would be possible for Jews to seek to interpret both Testaments from a standpoint determined by the Old Testament, and there has certainly been a whole series of Jewish scholars who have approached the theology of the New Testament from a Jewish perspective. Equally, however, there have been Christian biblical exegetes who have been just as concerned to let the Old Testament be heard in its own right.

[59] Vol. 6 (Berlin/New York, 1980).

[60] Zimmerli, 426-55, appealing to R. Smend, *Die Mitte des Alten Testaments* (ThSt [B] 101; Zürich, 1970), 48-9, 52, 54, etc., who was in turn quoting J. Wellhausen, "Israelitisch-jüdische Religion", in P. Hinneberg (ed.), *Die Kultur der Gegenwart*, 1.4.1 (Leipzig, 1905), p. 8 = R. Smend (ed.), *Grundrisse zum Alten Testament* (ThB 27; München, 1965), 73.

[61] Smend, *Die Mitte*, 58-9, quoted by Gräßer, "Fragen", 219. Smend in fact here quotes, with his endorsement, E. Jüngel in E. Jüngel, K. Rahner, M. Seitz (ed.), *Die Praktische Theologie zwischen Wissenschaft und Praxis* (München, 1968), 42-3.

However, the independence of New Testament theology remains unchallenged over against the pre-history which directly determines it, namely the religious history of Israel. This is because the New Testament community is a formation complete in itself with its own central point. It grew out of a new impulse which is more than simply a repetition of old material.[62]

Yet, if "biblical theology" is defined as an attempt to tie together both Testaments as one "Bible" and to seek the unity within it, is it not anachronistic to call the theology of Paul and his contemporaries "biblical" in this sense, for they knew as authoritative writings only those of the Old Testament, however its extent was defined at that time? Thus we would have to use "biblical" in a rather different sense, to refer to the appeal of Paul and others like him to the writings of the Old Testament rather than the twofold modern appeal to both Testaments: their theology was "biblical" in that they claimed that the God made manifest in Jesus Christ was the same God as made manifest in the Old Testament.[63]

Indeed they could not do otherwise without denying the identity and the continuity of the God who spoke in the Old Testament with the God who raised Jesus from the dead. As Koch puts it, they did not believe God would issue self-contradictory statements; rather they believed that the God disclosed in the Old Testament had in Christ provided them with a final and full self-disclosure.[64] Since that God was, they believed, more clearly discernible in Christ they interpreted the Old Testament and evaluated its contents from that perspective. Indeed, what Haenchen says of the community which stands behind Matthew's Gospel should be regarded as true of the New Testament church in general: the Old Testament was precious to them because, *and only because,* it dealt with Jesus Christ.[65] On that basis they focused on some parts more than others and had the confidence to interpret those former parts in a way often drastically different from that of Jewish exegetes.[66] After all they, like other Jews before them (e.g. the Qumran community), believed that the scriptures had been written "for them",[67] and, if that was the case,

---

[62] Ed./tr. R. Morgan, *The Nature of New Testament Theology* (SBT 25; London, 1973), 117-66, here 146 (original in BFChTh 13.2; Gütersloh, 1909, 7-82).
[63] Cf. Vielhauer, "Paulus", 219.
[64] *Schrift*, 348.
[65] "Alte 'Neue Testament'", 15; one should perhaps say "*so* precious", since it is *theoretically* conceivable that Jewish Christians might have failed to find Christ in the Old Testament and yet, as Jews, have continued to value the latter.
[66] Cf. Dugandzic, *"Ja" Gottes*, 42-3: from Paul's argument in Gal 3.16,19 concerning Christ as the (singular) $\sigma\pi\acute{\epsilon}\rho\mu\alpha$ of Abraham one can see how the decisive influence and guide for Paul was not the Old Testament but the Christ-event.
[67] Cf. Rom 4.24; 15.4; 1 Cor 9.10; 10.11.

then surely they would be the ones who should be best able to interpret scripture correctly, as it was meant to be interpreted.

Seen in that light, the problem of a "biblical theology", whether that phrase refers to the early Christians' appropriation of the Jewish scriptures or a modern Christian exposition of the message of the New Testament as in some way in continuity with that of the Old Testament, an exposition which shares the early Christians' conviction that Christ was the key to understanding the Old Testament, is this: how does that way of looking at the Old Testament relate to those views of the Old Testament and its thought which one obtains when one does not share that perspective? Put bluntly, the question is why the Christian way of looking at the Old Testament should be any more valid than, say, that of an orthodox Jew? It is a problem of verification.[68] For is the selecting of some texts in preference to others, and the often arbitrary-seeming exegesis of them, not enough to support the charge of "eisegesis"?

Ultimately there is perhaps no fully adequate answer to that question. Certainly Paul, with his drastic reinterpretations and "protest exegesis", gives us none. To give but one example: Koch, discussing 2 Cor 3.12-18, rightly observes that Paul's argument here is circular: to make his point that a proper understanding of scripture is only possible in Christ Paul must first interpret the Old Testament in Christ.[69] But one way of at least partially answering this question is to claim that the Old Testament in some way invites, calls for, this sort of treatment which Christians give it. And so some Christian Old Testament theologians talk of it being "open", looking forward to a completion which will at the same time provide the all-important clue to the interpretation of the whole.[70] Yet the completion may only be that of one of the plurality of lines of tradition which make up our Old Testament. For a Jew might equally claim that it is the rabbis of Judaism who have provided the Old Testament with its completion. We run a grave risk here of a plurality of circular arguments which at no point overlap with one another, of a multiplicity of intellectual ghettos, each self-contained and content to

---

[68] Luz, "Paulinische Theologie", 134. To introduce the dimension of the different communities of faith and their respective life-styles here as does R. W. L. Moberly, *The Old Testament of the Old Testament: Patriarchal Narratives and Mosaic Yahwism* (Overtures to Biblical Theology; Minneapolis, 1992), e.g. 170-1, only shifts the problem elsewhere, and does not solve it; for the communities and the life-styles are based on differing understandings of the same text and one must still ask which community and which life-style really accords best with the nature and will of God.

[69] *Schrift*, 339.

[70] Luz himself uses this language ("Paulinische Theologie", 119, 142-3) echoing that of Zimmerli (*Grundriß*, 205-7), H. Gese ("Erwägungen zur Einheit der biblischen Theologie", in *Vom Sinai zum Sion* [BEvTh 64; München, 1974], 11-30), and G. von Rad (*Theologie des Alten Testaments*, 2 [2nd ed.; München, 1965], 446-7; cf. also 331). Distinguish this from the sense in which Haenchen talks of the Old Testament as "open", in the sense of being susceptible to a variety of different interpretations ("Alte 'Neue Testament'", 27).

contemplate its own intellectual heritage from within its own inherited set of assumptions. If this self-contained isolation and ultimate absence of truly radical self-criticism were inherent in the nature of the business of "theology", then indeed there would be a strong case for abandoning it as a scholarly discipline. (Few theologians would admit that that was what they were doing; yet it is perhaps those who are least aware of this danger who are most imperilled.) Yet there is also the possibility that the theological discipline, with the aid of other disciplines, can free itself from this strait-jacket and, at least partly and temporarily, step outside the position of unconditional commitment in order to view things "from outside", as it were, and in relative detachment.

So another way of dealing with this problem would be to try to see both Testaments within a wider context, to stand outside both, as it were, and to seek to evaluate them, say from the standpoint of philosophy or phenomenology of religion or some such perspective. One example of such an external viewpoint would be the "philosophy of history" appealed to by Wolfhart Pannenberg, a philosophy which he links with that of Marx and Hegel, according to which history can only be properly seen in the light of its end; this enables him to advance the thesis that

> the universal revelation of the deity of God is not yet realized in the history of Israel, but first in the fate of Jesus of Nazareth, insofar as the end of all events is anticipated in his fate.[71]

Another example is the attempt of Gerd Theiβen to set the entire biblical history within the broader framework of a process of "cultural evolution".[72] This most suggestive account presents an understanding of faith that is "biblical" in the sense of being, as J. Barton puts it,

> a style of faith to which the Bible gives us access, rather than one to which it unequivocally witnesses in all its parts. Biblical faith is the faith we encounter especially in the Bible, even only in the Bible, but not a religion that takes the Bible as its primary datum or which can be found evenly distributed throughout the Bible.

As Barton also remarks, Theiβen fully recognizes how parts of the New Testament compromise aspects of what Jesus stood for, "by insisting on rigid structures of church authority", just as strains of thought in the Old

---

[71] "Dogmatic Theses on the Doctrine of Revelation", in W. Pannenberg et al., Revelation as History (London/Sydney, 1969; ET of Göttingen, 1961), 123-58, here esp. 133, 139. See the discussion in Hübner, Biblische Theologie, 152-61.
[72] Biblical Faith: An Evolutionary Approach (London, 1984; ET of München, 1984).

Testament "deny the cause of the poor and helpless, against the teaching of the prophets".[73]

> "Biblical faith", as Theiβen sees it, has to be ready to reject such compromises and denials. Yet, however attractive Theiβen's proposal may be, we have to recall the long history of "developmental" accounts of biblical faith, going back into the days before biological theories of evolution.[74] There is in these a constant dilemma: is this development one wholly immanent within human history, or does it leave some room for divine intervention or "revelation"? It is not clear to me that Theiβen has come up with an answer to this, any more than he has spelt out the implications of his proposals for our understanding of the nature of God. Until that is clearer, it is hard to be sure where we stand along a spectrum of perspectives ranging from a passive God, to whom humans try as best they may to approximate, to a thorough-going interventionist God who unerringly guides the human race towards a goal in a sort of evolutionary *Heilsgeschichte*.[75]

It is even possible, too, within the categories of a more traditional historical-critical approach, to stand back and view both Testaments "from outside" and indeed that sort of detachment is a necessary part of the historical critic's task *qua* historical critic; so, at the end of his study of *Paul and the Law*, Räisänen observes that

> The only reasonable way to cope with the Torah theologically (if you are not an orthodox Jew or a Fundamentalist Christian) is to admit that it was *not* a direct divine revelation to Moses. It consists of a long series of human attempts to respond appropriately to what God was believed to have done. Its commandments are therefore historically conditioned. From such a critical point of view one is enabled to make distinctions within the Torah and give some parts more importance than others. But this was *not* the starting point of Paul (or of Jesus, or of any Christian of the first generation) ... .[76]

---

[73] J. Barton, *People of the Book? The Authority of the Bible in Christianity* (Bampton Lectures, 1988; London, 1988), 52-3.

[74] Cf., e.g., Gunneweg, *Verstehen*, 67 ("eine *menschliche Fortschritts-geschichte*"): there is a place, too, in such a scheme for God as the Mover in this history (e.g., 150).

[75] Although at times Theiβen's language may seem to imply a passive God (e.g. *Biblical Faith*, 30: we are the living beings who may "articulate the relationship of life to an ultimate reality ... for which there is no better word than 'God'"), what he says on the Spirit clearly seems to imply a far more interventionist model: Christians are "seized" by the Spirit and "the Spirit aims at an inner transformation of humanity" (139-40).

[76] *Paul and the Law*, 266; cf. Barton, *People*, 46: "The Bible is human reflection on the mystery of God, sparked off indeed by the fresh divine input into the human situation, in ancient Israel and in the first-century Mediterranean world through Jesus and his first disciples, but still remaining through and through a human book".

We can add to this that the "series of human attempts to respond appropriately to what God was believed to have done" did not end with the Torah, but extends on into the New Testament and beyond, even up to the present day. Discerning the human responses, we may note, is the work of historical criticism; whether they are appropriate responses to what God was thought to have done, or whether those who so responded were right to think that God had so acted, is a theological matter. Those theological questions can be asked of the Old Testament in isolation from the New. They can and must be asked also of the New Testament.[77]

But in all these, and other, attempts to evaluate both Testaments from outside it is implicit that this evaluation involves a selection of certain elements within both Testaments as somehow bound together with a connecting thread of continuity. Other material is either quietly left to one side, or else is expressly rejected as a discordant voice or voices injuring the harmony of the whole. And there is the danger that what is rejected may in the eyes of some render futile or pointless the attempt to trace a continuity: so, if Räisänen is right to argue that Paul's insistence on salvation solely by faith in Christ constitutes a break with the Sinai covenant, even if the apostle himself failed to recognize it,[78] one cannot expect the posited continuity to impress Jews of today any more than it impressed James and the Jerusalem church and the Jews of Paul's own day. The new order does *not* preserve intact what was generally held to be of the essence of the old.

At the same time the tracing of a connecting thread running through both Testaments is in the last analysis not something that can be proved with utter objectivity. It is the person with faith and, Christians believe, specifically with faith in Christ and guided by Christ, who is able critically to discern the thread, a paradoxical thread whose sole basis is the grace of God.[79] And yet such a description of the unity of the biblical testimony should be able to commend itself to the outsider by the way that it "makes sense" of the whole, even if, to make sense of the "whole", parts of that whole must be rejected or played down. It will "make sense" if it not only accounts for the records of past experiences of God reflected in both Testaments, but also fits in with one's perception of God today. And that "making sense" is not something that is fundamentally alien to a historical-critical approach, since ultimately a historical critic's reconstruction of past events will commend itself too by

---

[77] That is one reason why I would find it hard to limit the discipline of New Testament theology to a thorough-going historical programme as does H. Räisänen in his *Beyond New Testament Theology: A Story and a Programme* (London/Philadelphia, 1990).
[78] "Bruch", 168, 171 (he parts company with E. P. Sanders in denying that Paul was aware of repudiating the covenant).
[79] Dugandzic, *"Ja" Gottes*, 308.

the way that it "makes sense" of a complex web of past events, and "makes sense" in the light of our present experiences of historical reality.[80]

A Christian theology must be biblical in the sense that it recognizes that the God proclaimed as the Father of Jesus and as the one who raised him from the dead was regarded by the New Testament writers, including Paul, as the same God who is disclosed in the Old Testament; although that God had done a new thing in Jesus, it was not a new God who did it, nor was faith in that God new, nor was the new thing done unheard of;[81] for they believed it to have been foreshadowed by the Old Testament scriptures. But Paul makes it clear that not all those scriptures foreshadowed this new thing, and some served to blind hearers to the news of it. If the radical rejection of the Old Testament by a Marcion finds no warrant in Paul's writings, neither does a wholesale endorsement of all that the Old Testament scriptures contain.

---

[80] As an example of such a historical-critical "making sense" cf. the admirably sane judgment of W. G. Kümmel on the matter of sifting out authentic Jesus-material in his *Die Theologie des Neuen Testaments nach seinen Hauptzeugen: Jesus, Paulus, Johannes* (GNT 3; Göttingen, 1969), 24: the decisive control over this process lies in the demonstration that the material sifted out yields a historically credible and coherent picture of Jesus and his message and makes the further development of Christianity credible.
[81] Cf. Dugandzic, *"Ja" Gottes*, 45.

CHAPTER THREE

# BIBLISCHE THEOLOGIE IM RÖMERBRIEF

Karl Kertelge, Münster

*I. Zur Aufgabe einer biblischen Theologie*

1. Das Thema "Biblische Theologie" wird in neuerer Zeit[1] hauptsächlich als theologische Grundfrage nach dem gegenseitigen Verhältnis der beiden Testamente, des Alten und des Neuen, im christlichen Kanon der zweigeteilten Bibel behandelt. Diese Frage stellt sich in der christlichen Theologie aus verschiedenen Gründen, besonders um die innere und äußere Einheit der beiden Testamente als die eine Heilige Schrift zu erklären, die eben als Ganze den Ausgangspunkt und Grundstock der christlichen Theologie bildet. Insofern sich christliche Theologie nicht damit begnügen kann, in der Bibel des Alten und Neuen Testaments nur eine Sammlung verschiedener, geschichtlich gewachsener theologischer Ansätze und Konzeptionen wahrzunehmen, insofern sie vielmehr Zusammenhänge zwischen ihnen aufzuzeigen hat, die es erlauben, von einem die verschiedenen Entwürfe zusammenhaltenden Faktor zu sprechen, stellt sich ihr die Frage nach der theologischen Einheit der Schrift.[2]

2. Angesichts dieser Bemühungen um die Einheit bzw. die "Mitte" der Schrift ist es nicht unwichtig, zu sehen, welchen theologischen Stellenwert die überlieferungsgeschichtlich schon vorgegebene "Schrift" des Alten Testaments, die γραφή, im Neuen Testament, näherhin bei dem

---

[1] Daß "Biblische Theologie" im theologischen Sprachgebrauch "kein eindeutiger Begriff" sei, betont m.R. G. Ebeling, "Was heißt 'Biblische Theologie'?", in: ders., *Wort und Glaube*, Tübingen 1960, 69-89, hier 69. Zu den Anfängen der "Biblischen Theologie" als einer hermeneutischen Bestimmung von Theologie nach dem reformatorischen Sola-scriptura-Prinzip und ihrer weiteren Entwicklung zu einer theologischen Disziplin siehe besonders H.-J. Kraus, *Die biblische Theologie - Ihre Geschichte und Problematik*, Neukirchen-Vluyn 1970, und O. Merk, *Biblische Theologie des Neuen Testaments in ihrer Anfangszeit* (MThSt 9), Marburg 1972.
[2] Dieser Frage gilt das besondere Interesse, das eine Reihe von Theologen, nicht nur Exegeten, mit dem Thema "Biblische Theologie" ausdrücklich verbindet. Ihre Beiträge sind zu einem großen Teil in dem seit 1986 erscheinenden "Jahrbuch für Biblische Theologie" (Neukirchener Verlag), bisher in sieben Bänden, veröffentlicht. Besonders einschlägig ist der Titel des zweiten Bandes: Der eine Gott der beiden Testamente (1987).

ältesten neutestamentlichen Autor Paulus hat. Für die neutestamentlichen Autoren ist die γραφή bei aller Unterscheidbarkeit nach Gesetz und Propheten bzw. Gesetz, Propheten und Schriften eine Einheit. Ihre Einheit findet sie in ihrem Anspruch als das Wort des sich seinem Volk offenbarenden Gottes, so wie es in den einzelnen Schriften seinen Niederschlag gefunden hat. Als solches hat die Schrift ihre Autorität im Leben und in der Geschichte des von Gott sich zum "besonderen Eigentum" (Ex 19.5) berufenen Volkes erlangt. Als solches ist sie das ständige Gedächtnis des Gottesvolkes: das Wort der Erinnerung an das besondere Verhältnis des Volkes zu seinem Gott, der Weisung und der Verheißung Gottes für sein Volk.

Im Lichte dieser Grundeinschätzung der Schrift als Gotteswort an sein Volk ist es ein kühner theologischer Sprung, wenn Paulus das als Schrift aus früherer Zeit überlieferte Gotteswort unmittelbar auf die Gegenwart bezieht, näherhin auf "uns". So Röm 15.4: "Denn alles, was vormals geschrieben worden ist, das ist zu unserer Belehrung geschrieben...". In Röm 4.23-24 sagt Paulus, daß das verheißungsvolle Wort Gen 15.6 nicht nur um Abrahams willen, "sondern auch unseretwegen aufgeschrieben worden ist, denen (der Glaube) angerechnet werden soll (wie Abraham)". In ähnlicher Weise überträgt Paulus auch an anderen Stellen Worte der vorgegebenen Schrift auf die Gegenwart mit dem ausdrücklichen Anspruch: "um unseretwillen steht geschrieben...", so 1 Kor 9.9-10; vgl. 10.11. Auch wenn er wie in Röm 4 Abraham als den ursprünglichen Adressaten des Gotteswortes nennt und im Auge behält, so zielt er mit seiner Zitierung als "Schrift" doch auf "uns" als die Adressaten in der Gegenwart, auf die in ihrem "endzeitlichen" Kontext (1 Kor 10.11) dieses Wort in letztgültiger Weise trifft. In diesem gezielten Gebrauch erweist die Schrift ihre Autorität nicht im Sinne einer "Verbalinspiration", sondern als in der Geschichte seines Volkes ergehendes Wort Gottes, das Vergangenheit, Gegenwart und Zukunft zusammenschließt.

Um dies zu erkennen, bedarf es allerdings auch des Interpreten, der den Zusammenhang zwischen dem geschichtlich ergangenen Gotteswort und seiner Zukunft eröffnenden Gegenwart herstellt. Dazu weiß Paulus sich autorisiert. Seine theologische Autorität, die er als Interpret der Schrift sehr wohl wahrzunehmen weiß, ist im Grunde keine andere als die apostolische Autorität, die er am Anfang des Römerbriefs (1.1-7,8-17) nachdrücklich herausstellt.

3. Für unsere Frage nach einer "Biblischen Theologie", die das Alte und das Neue Testament als eine theologische Einheit zu verstehen sucht, bietet der Römerbrief nicht schon die Lösung aller mit diesem Thema aufgegebenen Probleme. Für die Behandlung dieses Themas im Rahmen

christlicher Theologie ist es allerdings aufschlußreich zu sehen, welchen Stellenwert Paulus der vorgegebenen γραφή des Alten Testaments für die theologische Explikation des "Evangeliums Gottes... über seinen Sohn", mit dem er sich beauftragt weiß (Röm 1.1-4), zuspricht. Die paulinische Verhältnisbestimmung von "Schrift" und "Evangelium" mag uns so in die Aufgabe einer christlichen "Biblischen Theologie" einführen.

Im Rahmen des Symposions "Biblical Theology", das die Theologische Fakultät der Universität Aarhus zu ihrem 50-jährigen Jubiläum veranstaltet, fällt mir die Aufgabe zu, das Thema in zwei Seminarsitzungen exemplarisch zu behandeln. Aus Gründen, die oben schon angesprochen wurden, wähle ich das Paradigma des paulinischen Römerbriefs und führe im folgenden in zwei Textzusammenhänge ein, die Grundlage des Arbeitsgesprächs sein sollen.[3]

*II. "Das Evangelium Gottes - zuvor verheißen in den Heiligen Schriften" (Röm 1.1-2)*

1. Geradezu programmatisch verbindet Paulus im Präskript des Römerbriefs seine Berufung zum Apostel mit dem "Evangelium Gottes". Seine Berufung erfüllt er als Dienst am Evangelium. Auf dem Stichwort εὐαγγέλιον liegt ein besonderer Nachdruck, der in V. 1 schon mit dem Genitiv θεοῦ angezeigt ist, und danach in V. 2 und V. 3-4 zu zwei theologisch gewichtigen Qualifizierungen dieses Evangeliums führt. Das von Paulus verkündete Evangelium gründet letztlich in der Autorität Gottes selbst, der sein Evangelium "durch die Propheten vorher verheißen hat in Heiligen Schriften", und es ist das Evangelium "über seinen Sohn". Die christologische Inhaltsangabe des Evangeliums in V. 3-4 verdient in mehrfacher Hinsicht exegetische Aufmerksamkeit, nicht nur unter traditionsgeschichtlichen Gesichtspunkten, sondern auch im Hinblick auf die in V. 2 eröffnete verheißungsgeschichtliche Perspektive. Die christologische Würde, die Jesus mit der Herkunft von David und seiner Offenbarung als Sohn Gottes zugeschrieben wird, versteht sich aus der in den "Heiligen Schriften" des Alten Testaments bekundeten Verheißung Gottes selbst. Es ist ein und derselbe Gott, der durch die Propheten gesprochen hat, bezeugt in den Heiligen Schriften, und der sich letztgültig durch den Erweis seiner Macht in der Auferweckung seines Sohnes mitgeteilt hat.

Am Thema "Evangelium" bleibt Paulus auch weiterhin in Kap. 1 orientiert, indem er dieses Stichwort zum Thema des ganzen Briefes

---

[3] Aus der einschlägigen Literatur sei hier besonders genannt U. Luz, "Paulinische Theologie als Biblische Theologie", in: M. Klopfenstein u.a. (Hg.), *Mitte der Schrift?* (JeC 11), Bern 1987, 119-147.

macht, und zwar in der für diesen Brief charakteristischen soteriologischen Wendung. So in 1.16-17. Das Evangelium, das zu verkünden sich Paulus berufen weiß, ist

> Kraft Gottes zur Rettung für jeden der glaubt, dem Juden zuerst und auch dem Griechen; denn Gerechtigkeit Gottes wird in ihm geoffenbart - aus Glauben zum Glauben, wie geschrieben steht: Der Gerechte aber wird aus dem Glauben leben (Hab 2.4).

Die Verkündigung des Evangeliums erlangt mit diesen Sätzen eine fundamentale soteriologische Bedeutung. Rettende Kraft wird dem Evangelium zugeschrieben, weil sich in ihm δικαιούνη θεοῦ geoffenbart hat, die im Glauben an allen, die zum Glauben gelangen, wirksam wird. Dieses mit dem Glaubensbegriff bezeichnete "Prinzip" des Heiles sieht der Apostel im Wort der Schrift (nach Hab 2.4) bezeugt.

2. Schriftgemäßheit wird aber nicht nur mit der ausdrücklichen Zitierung der Schrift belegt. Schon die von Paulus hier eingeführten Stichworte, die als Leitbegriffe seiner Botschaft und ihrer lehrmäßigen Entfaltung dienen, lassen die tiefe Übereinstimmung mit dem vorgegebenen Wortzeugnis der Schrift des Alten Testaments erkennen. Dies wird besonders mit dem im Römerbrief wiederholt gebrauchten Begriff der "Gerechtigkeit Gottes" deutlich (1.17; 3.5; 3.21-26; 10.3). Paulus ist offenkundig bei der Darlegung des Evangeliums als Wort von der "Rettung" am Begriff der "Gerechtigkeit Gottes" besonders gelegen, allerdings in enger Verbindung mit dem Begriff des "Glaubens". Beides verdient im Sinne der "Schriftgemäßheit" Beachtung.

a) Der Begriff δικαιούνη θεοῦ ist im Alten Testament vorgegeben und kann nur vom Alten Testament her sachgemäß verstanden werden.[4] "Gerechtigkeit Gottes" meint vom Alten Testament her nicht einfach nur eine isolierbare Eigenschaft Gottes, aber auch nicht die dem Menschen von Gott zugesprochene Eigenschaft (Gerechtigkeit, die vor Gott gilt). δικαιούνη θεοῦ ist in dem Ausdruck vielmehr ein *nomen actionis*. Es bezeichnet Gottes gerechtes und gerechtmachendes Handeln am Menschen zugleich. So ausdrücklich 3.26: Gott erweist seine Gerechtigkeit "in der Jetztzeit, so daß er selbst gerecht ist und gerechtspricht den aus Glauben."

---

[4] Vgl. im einzelnen K. Kertelge, *"Rechtfertigung" bei Paulus. Studien zur Struktur und zum Bedeutungsgehalt des paulinischen Rechtfertigungsbegriffs* (NTA N.F. 3), Münster (1966) 1971², aber auch andere Werke wie vor allem P. Stuhlmacher, *Gerechtigkeit Gottes bei Paulus* (FRLANT 87), Göttingen 1965. Vgl. auch K. Kertelge, δικαιοσύνη, δικαιόω in: EWNT I (1980) 784-807.

Paulus hat dieses Verständnis von "Gerechtigkeit" bzw. den "Gerechtigkeitserweisen Gottes" (Jes 45.24; Ps 103.6) aus der Schrift richtig gelernt und nicht nur terminologisch, sondern auch sachgemäß übernommen. Die Verwendung des Begriffs "Gerechtigkeit Gottes" wird damit zum Beleg dafür, daß die Schrift, die wir das Alte Testament nennen, an entscheidender Stelle formal und inhaltlich zur Quelle für die Verkündigung und die Theologie des Paulus wird.

Paulus betont mit dem Ausdruck $\delta\iota\kappa\alpha\iota o\acute{\nu}\nu\eta\ \vartheta\epsilon o\hat{\nu}$ nicht nur die Aktivität, sondern auch die Initiative Gottes zur Rettung des Menschen. Der Mensch bedarf des rettenden Eingreifens Gottes, weil er von sich aus nicht gerecht ist. "Gerechtigkeit" bezeichnet dabei in Übereinstimmung mit dem alttestamentlichen Verständnis des Wortes das dem Bund gemäße Rechttun Gottes und daraus resultierend das dem Bund gemäße Rechtsein des Menschen. Der Begriff "Gerechtigkeit Gottes" signalisiert somit die Bedeutung der Bundeswirklichkeit des alttestamentlichen Gottesvolkes als Verstehenshintergrund für die eschatologische Rettungstat Gottes in Jesus Christus.

b) Mit dem Zitat aus Hab 2.4 wird in Röm 1.17 die tragende Bedeutung des Glaubensbegriffs im Verständnis vom Gerechtigkeitshandeln Gottes unterstrichen. Es ist bemerkenswert, daß der Glaubensbegriff hier zwar noch nicht christologisch bestimmt wird, zumindest nicht ausdrücklich, daß Paulus mit dem Glaubensbegriff aber besonders die Dimension der Universalität verbindet, so in V. 16: $\pi\alpha\nu\tau\grave{\iota}\ \tau\hat{\omega}\ \pi\iota\sigma\tau\epsilon\acute{\nu}o\nu\tau\iota$, konkretisiert als "Jude und Grieche". Hab 2.4 wird so zum Zeugnis für ein universales Heilsverständnis, das Paulus in 3.21-26 bzw. 3.21-31 zum eigentlichen Thema macht.

3. In Röm 4 wird diese für Paulus besonders charakteristische Bestimmung des Evangeliums von der "Gerechtigkeit Gottes" durch den Begriff des "Glaubens" mit einem "Schriftbeweis" aus der Abrahamgeschichte als Gottes von Anfang an bestehende und festgehaltene Intention unwiderlegbar gemacht. In V. 3 geht Paulus ausdrücklich von der $\gamma\rho\alpha\phi\acute{\eta}$ aus, die er mit Gen 15.6 zitiert. "Abraham glaubte Gott, und es wurde ihm zur Gerechtigkeit angerechnet". Paulus argumentiert mit der Schrift für die Rechtfertigung aus Glauben. Und wenn er in V. 6 das Zitat aus Ps 32.1-2 einführt mit: "wie auch David sagt", und die zitierte Psalmstelle auf die Rechtfertigung "ohne Werke" bezieht, dann läßt sich von einem "klassischen" Schriftbeweis sprechen, der in gleicher Weise Gesetz und Propheten heranzieht. Paulus bleibt allerdings vorwiegend im Bereich des Gotteswortes von Gen 15.6, mit dem er in V. 17 das andere Wort an Abraham aus Gen 17.5 verbindet: "Zum Vater vieler Völker habe ich dich eingesetzt". Zudem bewegt er sich mit den Motiven der

Beschneidung und der Verheißung im Textzusammenhang dieser beiden Stellen.

Paulus befindet sich in Röm 4 nach wie vor in Auseinandersetzung mit dem jüdischen Gesprächspartner wie schon seit 2.1. Das Thema der Auseinandersetzung ist die Geltung des Verheißungswortes Gottes auch für die Heiden. Abraham wird eingeführt als "unser Vorvater dem Fleische nach" (4.1). Nur Juden können sich in dieser Weise auf Abraham berufen, um an den an ihn ergangenen Verheißungen Anteil zu haben. Abrahamskindschaft bedeutet, zum Gottesvolk zu gehören. Paulus sucht nun mit Hilfe von Gen 15.6 zu zeigen, daß der Anteil an der Abrahamsverheißung nicht nur der fleischlichen Nachkommenschaft Abrahams gilt, sondern auf Glauben beruht und daß Abraham deswegen der eigentliche Vater-Titel als "Vater aller Glaubenden" (4.11) zukommt.

Paulus argumentiert mit dem Glauben Abrahams für die universale Geltung der Verheißung Gottes. Dem "Glaubensprinzip" steht das "Gesetzesprinzip" entgegen. "Denn wenn die aus dem Gesetz Erben wären, würde der Glaube entleert und (damit auch) die Verheißung zunichte" (V. 14). V.16 erklärt sodann, warum das so ist. Im Glauben kommt Gott in seinem ihm eigenen Gnadenhandeln zur Geltung, und darin realisiert sich die Verheißung für die ganze Nachkommenschaft Abrahams, "nicht nur für die aus dem Gesetz, sondern auch für die aus dem Glauben Abrahams". Glauben in der Weise des Glaubens Abrahams bedeutet also, Gott als den, der er ist, wirken zu lassen: als den, "der die Toten lebendig macht und das Nichtseiende ins Sein ruft" (V. 17b).

Der Glaube Abrahams wird damit zu dem von der Schrift selbst bezeugten und verbindlich vorgestellten Realbild für den rechtfertigenden Glauben an Jesus Christus in der Gegenwart. Der Schriftbeweis erschließt die vom Glauben an Jesus Christus bestimmte Gegenwart als die Zeit des Heilswirkens Gottes. Er belegt nicht nur in theologischer Entfaltung die Geltung einer theologischen These, sondern er überbrückt auch die Zeitabstände von geschichtlich ergangener Verheißung, an der Gott festhält, und ihrer Erfüllung in und durch Jesus Christus in der Gegenwart. Und er zeigt in der zeitlichen Unterschiedenheit von früher ergangener Verheißung und ihrer Realisierung im Evangelium die tiefere Identität von beiden als dem einen Wort Gottes auf, das nicht nur um Abrahams willen, "sondern auch unseretwegen" ergangen ist und "aufgeschrieben" wurde (V. 23-24).

4. Paulus verwendet die ihm vorgegebene Schrift (des Alten Testaments) im Rahmen der Darlegung des ihm aufgetragenen Evangeliums argumentativ. Es besteht eine Entsprechung zwischen dem Evangelium und der Schrift, so ausdrücklich in 1.17: καθὼς γέγραπται. Die Schrift, hier

Hab 2.4, wird zum Zeugnis für das Evangelium. Diese Entsprechung bestimmt sich nach 1.2 näherhin als Voraus-Verheißung des im Evangelium verkündeten endzeitlich-gegenwärtigen Heiles.

Biblische Theologie betreibt Paulus im Römerbrief vor allem als Auslegung der ihm vorgegebenen γραφή, wobei er nicht nur an einzelnen Textzitaten orientiert ist, sondern mehr noch an Sach- und Sinnzusammenhängen, die er durch den Wortlaut der Zitate angezeigt sieht. Auslegungsgrundsatz ist die von der Schrift selbst beabsichtigte Beziehung zu dem Heilsgeschehen der Gegenwart, das den Namen "Jesus Christus" trägt. In Röm 4 wird so der Glaube Abrahams zur Vorausdarstellung des Glaubens an Jesus Christus, zu dem in der Gegenwart - am "Ende der Äonen" (1 Kor 10.11) - Juden und Heiden durch das Evangelium gerufen sind. Die Schrift wird so zum Zeugnis für den universalen Heilsweg des Glaubens an Jesus Christus. Der Schriftbeweis in Röm 4 gehört in diesem Sinne zur theologischen Grundthese des Paulus im Römerbrief.

*III. "Biblische Theologie" im Horizont der Israelfrage (Röm 9-11)*

1. Die These von der Universalität des Heiles in Jesus Christus und damit der Universalität des Glaubens an ihn, wie Paulus sie im ersten Teil des Römerbriefes als Verdeutlichung seines Evangeliums vorgestellt (1.16-17; 3.21-31), schrifttheologisch begründet (bes. in Kap. 4) und in den folgenden Kapiteln (5-8) weiter entfaltet hat, muß sich an der Israelfrage, die er in Röm 9-11 entwickelt, bewähren. In Röm 9-11 geht es um das Schicksal des vorfindlichen Israel, das sich in seiner überwiegenden Mehrheit, um nicht zu sagen: in seiner Gesamtheit dem Glauben an Jesus Christus verschlossen hat, wie Paulus besonders in Kap. 9 beklagt.

> Israel, das dem Gesetz der Gerechtigkeit nachstrebte, ist zu dem Gesetz nicht gelangt. Warum? Weil nicht aus Glauben, sondern aus Werken des Gesetzes. Sie stießen an den Stein des Anstoßes (9.31-32).

Der Glaube an den Messias Jesus wird ihnen zur Schicksalsfrage.

Wohlgemerkt, es geht um das konkrete geschichtliche Israel der Gegenwart, dessen ablehnende Haltung gegenüber dem Evangelium Paulus oft genug persönlich erfahren hatte. So besonders nach 1 Thess 2.14-16. Deswegen setzt er in 9.1-5 dezidiert mit der Benennung und Charakterisierung der jüdischen Volksangehörigen als ἀδελφοί μου ... κατὰ σάρκα ein. Zu beachten ist, daß Paulus die Gegenwartsgröße Israel in seine theologische Reflexion positiv einzubeziehen sucht.

2. Die Darstellung der Israelfrage in Röm 9-11 verläuft sehr spannungsvoll.[5] In 9.6 sucht er sogleich zu unterscheiden zwischen "Israel" und "Israel"; "nicht alle, die aus Israel sind, diese sind (auch wirklich) Israel." Zur Unterscheidung gelten die Maßstäbe des frei erwählenden und souverän schaffenden Willens Gottes. Dies ist der durchgehende Tenor in 9.6-29. Gottes Wahl bestimmt, wer oder was Israel ist. Eine gewisse rationale Begründung für das frei erwählende Handeln Gottes bietet Paulus sodann in 9.30-10.21: Israel hat bei allem Eifer für das "Gesetz der Gerechtigkeit" (9.31) das Ziel nicht erreicht. Im Gegenteil, es ist der Gerechtigkeit Gottes, die in Jesus Christus offenbar geworden ist, ungehorsam geworden (10.3). Daß dabei die Verheißungstreue Gottes noch erhalten geblieben ist, stellt in Kap. 11 den positiven Anknüpfungspunkt für die These von der endzeitlich-endgültigen Rettung Israels dar. Schließlich wird - in Hoffnung gegen alle Hoffnung - doch "ganz Israel gerettet werden" (11.26), was, mit Nikolaus Walter[6] zu sprechen, "nur als ein eschatologisches Wunder" zu verstehen ist.

Mit Heikki Räisänen[7] mag man in Röm 9-11 von einem "geistigen Ringen" des Apostels sprechen, das es zu analysieren gelte (N. Walter: ein "gedankliches Ringen"). Jedenfalls stellen sich die Kap. 9-11 bei feststellbarer formaler und inhaltlicher Einheitlichkeit doch als eine spannungsvolle literarische und theologische Einheit dar. Uns stellt sich dabei die Frage, wo für Paulus der eigentliche Schwerpunkt in seiner Behandlung der Frage nach dem Schicksal Israels gegeben ist, mehr im Bereich des neuschöpferischen Handelns Gottes aufgrund des Glaubens an Jesus Christus (so in Kap. 9 und 10) oder mehr in dem erbarmenden Handeln Gottes an Israel entsprechend seiner Bundestreue (so in Kap. 11). Wenn wir die Hauptfrage des Paulus schon in 9.1-5 angelegt finden, dann erscheinen die Ausführungen in 9.6-29 und 9.30-10.21 als nur vorläufige Antworten, die dann in Kap. 11, über die Wende in 11.11 schließlich in 11.25-26 bzw. 11.25-32, zur Lösung gebracht werden.

Im Überblick über diese spannungsvolle literarische und theologische Einheit von Kap. 9-11 wird allerdings deutlich, daß es ein Gefälle von Kap. 9 über Kap. 10 hin zu Kap. 11 gibt. Die These von der endgültigen Rettung von "ganz Israel" in 11.25-26 ist nicht nur Ausdruck einer "Flucht nach vorne", um aus der theologischen "Sackgasse" eines rein

---

[5] Siehe hierzu (außer den Kommentaren) besonders F.W. Maier, *Israel in der Heilsgeschichte nach Römer 9-11* (Biblische Zeitfragen 12/11-12), Münster 1929; H. Hübner, *Gottes Ich und Israel. Zum Schriftgebrauch des Paulus in Röm 9-11* (FRLANT 136), Göttingen 1984; N. Walter, "Zur Interpretation von Röm 9-11", in: *ZThK* 81 (1984), 172-195; O. Hofius, "Das Evangelium und Israel. Erwägungen zu Römer 9-11", in: *ZThK* 83 (1986), 297-324; H. Räisänen, "Röm 9-11: Analyse eines geistigen Ringens", in: ANRW II, 25.4, Berlin 1987, 2891-2939 (Lit.).
[6] A.a.O, 183.
[7] A.a.O (im Titel).

christologischen Heilsverständnisses herauszukommen. Vielmehr zeigt sich hier, daß die christologische Kernbotschaft des von Paulus verkündeten Evangeliums vermittels des Erwählungsgedankens positiv in seiner Eschatologie aufgehoben wird. Das Stichwort μυστήριον[8] bekommt dadurch seinen präzisen Inhalt, daß es der Parusie-Christus ist, der als "Retter vom Sion her kommen wird" (V. 26 mit Jes 59.10), um "ganz Israel" in die vollendete Erlösung einzuholen. Am Ende wird sich so auch für Israel die Identität von εὐαγγέλιον und ἐκλογή (V.28) erweisen.

3. Paulus macht in Kap. 9-11 ausführlichen Gebrauch von der Schrift. Es ist eine Fülle von Schriftzitaten und Schriftanspielungen aus verschiedenen Büchern des Alten Testaments, die er hier verwendet, und die Schriftworte sind nicht einfach wie Farbtupfer auf den von ihm entwickelten Gedankengang aufgesetzt. Vielmehr kommt ihnen eine den Gedankengang des Paulus anregende und weiterführende, argumentative Bedeutung zu.

In Kap. 9 greift er zunächst auf die Abrahams- und Patriarchentradition aus Gen 18; 21 und 25 zurück, um den Gedanken von dem frei erwählenden Handeln Gottes darzulegen. Kritisch verstärkt wird dieser Gedanke in 9.25-26 mit dem Volk-Gottes-Motiv aus Hos 2.25 und 1.10: Gott schafft sich aus Juden *und* Heiden sein Volk neu.

Von 9.30-11.10 gewinnt Paulus besonders aus Deuteronomium und Jesaja die Fundierung seiner Aussagen über die Verstockung Israels (πώρωσις, 11.7,26) bis hin zu 11.8 mit Dtn 29.4:

Gott gab ihnen einen Geist der Betäubung, Augen, daß sie nicht sehen, und Ohren, daß sie nicht hören, bis auf den heutigen Tag.

Diese Aussage kann er dann in 11.9-10 noch ergänzen mit Ps 69.22-23 (und 35.8). Natürlich muß in theologischer Reflexion das willentliche Handeln Gottes im Vorgang der "Betäubung" bzw. "Verstockung" weiter reflektiert werden. Dies geschieht im folgenden Zusammenhang, vor allem in 11.11-16 mit dem Motiv, daß so "das Heil zu den Heiden kommen" sollte, aber nicht um Israel zu verdrängen, sondern um Israel "eifersüchtig" zu machen. Dieses Motiv sollte selbstverständlich nicht für das Missionsprogramm des Paulus in Anspruch genommen werden.[9]

---

[8] Zum μυστήριον-Motiv in ähnlicher Stellung als "Höhepunkt der ganzen Argumentationskette" ist auch 1 Kor 15,51 zu vergleichen: "Siehe, ich sage euch ein Geheimnis: Wir werden nicht alle entschlafen, wir werden aber alle verwandelt werden". H. Probst, *Paulus und der Brief* (WUNT 2. R. 45), Tübingen 1991, 348: "Dieses 'Geheimnis' erschließt ihm Gottes Handeln in der Endzeit".
[9] So mit Recht H. Räisänen, a.a.O., 2913, der dagegen etwas mißverständlich von einer "nachträglichen Rationalisierung" spricht.

Vielmehr ist es geeignet, die Universalität des Evangeliums in der "Zwischenzeit" zu signalisieren.

Was die Schriftverwendung angeht, so ist zu bemerken, daß die Zitate aus Jesaja in Röm 10 und 11 überwiegen. Jesaja (59.20-21; 27.9) steht dann auch in Röm 11.26-27 an entscheidender Stelle, um den zuversichtlichen Ausblick auf die eschatologische Rettung von ganz Israel schrifttheologisch festzumachen.

Zweifellos ist die christologisch-soteriologische Hermeneutik des paulinischen Evangeliums leitend für die Schriftinterpretation des Apostels - wie sonst in seinen Briefen, so auch hier. Es verdient allerdings Beachtung, daß er gerade an dieser Stelle bei der Behandlung des Israel-Themas bei aller christologischen Selbstbindung "die Eigenaussage der Schrift"[10] als Zeugnis von der Erwählung Israels nicht nur respektiert, sondern auf seine Weise auch exegetisch zur Geltung bringt. Er nimmt dafür auch die Spannung zu seiner Theologie der "Rechtfertigung aus Glauben an Jesus Christus" (außerhalb der Christusgemeinschaft kein Heil!) in Kauf. So wichtig ist ihm die Lösung des Israelproblems!

Aber er löst dieses Problem nicht gegen das "Heil in Jesus Christus", sondern indem er es mit Hilfe der Schrift auf den Gedanken der Verheißungstreue Gottes im Bund mit Israel zurückführt. Es sind nicht zwei verschiedene Stränge des Heilshandelns Gottes, die Paulus aus der Schrift eruiert, das Verständnis vom Heil im Glauben an Jesus Christus und das Verständnis von dem Heil um Gottes eigener Selbstzusage an Israel willen. Vielmehr setzt er auf die Identität von Christusevangelium und Selbstbindung Gottes im Bund mit Israel, die sich in ihrer letzten Konsequenz für Israel freilich erst im Eschaton erweisen wird. Einstweilen mag nach Paulus zur "Erklärung" genügen, daß Gottes freies, erwählendes Handeln (9.14-16) seiner Barmherzigkeit entspricht, auf die letztendlich auch Israel als das Volk des "Bundes" (11.27) verwiesen bleibt (11.30-32).

*IV. Abschließende Thesen zum Thema*
*"Biblische Theologie" nach Paulus*

1. Biblische Theologie und Exegese

Auf dem von Paulus begangenen Weg der Schriftauslegung ist biblische Theologie nicht eine nachträgliche theologische Reflexion über den Stellenwert der vorgegebenen Schrift, sondern ein integrierender Teil der vertieften Reflexion und Darlegung des Evangeliums von Jesus Christus. Daher sollte biblische Theologie auch bei uns nicht als ein separates

---

[10] U. Luz, a.a.O., 120-121.

Unternehmen neben der Exegese stehen, sondern ein Teil der Exegese selbst sein, näherhin als Sachreflexion der exegetisch erarbeiteten Textinhalte des Neuen Testaments im Horizont der vom Evangelium vorausgesetzten Heiligen Schrift des Alten Testaments.

Von Paulus haben wir vor allem zu lernen, unsere mit Hilfe der historisch-kritischen Methode gewonnenen historischen Erkenntnisse nicht schon als das eigentliche und letzte Ziel der Exegese anzusehen, sondern mit ihrer Hilfe die theologische Aussage des biblischen Textes zu erheben und sie im theologischen Ganzen der biblischen Überlieferung zu orten.

2. Paulinische Theologie als Biblische Theologie

Insofern Paulus sich in seiner Verkündigung und Theologie, die ihren Ausgangspunkt beim Evangelium nimmt und dieses im Lichte des vorgegebenen Offenbarungswortes der Schrift reflektiert, um die Wahrheit des in der Schrift überlieferten Gotteswortes bemüht und sie darin zur Geltung bringen will, ist von einer "biblischen Theologie des Paulus" zu sprechen, die im Kern "Schrift" und Evangelium und in diesem Sinne auch Altes und Neues Testament umgreift. Eine Altes und Neues Testament umfassende Biblische Theologie begründet sich so nicht nur in einem theologischen Interesse "jenseits" der beiden Testamente, sondern mit Paulus in der Verwurzelung des Evangeliums im Verheißungswort der Schrift.

3. Zur ökumenischen Relevanz einer Biblischen Theologie

Das Stichwort "Biblische Theologie" hat lange Zeit als Proprium des Protestantismus gegolten, insofern es die grundlegende Geltung des "Sola Scriptura" gegenüber Tradition und Dogma signalisieren sollte. So Otto Merk[11] über das Verständnis von Biblischer Theologie bei Johann Phillip Gabler: Die biblische Theologie sei (nach Gabler) eine protestantische Wissenschaft, die nur auf dem Boden der Reformation möglich sei. Dagegen zeigen die neueren Bemühungen um eine das Alte und Neue Testament umfassende Biblische Theologie eine stärkere Beachtung des Traditions- und Rezeptionsprozesses für die Formierung der biblischen Grundbotschaft schon in der Bibel selbst und auch in der von der Bibel eröffneten Wirkungsgeschichte innerhalb der Kirche.

In diesem Sinne kann sich Biblische Theologie als ein hervorragendes Beispiel einer konfessionsüberschreitenden ökumenischen Theologie erweisen.

---

[11] A.a.O., 268.

CHAPTER FOUR

# SALVATION-HISTORY IN THE GOSPEL OF MATTHEW

*An Example of Biblical Theology*

Mogens Müller, Copenhagen

*I. Introduction*

*1. Biblical Theology*

The term 'biblical theology' may be construed in two ways. On the one hand the adjective 'biblical' conveys conformity with the content of the Bible, that is, it can be used in the same way as the qualifying adjective 'Lutheran'. On the other hand 'biblical' may also be taken as a precise definition of the theology in question, *in casu* the one contained in the Bible; it is of course in this sense it will be used in the following about biblical theology. Even so, the adjective 'biblical' will have to be more clearly defined, depending on how the relationship between the Old and the New Testament is understood.[1] According to the so-called 'new Tübingen School', represented in the first place by Hartmut Gese and Peter Stuhlmacher, the word 'biblical' signifies that the two testaments represent a joint development of traditions, which virtually comprise a continuum, that is, a unity.[2] In the following I shall consider the relationship between the Old and the New Testament from the opposite viewpoint, namely that the Jewish Bible *de facto* became another book

---

[1] Cf. Gerhard Ebeling, "Was heißt "Biblische Theologie"?" (1955), in: *Wort und Glaube* (Tübingen, 1960, 3. Aufl. 1967), 69-89, esp. 88: "In der "Biblischen Theologie" hat der speziell der Erforschung des Zusammenhangs von Altem Testament und Neuem Testament sich widmende Theologe Rechenschaft zu geben über sein Verständnis der Bibel im ganzen, d.h. vor allem über die theologischen Probleme, die dadurch entstehen, daß die Mannigfaltigkeit des biblischen Zeugnisses auf ihrem Zusammenhang hin befragt wird".

[2] Cf. the thesis of Hartmut Gese: "das Alte Testament entsteht durch das Neue Testament; das Neue Testament bildet den Abschluß eines Traditionsprozesses, der wesentlich eine Einheit, ein Kontinuum ist". The quotation is from his programmatic article "Erwägungen zur Einheit der biblischen Theologie", first printed in *ZThK* 67 (1970), 417-436, cited here from H. Gese, *Vom Sinai zum Zion. Alttestamentliche Beiträge zur biblischen Theologie*, BEvTh 64 (1974), 11-30: 14. On Peter Stuhlmacher's views, see e.g. his *Versöhnung, Gesetz und Gerechtigkeit. Aufsätze zur biblischen Theologie* (Göttingen, 1981), a volume dedicated to Hartmut Gese. A critical attitude to the 'new Tübingen School' is found in Hans Hübner, *Biblische Theologie des Neuen Testaments*, Band 1. Prolegomena (Göttingen, 1990), 16-18.

when it was taken over by the Christian Church. Discontinuity came to overshadow the continuity.[3]

The reason for this was that the tradition, which only gradually was set down in writing in the various New Testament books, was primarily created by and dependent on faith in Christ. This means that the very existence of the communities that created and handed down this tradition is of the utmost importance when it comes to understanding what biblical theology embodies. Whatever the New Testament writings may represent, they also express individual attempts - primarily based on Holy Writ - to legitimize any Christian community's right to see itself as the fulfilment of the biblical promises, as possessing the key to a true understanding of the Jewish Bible and as the chosen people incorporating both Jewish and Gentile Christians. All New Testament books were written with a view to the life of these Christians and the preaching to them. To put it differently, they were not directed at an unqualified audience, on the contrary they spoke to people already familiar with the conditions of congregational life and the content of Christian faith. Because they had been baptized, they belonged to the people of the new covenant. Each in its own way the New Testament writings represent attempts to evoke and interpret the common basis, be it the Jewish Bible, the Jesus-tradition or a more catechism-like ethical teaching. In this mediation process the various authors seem like theologians. This not only applies to the author of the Gospel of John, who, in this connection, is usually parallelled with Paul; it applies as much to the other evangelists. It goes without saying that such implicit prerequisites cannot be left unconsidered, for if we did so, our interpretation of the various writings would go awry.

## 2. Salvation-history

The concept known as 'salvation-history' presupposes that salvation *has* a history, i.e. is manifest in a chain of events in which one state of things replaces another. One may also say that salvation is manifested in historical events which, thanks to their interpretation, are given the impress of revelation. New Testament theology characteristically consists in interpretations of the acts and fate of an historical person. Jesus of Nazareth is not only seen as the preacher of an eternal and unchangeable message, but his very person, his sufferings and death are irretrievably

---

[3] Cf Ernst Haenchen, "Das alte "Neue Testament" und das neue "Alte Testament"" in idem, *Die Bibel und Wir*. Gesammelte Aufsätze 2 (Tübingen, 1968), 13-27: 18, where it is said, that it is an unfamiliar thought for most evangelical Christians and exegetes, "daß das in seinem *ursprünglichen* Sinn verstandene Alte Testament noch nie zum christlichen Kanon gehört hat." I owe thanks for this reference to professor Otfried Hofius, Tübingen.

interlocked with his message of salvation. As the Christ, Jesus appears as the proclaimed preacher, whereby theology and soteriology become synthesized into christology.

It is thus characteristic of New Testament theology that the salvation preached by Jesus has a prehistory at the same time as it creates history. Its prehistory is instrumental in making New Testament theology into what is essentially a biblical theology as is also indicated by the prefix 'New'. The Bible of this theology is of course nothing but the holy writings of Judaism.[4] It might seem to be self-evident, but it should nevertheless be borne in mind that in this respect all New Testament writings should be seen as expressions of biblical theology. In a manner of speaking they have another status than the Bible they build on and try to interpret.

On the other hand, if the key to the New Testament interpretation of the Jewish Bible is Jesus' life, his suffering and death, then biblical theology must by definition deny the existence of a particular Old Testament theology as an independent and finished affair. For New Testament theology is biblical precisely because it maintains the import of the Jewish Bible as the prehistory of salvation, thus implying that it cannot stand alone. No New Testament author expresses this more clearly than Paul in 2 Cor 3.15-16, where he says that until this day, whenever Moses is read, a veil lies over peoples' minds; "but when a man turns to the Lord the veil is removed".[5] In other words the road does not lead from the Bible to Christ, but from Christ to the Bible.

With respect to the content of salvation-history three fundamental questions should be asked. The first is the question of the continuity with the prehistory, i.e. the history encompassing Israel's history from Abraham to Christ. There is of course also a high degree of discontinuity in this, but continuity is the essential under-current. The second question relates to the disagreement and rupture with contemporary Judaism. This induces a salvation-historically influenced explanation which leads to a new definition of who is God's chosen people, and also, *de facto,* to an annulment of the unique position of historical Israel. The third question, which is related to the second, is about the way of the salvation message to the Gentiles, since the new definition of who belongs to God's chosen people cancels the old barrier between Jew and Gentile.

Where these questions are taken up, they are characteristically answered in a salvation-historical way. It is not that Jesus is being

---

[4] On this and the following, see Ulrich Luz, "Das Matthäusevangelium und die Perspektive einer biblischen Theologie", *JBTh*, 4 (1989), 233-248. Here it is said, 233: "Auslegung der biblischen Dimension des Evangeliums könnte man von Neuen Testament her "biblische Theologie" nennen".

[5] This quotation and the following are taken from the Revised Standard Version of the Bible.

depicted as one who beforehand exceeds all bounds by preaching a universalistic message which does not distinguish between Gentiles and Jews. On the contrary, it is a question of a historical periodization which describes and explains the way of salvation from Israel to the Gentile world by means of a chain of events. It makes good sense to comprehend these descriptions and explanations as attempts at theological rationalization which are based on accomplished facts. The authors of the gospels of Matthew and Luke in particular are such salvation historians. The salvation-historical concept of Luke is the more comprehensible, not least because his Gospel was continued in Acts, and it was also the first to attract attention. A similar concept is, however, embodied in the Gospel of Matthew, though here it is expressed in another way. In the following I shall go into this in more detail.[6]

The accomplished facts which Matthew endeavours to explain within the compass of a description of Jesus' life - apart from the conclusion of the new covenant - thus represent the definitive break with Judaism and determine the Gentiles' admission to salvation. The 'code' used by the evangelist to incorporate these events in his salvation-history is the Bible he shares with Judaism. This Bible is also the factor that ensures the continuity in the sequence of events, although, on the face of it, discontinuity seems to be the rule. This 'project' will be examined in more detail below as 'an example of biblical theology', because in this sense New Testament theology is biblical theology. To the early church, the writings of the old covenant were the Bible as such, and the creation and addition of a New Testament scripture cannot abolish the fact that in principle only the Jewish Bible is Holy Writ, and that the New Testament writings can never rank alongside it. For this would mean that the writings of the old covenant would be accorded an independent position, which cannot be sustained in a Christian theological connection. Here it must necessarily become the *Old* Testament, a position Judaism would never acknowledge. At the same time it would lead to a misrepresentation of the New Testament as a 'continuation' of the Old Testament which reveals and expands its actual significance.

---

[6] The question of the presentation and importance of salvation-history in Matthew has been rather neglected in the voluminous secondary literature as reflected in two recent surveys, Graham Stanton, "The Origin and Purpose of Matthew's Gospel. Matthean Scholarship from 1945 to 1980" in *ANRW* II,25,3 (1985), 1889-1951, and Alexander Sand, *Das Matthäus-Evangelium*, *EdF* 275 (Darmstadt 1991), where this problem is not dealt with in a separate chapter.

## II. Prehistory

To understand the Gospel of Matthew it is essential to realize that its aim is not to start a new history, but to terminate the history that began with Abraham. This is evident already in the genealogical table which introduces the book. The purpose is of course to proclaim that Jesus Christ is the inheritor of the promises to Abraham and David, according to which Abraham was to be the founder of a multitude of nations and the one by whom all nations of the earth were to be blessed (Gen 17.5-6; 18.18), while David was to become the founder of a kingdom that would be established for ever (2 Sam 7.12-16). But, as it is placed, the genealogical table also serves to emphasize the fact that the evangelist includes the history from Abraham to Christ in his gospel, although, in analogy with the Chronicler's incorporation of the history from Adam to Saul's death, he does so in the form of an enumeration, which has been periodized into three periods of fourteen names. Like Chronicles, Matthew takes this history for granted and in no need of repetition.

The transition from the prehistory to the section covering Jesus' life is provided by John the Baptist as the forerunner of Messiah. "All the prophets and the law prophesied until John" (Matt 11.13). In Matthew, John the Baptist belongs to the epoch of salvation; with him begins the preaching of the kingdom of Heaven (see 3.2); in v. 12 ἀπό is thus to be understood inclusively. The epoch preceding that of Jesus is marked by its preliminary character.

If the genealogical table emphasizes the more 'formal' continuity, then the continuity as regards contents is underlined by a saying like 5.17: "Think not that I have come to abolish the Law and the prophets; I have come not to abolish them, but to fulfill them". This saying may put the Law and the prophets within brackets of temporarity, but at the same time it says that what is now being launched was in fact their fundamental intention.

## III. The Time of the Saviour

### 1. The Fulfilment

In Matthew the connection to the prehistory is established for instance by the so-called fulfilment quotations. These have occasioned an abundance of literature, largely concentrated on their textual form.[7] The idea has gained a foothold that, in comparison with other known forms, the deviations peculiar to the Gospel of Matthew are mostly due to the

---

[7] Cf. G. Stanton, "The Origin and Purpose of Matthew's Gospel", 1930-1934.

evangelist's liberty in relation to his originals. In our connection it may be more interesting to ascertain their significance and function.[8] To be sure, the term 'fulfilment quotations' does suggest that what we have here are chiefly prophetical sayings which have been fulfilled, and thus established as proofs of Holy Writ. It is open to question, though, whether this idea will not lead us into a blind alley. More likely the fulfilment quotations should be seen as expansions on the words of Scripture. The fulfilment is actually more of an interpretation which invests the sayings in question with a new content. In other words, it is the events that interpret the prophesies, and in the process these practically lose their 'original' meaning. Or, to put it differently, when prophecy is replaced by 'fulfilment', the former is no longer interesting in itself. In this connection Hans Hübner's formulation might be used, to the effect that the Old Testament is *Vetus Testamentum in Novo receptum*.[9]

It is therefore of crucial importance to know the correct meaning of the verb πληρόω. In this connection there is reason to refer to Henrik Ljungman's monograph *Das Gesetz erfüllen,* from 1954.[10] Certainly this monograph, as indicated by the subtitle, is primarily dedicated to the understanding of Matthew 5.17ff. and 3.15, but Henrik Ljungman does involve the use of πληρόω/πλήρωμα in the New Testament as such. By including also then-contemporary Jewish literature he is able to prove how extensively it is to be understood. Jesus himself is part of the fulfilment, which thus becomes a realization.[11] The same aspect comes out in the so-called more-than-christology in Matthew 12.41,42; cf. 12.6.[12] Metaphorically, one might say, the relationship between the Scripture and the fulfilment may be likened to the relationship between an egg and what comes out of it: what remains of the egg is nothing but a shell.

---

[8] Cf.the latest discussion in Ulrich Luz, "Das Matthäusevangelium und die Perspektive einer biblischen Theologie", 236-240.
[9] *Biblische Theologie des Neuen Testaments*, 62-70.
[10] Appeared as *Lunds Universitets Årsskrift.* NF. Avd. 1 Bd. 50. Nr. 6.
[11] Cf. H. Ljungman, *Das Gesetz erfüllen,* 114-126., e.g. 123: "Jesus ist gekommen, um die ganze Schrift zu "füllen". Mit ihm ist die ganze Schrift da. Auf ihn deutet die Schrift in allem".
[12] The designation is taken from the title for an article by René Kieffer, ""Mer-än"-kristologin hos synoptikerne" in *SEÅ* 44 (1979), 134-147. Kieffer understands this christology within the framework of a hierarchically structured view of the world, and its *Sitz im Leben* as the scriptural reading (from the Old Testament) in the service, which in this way set off what was related to Jesus.

## 2. The New Covenant

Continuity and discontinuity are also apparent in what I see as the hidden substructure of Matthew, and of other New Testament writings,[13] namely the concept of the death of Jesus as the event that puts the new covenant into force. To me it seems tempting to understand the prophetical sayings about a new covenant in the last days (expressed in particular in Jer 31 and 32 and Ezek 11 and 36, though also elsewhere) as *the* fundamental theological concept, the principal dogma, on which the Gospel of Matthew builds its ethics and soteriology. Hence, what is, judging by appearances, absent from the gospel, exists as presuppositions of this gospel in the community it addresses, presuppositions with which it has a complementary relationship.

In the Gospel of Matthew this new covenant was established at Jesus' last supper with his disciples in the shadow of his impending death. Jesus says expressly that his blood shall be poured out for the many εἰς ἄφεσιν ἁμαρτιῶν (26.28); in its description of John's baptism the gospel omits this prepositional phrase. Together with the ransom saying of 20.28 - perhaps also the reply to John the Baptist in 3.15 - it sums up the salvational importance of Jesus' life and death, namely that God gives man the fulfilment of the Law.[14]

The use of a prophetical allusion to the conclusion of a new covenant to identify an innovation in Judaism is not without precedent, although similarities with the community of Qumran are merely formal. More decisive in this respect is the way both the Qumran and the early Christian communities conceived themselves as being the fulfilment of the prophecy and therefore true interpreters of the Scripture. It should be remembered that the truth of Holy Writ was not considered a historical problem, indeed, it was perceived to be hidden in the true interpretation, i.e. not in the written words, but in the way these were read in the light of contemporary events. For Holy Writ spoke, not only to people of the past, but in particular to a contemporary audience; cf. Rom 15.4.

---

[13] In my article "Ånden og Loven. Pagtsteologi i Romerbrevet in" *DTT* 52 (1989), 251-267, I have tried to elucidate this complex of concepts and its meaning for Paul's argument in his epistle to the Romans.
[14] Cf. H. Ljungman, *Das Gesetz erfüllen*, 33. Inspired by A.N. Whitehead's linguistic philosophy, Russell Pregeant, *Christology beyond Dogma. Matthew's Christ in Process Hermeneutic*, Semeia Supplements 7 (1978), arrives at an interpretation, which in many respects comes close to these results. So the two theses which he defends in Part III of his book, The Components of Matthew's Christology: Torah, Salvation, Grace, run (61): "1) Matthew's soteriology is based upon Torah; while it is Jesus who brings salvation, by interpreting the Law, it is finally the Law itself that is the efficient means of salvation, and not any kind of vicarious atonement; 2) salvation, nevertheless, is not "legalistic", but actually rests upon a functional equivalent of the Pauline "grace"." Indeed, R. Pregeant does not include the concept of the conclusion of the new covenant and on the whole directs his efforts to other goals.

## 3. The Epoch of Revelation as the Centre of Times

In Hans Conzelmann's construction of the salvation-historical concept of the Lukan writings, the ministry of Jesus is "die Mitte der Zeit".[15] It is preceded by the epoch of Israel (see Luke 16.16: "The Law and the prophets were until John; since then the good news of the kingdom of God is preached and every one enters it violently"); this epoch is followed by a third, beginning with Jesus' exaltation. This is the epoch of the Church. This tripartition of salvation-history has been applied to the Gospel of Matthew by Georg Strecker in his classical monograph *Der Weg der Gerechtigkeit* (1962).[16] Strecker rightly points out that also in this gospel the epoch of the life of Jesus is described as a past epoch, not to be repeated, sacred and ideal; it was a unique epoch, indeed; on the other hand it was immanent in its time and did not end it, but it is separate from the termination of all history which is yet to come, and which will bring judgment and salvation.[17] According to Georg Strecker there is in the Gospel of Matthew "eine in drei Epochen sich entfaltende Historie, deren Mitte die Zeit Jesu als die Zeit der Offenbarung ist".[18] Within the scope of these epochs the work of Jesus is eminently construed as a legitimization of the Matthean communities' life and self-understanding, including the historical events that determines the actual circumstances.[19]

Accordingly, I do not agree with Jack Dean Kingsbury when he insists on a "Salvation History in two Epochs".[20] When Kingsbury says that the epoch of the Church started with the ministry of Jesus, he misses the aspect that the new covenant was not established until Jesus' crucifixion.

---

[15] Cf. *Die Mitte der Zeit. Studien zur Theologie des Lukas*, BHTh 17 (1954, 5. Aufl. 1964), espec. 9-10. Se also 172-173.
[16] *Der Weg der Gerechtigkeit. Untersuchung zur Theologie des Matthäus*, FRLANT 82 (3. Aufl. 1971).
[17] See *Der Weg der Gerechtigkeit*, 122, where it is said about the redactor of the gospel of Matthew, "daß er die Zeit Jesu als zurückliegende, heilige Vergangenheit zeichnet." And further: "So erscheint das Leben Jesu [in Matthew] als ein Zeitabschnitt, der zwar im Zeitablauf eine besondere Stellung einnimmt, aber ihm doch immanent ist, ihn nicht beendet, sondern von dem noch ausstehenden, Gericht und Heil bringenden Ende der Geschichte abgehoben ist." See on the whole 86-122. In a later article, "Das Geschichtsverständnis des Matthäus", EvTh 26 (1966), 57-74, reprinted and here quoted after *Das Matthäus-Evangelium*, hg. von Joachim Lange, WdF 525 (Darmstadt 1980), 326-349: 334, it is said: "Die Zeit Jesu [ist] ein einmaliger, unwiederholbarer, heiliger, idealer Abschnitt im Ablauf der Geschichte".
[18] "Geschichtsverständnis des Matthäus", 334.
[19] Cf. also Rolf Walker, *Die Heilsgeschichte im ersten Evangelium*, FRLANT 91 (1967), 146, where it is claimed that the description in Matthew of the history of Jesus contains "verschiedene Textelemente in heilsgeschichtlich-ätiologischer Funktion, die als solche zum Abschluß der Vergangenheit und zur Begründung der Gegenwart dienen, die also für die Gegenwart des Evangelisten keinen direktkerygmatischen, sondern nur noch geschichtlich-funktionalen Sinn haben".
[20] See "The Structure of Matthew's Gospel and His Concept of Salvation History", CBQ 35 (1973), 451-474, here quoted after the revised edition in Kingsbury, *Matthew: Structure, Christology, Kingdom* (London, 1976 = American edition 1975), 1-39: 31-36. Kingsbury arrives at this conclusion because he ranks christology higher than soteriology.

Not until this event, including the subsequent resurrection and exaltation, did the epoch of salvation begin, *de jure* so to say, as is also apparent from the retention of the prohibition against mentioning "the vision" on the mountain "until the Son of Man is raised from the dead" (17.9). Only then did the temporary mission to Israel end (ch.10), and the epoch of the mission to the Gentiles begin (28.16-20). John P. Meier is right, although on other premises, when he says that "Matthew sees the death-resurrection as an eschatological event in which the kingdom breaks into this aeon in a new, fuller way".[21]

## IV. The Epoch of the Church

There may thus be every reason to adopt Hans Conzelmann's tripartition of the salvation-history of the Lukan writings, but it is conspicuous that when it comes to defining what is essential in the third epoch, that of the Church, the two authors part company. Both describe the work of Jesus as belonging to the past and as a presupposition for the Church. But, as is proclaimed at the end of the Gospel of Luke, the foundation of the church was laid in Acts when it received the Holy Spirit; in a way the Holy Spirit takes over Jesus' part in this book. Thus, far from being a casual continuation of the story, this volume, which Franz Overbeck termed "a tactlessness of worldhistoric dimensions",[22] is a very essential supplement.

The picture is somewhat different in the Gospel of Matthew. As has been pointed out by Rolf Walker in the monograph *Die Heilsgeschichte im ersten Evangelium* (1967), this gospel is in no need of a continuation. On the contrary, the evangelist involves his "Acts" in his description of the life of Jesus in a way that would make a sequel quite superfluous.[23]

Accordingly, the Gospel of Matthew does not treat the life and work of Jesus exclusively as something to be looked back upon. But, as emphasized by the final missionary command, this gospel everywhere aims at impressing upon its audience the picture of the resurrected and exalted Lord. As Rolf Walker has expressed it: the "Spirit" that spoke

---

[21] "Salvation-History in Matthew: In Search of a Starting Point", *CBQ* 37 (1975), 203-215: 212.

[22] "Nichts ist bezeichnender für die Auffassung des Lukas von der evangelischen Geschichte, sofern er darin ein Objekt der Geschichtsschreibung sieht, als sein Gedanke, dem Evangelium eine Apostelgeschichte als Fortsetzung zu geben. Es ist dies eine Taktlosigkeit von welthistorischen Dimensionen, der größte Exzeß der falschen Stellung, der sich Lukas zum Gegenstand gibt". The quotation is from Franz Overbeck, *Christentum und Kultur* (1919), but is here quoted after Philipp Vielhauer, *Geschichte der urchristlichen Literatur* (Berlin, 1975, 3. Aufl. 1981), 404.

[23] *Heilsgeschichte im ersten Evangelium*, 114: "Matthäus arbeitet seine "Apostelgeschichte" ([...]) so organisch in die von ihm vorgelegte vita Jesu ein, daß sein Evangelium keiner Ergänzung durch ein zweites Werk bedarf. Das Matthäus-Evangelium enthält die matthäischen vita Jesu und "Apostelgeschichte" in einem". Cf. 126.

after Easter has been replaced by the word spoken before Easter, i.e. the Christ tradition in the shape it has been given in the sayings of the Gospel of Matthew and in its salvation-history, is the basic norm of all faith and all "church".[24]

Thus interpreted, the sequence of events in Matthew is on the whole the essential presupposition for the foundation of a church that will embrace both Jews and Gentiles. In Acts this is described as the result of an independent development. The Matthean Jesus speaks directly to his (future) congregations. The theme of the apostles' and disciples' folly, which we find in the Gospel of Mark in connection with the motif of the Messianic secret (though also in Luke, cf 9.45; 18.34; 24.25,45), has been superseded in Matthew by an image of the disciples as paragons to the future Christians.[25] In this gospel, the disciples already, proleptically, act as a congregation. This is expressed very clearly when first Peter is given the *potestas clavis* in connection with his confession (16.19), then the disciples in general according to the disciple speech (18.18). The duality is also conspicuous in chapter 10, where the speech is about a temporary mission to the lost sheep of the house of Israel, though it changes very soon into a speech about the circumstances awaiting the disciples in the world and about their appearance before governors and kings to testify before them and the heathen (v. 18 = Mark 13.9!); accordingly, it also contains an admonition to endure until the end, i.e. when Jesus comes (v. 22-23).

This duality is further reflected in the use Matthew makes of christological titles. Where non-disciples generally address Jesus as $διδάσκαλος$, the disciples quite consistently say $κύριος$, which is clearly meant as a title. Significantly, Judas Iscariot uses $ραββί$ instead of $κύριος$ (26. 25,49). The use of the title 'Son of David' is also to be understood in this context; it occurs more frequently in this gospel than in the others, partly as a title connected with the historical Jesus, partly apologetically, as a means to depict Jesus as the one who has fulfilled Israel's expectations of a Messianic Son of David. In this way the title also serves to remind Israel of its guilt, because it did not receive its Messiah, but, on the contrary, charged him with being an accomplice of the prince of demons (see 12.34; cf. 9.34). The title 'Son of God' is thus superior in relation to the idea of Jesus as the Son of David; in the Gospel of Matthew it appears, first on a 'redactional' level (2.15), and in the mouth

---

[24] See *Heilsgeschichte im ersten Evangelium*, 116: "Der nachösterliche redende "Geist" ist verdrängt durch das vorösterlich gesprochene Wort...: die Christus-Tradition in Gestalt der matthäischen Wort- und Heilsgeschichte ist die einzige und grundlegende Norm allen Glaubens und aller "Kirche"".
[25] Cf. Ulrich Luz, "Die Jünger im Matthäusevangelium", *ZNW* 62 (1971), 141-171, here quoted after *Das Matthäus-Evangelium*, hg. von Joachim Lange, *WdF* 525 (1980), 377-414: 386: "Gerade als Schüler des historischen Jesus werden die Jünger transparent, Typen für das Christsein überhaupt".

of God (3.17; 17.5); but it is also voiced by Satan and the demons (4.3,6; 8.29). We find it in the confessions of the disciples and Peter (14.33; 16.16), and, additionally, it occurs in the high priest's question at the interrogation (26.63) and as the reason for the high priests' and the elders' mocking exhortations to the crucified one to save himself (27.43). Finally, it is affirmed by the confession of the centurion and his companions when they witnessed Jesus yield up his spirit (27.54). Thus the Son of David, representing the particularist expectations, is throughout the gospel revealed as the Son of God whose reign is universal.[26]

This comes out very clearly in 11.25-30 in Jesus' eulogy to his Father, his confession of himself as the one who alone reveals the Father, and his invitation to all who labour and are heavily laden. Here, as in 28.18-20, it is the exalted one who speaks and calls for the rest that springs from taking his yoke and learning from him. When he describes his yoke as useful and his burden as easy, it follows that obedience to the Law is God's gift, a sign of his mercy. What this means appears from the peculiar story of the shekel in the mouth of the fish in 17.24-27. The ordinance of the temple offering, Exod 30.13-14 (which belongs to the ceremonial law), is being relativized when Jesus says that the sons are free. Not to offend "them", i.e. the Jews, God sees to it that the tribute is paid, namely by Peter's miraculously acquisition of the money needed for the temple tribute.

If the Gospel of Luke sees the history of Jesus principally as bygone events, which had to be equipped with a "continuation" in order to reach the present, in Matthew the history applies directly to the present. The Gospel of Matthew is thus, unlike to the Gospel of Luke, a complete gospel. It is no coincidence that where the Lukan writings have a description of the Ascension (Luke 24.51; Acts 1.9-11), there the Gospel of Matthew lets the exalted one issue his final command. This is illustrated by Ernst Käsemann in his lecture *Das Problem des historischen Jesus* from 1953,[27] where he marks the difference between Luke and the other three gospels by saying that in these history is best characterized by an eschatological catchword from the New Testament itself, "nämlich mit dem ἐφ' ἅπαξ, in welchem sich die beiden Bedeutungen, "einmal" und "ein für alle Male" so merkwürdig verschmelzen".

---

[26] Cf. Jack Dean Kingsbury, "The Composition and Christology of Matt 28:16-20", *JBL* 93 (1974), 573-584. He claims that this pericope expresses the Son of God-christology which Kingsbury generally thinks is basic in this gospel.

[27] First printed in *ZThK* 51 (1954), 125-153. Hier quoted from E. Käsemann, *Exegetische Versuche und Besinnungen* I (1960, 4. Aufl. 1965), 187-214: 200.

## V. The Church and Israel

This incorporation in the story of Jesus' life, including the part of salvation-history, which applies to the epoch of the Church and the Gentiles' admission to salvation, raises the question how the Gospel of Matthew actually treats Israel's fate during this sequence. For the sake of comparison I shall again start with the Lukan writings. Broadly speaking, the picture here is that after the crucifixion of Jesus, Israel is given another chance of salvation when the resurrection is proclaimed. Ostensibly the Jews had acted in ignorance (Acts 3.17), but after the resurrection ignorance is no longer an excuse. In Acts the gospel is communicated first to the Jews (Acts 13.46), though very soon it is followed up, if not by an immediate mission to the heathen, then at least by the conversion of Samaritans and Gentiles. The respite granted to the Jews as a nation lasted until the events of the year 70. What happened then was interpreted by the author of the Lukan writings as God's final reckoning with a wicked and obstinate people. The future thus belongs to the Gentile church, whilst Judeo-Christianity is encapsulated as a thing of the past. The individual Christian Jew may, of course, like Paul, continue to observe the Mosaic Law in its entirety, but after the year 70 the picture of this people, constituted by their obedience to the law, becomes a 'negative'.

In the Gospel of Matthew a similar chain of events has been incorporated in the story about the life of Jesus, namely in the form of predictions. If, in Luke, the ceremonial part of the Mosaic Law is conspicuous, the reference, in Matthew, to the heathen nations is no less so. Considered as a nation, Israel is *de facto* lost from the beginning. Its representatives, reckoned from king Herod, over the high priests, the Sadducees and the elders to the Pharisees, were all hostile to Jesus,[28] whereas the representatives of the Gentiles appear in a strangely parallel sequence - as a fulfilment of the promises to Abraham - as those who acknowledge and are themselves acknowledged by Jesus; thus the Magi were the first to adore the child, and the centurion and the Canaanite woman are noticed at the cost of those born to the Kingdom (cf. 3.9; 8.11).

To put it differently: Israel as a nation appears in Matthew on 'borrowed' time. The 'course of events' is summarized in three parables, preceded by two pericopes leading up to them. The second of these

---

[28] See to this R. Walker, *Die Heilsgeschichte im ersten Evangelium*, kap. II. "Israel im Matthäusevangelium" (11-74). Cf. also "Problemstellung", 10, where Walker is talking about Matthew's "Tendenz, Israel als geschlossene Einheit darzustellen, als massa perditionis, die für den Messias Jesus nur das Kreuz übrig hat und deren Gerichtsverfallenheit von daher offenkundig ist."

pericopes asks the question who gave Jesus authority (Matt 21.23-27), whereas the first is about the curse on the fig tree, a symbolic act aimed at Israel and accompanied by the words; "May no fruit ever come from you again" (v. 19). The parables about the two sons (21.28-32), the unfaithful vineyard tenants (21.33-46) and the marriage feast of the king's son (22.1-14) indicate a salvation-historical periodization illustrating both Israel's fate and the opportunity offered to the Gentiles.

The salvation-historical ponderings underlying the various textual emendations in the parable of the two sons cannot have sprung from nothing, although they are not apparent in the pericope, but only become explicit in the parable of the marriage feast. The first parable, on the other hand, exemplifies the criteria. He who said no but afterwards repented and came back to the vineyard represents, according to the context, the rejected by Jewish society, who have entered upon the road to justice which John the Baptist had revealed. By contrast, he who said yes, but who was all talk symbolizes the Judaism which did not do the will of the Father and was not even moved by the sight of those who did.[29]

The subsequent parable of the unfaithful vineyard tenants puts this in its true perspective in a sketch of the 'Israelite-Jewish epoch', the termination of which apparently coincides with the murder of the son. The question as to *when*, more precisely, the owner of the vineyard will come to settle his accounts with the murderous tenants (v. 40) is only answered in the last parable. Before this a quotation from Ps 118.22-23 has been inserted, as an appendix to the parable and in continuation of the audience's judgment upon themselves. With its reference to the stone that was rejected by the builders and yet became the head of the corner, it functions as a clue, as is further emphasized by the lines; "This was the Lord's doing, and it is marvellous in our eyes". How this was fulfilled is explained in the saying, introduced by a διὰ τοῦτο, that God's kingdom shall be taken away from 'you', i.e. the Jewish people, and be given to a people (ἔθνος) who will 'produce' its fruits. This people is identical with the other tenants, of whom the Jews themselves say in v. 41 that they should give 'him', i.e. the owner of the vineyard, the fruits

---

[29] Michael D. Goulder claims in *Luke. A New Paradigm*, II, *JSNT.SS* 20 (1989), 609-616, that Matt 21.28-32 (21.18ff. must be a misprint) was "a matrix" for the Lucan parable about the prodigal son in Luke 15.11-32. Heikki Räisänen, who also looks upon Luke 15,11-32 as essentially created by the evangelist and who would like to follow Goulder, if he were able to believe that Luke had had Matthew among his sources, finds it "possible, and even likely, that the story was composed to drive home the point that *converted Gentiles* are accepted by God and *should be joyously accepted* by the community, even by observant Jewish Christians". See his contribution "The Prodigal Gentile and his Jewish Christian Brother. Lk 15,11-32", in *The Four Gospels 1992. Festschrift Frans Neirynck*, *BETL* 100, Vol. II (1992), 1617-1636: 1635-36. In that case the intention has been altered.

in their seasons. Presumably this αὐτῶν is to be understood about the new tenants, not the fruits, and accordingly it should be taken to refer to the times of the Gentiles. The significance of this is emphasized in v. 44, where it is proclaimed, in the form of an allusion to Dan 2.34,44-45, that "he, who falls on this stone will be broken to pieces, but when it falls on any one, it will crush him".

Here a 'stage direction' has been inserted to the effect that after having listened to these parables, the high priests and the Pharisees understood that Jesus was talking about them, and they tried to arrest him, but for fear of the masses, who considered him a prophet, they hesitated. Then follows a parable, which even more clearly illustrates the course of events. The parable of the marriage feast, in the shape it has in Matthew, certainly invites to an allegorical interpretation of the history created by Jesus' coming. Here it is also a question of what heaven is like (not, as elsewhere, what it is going to be like). The dispatching of the servants probably relates to the prophets (cf. 21.34ff.) and to the sending of the twelve (see 28.18-20), respectively. It is also more reasonable to interpret v. 7 as referring to the conquest and subsequent destruction of Jerusalem in the year 70, an event which the evangelist interprets as God's judgment over Israel, because it spurned his Messiah. The same theme is repeated in the prophetic lament over Jerusalem in 23.37-39, where it is also said that "their" house, that is the temple, will be deserted (cf. 24.1-2). From then on the people of Israel definitively became "the Jews" in the negative sense of the word, which we find in the Gospel of John, and in Matthew 28.15.[30]

There can hardly be any doubt that the second dispatch of the servants in Matt. 22.8-10 relates to the Gentiles, and it might well tempt one to the conclusion that the mission to the Gentiles did not start till after the year 70. However, this is obviously to treat the allegory too rigoristically. On the other hand, considering the speech in v. 7, the chain of events cannot be taken to mean that the death of Jesus interrupted the mission to Israel. The command of 28.18-20 does not exclude Israel,[31] but it does range it with πάντα τὰ ἔθνη (cf. 25.32, but also 24.9,14). There is an implication of tension in the salvation-historical concept of the gospel between the mission to the Gentiles, which replaced the mission

---

[30] Cf. G. Strecker, *Der Weg der Gerechtigkeit*, 116-117: "Damit ist ein Sprachgebrauch aufgenommen, der sonst nur im Mund der Heiden erscheint. Nicht mehr von Israel, dem auserwählten Volk ist die Rede, sondern die "Juden" erscheinen als ein Volk unter anderen".
[31] So e.g. Bernhard Weiss, *Das Matthäus-Evangelium*, KEK I,1 (10. Aufl. 1910), 508: "Der Befehl 10,5f. ist also nicht bloss erweitert (Nösg[en]), sondern zurückgenommen (H[o]ltzm[ann])". R. Walker, *Die Heilsgeschichte im ersten Evangelium*, 111-112, share this opinion: "Gab es zur Jesuszeit keine Mission unter den Heiden, sondern allein unter dem "auserwählten Volk", so ist jetzt die Zeit der "Mission" Israels zu Ende und die Heidenvölker treten an ihrer Stelle" (112).

to Israel, and a parallel mission lasting from the death of Jesus until the year 70.[32] This may be due to the fact that the Gospel of Matthew dates from a time when the break with Judaism was an accomplished fact. In that case this tension is 'literarily' conditioned.

## VI. The Church and the Gentiles

On the one hand the evangelist must necessarily maintain the continuity with Israel as the bearer of the promises, while on the other hand he needs a theological justification for abolishing his followers' identification with the historical Israel.[33] Accordingly, the factor that creates continuity and identity is redefined, so that, rather than expressing an affiliation to a particular people, it becomes the faith that is evoked by Jesus or the preaching of him.[34] This faith gives access to the new covenant, which was concluded on the death of Jesus, and which is remarkable by the way in which it perfects the old covenant by creating conditions instead of imposing them. God's will remains the same in the Decalogue and the double commandment of love, whereas the so-called ceremonial part of the Mosaic Law is allowed to lapse.[35] The new covenant makes that justice possible which is not only its ultimate goal, but also the basis of life within it. However, considering the view of the congregation held by the Gospel of Matthew we would misjudge it if we were to see it as 'enthusiastic' about an *ecclesia triumphans*. On the contrary, the gospel is saturated with the admonition to adhere to the new justice; the preaching of the judgment to the community is almost exclusively parenetic. It is absolutely crucial to do justice by doing the will of the Father who is in heaven. Without such acts as originate from faith, it is as dead as a body without spirit (cf Jas 2.26) and therefore useless (see in particular 7.23; 22.11-12; 25.11,24-30,31-46). All exterior manifestations like e.g. circumcision (not mentioned at all in this gospel) and the observance of the commandments of purity have been replaced by a legal observance inspired by the heart.

Thus falls the wall around Israel already in the gospel's story of Jesus' work, at the same time as it is claimed that Jesus himself had been sent

---

[32] Cf. R. Walker, *Die Heilsgeschichte im ersten Evangelium*, 115.
[33] Cf. the thorough exposition in R. Walker, *Die Heilsgeschichte im ersten Evangelium*, kap. III. "Die Heiden im Matthäusevangelium" (74-113).
[34] Cf. R. Walker, *Die Heilsgeschichte im ersten Evangelium*, 80: "Die Kontinuität der Heilsgeschichte liegt nicht im Volk oder religiösen "Volksbegriff", sondern auf der höheren Ebene eschatologischer Erwählung - in dem handelnden und berufenden Gott". And further, 81: "Mögen auch die Adressaten der Basileia wechseln, die Gabe der βασιλεία τοῦ θεοῦ bildet das Kontinuum zwischen Israel und der neuen heilsgeschichtlichen Größe".
[35] Cf. my article "The Gospel of St Matthew and the Mosaic Law - A Chapter of a Biblical Theology", *StTh* 46 (1992), 109-120.

to the lost sheep of Israel. This apparently particularistic saying does, however, leave a door ajar. For the lost sheep of Israel were none but those who were not held in any esteem in Israel, those who belonged in the grey zone between Israel and the Gentiles (cf. John 7.49). Also, when Jesus (at a distance) cures the son of the centurion and the daughter of the Canaanite woman, these two Gentiles are praised, respectively, for a faith, not even found in Israel (see 8.10), and for a "great faith" (see 15.28). In the same way, the first to acknowledge that the Crucified was indeed the Son of God were the centurion and those with him, again representatives of the Gentiles (see 27.54). The eschatological significance of this event is made the more conspicuous in Matthew, because the confession of the centurion and the others was not occasioned by Jesus' way of dying, but by what they saw, τὸν σεισμὸν καὶ τὰ γινόμενα, which filled them with awe.[36]

It is characteristic of the Gospel of Matthew that it has built into its story of the life of Jesus the conflict about the commandments of purity, which the Lukan writings reserve for Acts. The Gospel of Luke has neither the pericope on clean or unclean, or on the Syro-Phoenician/Canaanite woman (Mark 7; Matt 15), but rather postpones this step until the Cornelius episode in Acts 10. Thus it becomes an achievement by the Holy Spirit, which, according to this gospel, carries on Jesus' work. The Gospel of Matthew cannot afford such 'postponements', for here Jesus is already the exalted one, i.e. he ranks as such, cf. 13.37-38; 19.28; 26.64[37] and 28.16-20. For this very reason a positive picture of the ceremonial law cannot be accomodated in this gospel, for when it was written this part of the law had lost its 'predicatory value'.

It is thus correct that the Gospel of Matthew delimits Jesus' own ministry geographically and nationally. It is also correct, as pointed out by John P. Meier that the same disciples, who were told in the missionary discourse to go nowhere among the Gentiles and enter the town of the Samaritans, are in 28.16-20 told to go and make disciples of all nations.[38] Meier also emphasizes that while Jesus is described as teacher during his life on earth, nothing is said about the disciples teaching before they are told to in 28.20, where it is also said that they are to

---

[36] Cf. again J.P. Meier, "Salvation-History in Matthew", 207-210, the section "The Death-Resurrection as *die Wende der Zeit*", where, among other things, it is said about 27.51-54 (207-208): "Here, with the full panoply of apocalyptic imagery, Matthew portrays the death of Christ as the end of the OT cult, as the earth-shaking beginning of the new aeon (bringing about the resurrection of the dead), and as the moment when the Gentiles first come to full faith in the Son of God".

[37] Context and wording in 19.28 invite us to understand it with respect to the exaltation, and a similar interpretation is the most likely regarding 26.64; cf. here my *Der Ausdruck "Menschensohn" in den Evangelien. Voraussetzungen und Bedeutung*, AThD 17 (1984), 106-108 (My interpretation of 19.28 in the same book, 116-117, is hereby withdrawn).

[38] See "Salvation-History in Matthew", 204-205.

teach all that Jesus has commanded them. This is where we find the decisive transition from the mission to Israel to the mission to the Gentiles. Though it is not said so explicitly, it is implicitly understood that the 'Jewish restriction' presupposing the validity of the Mosaic Law, has now been abolished in favour of Jesus' law preaching κατὰ Μαθθαῖον. Accordingly, when it is said that the gospel should be preached first to the Jews, this is not tantamount to 'Jew first - Christian then'.

In the final words of the gospel, Jesus' death and resurrection exaltation become explicit as the primary eschatological events, as implied all through in the preaching of Jesus. The members of the new covenant are referred to here as no longer being subject to geographical and national limitations. This is the kingdom of the son of man, which will stand as a *corpus mixtum* until Jesus' second coming when the Father's kingdom, in which the righteous are to shine like the sun, will be universal (cf. the "parallel" in 1 Cor 15.22-25).

The rupture with Judaism, inherent in the Gospel of Matthew and thus part of it from beginning to end, implies nothing about the evangelist's own nationality. Rolf Walker, and others with him, claim that the evangelist must be a Gentile,[39] an assertion which he bases on the author's attitude to Judaism. This is in continuation of esp. Georg Strecker's investigations, but in my opinion this is not necessarily the case. It could just as easily be a question of a Jew departing, though sorrowfully, from the people which has spurned its saviour and thus relinquished whatever created its identity as God's own people. The intensity peculiar to the Gospel of Matthew need not be construed as an estrangement or animosity. Rather, it seems to reflect the need, felt especially by a Christian Jew, for a theological 'explanation' of the outward rupture, seeing that he will have to contend with his own 'inward synagogue'. The idea of the hardened heart offers itself readily here (see esp. 13.13-15; characteristically this Isaiah-saying is not quoted in the Lukan writings until Acts 28.26-27); the 'animosity' towards Judaism is hardly more pronounced than the animosity demonstrated in the Qumran scrolls against the Judaism, from which the Qumran sect had segregated itself.

Everything considered, the mission to the Gentiles is the sole perspective dominating past and future in Matthew. The period of salvation-history, which the evangelist and his followers belong to, and which is the kingdom of the son of man and the time of the new

---

[39] See R. Walker, *Die Heilsgeschichte im ersten Evangelium*, e.g., 126, and G. Strecker, *Der Weg der Gerechtigkeit*, 15-35.

covenant, will last until the "close of the age" (συντέλεια τοῦ αἰῶνος; Matt 13.39,40,49; 24.3; 28.20). It is also illustrated in the words of 24.14 that this gospel of the Kingdom will be proclaimed all over the earth as a testimony to all nations, καὶ τότε ἥξει τὸ τέλος (see also 26.13). This close of the age is, however, overshadowed by Jesus' exaltation as the real eschatological event. As it has been said, there is more 'realised eschatology' in Matthew than in Mark e.g., and it seems very likely that, in the final sentence of 28.20, the emphasis should be on πάσας τὰς ἡμέρας rather than συντέλεια τοῦ αἰῶνος.[40]

## VII. An Outstanding Question

Where Israel, e.g. in the letters of Paul, preserves its identity thanks to the birthright, the glory, the covenants, the giving of the law, the worship, the promises and the patriarchs (Rom 9.4-5), there the Jews of the Gospel of Matthew (and, for that matter, the Lukan writings) have lost all prerogatives. The events of the year 70 were interpreted as the expiration of the time-limit and the ratification of God's final judgment of rejection. The fatal cry of Matt 27.25: "His blood be on us and on our children!" had been "heard"! According to this salvation-historical concept, Israel's history as God's own people was over.[41] Judaism could not continue to be the religion it was once.[42] Christianity left it transformed, now to be the religion of an obstinate, callous and therefore rejected people.

This leads quite easily to a view of Israel as an interlude in salvation-history, but as such it allows salvation-history to get behind it. This comes out very clearly in Matthew's version of the divorce pericope, Mark 10.1-12 (Matt 19.1-12). When Mark, 10.6-9, says that Moses wrote the commandment of the certificate of divorce πρὸς τὴν σκληροκαρδίαν ὑμῶν, he argues for it by quoting Gen 1.27 and 2.24 verbatim, beginning with the words "from the beginning of creation" (ἀπὸ δὲ ἀρχῆς κτίσεως). In Matt 19.4-5 these quotations constitute a first reply to the Pharisees' question as to whether divorce is allowed or not. Only when his adversaries insist, quoting Moses' commandment of the

---

[40] See J.P. Meier, "Salvation-History in Matthew", 213-214.
[41] Cf. R. Walker, *Heilsgeschichte im ersten Evangelium*, 126, where it is said about the gospels of Matthew and Luke: "Hier stoßen wir auf verschiedene Ausformungen einer "heidenchristlichen" Theologie vom Ausgang des 1. Jahrhunderts, die mit dem Israel-Problem, horribile-dictu, auf ihre (heilsgeschichtlich begründete) Weise "fertig" war".
[42] It is interesting that a Jewish theologian like Jacob Neusner in his book, *Jews and Christians. The Myth of a Common Tradition* (London, Philadelphia, 1991), is able to talk about Rabbinic Judaism after the year 70 as a movement parallel to Christianity: "The upshot was two religions out of one, each speaking within precisely the same categories but so radically redefining the substance of these categories that conversation with the other became impossible" (5).

certificate of divorce, does Jesus reply, in v. 8, that Moses allowed this "for your hardness of heart", and he adds that "from the beginning it was not so" (ἀπ' ἀρχῆς δὲ οὐ γέγονεν οὕτως). Matthew thus restricts the validity of this commandment to the period of salvation-history, which coincides with the history of Israel until Jesus' coming. In this way the evangelist lays the foundation of the belief, which became prominent in the Church Fathers, that when Moses accepted divorce, this was because of the Jews' peculiar callousness and obstinacy (see esp. Irenaeus, *Adversus haereses* IV.15.2).

The history of the Israelite-Jewish people up to the time of Christ - i.e. in practice until the final rejection in the year 70 - is treated in the gospels of Matthew and Luke as a chapter of salvation-history - although a finished chapter - but later on this same chapter was interpreted by some theologians as a flagrant misunderstanding. Judaism became demonized, partly in gnosticism where the Old Testament Yahweh was identified with the demiurge, partly in the Letter of Barnabas, which interpreted the Old Testament as an entirely Christian book never understood by the Jews. Such ahistorical attempts at an interpretation must of course be denied. But, due to its salvation-historical character, the New Testament itself makes a dialogue between Judaism and Christianity impossible on other premises than the salvation-historical. Christianity signifies a complete innovation in relation to Judaism, which is thus referred to a place outside the history of salvation. There is but one way to salvation.

## VIII. Conclusion

Hopefully, I have succeeded in showing, by means of this example of biblical theology, that salvation-history is an indispensable and integral part of Matthew's preaching of Christ. For it is through the historical periodization that the work of Jesus assumes importance, meant exclusively for the people of Israel as it was, while at the same time laying the foundation of the mission to the Gentiles. The chapter of salvation-history devoted to Israel was concluded with the rejection of the Messiah, whose crucifixion marked the conclusion of the new covenant with its promise of the kingdom of heaven for all who carry its fruits, Jews as well as Gentiles. In this way he, the exalted one, who was called Emmanuel, "God with us", in Matt 1.23, is with his people always until the close of the age.

CHAPTER FIVE

# THE LUCAN INTERPRETATION OF JESUS AS BIBLICAL THEOLOGY

Jacob Jervell, Oslo

I

Is Luke a theologian? If the answer is no, it would be impossible to speak of biblical theology[1] when dealing with Luke. In the last 40 years scholars have been more interested in Luke's contribution to theology than to history.[2] The historian Luke has been almost completely absorbed by the theologian.[3] Still the question is valid: Luke a theologian?

Luke is, however, more of a poet, an artist and a narrator with great skill in composing a story, giving us the history of the church in the first century by means of pictures, lively, dramatic and broad scenes and fragments of scenes. And so he acts as an evangelist. At least he is not a systematic theologian, giving us a systematic, defined and uniform exposition. He does not give an account of fundamental conceptions. We do not by him find the explicit theological statements. Still we may say that if not within, so at least behind his narrative account we do have certain theological presuppositions. And he understands history theologically.[4] So we may justifiably speak about him as a theologian. In the same way as we may find theology in a sermon or in a historiographical work. It is correct to say that he is a theologian of no mean stature who very consciously executed his work.

But in speaking of him as a theologian I do not share the widespread opinion that Luke's theological contribution lies in his supposed innovation of eschatology and so his historicism, ("Historisierung"), of

---

[1] "Biblical theology" can here only be used with reservations as no Bible existed for Luke apart from the Old Testament.
[2] So due to the influence of German interpreters like Conzelmann, Dibelius, Haenchen, Vielhauer.
[3] Cf. the survey in H. Gasque, *A History of the Criticism of the Acts of the Apostles*, BGBE 17, Tübingen 1975; I.H. Marshall, *Luke: Historian and Theologian*, Grand Rapids 1970; E. Plümacher, *Lukas als hellenistischer Schriftsteller. Studien zur Apostelgeschichte*, StUNT 9, Göttingen 1972; J. Thornton, *Der Zeuge des Zeugen. Lukas als Historiker der Paulusreisen*, WUNT 56, Tübingen 1991.
[4] M. Hengel, *Zur urchristlichen Geschichtsschreibung*, Stuttgart 1984².

the message and ministry of Jesus.[5] In eschatology Luke's ideas are traditional with no innovations. And he is not the inventor of Salvation history. His actual theological contribution lies in ecclesiology, and within this frame his original interpretation of Jesus.

I am not dealing with "Luke-Acts", this expression signalizing Luke's Gospel and Acts as once a single book only divided when it was taken into canon.[6] We have to do with two works of one author, Acts written many years after the Gospel, adressing a somewhat different set of concerns.[7] There is a shift in emphasis (f.ex. in the use of the Scriptures, poverty/wealth, the Spirit, the women in the church, the pharisees, the way of treating sinners etc) in Acts. Still there is to a great extent a theological unity in the presuppositions behind the books of Luke, especially when dealing with christology.

IIa

Luke is an historian.[8] He uses history as a tool for his theology. This is a mostly undisputed fact among New Testament scholars today, even if some scholars do not believe, that Luke ever intended to write history.[9] He is the only historian[10] among the New Testament authors. Not that the other ones had no idea about history, but only Luke writes history on a larger scale. The other ones reflect history more indirectly, and you have to read between the lines in order to get at it, whereas Luke gives it directly.[11]

There has of course been a discussion what kind of historian he actually is and what type of history he writes. If he is a pragmatic historian, a tragic one, a Hellenistic historian or a Jewish influenced

---

[5] So after the famous book of H. Conzelmann, *Die Mitte der Zeit*, BHTh 17, Göttingen 1953, 1964⁵ ; English: The Theology of St.Luke, New York 1961.

[6] So a majority of interpreters after H.J. Cadbury, *The Making of Luke-Acts*, New York 1927 (repr. London 1961); cf. R. Maddox, *The Purpose of Luke-Acts*, FRLANT 126, Göttingen 1982, 3-6.

[7] Each of the two parts corresponds approximately to the largest size of a standard scroll.

[8] This must be taken cum grano salis because Luke writes salvation history and so transcends the limits of antique historiography, cf. J. Jervell, "The Future of the Past - Luke's vision of Salvation History and its bearing on his writing History", in B. Witherington, III, *The Acts of the Historians - Acts and Ancient Historiography*, Cambridge 1994.

[9] L. Alexander, *The Preface to Luke's Gospel. Literary Convention and Social Context in Luke 1.1-4 and Acts 1.1*, SNTS.MS 78, Cambridge 1993; R.I. Pervo, *Profit with Delight. The Literary Genre of the Acts of the Apostles*, Philadelphia 1987; C. Talbert, *What is a Gospel? The Genre of the Canonical Gospels*, Philadelphia 1977; cf. E. Trocmé, *Le "Livre des Actes" et l'Histoire*, 1957, 41-50, 113.

[10] This must not be confused with the question if he is a capable or poor historian.

[11] Luke is not the inventor of Salvation History because we find it in prefigurations and fragmentary in the Pauline letters and in the other Gospels.

one.[12] He is surely not a modern historian, and we can't judge him by our standards. But it has too often been overlooked that Luke as an historian can not act as historians of his own time. So when we without further ado talk about Luke as historian, we do forget that this is only the half of the truth.

This has to do with the fact that Luke writes salvation history and as historian is doing nothing but interpreting the Scriptures. And so he is in a different situation from that of other historians in antiquity. You can not separate the historian Luke from the theologian. The holy Scriptures are of course books of history, at least to us, but these books of history are to Luke the words of God, therefore normative and binding. History can not be separated from preaching. And these books of the Scriptures are more than a reflection of what has happened, they are more than a mirror of history as they themselves create history. They do not only tell of the past, but of the present and the future. Then you are not solely dealing with phenomena of the past, but those phenomena of the past are as the words of God normative even for people living in the aftertime. That is in our context: the early church or the church of Luke. It is a commonplace that history can give us self-knowledge, telling us where we come from and who we are.

It is a commonplace that history can be our teacher, but there is far more to it for Luke. We can make our choice wether we are willing to learn from history or not and what to learn. When history is Scripture, you are not left with any choice. You are then dealing with history as the word of God, binding and normative. What applied yesterday, applies equally today. Nothing essentially changes, history does not mean changes. That is strange to us as we see historical consciousness as meaning relativety, the past was different, and we accept different ways of living, thinking, feeling, from epoch to epoch, in various cultural and geographical areas. Luke is of another opinion, as he is a fundamentalist, with without any criticism of the Scriptures and the traditions.

We often make the error, when dealing with Luke as an historian, that he has something of a modern historical consciousness, seeing the past as different from the present. F.ex. the church in Jerusalem lived and acted as pious Jews, within the piety of temple and law, faithful to the Jewish law, but that is not binding for the church of Luke. Then here is is not talking as a theologian, but as an historian.[13] And then we get a

---

[12] Cf. B. Gärtner, *The Areopagus Speech and Natural Revelation*, ASNU XXI, Uppsala 1955, 7-36; E. Plümacher, *Lukas als hellenistischer Schriftsteller*; J.Thornton, *Der Zeuge des Zeugen*, 355-368. On tragic and pragmatic historiography: B. Gentili - G. Cerri, *History and Biography in Ancient Thought*, Amsterdam 1988, 7-33.

[13] So last: F. Bovon, *Das Evangelium nach Lukas I*, EKK III/1, Neukirchen 1989, 25.

false picture of what he is actually saying. This because there is nothing to Luke that we can label "only history". It is impossible to separate Luke the historian from Luke the theologian, that is the interpreter. History does not confirm the Scriptures, but the Scriptures confirm history.

IIb

It is easy to recognize that we can not divorce the historian from the theologian, when dealing with the question of the law in Luke and Acts.[14] We will return to the question of christology. The law is given by God and has so to say everlasting life, is always valid. This why it is a part of the Scriptures. Luke 16.17[15] confirms the law in a very conservative way:

> It is easier for heaven and earth to come to an end than for one dot or stroke of the law to loose its force.

The law does not only belong to the past epoch of redemptive history, but has validity in the present and in the future. Some interpreters have been so unhappy about this saying that they have labeled the saying "irony", as they don't know what to do about it.[16] A superficial look into Acts shows the unbroken authority of Moses in the church of Luke. He has no summary of the law f.ex. in the commandment of love or the golden rule; the law is valid in its totality for the church as it has always been and always will be. There is no question of its being abolished,[17] with no validity anymore, or being replaced by the apostolic decree[18] or what me may call "general ethics".[19] The apostolic decree is in itself a part of the law. And above all are the ritual commandments important

---

[14] This question was for years neglected by exegetes, but has since 1972 been the subject of intense scholarly efforts. The newest contributions: M. Klinghardt, Gesetz und Volk Gottes. Das lukanische Verständnis des Gesetzes nach Herkunft, Funktion und seinem Ort in der Geschichte des Urchristentums, WUNT 32, Tübingen 1989; K. Salo, Luke's Treatment of the Law. A Redaction-Critical Investigation, AASF 57, Helsinki 1991; M.A. Seifrid, Jesus and the Law in Acts, JSNT 30, 1987, 39-57; M. Syreeni, Matthew, Luke, and the Law, PFES 51, Helsinki 1990, 125-155.
[15] To the scholarly discussion on this passage: K. Salo, Law, 136-150.
[16] Cf. R. Banks, Jesus and the Law in the Synoptic Tradition, SNTS.MS 28, Cambridge 1975, 218; W.G. Kümmel, Promise and Fulfilment. The Eschatological Message of Jesus, SBT 23, London 1957, 124; S. Wilson, Luke and the Law, SNTS.MS 50, Cambridge 1983, 45.
[17] H. Hübner, Das Gesetz in der synoptischen Tradition. Studien zur These einer progressiven Qumranisierung und Judaisierung innerhalb der synoptischen Tradition, Witten 1973, 15-35; R. Nixon, "Fulfilling the Law: The Gospels and Acts", in: B. Kaye/G. Wenham, Law, Morality, and the Bible, Leichester 1978, 55; W.G. Kümmel, Promise and Fulfilment 124; Wilson, Luke and the Law, 13.
[18] H. Conzelmann, The Theology of Luke, New York 1961, 145ff.and 212f.
[19] K. Berger, Die Gesetzesauslegung Jesu. Ihr historischer Hintergrund im Judentum und im Alten Testament, I, WMANT 40, Neukirchen 1972, 222-227.

in the law consisting of "living words", Acts 7.38,53. An idea as the one in Galatians 3 about the law being limited in time, a temporary measure, and that the period of the law has come to an end with Christ, is to Luke inconceivable. But we always run into problems here, as we are used to deal with the law in the context of salvation, which Luke does not![20]

IIIa

Biblical theology means to Luke the interpretation of the Scriptures, it is scriptural theology.[21] Luke can not add anything to the Scriptures, anything having in itself the rank of the Word of God or even the acts of God. Even when it comes to the resurrection of Christ, Luke, as the only author within the New Testament, has to demonstrate that the ressurrection of Christ is given in the Scriptures; it has to have proof from the Scriptures, Luke 18.33; Acts 2.25ff.; 13.32ff.; the resurrection is called "the hope of Israel", Acts 26.6f.; 28.20.[22]

In order to understand the meaning of biblical theology in the sense of scriptural theology, we have to be aware of the fact, that to Luke the word of the Scriptures is not primarily a written word, but a spoken one.[23] This is clear from the from the form of Luke's quotations from the Scriptures, that is: in Acts. He may introduce a quotation with: "it is written", Acts 1.20; 7.42; 13.33; 15.15. But that is the exception, coming from his tradition, so above all in the Gospel, where Luke makes almost exclusive use of "it is written". Luke introduces in Acts generally (22 of 26 quotations) his quotations with words denoting the verbal element: it is said, spoken, commanded, preached, proclaimed etc.[24] He is talking in his introductions to the quotations - as the only one in the New Testament - about the "mouth" and the "voice" of the prophets, Acts 3.18,21; 4.25; 13.27.

---

[20] The issue has always been dealt with by contrasting Luke with Paul with regard to soteriology. And: Luke as a representative of Gentile Christianity treats the law as a purely historical matter in so far as the law no longer represents an actual problem.

[21] Luke's interpretation of Scriptures: D.L. Bock, *Proclamation from Prophecy and Pattern. Lucan Old Testament Christology*, JSNT.SS 12, Sheffield 1987; T. Holtz, *Untersuchungen über die alttestamentlichen Zitate bei Lukas*, Berlin 1968; J. Jervell, *The Unknown Paul. Essays in Luke-Acts and Early Christian History*, Minneapolis 1984, 122-138; B.J. Koet, *Five Studies on Interpretation of Scripture in Luke-Acts*, SNTA 14, Leuven 1989; M. Rese, *Alttestamentliche Motive in der Christologie des Lukas*, StNT 1, Gütersloh 1969; P. Schubert, "The Structure and Significance of Luke 24", in FS R. Bultmann, *BZNW* 21, 1954, 125-144.

[22] Cf. K. Haacker, "Das Bekenntnis des Paulus zur Hoffnung Israels nach der Apostelgeschichte", *NTS* 31, 1985, 437-451.

[23] Cf. J. Jervell, *Unknown Paul*, 124.

[24] The only parallel to this approach in the New Testament is the Epistle to the Hebrews. All 23 references are to what is "said", not a single one to "what is written" or the like.

The idea is not that of a initially spoken word later written down, but it has to do with the service in the synagogue, to which Luke repeatedly points, Acts 13.14ff.; 14.1ff.; 16.13ff.; 17.1ff.,10ff.,17; 18.4; 19.8. Here the Scriptures are read, interpreted and heard every sabbath, in the regular services and in missionary preaching. The missionary preaching is a part of the regular services .This is Scripture in function, where God speaks again and again. They are words for the moment. That underlines once more the normative and binding charakter, sit venia verbo: unhistorical character, in the modern sense of the word, of the Scriptures. And Luke is never talking about the Scripture in the singular, as if he is able to extract some sort of systematic ideology from the entity called "Scripture", but he always talks about the Scriptures in the plural, where everything and anything is important.

It is not possible to separate the historian Luke from the scribe Luke. In his account he is doing nothing but interpreting the Scriptures. We do not see this clearly if we label him the first church historian, as if he is writing the history of the church, or better: his own early church, as he does not cover the whole. But Luke is not writing the history of the church in the sense we talk about church history.[25] There is to Luke nothing like an established church as an own entity. Luke does not look back on a history which has come to its end, Israel and the Old Testament, and then a new history, the history of the church, has started.

Luke is dealing with the one and only people of God, that of the history of Israel, and this history includes the history of the church. The latter is nothing but a new and final epoch in the one history of the old people of God. According to Luke you can actually find the history of Jesus and the church in the details in the Scriptures,[26] put down in writing long before the things actually happened.

This is Luke's subject matter: God and his people, from the beginning until today. He shows no interest in world history.[27] God has acted and spoken as saviour only in the history of his one and only people. Luke may mention that even other peoples have a history too, Acts 14.14ff.; 17.26ff., but to this God is indifferent and in it only passive present. It is not necessary to demonstrate that Luke is interested in the history of

---

[25] The honor of being the first church historian should be given to the one who actually deserves it, namely the Palestinian Eusebius from the third century.

[26] J. Jervell, *The Unknown Paul*, 135ff.

[27] The widespread opinion that Luke relates the Christevent to persons and times of world-history in order to make Jesus a figure of world-history and the church a part of Greek-Roman culture is false. There are some scattered references to world-history, Luke 2.1-3; 3.1-2; Acts 11.28; 18.2,12; 25.11; 27.1. But the history of other peoples than Israel, inclusive the church, is not worth mentioning as it is an "empty" history, peoples God had "all left alone to go their own ways" Acts 16.14. Cf. J. Jervell, "Gottes Treue zum untreuen Volk", in FS G. Schneider, Freiburg-Basel-Wien 1991, 15-18. To the relationship between salvation history and world history: J. Jervell, "The Future of the Past".

Israel before the coming of Christ, that is the previous history of the church, or the first phase in the history of the church. He is even more interested in it than all other authors in the New Testament, Paul included. As the only one among them he recapitulates and summarizes the whole history, Acts 7.2-53 and 13.16-25.[28]

Luke is not occupied with one or few ideas in the Scriptures, f.ex. the prophecies about Messiah, the promises. He is not picking up ethical ideas, and the history is not important as illustrative material f.ex. in connection with ethics. Not some theological ideas in the Scriptures are important to him, but the history as such. The history about God and his people is determined and led by God's everlasting faithfulness to his people in spite of human faithlessness and even idolatry, Acts 7; the whole history of Israel is predestined solely by God's benevolent guidance, Acts 13.17-25. This history as such is theology.

In the last survey, Acts 13.17-25, the Christ-event, characterized as the salvation of Israel, is in itself a part of the history of Israel, 13.23. That is in itself astonishing. And the way Luke connects Christ with the history of Israel as a part of it, 13.22-23, shows that Luke does not attach something new and strange, a new idea of Messiah, a new institution different from the ones of Israel, a new religion, to the history of Israel. It is often in New Testament research taken for granted that to Luke the history of Israel has come to an end. That is nonsense to Luke. If this were the case, there would be no chosen people and no church.

### IIIb

The gospel of the church is there in detail in the Scriptures. It is not there simply as a prophecy o r a promise of the future Messiah. But the whole history of Jesus is written down:

> His life and mission, words and wonders: Luke 4.18ff., Acts 3.22; 7.37.
> His predecessor, the baptist: Luke 3.4ff.; 7.26ff.
> His passion, crucifixion and death: Luke 18.31ff.; 24.25ff.,44ff.; Acts 3.18,24; 4.25ff.; 8.32ff.; 17.3; 26.22.
> His resurrection and exaltation: Luke 18.31,33; 24.26,46; Acts 2.25ff.,30; 3.13,24; 13.33ff.; 17.3; 26.22f.
> The Scriptures even identify the promised Messiah as Jesus of Nazareth, Acts 17.3; 18.28.

---

[28] Hebr 11 is different, a historic list of parenetic examples.

But you have even more than the history of Jesus in the Scriptures according to Luke. You can find other parts of the Gospel and even the history of the church:
The story of Pilate, the Romans and Herod is there: Acts 4.25ff.
The story of Judas is reported: Acts 1.16f.,20.
The election of a new Apostle, Acts 1.20ff.
The forgiveness of sins for the believers in Jesus: Acts 10.43; Luke 24.26.
The outpouring of the Spirit is told by the prophets: Acts 2.17ff.
The prophecies in the church and the miracles: Acts 2.17ff.
The mission and missionaries among Jews and Gentiles, starting in Jerusalem, Luke 24.26,46f.; Acts 13.47; 15.15ff.; 26.22f.
That parts of Israel will not accept the gospel is there: Acts 3.23; 13.41; 26.22; 28.26ff.
The end of history, the parousia: Luke 21.22; Acts 3.21.

The whole Gospel is read every sabbath in the synagogues as they read the Scriptures, Acts 15.21. In order to understand the Gospel you have to turn to the Scriptures, 17.3. If it is not there in the Scriptures, it is not a true Gospel. So when Luke is writing the history of the church, he is all the way interpreting the Scriptures. History as normative and binding is always present, and the history of Israel, so even in the period of the church, is holy history, normative history. There is no legitimacy in the church unless you can display it from the Scriptures. Theology is nothing but scriptural theology.

## IV

And now more explicitly to Luke's interpretation of Jesus. We have no parallel in the New Testament to Luke's christology as a whole. The setting for Luke's christology is the question: Had Jesus actually Messianic status? Then salvation is given only to the people of God and coming from no one but the Messiah stemming from that people. Luke knows that his church has doubts and a great need for "assurance for the instruction, they have received", Luke 1.4.[29] Consequently Luke's interpretation of Jesus is intended to be taken from the Scriptures.

In the gospel of Luke the christology is worked out above all by a series of stories, most of them stemming from the tradition. Luke here rarely employs titles and never exact definitions about the identity of

---

[29] To the interpretation of Luke 1.4: L. Alexander, *The Preface to Luke's Gospel. Literary Convention and Social Context in Luke 1-4 and Acts 1.1*, Cambridge 1993; Fr. Bovon, *Das Evangelium nach Lukas*, 40ff.; J.A. Fitzmyer, *The Gospel According to Luke*, I, AB, New York 1981, 300f.

Jesus. Luke does in his gospel not teach christology, he tells it. When writing Acts Luke obviously assumed that his readers knew these stories, Acts 2.22f.; 10.36ff.; 13.27f. From obvious reasons we don't find the stories from the life of Jesus in Acts. Christology is preferably formed by the use of titles and epithets. There is a highly independent and distinctive selection and use of christological titles.[30] It goes without saying, that all Jesus has said and taught is in toto normative for the church. But even this is for Luke tied to the Scriptures. Jesus is to him, f.ex. in his words, no authority on a par with the Scriptures, but there must exist proofs of what he says from the Scriptures. His words are normative because they all the way are "according to the Scriptures." Therefore there is of course no criticism of Scripture and tradition in the words and acts of Jesus.

And this even has to do with the clear subordination of Jesus in relation to God.[31] Jesus is in himself a part of the history of the people of God, he is the Messiah of Israel. He is a link in a preceding history. Jesus is not above or outside history. He is not divine, not creator or the tool in the creation, not preexistent, not the universal reconciler, not the imago dei etc. Absent is any form of metaphysical speculation in Luke's interpretation of Jesus.

The idea of the history of the people of God and the idea of God being the God of Israel - not the God of the nations - determine the christology.

You see this in the distinctive and independent use of christological titles, closer to Old Testament and Jewish conceptions than elsewhere in the New Testament. But Luke avoids titles intelligible to non-Jews.[32] You find the most archaic and very old titles going back to the church in Jerusalem exactly in Acts and very often only here in the New Testament:

- ὁ ὅσιος, ὁ ἅγιος, Jesus is the "holy one", Acts 2.27; 3.14; 13.34-35, that is the lawobedient,
- ὁ δίκαιος, 3.14; 7.52; 22.14, that is: the true agent of God to Israel

---

[30] A survey of the literature on christological titles: Fr. Bovon, *Luke the Theologian. Thirty-Three years of research*, Allison Park, PA, 1987, 177-179; J.A. Fitzmyer, *Luke I*, 263-265.
[31] Cf. H. Braun, "Zur Terminologie der Acta zur Auferstehung Jesu", ThLZ 77, 1952, 533-536; H. Conzelmann, *Mitte der Zeit*, 161ff.
[32] The title υἱὸς τοῦ θεοῦ appears only once in Acts 9.20, we have it in some late manuscripts to Acts 8.37, and 5 times in Luke's gospel. The title does not demonstrate " the unique relationship between Jesus and God", so J.D. Kingsbury, *Jesus Christ in Matthew, Mark, and Luke*, Minneapolis 1981, 98-110; further J.A. Fitzmyer, *Luke I*, 207; J. Kremer, ""Dieser ist der Sohn Gottes" (Apg 9.20). Bibeltheologische Erwägungen zur Bedeutung von "Sohn Gottes" im lukanischen Doppelwerk", in FS G. Schneider, 1991, 150f.155. The content of the title is the divine miraclepower of Jesus.

- παῖς,[33] the servant of God, Acts 3.13,26; 4.25,27,30; Luke 1.54, Jesus as one of the men of God in the Scriptures,
- ὁ προφήτης, Jesus as Prophet, Acts 3.22; 7.37f., cf. Luke 9.8,19.
- ὁ ἀρχηγός, leader,prince, Acts 3.15; 5.31, Jesus as the fulfilment of the Davidic hope.[34]

The most significant title to Luke is χριστός, stemming from the Palestinian Jewish tradition, and this title is decisive for the other forms of titles. Luke employs it as a title, and not in accord with the christological development in early Christianity, as a proper name.[35] Luke utilizes the title not primarily to show the relationship between God and Jesus, but attaches it to the story of Israel in terms of the scheme promise- fulfilment. Jesus fulfills the promises to the people of God, he is the anointed one of Israel. The title is for Luke not tradition; he uses it etymologically and gives a definition unintelligible to non-Jews, Luke 4.18; Acts 4.27; 10.38. The Messiah is thoroughly the Old Testament figure, Luke 2.36; 3.15; 24.24-26; Acts 2.31. He is "the Lord's (God's) Messiah", Luke 2.26; 9.20; 23.35; Acts 4.26.[36] Messiah-Jesus is God's agent as the bearer of salvation to Israel. Peculiar to Luke is that this Messiah of Israel is a suffering Messiah, Acts 3.18; 17.3; 26.23; Luke 24.24,46. Each reference to the suffering Messiah is accompanied by the assertion, that this is exactly what the Scriptures say. The suffering Messiah is not an invention of the church, but the testimony from of old from God himself.

A variant to "Messiah" is "the Son of David", used by Luke more than any other New Testament writer. This title again is not tradition to Luke, something from the past to the historian Luke, useful to describe the oldest christology in the church. Luke knows the title "Son of David", Luke 18.38f.; 20.41, but he does not ones use it in Acts, but rewrites it there and in the Gospel when he repeatedly talks about David.[37] Luke uses the title in the most independent way, not primarily from his Christian tradition, but viewed against the background of the

---

[33] The translation "child" is impossible as Luke even characterizes David and Israel as παῖς, Luke: 1.54,69; Acts 4.24. In Luke 2.43 it means "child", that is Jesus as a small boy, this is a different form from those we have in Acts.

[34] Equivalent to עבד ; the Old Testament and Jewish sources in: G. Johnson, "Christ as Archegos", NTS 27, 1981, 381-385; cf further P.-G. Müller, ΧΡΙΣΤΟΣ ΑΡΧΗΓΟΣ. Der religionsgeschichtliche und theologische Hintergrund einer neutestamentlichen Christusprädikation, EHS.T 28, Bern and Franfurt 1973.

[35] When Luke uses Christos as a second name in Ἰησοῦς Χριστός, this is dependent upon his use of the term as title.

[36] Luke can even use Christos for the Old Testament Messiah without a special reference to Jesus, Luke 2.26; 3.15; 24.24-26.

[37] Examples: Luke 1.32,54,67,69; 2.4; Acts 1.16; 2.29; 4.25; 13.34; 15.16.

Old Testament and Jewish tradition.[38] As the Son of David Jesus fulfills the promises to David, restoring David's kingdom for Israel, Luke 1.32,69; Acts 2.29-36, further Luke 2.4,11,14; 18.38f.; 19.38; Acts 13.32,34-37; 15.15-18. So Jesus ist ὁ βασιλεύς, the King, and of course the King of the Jews, Luke 19.38; 23.2,3,37,38; Acts 17.7. When σωτήρ, Heiland, is mentioned, it refers to the saviour of Israel and descendant of David, Luke 1.47; 2.11; Acts 5.31; 13.23, and Luke applies the title to the resurrected Jesus. The background is obviously the Old Testament.[39]

The title Luke numerically prefers is κύριος, Lord, stemming from the church in Jerusalem, connoting not Jesus as divine, but his dominon over Israel, Luke 1.32,35; 2.11; 20.44; Acts 1.6; 2.25ff.,26, and he often combines χριστός and κύριος, Luke 2.11,26; 24.3; Acts 2.36; 4.26; 11.17; 15.2. The title has "an essentially Messianic resonance".[40]

It is seldom noted that Luke even works with the christological notion of Jesus as the Son of the people, of Israel. Jesus is christologically presented as a Palestinian Jew.[41] There exists nothing like a title "Son of Israel", but the idea is present. The simple fact that Jesus was a Jew - a fact that no author in the New Testament denies or discusses - Luke elaborates in a most independent way. It is important to him to show, not that Jesus was a man, but that he was a Jewish man. He did not come down from heaven, but was a Jew born in Betlehem of Davidic lineage; Luke 1.27. 2.4; 3.31. In Luke's gospel the emphasis is found in the material peculiar to Luke:

- 2.21: the circumcision of Jesus
- 2.22-24: the presentation of Jesus as a firstborn in the temple
- 2.41-52: Jesus as a boy in the temple
- 3.21-22: Jesus' baptism together with the people
- 3.23-28: Jesus as one in the succession of many sons of David, in the genealogy of Jesus.[42]

---

[38] Cf Chr. Burger, *Jesus als Davidssohn. Eine traditionsgeschichtliche Untersuchung*, FRLANT 98, Göttingen 1979, 137-152. The Old Testament dominance on Luke's Christology is so clear, that he does not always give "full expression to the experience of the early Christian community" (E. Franklin, *Christ the Lord. A Study in the Purpose and Theology of Luke-Acts*, London 1975). A study of the later manuscripts shows their dissatisfaction that Luke use the title in accordance with Jewish thought.

[39] Cf. G. Voss, *Die Christologie der lukanischen Schriften in Grundzügen*, SN 2, Paris/Bruges 1965, 45ff.

[40] I. de la Potterie. "Le titre *kyrios* appliqué à Jésus dans evangile le Luc", FS P. Beda Rigaux, Gembloux 1970, 45.

[41] J. Jervell, "Der Sohn des Volkes", in FS Ferd. Hahn, Göttingen 1991, 245-254.

[42] The genealogies in Judaism served not to show that a person belonged to a certain family, but to the people, cf. Chr. Burger, *Jesus als Davidssohn*, 171; O. Cullmann, *Die Christologie des Neuen Testaments*, Tübingen 1979[5], 131, N.3; Ferd. Hahn, *Christologische Hoheitstittel. Ihre Geschichte im frühen Christentum*, FRLANT 83, Göttingen 1966[3], 241, N.1; M.D. Johnson, *The Purpose of Biblical*

In Acts the emphasis is present in the two historical surveys, 7.37 and 13.23. Jesus falls into the line with the history of the people. He is incorporated in Israel.

Characteristic is the accumulation of christological titles and epithets. This has nothing to do with Luke's dependence on the tradition, as if he tries to collect all christological titles in the church. This he has obviously not done: we miss some titles known from the church. And Luke employs the titles in a most independent way, not going back to the Christian tradition, but to the Scriptures. And it has to do with with Luke's stressing the πᾶς, πάντες.[43] He is talking about all the prophets, Acts 3.18,24; 10.43; all God's word, Acts 13.29; 20.27; 24.14, all Jesus has said and done, Acts 1.1; 3.22. And so there is no messianic title, epithet or name from the Scriptures which does not apply to Jesus. The multiplicity testifies to Luke's biblicism, his appeal to the Scriptures of Israel: only so biblical theology is possible.

In Jesus is God's activity in the history of Israel manifested. The key figure in this history and so even in christology is God himself. God himself is the saviour, Acts 28.28; Luke 1.47; 2.30; 3.6, even when salvation is tied to the Christevent. The notion that God himself is the very center of Christology is demonstrated by Luke's heavy employment of the Scriptures in his christology, the Scriptures understood as the revelation of God's will, works and words throughout history, including the Christevent. Luke only within the New Testament describes the main events in christology, the suffering, death and resurrection of Jesus by proofs from the Scriptures, Acts 2.24ff.,30ff.; 3.18ff.; 4.10ff.; 13.33ff.; 17.21ff.; 26.22f.; Luke 18.31ff.; 24.26ff.,44ff.. The climax of God's acts in Christ is the ressurrection, and everything hangs on this act as the act of God.

Apart from the proof from the Scriptures Luke gives his account in a language peculiar to him: He uses the transitive verbs ἀναστῆσαι and ἐγείρειν;[44] the last verb he uses in the active with God as the subject, Acts 3.15; 4.10; 5.30; 10.41; 17.3. The transitive ἀναστῆσαι, "raise", is used in the active, God as subject for the resurrection, Acts 2.22,32; 3.26; 13.33,34; 17.31. The intransitive ἀναστῆναι, "rise", is used Luke 18.33; 24.7,46; Acts 10.41; 17.3, and is the traditional way of refering to the resurrection. Luke knows this, but prefers a different vocabulary. His form ascribes the causality of the resurrection of Christ to God,

---

*Genealogies with Special Reference to the Setting of the Genealogies of Jesus*, SNTS.MS 8, Cambridge 1969, 97.
[43] Used 1244 times in the New Testament, Luke alone 329.
[44] Luke uses the passive ἠγέρϑη only twice, Luke 9.22; 24.34, from the tradition; in the passive God is the implied agent, cf. J.A. Fitzmyer, *Luke I* 195f.

whereas the other implies that Jesus rose by his own power.[45] The oldest form of the kerygma is the one, which stresses God's causality: God is the one who raises the dead, God has intervened, and Luke has returned to and stresses that form. For him everything hangs upon the God of Israel having raised Jesus from the dead: "The God of our fathers raised up Jesus", Acts 5.30; 3.13-15. We find the same when dealing with the ascension, Acts 1.2,9,11; 2.33; 5.31; 7.56; Luke 9.51; 22.69; 24.51.[46] God himself has intervened, and he alone has given Christ the proper status.

How can this kind of Christology, especially the Lucan use of titles, be suitable for non-Jewish readers of Luke's work? What about his readers if they were Gentile Christians? No wonder that exegetes have found his christology peculiar,[47] with a view to Luke's presumed status as a Gentile writing to Gentile readers. The solution often given is that Luke is an historian. He gives us a description of how the first Jewish Christians thought of Christ, and therefore we have those very old elements. But then we do overlook that this christology from Luke's point of view is nothing but interpretation of the Scriptures. Has Luke any interest in an archaic christology without relevance for his church?

We would have an indicator if we found this spesific christology only in the first parts of Acts, let us say before the conversion of Paul, and after that a christology which we could label Hellenistic-Christian. Even that would have been peculiar. Could Luke's church differ in christology from the church in Jerusalem with its christology stemming from the Scriptures? To Luke that would have meant to dismiss the Scriptures or part of the Scriptures. There is, however, no difference in the two parts of Acts when it comes to Christology. There is nothing like a development in christology for Luke as it stems from the Scriptures. History as such has no theological significance, only salvation history with Scripture as its basis.

Some words about the notion of salvation,[48] as this is tied to the interpretation of Jesus. God himself is to Luke the saviour, Luke 1.47; 2.30; 3.6; Acts 28.28. God has acted as saviour through the history of

---

[45] 1 Thess 4.14; Mark 8.31; 9.9,31; 10.34; 16.6; Joh 20.9.
[46] The vocabulary is characteristic: all the verbs in question are used in the passive: ἀναλαμβάνειν, ἀναφέρειν, ἐπαίρω, ὑψόω, Acts 1.2,9,11; 2.33; 5.31; Luke 24.51.
[47] H. Conzelmann, *Mitte der Zeit*, 158ff.
[48] The Old Testament as background: J.A. Fitzmyer, *Luke I*, 223f.; P. Minear, *To Heal and to Reveal. The Profetic Vocation According to Luke*, New York 1975, 102-111; G.Voss, *Die Christologie der lukanischen Schriften*, 45-60. The Greek sense as primary: F.W. Danker, *Luke*. Proclamation Commentaries, Philadelphia 1987², 28-45; 82-99; Ch. Talbert, "The Concept of Immortals in Mediterreanean Antiquity", *JBL* 1975, 419-436.

Israel, so that this history is determined by a serious of God's saving acts, Acts 7.2-53; 13.16-25; Luke 1.46-54. The history of Israel is "Heilsgeschichte", and only this history is, as there is no salvation in the history of the Gentiles; Acts 14.16. Now, with the appearance of Jesus, we have reached the eschatological time for salvation. Mostly Luke talks in general terms of salvation, as he presupposes that his readers know what it is about. Salvation consists of various elements:

cure Acts 4.9; 14.9; Luke 6.9; 7.50; 8.48,50,
peace, Luke 2.14; 19.38,42,
life Luke 10.25ff.; Acts 5.20,
spirit, Acts 2.19-21; 10.47; 15.8; 19.2ff.,
and above all remission of sins, Luke 1.7; 5.21ff.; 7.47ff.; 24.46f.; Acts 2.38; 5.31; 10.43; 22.16; 26.18.

Decisive is, that salvation is to be found in Israel, that is Israel at the end of times, namely the church, and that God has transferred the divine prerogatives in salvation to Jesus, Acts 3.13; 4.12; 5.31; 13.23; Luke 1.47,69,77; 2.11. Jesus ist the saviour of Israel, Acts 2.36-41; 5.31; 13.23,36; Luke 1.69,71,77; 2.10f.; 19.9f. Salvation is exclusively connected with the coming and acts of the Messiah-Jesus, Acts 2.21; 4.12; 13.23; Luke 1.69; 2.11; 19.9. But salvation is not the outcome of one single act or aspect of the work of Christ,[49] but has to do with all the phases of his life and work:[50]

- His life: Luke 2.11,30-32; 4.18f.; 5.21ff.; 7.20ff.,47ff.; 19.9; Acts 10.38
- His death: Luke 22.19f.,37; Acts 20.28; 26.28
- His resurrection and exaltation: Luke 24.47; Acts 2.25ff.,38; 3.15, 19,26; 5.30; 10.43; 13.37ff.; 22.16; 26.23.

How is salvation related to these different aspects of the work of Christ? There is no answer to this in Luke-Acts.

---

[49] The most discussed problem is if the death of Jesus has saving significance for Luke. That no soteriological significance is drawn from Jesus' death is a widespread opinion . It is clear that Luke does not regard Jesus' death as a sacrifice or as an expiation from sin, but it is evident that Luke knows about the sacrificial death of Jesus, Acts 20.28 (the blood of Christ); Luke 22.19f. For some inscrutable reason Luke thrusts the sacrificial death of Jesus into the background. But the death of Christ is to Luke related to God's salvific plan, Acts 3.18; 13.28-30,33; 17.3; Luke 13.33; 17.25; 24.46f.
[50] R. Glöckner, *Die Verkündigung des Heils beim Evangelisten Lukas*, Mainz 1976.

## V

Luke presents to us biblical theology. That is to him literally theology from the Scriptures, the Old Testament, coming from the interpretation of these Scriptures. The character of the Scriptures determines the character of Luke's theology. It has not the form of a credo or systematic abstract or treatise; it is not an explanation and development of ideas and conceptions, from God the creator to the return of Christ, in logical order with consequenses and with coherence. It is an historical narrative in pictures, not dealing with conceptions, but with texts in the process of an ongoing interpretation and preaching. It is like a kaleidoscope - as the Old Testament is one - with a serious of pictures and scenes and fragments. There is no developed doctrine of God or Christ, but the subject is always Jesus who acts and speaks in various situations.

And for Jesus there is not only one name or title, but a whole serious, as we find it in the Scriptures when dealing with Messiah. There is no need for coherence or for logical consequenses. It is not necessary for Luke f.ex. to explain how salvation is related to Christ, or to his life, death or resurrection. He does not bother to explain how forgiveness of sins is possible. There are inconsistencies and contrasts, as you find them in the Scriptures, and Lukes does not bother to harmonize. He does not even bother to explain in his interpretation of Jesus his proclamation and confirmation of the Mosaic law and at the same time his insistence on God's mercy. This does not mean, that his report consists of disparate elements, but they are tied together as Scripture and by a story.

I don't expect systematicians to acknowledge this as theology, but to Luke it is, even if he is not familiar with the word "theology". If Luke had been more like a systematic theologian we would probably not have had such hard disagreements on the content of his theology, representing a stormcenter in exegetical theology today.

Luke claims to have reported everything there is to be said about Jesus and his people. His frequent use of the word $\pi\hat{\alpha}\varsigma$, as demonstrated from the very beginning of his gospel, Luke 1.3, makes this evident. There is to him but one theology, represented by himself. There are, however, other concepts, only to mention Paul, John and the letter to the Hebrews. Then we are dealing, not with biblical theology, but with biblical theologies. To extract from the various conceptions in the New Testament, or in the Scriptures, one single biblical theology, is probably possible, but I don't see what the gain should be. You do find in the New Testament side by side different conceptions, and not only different ones, but even contrasting conceptions, f.ex. the ideas about Israel and its fate. But this did not harm the church or bring it to a downfall.

Luke's contribution to biblical theology, that is the theology we today have to work out, is invaluable even if we can resume neither his material christological conception nor his use of the Scriptures. The titles have only historical value to us and his fundamentalist ideas of interpreting the Old Testament are obsolete. But of contemporary, biblical-theological significance is his way of creating Christology, demonstrating the identity of Christ as *the* man in history, and the testimony of the Old Testament about God and his dealing with the world and mankind as a pattern for our understanding and confession to God. And last but not least: A theology of history is indispensable. Luke gave us one.

CHAPTER SIX

# BIBLICAL THEOLOGY AND THE JOHANNINE LITERATURE

Judith M. Lieu, London

*I. Introduction*

The title of this paper has been deliberately left as neutral as possible, reflecting the uncertainties it provokes. Certainly the Johannine Literature has not been the most fertile ground for explorations of Biblical Theology in the past. This is particularly true for someone from the English speaking world for whom 'Biblical Theology' at first raises images of the movement whose crisis, perhaps deaththrows, Brevard Childs recorded in 1970.[1]

Oscar Cullmann made much of John 7.8 where Jesus says to his brothers, "Go to the feast yourselves; I am not going up to this feast, for my time has not yet come (οὔπω πεπλήρωται)", in the interests of salvation history - a perspective congenial to that Biblical Theology movement.[2] Yet although his distinction between καιρός time and χρόνος time proved attractive to some,[3] few found in his approach a convincing framework for understanding the Fourth Gospel as a whole. Cullmann was already protesting against Rudolf Bultmann's demythologising programme of interpretation which declared that John had renounced any salvation-historical perspective,[4] but it is probably the lasting influence of Bultmann's approach which has inhibited much further work from a Biblical theological perspective.[5] An existentialist interpretation combined with a reconstruction of a gnostic or proto-gnostic background left little room for any serious engagement with the Gospel's 'Biblical' roots.[6]

---

[1] B. Childs, *Biblical Theology in Crisis* (Philadelphia, 1970).
[2] O. Cullmann, *Christ and Time* (ET London, 1951), 41-44.
[3] See J. Marsh in ed. A. Richardson, *Theological Wordbook of the Bible* (London, 1950), 258-267.
[4] O. Cullmann, *Salvation in History* (ET London, 1967), 268-291.
[5] So also M. Hengel, "Die Schriftauslegung des 4. Evangeliums auf dem Hintergrund der urchristlichen Exegese", *JBTh*4 (1989), 249-88, 260-61.
[6] Despite their fundamental differences in the interpretation of the Fourth Gospel Ernst Käsemann at least agreed with Bultmann on the absence of any salvation history in it.

While modern study has moved on, at least in the English speaking world, to rather more interest in the socio-historical background - the Johannine community, - the creative theological impulses of the Gospel, and even more of the Epistles if they are allowed any, have been traced to outside the Biblical tradition. There are however other voices and the current situation can best be illustrated by comparing two recent studies of the Fourth Gospel. John Ashton in his magisterial study of *The Interpretation of the Fourth Gospel* [7] acknowledges his debt to Bultmann with whom he maintains a fruitful dialogue. Despite occasional acknowledgement of the importance of the Old Testament background, the Old Testament itself contributes virtually nothing to his understanding of the Gospel; the passages he highlights as the key to its understanding, the 'blue print' of the Gospel, are those which declare most sharply the dualism of decision and the detachment from any sense of continuity - 3.16-21,31-36; 7.33-36; 8.21-27; 12.44-50.[8] Contrast A.T. Hanson in *The Prophetic Gospel*:

> For the author of the Fourth Gospel scripture is not just a prop, an addition. It is constitutive for this work, or again, Thus Scripture, far from being used merely as illustrative material in his work, is part of its very woof and warp.[9]

This contrast is not just that between two scholars or approaches but reflects a tension within the Gospel itself; any exploration of Biblical Theology and the Johannine literature, then, must both discover how we can fruitfully speak of the two in one breath and yet also ask what questions the one poses to the other.

Hanson's claim comes as the culmination of a detailed study of if not all possible then of an impressive range of references, echoes and allusions to Scripture in the Fourth Gospel, engaging with or claiming the support of a wealth of other secondary literature. Faced with such a substantial bibliography, it would clearly serve little purpose to review Johannine indebtedness to Scripture in the brief space here possible; indeed, however defined - and we may refer to the discussion covered by other papers - Biblical Theology must go beyond that. One distinctive characteristic however is what might be termed 'the wave effect', the integration of and the impact of scriptural exegesis in the tradition history of the Johannine literature - extending beyond the Gospel into the Epistles; this too introduces a question which has been levelled at some

---

[7] Oxford, 1991.
[8] *The Interpretation of the Fourth Gospel*, 531-45.
[9] Edinburgh, 1991, 253; 245.

contemporary searches for a Biblical Theology, namely how does it relate to or differ from a tradition history?[10]

## II. Isaiah 6.9-10

That Isaiah 6.9-10 stimulates such a 'wave effect' prior to as well as within the Johannine literature is easily demonstrated.[11] Here we may leave the detail and merely highlight the pattern left by the 'waves'. The tradition is already growing within the Old Testament texts, particularly within the Isaiah school (eg. 29.18-19; 42.6-7; 59.9-11; 43.8-10) but also in other prophetic and Deuteronomic material.[12] Growth does not mean repitition but new applications, sometimes including reversal, as in some of the Deutero-Isaiah passages where judgement becomes a prelude to hope because it is the same, creative God at work. New elements may be added: light and darkness may seem obvious correlates of sight and blindness but they do not appear explicitly until Isaiah 42.6-7 and 29.18. What begins as a divine declaration through the prophet may be picked up by the people as a question thrown back at God through the prophet in the face of the apparent failure of the promises (59.9-10).

The creativity of the tradition is evidenced by its continuing use beyond our Old Testament, for example at Qumran, where it appears in a dualistic setting in the much quoted 1QS 4.11: "But the ways of the spirit of falsehood are these: greed, slackness in the search for righteousness.......a blaspheming tongue, blindness of eye and dullness of ear, stiffness of neck and heaviness of heart so that man walks in all the ways of darkness and guile";[13] similarly the Damascus Document 1. 9 speaks of those who "for twenty years were like blind men groping for their way", where the word translated groping is that found only in the MT at Isaiah 59.10 ('gss').[14]

The impact of this tradition - an important one elsewhere in the New Testament - within the Johannine literature reaches further than is at first apparent. Most obvious, ofcourse, is John 12.40, where it comes at the

---

[10] See for example H.G. Reventlow, *Problems of Biblical Theology in the Twentieth Century* (ET London, 1986), 173-174.
[11] See J.M. Lieu, "Blindness in the Johannine Tradition", *NTS* 34 (1988), 83-95; "What was from the Beginning: Scripture and Tradition in the Johannine Epistles", *NTS* 39 (1993), 458-477.
[12] Deut 29.4; Jer 5.21 etc. For a study of this text in John and for its earlier history see now R. Kühschelm, *Verstockung, Gericht und Heil* (BBB 76. Frankfurt am Main, 1990) and on wider use of the theme in the OT, 85-88.
[13] Quoted from G. Vermes, *The Dead Sea Scrolls in English* (Harmondsworth, 1987), 65-6.
[14] Approaches to Biblical Theology such as that adopted by H. Gese make much of the continuing development beyond what eventually became the Old Testament Canon, although it is this which makes them appear like a sanctified history of tradition.

close of Jesus' public ministry and acts as a judgement on a response which, despite the intrusive v.42, is almost unanimous in its negativity. The unashamed active indicative verbs (τετύφλωκεν....ἐπώρωσεν) are closer to the imperatives of the MT and Targum than the circumlocutionary passive of the LXX which is followed by Matthew (13.13-15) and Luke (Acts 28.25-28).[15] In the context of vv.37-40 the subject of the verbs can only be Christ himself whose sovereign authority remains intact. Just as in its original setting, the Isaiah passage as cited in John 12.40 raises serious theological issues for both Johannine thought and for a Biblical theology.[16] The theme is anticipated in John 9.39 where Jesus claims explicitly to effect blindness, echoing the preceding verse in Isaiah 6.9, possibly in conjunction with Isaiah 29.18 where the positive is expressed.[17] In its turn, John 9.39 does not stand alone as an afterthought but is an integral part of chapter nine, forming a balance or inclusio with vv.4-5 where Jesus speaks of himself as the light of the world, and appropriately illustrated by the opening of the eyes of a blind man.

Both theme and vocabulary also identify 1 John 2.11, "because the darkness blinded his eyes", as part of the trajectory, again not in the form of a quotation but clearly an echo, and yet not drawn directly from the Gospel but rather from a common tradition. Most significantly the responsible subject is not God or Jesus but darkness: it is easy to draw parallels to this development of the imagery in a dualist direction within hellenistic Judaism.[18] In the immediate context comes more 'Isaianic' language - walking in the darkness (v.11), a σκάνδαλον (v.10), the victim not knowing where he is going (v.11). Walking as if in darkness is an obvious problem for the blind, and it is hardly surprising that the image surfaces in the Isaiah tradition, at 59.9-10, although the equally obvious result of not knowing where he is going is not so explicit.

The same images occur within the Gospel although rather more scattered: in John 12.35 the one walking in darkness does not know where he/she is going (ποῦ ὑπάγει), and the threat is that "darkness might seize (καταλάβῃ) you".[19] From here the trail leads to John 1.5 where the darkness did not 'seize' (κατέλαβεν) the light,[20] and to a

---

[15] On this see also Kühschelm, *Verstockung*, 91-6.
[16] As indicated by the subtitle of Kühschelm's study, "Exegetische und bibeltheologische Untersuchung zum sogennanten "Dualismus" und "Determinismus" in Joh 12,35-50".
[17] The parallel is clearer in the light of the LXX of Isa 6.9, 'βλέποντες βλέψετε'. Isa 29.18 reads ὀφθαλμοὶ τυφλῶν βλέψονται..
[18] See Lieu, "Blindness", 87-88, with reference to TJudah 18.6; TGad 3.3; TSim 2.7 and 2 Cor 4.4.
[19] This is the closest parallel to the agency of darkness blinding in 1 John 2.11.
[20] A number of commentators deny that καταλαμβάνειν has the same meaning in 1.5 ('grasp') as in 12.35 ('seize') while recognising that it is Johannine in 1.5 (cf. σκοτία rather than σκότος), eg. R. Schnackenburg, *The Gospel according to St John* (ET. New York, 1982), I, 245.

chain of light passages in John including 8.12 and 11.9 where in place of the σκάνδαλον of 1 John, the one who walks in the day does not stumble (προσκόπτειν): both Greek roots are used to translate the Hebrew 'kshl' (cf. Isa 59.10).[21] In this Gospel there is but one who does know where he is going (ποῦ ὑπάγει) - Jesus himself (8.21; 13.33,36; 14.4,5; 16.5).

Isa 59.9-10, which has proved itself already a fruitful part of the Isaiah wave, offers further possibilities.[22] Those who walk in the gloom lament (v.10) that like the blind 'we grope' - just as does the blind Isaac (in the LXX) fumbling for a hairy Jacob (Gen 27.12,21,22);[23] it is then surprising to find 1 John using the same LXX term (ψηλαφάω) in its opening salvo: "that which was from the beginning, which we have heard, which we have seen with our eyes,[24] which we have looked at, which our hands have *groped*". The rest of the declaration, with its language of witness and proclamation, has other stronger Isaianic echoes, notably of Isa 43.8-10, which in turn is picked up by 1 John 5.13 and by John 15.27 and 20.31.

It is not easy to fit what is happening here into traditional models of Old Testament: New Testament relationships. Clearly language of promise and fulfilment would be inadequate: while John 12.38 does use fulfilment language of Isa 53.1, the citation of Isa 6.9-10 in the following verses seems rather to be a statement in anticipation of the completed action of Jesus. The further evolution of the tradition follows a pattern of adopting and reworking rather than of fulfilling. The Old Testament is here more than a background or a quarry for the Johannine writers. The tradition of interpretation and reflection has fed into an ongoing tradition within the Johannine school, with far-reaching effects. Sometimes it has become totally entwined with what we see as distinctive Johannica - as with the theme of "(not) knowing where he is going". Surely we see here the activity of the "Johannine school", interpreting Scripture in the light of experience, experience in the light of scripture in a continuing and dynamic process.[25] Sometimes other Old Testament passages have also made their contribution - such as the influence of Genesis 1 on the light and darkness imagery of the opening of the

---

[21] See *TDNT* VI. 572-573; VII. 356-357; σκάνδαλον is used at Isaiah 8.14 for '*mikshol*' by Aquila, Symmachus and Theodotion.

[22] It may only be chance that the LXX uses καταλαμβάνειν for 'Righteousness does not reach us'.

[23] The Hebrew here ('*mus*') is a different root from that (a hapax) used at Isa 59.10 ('*gss*'); however the Greek ψηλαφάω is regularly used in contexts of darkness and blindness; see Job 5.14; 12.25 and Deut 28.29 where there may be some Isaianic influence.

[24] The reference to hearing, omitted from the quotation of Isa 6.10 at John 12.40 is here retained; moreover, although it is thoroughly Johannine to speak of what "we have seen", the additional "with our eyes" is peculiar to 1 John 1 and strengthens the echo of Isaiah.

[25] See Lieu, "Blindness" on the place of the exclusion from the synagogue in this process.

Johannine prologue.[26] Sometimes the reapplication becomes a reversal - most strikingly in the groping which is no longer a mark of punishment and of the blind, but of those who now see. There is, then, not a single pattern or wave. This means that description in terms of a salvation history is also inappropriate. Although all that has been described could be incorporated under the heading of themes - "blindness, light and darkness as a Biblical theology theme in the Johannine writings" - that too may be unsatisfactory and imply more of a coherence and system than we have discovered. For example, in John light is christologically anchored (8.12) while in 1 John it has an ecclesiological framework (2.10-11). The active dualism of 1 John, where it is darkness which blinds, stands alongside the sovereign agency of Jesus in John 12. Are the two compatible? What is needed is a dynamic description which matches the dynamic process which lies behind the texts.

A further factor is that the Johannine tradition does not simply reach back directly into the Old Testament. The Isaiah tradition is developing within the Old Testament and beyond it - as we have seen in the appeal to Qumran and to hellenistic Judaism. This is an issue that has been met in some Biblical Theology by the claim that the "Old Testament" was not closed at the time of the writing of most of the documents of the New.[27] Yet does this recognition, if true, really allow us to include Qumran and other material within a Biblical Theology trajectory without it simply becoming a history of religions? Other questions or observations might also be drawn from this exploration, but I would like to postpone them until we have studied the second set of waves.

### III. The Cain tradition

In this case it is 1 John which betrays the significance of the Cain narrative of Genesis 4 for the Johannine tradition. If we were guided by the Gospel we would expect 1 John (3.11-12) to say that "we are to love one another 'as he loved us'" (cf. John 13.34; 15.12). Instead it is 'not as Cain' who, rather than loving, murdered his brother. Cain was "of the evil one" (ἐκ τοῦ πονηροῦ) and his deeds were evil (πονηρά) while those of his brother were righteous; he was, then, like anyone who hates his brother, a murderer (v.15: ἀνθρωποκτόνος). Hans Windisch[28] argued that the Cain narrative continues in the background up to v.22 which recalls Cain's encounter with the all-knowing God, but the story can

---

[26] So P. Borgen, "The Use of Tradition in John 12.44-50", *NTS* 26 (1980), 18-35, 33.
[27] See for example H. Gese, *Essays on Biblical Theology* (ET. Minneapolis, 1981), 11-12.
[28] H. Windisch, *Die Katholischen Briefe* (3rd ed. H.Preisker. Tübingen, 1951), 224.

equally well be traced back into the earlier part of the chapter. Abel, whose deeds were righteous is anticipated by the one who does righteousness in v.7 and is implicitly to be counted among the children of God in v.10; Cain, by contrast, failing to love his brother, is among the children of the devil (v.10), who, according to v.8, sins from the beginning. Even before Cain appears explicitly on the scene, he casts his shadow back over the stark dualism of this chapter, over the absolute contrast between the children of God and the children of the devil (v.10), those who have been born of God and those of the devil (vv.8-9).

If we are to understand some of this we must turn back both to the Biblical narrative about Cain and to its earlier exegesis - and here I must refer to the work of Nils Dahl among others.[29] The silence of the Biblical narrative as to the reasons for the divine preference for Abel's offering is filled by both Josephus (*Ant.* I,2.1; § 53) and Philo (*Quaest. in Gen.* I.59) who speak of Cain, even before the event, as evil or πονηρός, and of Abel as righteous, δίκαιος, or concerned for righteousness. The targumic tradition elaborates this, and the apparent lacuna in the MT at Gen 4.8, by putting in the mouths of the brothers, in different forms, a debate over theodicy, the justice as well as the love of God in the creation and judgement of the world. A further tradition - but not a unanimous one - answers the still unresolved question of the source of Cain's evil potential by explaining at Gen 4.1 that Cain was in fact the child not of Adam but of the evil one.[30] Thus far we may see 1 John as standing within such a tradition of exegesis - Cain is of the evil one; he is the archetypal child of the devil.

As I have argued alsewhere,[31] other elements of the tradition have also left their trace. Gen 4.25 celebrates a new beginning with the birth of Seth; Eve's unusual acclamation of this event, "God has appointed me another seed" ('*zera*''; LXX σπέρμα) echoes the earlier sentence of judgement pronounced by God at Gen 3.15, "I will appoint enmity between you and the woman, between your seed and her seed". Small wonder that later Jewish tradition, followed also by Christian Gnostics, made of Seth, who is according to Gen 5.3 in the image and likeness of God, a type or progenitor of the righteous, even, in Gnostic material, of the elect and the bearer of the Messianic seed who would fulfil the eschatological promise of Gen 3.15. 1 John knows this tradition too as

---

[29] N. Dahl, "Der Erstgeborene Satans und der Vater des Teufels", in *Apophoreta* (FS E. Haenchen, BZNW 30. Berlin, 1964), 70-84; see also J.M. Lieu, "What was from the Beginning", 467-72.
[30] So Ps.Jonathon on 4.1 and 5.3; *Pirke R. Eliezer* 21; 22; and in the (Christian) Gnostic tradition *EvPhil* 61.6-10. The tradition may already be in view in 2 Cor 11.2-3; 4 Macc 18.9.
[31] "What was from the Beginning", 469.

he speaks of the one born of God who cannot sin as bearing "his seed" (v.9) - a Seth type.

We shall need to go further, but let us turn first to John 8, also one of the most explicitly dualistic passages of the Gospel. It too speaks of the murderer (ἀνϑρωποκτόνος) in v.48 where the Greek is awkward and the uneveness may reflect the exclusion of an intermediary figure, Cain, although there are no compelling grounds for emending the text: "You are of the father, the devil, and you want to do the desires of your father. He was a murderer from the beginning." In what, in the light of later Jewish charges of Jesus's illegitimacy or Samaritan descent (v.48), may be a multiple Johannine irony, the Jews had denied that they were born of adultery and had claimed God as their only father (v.41).[32] But what were the desires of their father - other than wanting to murder a man, Jesus (so v.40)? At Gen 4.7, interpreting the enigmatic "sin crouching at the door", the Palestinian Targumic tradition introduces the concept of the evil inclination ('*yetzer hara*'') which Cain does have control: "I have placed in your hand power over the evil inclination (and its desire shall be towards you: Ps Jon only) that you may govern it so as to be just or to sin".[33] As elsewhere in the New Testament,[34] behind ἐπιϑυμία (desire) may lie the idea of the evil inclination.

Despite this common ground between the Epistle and Gospel, the latter here has not only excluded any direct reference to Cain but also speaks only of "fathers", not of "children" or of "those born of God". Neither does John speak of "works" (although they are significant in the earlier passage, vv.39-41), for the concern is about hearing and about truth or falsehood. Yet both themes do come elsewhere in the Gospel. For "children", τέκνα, we can turn to 11.52, gathering the scattered children of God into one, and more pertinently to 1.12-13 where the children of God are those who have been born of God (only here in John). It is difficult to find an obvious Old Testament background for the idea of children of God, or being born of God;[35] an underlying association with the Cain narrative may be confirmed in that in these verses such are not born of *bloods* - the unusual plural recalls the plural (natural in the Hebrew of slain blood) of Gen 4.10, "the voice of the bloods of your brother"; in early Jewish exegesis, found both in the Targums and in the

---

[32] Other links with the tradition have been traced in the dating of the murder at Passover (Ps.Jonathon) and its execution by stoning (Jubilees), cf. John 8.59. See N. Dahl, "Erstgeborene", 78, n.29.

[33] So also *Sifre Deut* 45. See G. Vermes, "Targumic Versions of Genesis 4:3-16", in *Post Biblical Jewish Studies* (Leiden, 1975), 92-126. Although the LXX translates '*teshuqato*' as ἀποστροφή (also at 3.16) understanding it as 'turning', Symmachus translates ὁρμή.

[34] See *TDNT* III, 170.

[35] So C.K. Barrett, *The Gospel of John and Judaism* (London, 1975), 30; the closest parallel is offered by Deut 32.18.

Mishnah (*mSan.* 4.5), this blood became the blood of future generations (or seed) of the righteous who were to have been born of Abel.

For those "whose deeds are evil" we may turn to John 3.19-20 and 7.7, the same wording as in 1 John 3.12.[36] Here too evil deeds are brought together with hatred - of the light by those who do evil, or of Jesus by the world. Hatred, we know from this Gospel, will lead to murder, just as in 1 John 3.13, following the declaration of Cain's evil deeds, "the world" makes a sudden and unexpected appearance in the midst of a section apparently dealing with love or hatred of brethren: "Do not be surprised if the world hates you". That Cain should be embodied now in the Jews, now in the world, merely echoes the congruence between the two parties throughout the Gospel and points us to a question to which we must return. A final faint echo of the theme may be heard in 2 John 11 where those who even greet one bearing alien teaching shares in "their evil deeds" - here the tradition has become the basis for denying any contact and has lost all its theological or Scripture grounding.

By contrast, the theme of truth and falsehood, integral to (and found only in) the Cain typology of John 8 is missing from 1 John 3; yet that theme is of course particularly important elsewhere in the letter in the debate with true and false claims (1.6,10; 2.4,21-22,27; 4.20; 5.10). 4.20 declares "If anyone says I love God and hates their brother, they are a liar" - Cain after all!

This analysis has shown, to speak in most general terms, the power of the impact of Genesis 3-4 on the Johannine understanding of their own life and of the conflict in which they were involved. It is conflict which forms the starting point for the patterns of the waves left by these chapters of Genesis. That Cain and Abel should offer an archetypal model of jealousy between brothers with its lethal consequences is no surprise - we find that elsewhere in the New Testament, in contemporary Jewish literature (*TBenj* 7-8), and in early Christian literature (*I Clement* 4.1-7). Yet in the Johannine tradition it is not a matter of types or models for comparison; here to declare one's opponents to be children of the devil is not simply rhetoric, it is an integral part of the theological world view of the writings. This is particularly true of 1 John with its more developed dualism; this dualism has probably not been created by the use of the Cain tradition but integrated with it. The theological consequences of the line taken there are momentous. 1 John 3.9, "Everyone who has been born of sin does not do sin because his seed remains in him, and is

---

[36] ἔργα without reference to Jesus' deeds comes only in these verses and in 8.39,41 in the Gospel and in 1 John only in 3.8,12,18.

not able to sin because he/she has been born of God" has exercised the minds of most commentators! And to speak of others as children of the devil leaves little room for change or freedom of choice; is it chance or theological sensitivity which has saved our author from speaking of them as "born of the evil one"? It is not chance that it is Gnostic sources which have provided the best parallels.

However, the preconditions for the Johannine interpretation are also found within Jewish tradition, and not only in what a previous generation of scholars would have dismissed as hellenistic Jewish. Again these texts can in no way be made part of a Biblical trajectory, however loosely the Old Testament canon is defined. Moreover, here it is not a case, as it was in Isaiah 6, of a tradition which is already developing within the Biblical tradition, so much as with attempts to wrestle with the problems raised by the text. Genesis 4 remains silent both about the reasons for God's preference for Abel's offering and about the source of Cain's malevolent intent, just as in the previous chapter it fails to explain how one of the creatures which God had made could become the source of the temptation to disobey God. Yet the question had to be asked and we discover - even today - a range of attempts to answer it.

Some would feel that to assign Cain diabolic paternity was in fact a denial of the Biblical (and later Jewish) understanding of God before whom all humanity stands with equal responsibility;[37] such an interpretation raises serious questions about the role of critical assessment of any 'Biblical-theological' trajectory. The fact that dualism is not alien to the Jewish world does not necessarily make it Biblical in a theological sense. When we consider the way that later church exegesis developed the identification of the Jews with Cain and the assertion of their diabolic paternity, then we realise the seriousness of the question - although we cannot hold the Biblical text responsible for the misuse made of it by its interpreters. Thus a Biblical Theology must surely not simply describe development or reapplication, but critically engage with fundamental theological shifts; here one might look for a dialogue between Genesis 1 and 1 John 3.

A further qualification will be made by many that in the context of the Gospel the harshness of the use of the Cain trajectroy must be set both against a reconstruction of the situation of the Johannine community and within the framework of the function of the Gospel's dualism as a dualism of decision. Whether recognition of an original historical context - in this case the bitterness of the split from the synagogue or (and) of the

---

[37] So A. Goldberg, "Kain: Sohn des Menschen oder Sohn der Schlange?" *Judaica* 25 (1969), 203-21 of the Jewish tradition.

defection of some with too 'soft' a Christology - should mitigate the theological consequences is an important question. The validity of the reconstruction - drawn in any case from the text it is then used to justify - is a critical issue in its own right. Yet this principle of the priority of historical context itself must either be applicable to all texts or to none, and this is not avoided even when appeal is made to a 'Biblical' or 'Gospel' norm or core by which to judge theological centrality. Equally important, the discovery of a historical context does not totally explain the theological response taken, unless every comparable context is proven to generate an identical response. If history does not create theology but offers a context where certain elements may best develop, creating new historical possibilities and provoking a dialogue between them, there must be room for theological judgement of the choices made.

## IV. Biblical Theology

This leads into to a broader consideration of how we may speak of Biblical Theology in a Johannine context - or the Johannine literature in a Biblical Theology context. The issue just discussed provides a helpful starting point: John 8.44 has been declared "probably the most anti-Jewish assertion of the New Testament" (J.Becker),[38] and the Gospel as a whole has earned the same charge. How compatible is its anti-Jewishness, 'anti-Semitism', with a Biblical Theology? Here it is not enough to note that John can speak neutrally, even positively - John 4.22, "salvation is of the Jews"; neither does it help that he can use "Israel" in a more affirmative way, or emphasise Jesus's Jewishness.[39] Even if this is so, Jesus and his disciples, those who decide for him like the blind man of ch. 9, are not among "the Jews" of St John. To give this a historical explanation or to narrow the reference of the Jews to their leaders does not answer the fundamental theological problem, what positive value does John give the heirs of God's promises - if indeed one can speak of them as such.

Here M. Hengel would point to the key interpretative role of John 10.34-35 with its affirmation of both Scripture and of the Jews as its recipients: "Is it not written in your law, 'I have said: You are gods'. If he called them gods to whom the word of God came, and the Scripture cannot be annulled...".[40] This only leads us to a second, closely related

---

[38] Quoted by G. Reim, "Joh 8.44 - Gotteskinder/ Teufelskinder. Wie antijudaistich ist "die wohl antijudaistichste Äusserung des NT"?", *NTS* 30 (1984), 619-24.
[39] As argued by Hengel, "Schriftauslegung", 261-2.
[40] "Schriftauslegung", 263.

problem. Hengel rightly relates these verses with the appeal to the word of God to the claims of the prologue, ἐν ἀρχῇ ἦν ὁ λόγος; he goes on to describe the Prologue as presenting the whole Salvation History from the Uranfang before creation to the epiphany of the *logos ensarkos* in the present "in an extremely condensed form" and in so doing he betrays the heart of the problem. In John Salvation History is so condensed as to have no content except Jesus; indeed to speak of Salvation History in John is to mislead for the past has no content, of growth or even of preparation, except Jesus. It may be true that from this Gospel we know of Abraham's vision, of Jacob's gift of the well, of Moses and the manna, yet all these had of themselves no salvific content.[41] Even John the Baptist is a man without a context, a voice without an identity.

Equally important, there is no negative salvation history, no history of rejection. The disbelief of the Jews does not fulfil prophecy or their fathers' model, it fulfils Christ's activity as seen by Isaiah; the disappearance of Cain from the text of John 8 signals that identity is not characterised by history but by response to Jesus.[42] This then is the importance of the preexistent christology of John 1 which qualifies any salvation history so absolutely that it destroys it. "Before Abraham was I am", and, in the passage we were reviewing earlier, "Isaiah said this because he saw his glory and spoke about him" (12.41).[43] The same must be said about the fulfilment language which does indeed come in this Gospel; in 19.28-30 what is of concern is not that Jesus is thirsty - which we are not told - but that he speaks in order to demonstrate his sovereignty over Scripture, a sovereignty which is fulfilled in his own τετέλεσται. So with Walter Wilkens:[44] "In dieses "es ist vollbracht" wird die ganze Schrift einbezogen: Sie ist hier an ihr Ziel gebracht. *Der Skopus der Schrift ist das Kreuzesgeschehen*" - it might be better to say *Jesusgeschehen*. We have on the one side of the coin then the absolute exclusivity of the claim of Jesus, on the other, Jesus as the sum total of meaning or experience.

Yet we may also take a further clue from that earlier quotation from Hengel when he speaks of this salvation history as stretching from the "Uranfang vor der Schöpfung". Even more than in Luke's genealogy

---

[41] Against Hengel, "Schriftauslegung", 266; 268, who stresses the frequency of γραφή, νόμος etc. in John.

[42] Also in ch. 8 we may note the absence of any salvation historical use of the themes of Abraham, seed, children etc.

[43] As we have seen Cullmann's attempt to argue for a salvation history in John fails to convince; in the following sentence the first part more closely corresponds to the Johannine perspective than the second: "In this life the whole history of salvation, past and future, is summed up vertically, and yet this life is incorporated into a horizantal line" (*Salvation in History*, 2).

[44] W. Wilkens, *Zeichen und Werke* (AThANT 55. Zurich, 1969), 75.

which goes back to Adam, we are in a framework which is properly universal. Ofcourse this is the importance of the wisdom trajectory which has been found behind the Prologue. We may add to that the importance of Genesis 1-4 in the Cain and Eve traditions reviewed earlier, and also, if we had time to see, elsewhere. It is here too that the congruence between the Jews and the world becomes significant. Even in the context of a visit to Jerusalem in chapter 7 it is 'the world' which hates Jesus because he testifies that its deeds, like those of Cain, are evil. Is there, then, for John any real distinction between the Jews and the world - a question which might already be asked at 1.11, "he came to his own (neut) and his own (masc) did not receive him"?[45] This does not mean that it would be right to follow Bultmann when he puts 'the Jews' in inverted commas throughout his discussion of John 8, preferring to say of v.44, "Confronted by the revelation man, by his decision, chooses his origin";[46] this is to loose the scandal of the particularity of the Gospel genre, and indeed of the Christ event. Nevertheless, the question remains: do this people, of the same race and set of customs as Jesus "have no other claim to make"?[47]

These are proper questions to ask of the Fourth Gospel when we seek a Biblical Theological understanding, but they are equally proper questions to ask of Biblical Theology itself, as a survey of some recent discussion readily illustrates. When in his *Essays on Biblical Theology* Hartmut Gese says the New Testament "brings Old Testament concerns to their appropriate conclusion and even constitutes the goal or *telos* of the Old Testament's development", he uses language that John would find particularly congenial - although John probably would not speak of development.[48] Yet this implicitly raises a question which he himself answers at the end of the same essay: "By the same token, study of the Old Testament that does not take into account the organic growth of tradition down to and into the New Testament is incomplete and leads to false conclusions" (222). Inevitably the confessionalist concern of Biblical Theology is implied here and demands further debate. By contrast it is doubtful whether John could concur with James Barr when he says, "the One God of Israel is proceeding with his purpose. Our Christian faith is that the sending of Jesus Christ is the culmination of

---

[45] See J.W. Pryor, "Jesus and Israel in the Fourth Gospel - John 1:11", *NT* 32 (1990), 201-18 who argues that ἴδιοι/οι means his own kinsfolk, a relationship of race but not of covenant.
[46] R. Bultmann, *The Gospel of John* (ET. Oxford, 1971), 317.
[47] Pryor, "Jesus and Israel", 218.
[48] H. Gese, Essays on Biblical Theology, 167, appropriately at the beginning of an article on "The Prologue to John's Gospel".

this purpose. This does not mean that Jesus Christ becomes the criterion for the meaningfulness of that which is done before he is sent".[49]

This means that any theological, as opposed to history-of religions, claim for the belonging together of Old and New Testament must ask what other significance might the Old have; and it is this which makes the question of Israel unavoidable. Making the point explicit, Erich Grässer has objected to the Biblical Theology perspective (particularly as represented by Peter Stuhlmacher) with its implication that the Old Testament *must* lead to the New; he sees in this a serious danger for those "who for the sake of overcoming 'Christian anti-Judaism' are ready to criticise theologically the totalitarian claims of the Gospel of Jesus Christ".[50] As with John's Gospel we are forced then to ask how the recognition of the unity of Scripture and the revelation in Jesus addresses both the claims of Judaism and the Christian (?Johannine) heritage of anti-Judaism.[51] It is not merely that John and Biblical Theology stand in parallel here; a Biblical Theology that seeks to incorporate John can not avoid the question.

Stuhlmacher's response to this charge was rightly to affirm that any debate between Jews and Christians must be on the basis of the common Old Testament, but maintains that a fundamental issue will be "whether the Torah really is the way of life leading to its goal...";[52] while John could provide a response here - 5.39-40 - the Gospel would be unable to follow when elsewhere Stuhlmacher affirms that the Old Testament belongs not only to the Synagogue but also to the Christian community (and presumably also vice versa), and accepts that a Biblical theology of the New Testament must take upon itself the burden of leaving this Christian-Jewish conflict over the true sense of the Old Testament "ungeschlichtet offen".[53]

The title of this paper, then, must bear both an exclamation mark and a question mark. The Johannine Literature cannot be understood apart from its Biblical heritage; no attempt to explore the Theology(ies) of the Bible or the Biblical challenge to Theology can ignore the Johannine Literature. Yet Biblical Theology also cannot ignore the challenge of

---

[49] J. Barr, Old and New in Interpretation (London, 1966), 153.
[50] E. Grässer, "Offene Fragen im Umkreis einer Biblischen Theologie", ZThK 77 (1980), 200-21, 215-16.
[51] Grässer's own preference for a historical reading is illustrated by his treatment of John 8.
[52] Stuhlmacher, '"..... in verrosteten Angeln"', ZThK 77 (1980), 222-238, 232.
[53] Stuhlmacher, Vom Verstehen des Neuen Testaments (Göttingen, 1979), 244. Still less could John follow the even stronger comment of W. Zimmerli, "Biblical Theology", HBT 4.1 (1982), 95-130, "(a genuine Biblical theology) alone can lead to a promised fraternal dialogue with Israel which cleaves to the Old Testament and which is not to be deprived either of the Old Testament or of the God who calls Israel....It could be that in the dialogue with an Israel taking seriously its Old Testament the Christian partner may be confronted with very serious questions" (125).

encounter with, dialogue with Judaism, - indeed it is demanded by it; here the Johannine Literature, which, we may suspect, was born out of rather less than dialogue, faces us with as many questions as answers.

CHAPTER SEVEN

BIBLISCHE THEOLOGIE
IM LICHTE DES HEBRÄERBRIEFES

Otfried Hofius, Tübingen

I

Zu den zentralen Problemen einer Biblischen Theologie gehört die Frage nach dem inneren Zusammenhang zwischen dem Alten und dem Neuen Testament. Biblische Theologie "*im Lichte des Hebräerbriefes*" zu bedenken, das heißt deshalb, nach dem spezifischen Beitrag zu fragen, den dieser Brief für die Bestimmung des Verhältnisses beider Testamente zu leisten vermag.

Gleich die ersten Worte des Briefes sind hier von besonderer Relevanz. In dem "theologischen Fundamentalsatz",[1] mit dem das kunstvoll gestaltete Exordium Hebr 1.1-4 einsetzt, erklärt der Verfasser: "Nachdem Gott vorzeiten vielfach und auf vielerlei Weise zu den Vätern geredet hat durch die Propheten, hat er in dieser Endzeit zu uns geredet in dem Sohn."[2] Diesen Worten zufolge hat Gott sich in zweifacher Weise geoffenbart: zunächst - in vielfältigem und vielgestaltigem Reden - in der Geschichte Israels, und dann zuletzt - in endgültiger Selbsterschließung - in der Person und dem Werk Jesu Christi. Folgt Biblische Theologie der Sicht des Hebräerbriefes, so findet sie das Reden Gottes "zu den Vätern" in den Schriften des *Alten Testamentes* bezeugt, - und zwar keineswegs nur in der Hebräischen Bibel, sondern in gleicher Dignität auch in der Griechischen Bibel, der Septuaginta.[3] Die Urkunde des Redens Gottes ἐν υἱῷ wird Biblische Theologie dann analog in jenen Schriften erkennen, die sich - wie der Hebräerbrief selbst - der christli-

---

[1] E. Gräßer, *An die Hebräer I. EKK XVII/1* (Zürich-Braunschweig bzw. Neukirchen-Vluyn, 1990), 48.
[2] Hebr 1.1+2a. Zur Übersetzung der Wendungen ἐν τοῖς προφήταις v. 1 und ἐν υἱῷ v. 2a s.u. Anm. 21 und Anm. 22.
[3] Daß die neutestamentlichen Autoren das Alte Testament ganz überwiegend nach der Septuaginta bzw. nach einer der Septuaginta ähnlichen griechischen Fassung zitieren, ist durchaus von hermeneutischer Relevanz!

chen Kirche imponiert haben und deshalb das Korpus des *Neuen Testamentes* bilden.[4]

So sehr sich nun Altes und Neues Testament hinsichtlich ihres "Gegenstandes" unterscheiden, so sehr gehören sie dem zitierten Fundamentalsatz zufolge doch unlöslich zusammen. Die Worte "Deus locutus est", die jenem Satz sein besonderes Profil verleihen, verbinden ja die beiden Aussagen von V. 1 (λαλήσας τοῖς πατράσιν ἐν τοῖς προφήταις) und V. 2a (ἐλάλησεν ἡμῖν ἐν υἱῷ) aufs nachdrücklichste miteinander, so daß nicht überhört werden kann: Es ist der *eine* und *selbe* Gott, der einst durch die Propheten zu seinem Volk Israel (=τοῖς πατράσιν)[5] und jetzt in seinem Sohn zu der christlichen Gemeinde (=ἡμῖν)[6] geredet hat. Wo immer der auctor ad Hebraeos in seinem Brief von dem in Christus offenbaren "Gott" spricht, da ist also dezidiert *der* Gott gemeint, der sich den "Vätern" unter dem Namen "Jahwe" kundgegeben und damit in Israel anrufbar gemacht hat und der dementsprechend im Alten Testament mit diesem geoffenbarten Namen bzw. mit seiner Umschreibung ὁ κύριος benannt wird.

Ist dieses nachdrückliche und grundlegende Bekenntnis zu der Selbigkeit Gottes gesehen und festgehalten, dann will und muß allerdings zugleich auch das Andere bedacht sein: *Wer* der bereits im Alten Testament bezeugte Gott letztlich und in Wahrheit *ist*, das wird nach der Überzeugung des auctor ad Hebraeos allererst *da* erkannt, wo dieser Gott sich in dem "Sohn" offenbart, der "der Abglanz seiner Herrlichkeit und die Ausprägung seines Wesens" ist.[7] Der Akzent des Fundamentalsatzes liegt ja ohne jeden Zweifel ganz und ausschließlich auf den Worten ὁ θεὸς . . . ἐλάλησεν ἡμῖν ἐν υἱῷ, und alle weiteren Aussagen, die sich im 1. Kapitel des Briefes daran anschließen, haben einzig den Sinn, die unvergleichliche Würde und Hoheit des Sohnes herauszustellen und damit zugleich sein Persongeheimnis zur Sprache zu bringen.[8] Bereits das

---

[4] Die - K. Barth, *KD I/1*, 110 verpflichtete - Feststellung, daß sich die kanonischen Schriften und damit der Kanon selbst "der Kirche imponiert" haben, schließt weder die Frage nach der "Mitte" der Heiligen Schrift (bzw. des Neuen Testamentes) noch auch eine von dieser Mitte her vollzogene "interne Kanonkritik" aus.

[5] Der Ausdruck οἱ πατέρες 1.1 meint nicht speziell die Patriarchen, sondern das Israel der vorchristlichen Zeit als Ganzes; vgl. den Begriff οἱ πρεσβύτεροι in 11.2.

[6] Daß das ἡμῖν nicht bloß die unmittelbaren Augen- und Ohrenzeugen des irdischen Jesus im Blick hat, ergibt sich aus 2.3 (vgl. auch 12.25).

[7] 1.3a: ὃς ὢν ἀπαύγασμα τῆς δόξης καὶ χαρακτὴρ τῆς ὑποστάσεως αὐτοῦ.

[8] Zu Hebr 1.1-14 vgl. meine Ausführungen in: O. Hofius, *Der Christushymnus Philipper 2,6-11*. WUNT 17 (Tübingen, 1991²), 76-92. 131-136. Mit Nachdruck verweise ich ferner auf die tiefgründigen Auslegungen von H.-J. Iwand und F. Lang: H.-J. Iwand, *Predigt-Meditationen [I]* (Göttingen, 1963), 115-120 (zu Hebr 1.1-6); ders., *Predigt-Meditationen II* (Göttingen, o.J.), 219-225 (zu Hebr 1.1-12); F. Lang, "Hebräer 1.1-6", in: G. Eichholz (Hg.), *Herr, tue meine Lippen auf IV: Die neuen Episteln* (Wuppertal - Barmen 1955 = 1965⁵), 58-65.

artikellose υἱός in V. 2a[9] "kennzeichnet den Sohn in seiner Einzigartigkeit".[10] Wie bei Paulus und Johannes (und m.E. ebenfalls im Markusevangelium), so ist auch im Hebräerbrief der "Sohn Gottes"-Begriff[11] eine Ursprungs- und Wesensbezeichnung, die als solche notwendig die Präexistenz des Gottessohnes voraussetzt. Der "Sohn Gottes"-Begriff bringt somit die ursprüngliche und wesentliche Zugehörigkeit Jesu zu Gott zum Ausdruck - und eben damit seinen göttlichen Ursprung, sein göttliches Wesen, sein präexistentes Gottsein.[12] Um das ewige göttliche Sein geht es auch, wenn der Sohn Gottes als "der Abglanz seiner Herrlichkeit und die Ausprägung seines Wesens" bezeichnet wird (1.3a).[13] Die beiden synonymen Prädikationen, die hier begegnen, charakterisieren den Sohn als das vollkommene Ebenbild Gottes,[14] und sie betonen damit wie Phil 2.6 und Joh 1.1-2 die Gottgleichheit des Sohnes. In die gleiche Richtung weisen schließlich auch die Aussagen über die Schöpfungsmittlerschaft des Gottessohnes und über sein ewiges Weltregiment. Wenn es von dem Sohn heißt, daß Gott "durch ihn die Äonen geschaffen" habe,[15] so soll der präexistente Christus keineswegs bloß als das Werkzeug der göttlichen Weltschöpfung gekennzeichnet werden; von dem auf Christus bezogenen Psalmzitat in 1.10 her[16] ergibt sich vielmehr in wünschenswerter Klarheit, daß der Sohn *selbst* - in der Einheit mit dem Vater - *Schöpfer* ist. Dem Theologumenon vom Schöpfer-Sein des Sohnes tritt dann die Aussage an die Seite: "Er trägt das All durch sein machtvolles Wort."[17] Wie zahlreiche Parallelen aus der Literatur des antiken Judentums belegen, ist hier eine Gottesprädikation auf Christus übertragen worden, die Jahwe als den König bekennt, der die von ihm geschaffene Welt machtvoll regiert.[18] In der Übertragung auf den präexistenten Christus beschreibt diese Prädikation das göttliche *Tun* des Sohnes, das seinem zuvor beschriebenen göttlichen *Sein* entspricht.

---

[9] Ebenso in 5.8 (vgl. auch 7.28).

[10] H. Windisch, *Der Hebräerbrief*. HNT 14 (Tübingen, 1931²), 10.

[11] Außer 1.2a noch: 1.8; 4.14; 5.8; 6.6; 7.3,28; 10.29; s. ferner 3.6 sowie die Zitate in 1.5 und 5.5.

[12] Iwand formuliert in der Sache durchaus zutreffend: υἱός ist im Hebräerbrief "der Sohn im Sinne der zweiten Person der Trinität, der Sohn nach seinem ewigen, aller Zeit überlegenen Sein" (*Predigt-Meditationen II*, 222).

[13] Vgl. o. Anm. 7. Das Wort δόξα (= kbwd) bezeichnet in 1.3a die *Gottheit* Gottes; vgl. dazu Ex 33.18-23, aber z.B. auch die Austauschbarkeit der Begriffe jhwh (κύριος) und kbwd jhwh ([ἡ] δόξα κυρίου) in Lev 9.4,6 bzw. 9.23b,24.

[14] Vgl. dazu O. Hofius, *EWNT I* (1992²), 281-283.

[15] 1.2β: δι' οὗ καὶ ἐποίησεν τοὺς αἰῶνας. Vgl. dazu Joh 1.3,10; 1 Kor 8.6; Kol 1.16.

[16] σὺ κατ' ἀρχάς, κύριε, τὴν γῆν ἐθεμελίωσας, καὶ ἔργα τῶν χειρῶν σού εἰσιν οἱ οὐρανοί (= Ps 101.26 LXX).

[17] 1.3b: φέρων τε τὰ πάντα τῷ ῥήματι τῆς δυνάμεως αὐτοῦ.

[18] Die Nachweise s. bei Hofius, *Christushymnus*, 81-83.131-136.

Auf dem Hintergrund der skizzierten christologischen Hoheitsaussagen wollen die Worte des Fundamentalsatzes gehört sein, daß Gott "in dieser Endzeit zu uns geredet hat in dem Sohn". Diese Worte können demnach nur dann recht verstanden werden, wenn beachtet und ernstgenommen wird, daß der Mensch Jesus von Nazareth der wahre und ewige "Sohn Gottes" ist, der seinem Ursprung und Wesen nach auf die Seite Gottes gehört und im Wunder seiner Inkarnation auf die Seite der Menschen getreten ist.[19] In dem damit angesprochenen Persongeheimnis Jesu Christi liegt es begründet, daß für den Verfasser des Hebräerbriefes zwischen dem Reden Gottes "durch die Propheten" und seinem Reden "in dem Sohn" nicht bloß ein quantitativer, sondern ein qualitativer und somit fundamentaler Unterschied besteht. Die Propheten, zu denen der Hebräerbrief auch Mose und David zählt,[20] sind *Mittler* des göttlichen Wortes, - als solche von Gott aus den Menschen heraus berufen und zu seinen Boten und Werkzeugen gemacht.[21] Der Sohn aber ist "von oben her", - "eines Wesens mit dem Vater". Als solcher *redet* er nicht nur Gottes Wort, sondern *ist* er in *Person* das an "uns" gerichtete Wort Gottes selbst.[22] Eben deshalb steht Christus *nicht* in einer Reihe mit den Propheten, sondern er steht ihnen allen als der eine und einzigartige "Sohn" *gegenüber*.[23] Und das Reden Gottes "in dem Sohn" ist dementsprechend keineswegs einfach die Fortsetzung, aber auch nicht bloß die Steigerung oder Überbietung seines Redens "durch die Propheten"; es ist vielmehr ein qualitativ Anderes und Neues. Dieses qualitativ Andere und Neue ist präzise auf den Begriff gebracht, wenn Hans-Joachim Iwand erklärt: Gottes Offenbarung und die Erscheinung seines Sohnes auf Erden "sind nicht zwei irgendwie, und wenn auch nur in Gedanken, voneinander zu lösende Ereignisse", sondern "sie sind eins".[24] "Hier, im Sohn, entspricht die Form der Sache. Hier ist der Redende und der, durch den wir angesprochen werden, ›wesensgleich‹ . . . Hier wird also keiner von unten herausgeholt, um Gottes Zeuge zu sein, wie Amos von seiner Herde und Jesaja aus seinem Volk mit den unreinen Lippen,

---

[19] Die Inkarnation des präexistenten Gottessohnes ist im Hebräerbrief in 2.5-18; 5.5-10; 10.5-10 thematisch.
[20] Mose: 3.1-5; 7.14; 9.19; 10.28; aber auch 2.2; 12.25. - David: 4.7; vgl. 11.32.
[21] Die Wendung ἐν τοῖς προφήταις 1.1 hat deshalb - wie ἐν Δαυίδ 4.7 - *instrumentalen* Sinn ("durch die Propheten als die Mittler des göttlichen Wortes"); sie entspricht also dem διὰ τῶν προφητῶν von Röm 1.2 (vgl. auch Lk 1.70; Apg 3.18).
[22] Die Wendung ἐν υἱῷ 1.2a ist deshalb dem ἐν τοῖς προφήταις 1.1 nur in *formaler* Hinsicht parallel. Sachlich ist sie ganz umfassend gemeint ("in dem Sohn", der in Person die Offenbarung Gottes ist).
[23] Auch *dieser* Aspekt kommt in dem artikellosen ἐν υἱῷ 1.2a zum Ausdruck. Vgl. M. Zerwick, *Analysis philologica Novi Testamenti Graeci. SPIB 107* (Rom, 1984⁴), 492 z.St.: "opponit filium *ut talem* prophetis".
[24] Iwand, *Predigt-Meditationen I*, 116.

sondern hier sind Subjekt und Prädikat im Worte Gottes gleich. Der, in dem Gottes Wort uns hier auf Erden erreicht, ist selbst Gott."[25]

Es liegt in der Konsequenz der aufgezeigten Sicht, daß der Verfasser des Hebräerbriefes das Reden Gottes "in dem Sohn" als Gottes *letztes* und *abschließendes* Wort begreift, daß er die Offenbarung Gottes in Jesus Christus also für *endgültig* und *unüberbietbar* erachtet.[26] Von daher werden dann die an die "Väter" ergangenen und in der Heiligen Schrift Israels bezeugten Offenbarungen Gottes als etwas Vorläufiges und Unvollkommenes, ja zum Teil sogar als etwas durchaus Defizitäres und deshalb in seiner Geltung sehr Begrenztes erkannt und beurteilt.[27] Dieser erstaunliche Tatbestand kann in seiner Bedeutung für die biblisch--theologische Frage nach dem Verhältnis von Altem und Neuem Testament schwerlich überschätzt werden. Er bedeutet nämlich nicht weniger als dies, daß nach der Überzeugung des auctor ad Hebraeos das abschließende Reden Gottes "in dem Sohn" überhaupt erst den wahren Sinn und Gehalt dessen erschließt, was zuvor "zu den Vätern" geredet war. Christus ist demzufolge der Schlüssel zum rechten Verständnis der Heiligen Schrift Israels. Für den Verfasser des Hebräerbriefes selbst stellt sich das u.a. so dar, daß bereits das Alte Testament ein Buch ist, das *von* Christus redet[28] und *in* dem Christus redet.[29]

Auf die eigentümliche Art der "Schriftauslegung", die solcher Sicht zugrunde liegt, brauchen wir jetzt nicht weiter einzugehen.[30] Für unsere Fragestellung ist ausschließlich die *hermeneutische* Entscheidung wichtig, die hier greifbar wird. Ihr zufolge ist - ich wiederhole und präzisiere es - die Offenbarung Gottes in Jesus Christus und somit Christus selbst in seiner Person und in seinem Werk das eine und entscheidende Kriterium

---

[25] Ebd., 117; vgl. auch ders., *Predigt-Meditationen II*, 220: "In dem, der hier zum Träger und Organ der Offenbarung wurde, umfängt uns die Herrlichkeit und das Wesen Gottes selbst. Der, der redet, und der, in dem er redet, sind einander gleich! Die vollkommene Deckung von Form und Inhalt der Offenbarung ist erreicht."

[26] Das Kommen Christi gilt dem Hebräerbrief deshalb als die Äonenwende (9.26). Mit ihm ist die "Endzeit" angebrochen ($\dot{\epsilon}\pi$' $\dot{\epsilon}\sigma\chi\acute{\alpha}\tau o\upsilon$ $\tau\hat{\omega}\nu$ $\dot{\eta}\mu\epsilon\rho\hat{\omega}\nu$ $\tau o\acute{\upsilon}\tau\omega\nu$ 1.2a!), die ganz im Horizont der nahen Parusie Christi gesehen wird (s. 10.37-38).

[27] Deutliches Zeichen für die Vorläufigkeit und Unvollkommenheit der in der Geschichte Israels geschehenen Offenbarungen ist nach Hebr 1.1 die Vielzahl der prophetischen Wort-Mittler bzw. Offenbarungsträger einerseits (= $\pi o\lambda\upsilon\mu\epsilon\rho\hat{\omega}\varsigma$) und die Vielfalt der Wort-Kundgaben bzw. Offenbarungsweisen andererseits (= $\pi o\lambda\upsilon\tau\rho\acute{o}\pi\omega\varsigma$).

[28] Gott redet *zu* Christus: Ps 2.7: Hebr 1.5a/5.5; Ps 45(44).7-8: Hebr 1.8-9; Ps 102(101).26-28: Hebr 1.10-12; Ps 110(109).1: Hebr 1.13; Ps 110(109).4: Hebr 5.6/7.17,21. - Gott redet *von* bzw. *über* Christus: Dtn 32.43 LXX bzw. Ps 96.7 LXX: Hebr 1.6; 2 Sam 7.14: Hebr 1.5b; Ps 104(103).4: Hebr 1.7; Jes 26.20/Hab 2.3-4: Hebr 10.37-38. - Der Heilige Geist redet *von* Christus: Ps 95(94).7-11: Hebr 3.7-4.13. - Ps 8.5-7 redet *von* Christus: Hebr 2.6-9. - Gott bzw. der Heilige Geist kündigt die neue Christus-$\delta\iota\alpha\theta\acute{\eta}\kappa\eta$ an: Jer 31.31-34: Hebr 8.8-12; 10.15-17. - S. schließlich auch das ganz grundsätzlich gemeinte $\dot{\epsilon}\nu$ $\kappa\epsilon\phi\alpha\lambda\acute{\iota}\delta\iota$ $\beta\iota\beta\lambda\acute{\iota}o\upsilon$ $\gamma\acute{\epsilon}\gamma\rho\alpha\pi\tau\alpha\iota$ $\pi\epsilon\rho\grave{\iota}$ $\dot{\epsilon}\mu o\hat{\upsilon}$ Hebr 10.7.

[29] Ps 22(21).23: Hebr 2.12; Ps 40(39).7-9: Hebr 10.5-8; Jes 8.17-18: Hebr 2.13.

[30] S. dazu etwa: F. Schröger, *Der Verfasser des Hebräerbriefes als Schriftausleger*. BU 4 (Regensburg, 1968).

für den Umgang mit dem Alten Testament. Von Christus her wird es gelesen, beurteilt und rezipiert. Das schließt ein, daß der Verfasser des Hebräerbriefes von seiner Christologie und Soteriologie her an bestimmten Aussagen der Schrift durchaus auch ganz bewußt Sachkritik übt. Was im Zeugnis der Schrift auf Christi Person und Werk bezogen werden kann, das wird von *ihm* her als gültig und wahr anerkannt. Was *nicht* auf Christus bezogen werden kann oder gar inhaltlich in Spannung zu ihm steht, von *dem* kann jedenfalls nicht gelten, daß es die Wirklichkeit göttlichen *Heils* zur Sprache bringt, sondern das muß - wiederum: von Christus her - in einem anderen Lichte gesehen und also anders interpretiert werden.

Die Bezugnahme des Hebräerbriefes auf das Alte Testament ist somit durch *beides* gekennzeichnet: durch Kontinuität *und* Diskontinuität, Anknüpfung *und* Widerspruch. Das sei jetzt exemplarisch aufgezeigt, - und zwar zunächst hinsichtlich der Christologie, d.h.im Blick auf Christi Person, und sodann hinsichtlich der Soteriologie, d.h. im Blick auf Christi Werk.

II

Was die *christologischen* Aussagen des Hebräerbriefes betrifft, so sind vor allem jene Stellen zu bedenken, an denen der Verfasser einige Psalmtexte auf Christus bezieht, die im Alten Testament selbst entweder vom Menschen allgemein[31] oder aber von einem bestimmten Menschen, nämlich dem König Israels,[32] sprechen. Man begibt sich von vornherein auf einen falschen Weg, wenn man sich zur Erklärung dieser Stellen um den Nachweis bemüht, daß die dort aufgenommenen alttestamentlichen Texte bereits im antiken Judentum messianisch rezipiert und interpretiert worden seien. Der auctor ad Hebraeos benötigt nämlich die traditionsgeschichtliche Brücke der Messianologie nicht nur nicht, sie wäre ihm vielmehr geradezu als unbrauchbar erschienen. Das christologische Verständnis der genannten Psalmtexte hat ausschließlich darin seinen Grund, daß der Verfasser unseres Briefes diese Texte in einer Weise *wörtlich* nimmt, die über das ursprünglich Gemeinte weit hinausgeht. Eben deshalb findet er in den Texten ausgesagt, was von *keinem* Menschen - gerade auch von dem Messias nicht! - ausgesagt werden kann.

Aus dem 2. Psalm zitiert der Hebräerbrief zweimal (1.5a; 5.5) den

---

[31] So Ps 8.5-7 (zitiert in Hebr 2.6-8).
[32] So Ps 2.7 (zitiert in Hebr 1.5a; 5.5); Ps 45(44).7-8 (zitiert in Hebr 1.8-9); Ps 110(109).1 (zitiert in Hebr 1.13); Ps 110(109).4 (zitiert in Hebr 5.6; 7.17,21). - Das im folgenden zu Ps 2.7 Gesagte gilt entsprechend auch für 2 Sam 7.14 (zitiert in Hebr 1.5b).

Gottesspruch von V. 7:

"Mein Sohn bist du,
ich habe dich heute gezeugt."

(υἱός μου εἶ σύ,
ἐγὼ σήμερον γεγέννηκά σε.)

Den Ausdruck "mein Sohn" versteht der Verfasser dabei nicht im Sinne des königlich-messianischen "Sohn Gottes"-Begriffs, der eine Amts- und Funktionsbezeichnung darstellt und als solche die Adoption eines Menschen durch Gott voraussetzt. Er faßt das Wort υἱός vielmehr im Sinne seines eigenen "Sohn Gottes"-Begriffs auf, d.h. als eine Ursprungs- und Wesensbezeichnung, die dem "Sohn" göttliches *Sein* zuerkennt. Von daher kann er in Ps 2.7 niemand anderen als Christus angeredet finden. Auf ihn bezieht er auch den 8. Vers des Psalmes, in dem es heißt:

"Ich werde dir die Völker zu deinem Eigentum geben
und zu deinem Besitz die Enden der Erde."

(δώσω σοι ἔθνη τὴν κληρονομίαν σου
καὶ τὴν κατάσχεσίν σου τὰ πέρατα τῆς γῆς.)

An diesen Vers knüpft nämlich die Aussage von Hebr 1.2bα an, wonach Gott den Sohn bei der Erhöhung "zum Eigentümer von allem eingesetzt hat" (ὃν ἔθηκεν κληρονόμον πάντων). "Alles" - das meint nach der Auffassung des Hebräerbriefverfassers die ganze Schöpfung Gottes, die den gegenwärtigen *und* den noch verborgenen zukünftigen Äon umfaßt.[33] Wie könnte und sollte dann in Ps 2.8 ein anderer angeredet sein, als eben jener Schöpfungsmittler, "durch" den Gott "die Äonen geschaffen hat" (1.2bβ) und der deshalb bei seiner Erhöhung nur das zu seinem Besitz empfängt, was ihm aufgrund der Schöpfungsmittlerschaft von "Anfang" an (1.10) bereits gehört?! Ganz entsprechend hat der Verfasser des Hebräerbriefes die in 2.6-9 zitierten und dann ausgelegten Worte von Ps 8.5-7 verstanden:

τί ἐστιν ἄνθρωπος ὅτι μιμνήσκῃ αὐτοῦ,
ἢ υἱὸς ἀνθρώπου ὅτι ἐπισκέπτῃ αὐτόν;
ἠλάττωσας αὐτὸν βραχύ τι παρ' ἀγγέλους,
δόξῃ καὶ τιμῇ ἐστεφάνωσας αὐτόν,

---

[33] S. dazu Hofius, *Christushymnus*, 77-78.

πάντα ὑπέταξας ὑποκάτω τῶν ποδῶν αὐτοῦ.

Da der Verfasser die Worte "alles hast du unterstellt unter seine Füße" auf die Herrschaft über die ganze - gerade auch die *zukünftige* Welt einschließende[34] - Schöpfung deutet, ist es ihm schlechterdings unmöglich, die zitierten Verse in ihrem ursprünglichen Sinn zu begreifen und in ihnen das Lob des Menschen allgemein gesungen zu sehen. Er vermag in den Psalmversen nur das prophetische Zeugnis[35] von dem ewigen Sohn Gottes zu erblicken, der - "eine kurze Zeit unter die Engel erniedrigt"[36] - Mensch *wurde*, um zum Heil aller Menschen den Tod zu erleiden, und der dann um des erlittenen Todes willen "mit Herrlichkeit und Ehre gekrönt" wurde (2.9).[37] Daß der Verfasser des Hebräerbriefes die in 1.8-9 zitierten Worte Ps 45(44).7-8 ausschließlich auf den Sohn Gottes beziehen konnte, liegt auf der Hand. Wird hier eine von Gott selbst unterschiedene Person als "Gott" angeredet,[38] so kann eben nur der eine und einzige gemeint sein, der "der Abglanz der Herrlichkeit Gottes" und "die Ausprägung seines Wesens" ist (1.3a). Von keinem Menschen, sondern nur von dem gottgleichen Sohn kann ja in Wahrheit gelten und gesagt werden:

"Dein Thron, o Gott, hat Bestand in alle Ewigkeit."[39]

Einzig und allein den Sohn Gottes sieht der Verfasser des Hebräerbriefes schließlich auch im 110. Psalm angeredet, aus dem er die Verse 1 und 4 zitiert.[40] Der Inthronisationsbefehl von V. 1 lautet:

"Setze dich zu meiner Rechten,[41]
bis ich deine Feinde zum Schemel deiner Füße hinlege!"

(κάθου ἐκ δεξιῶν μου,

---

[34] S. dazu 2.5: οὐ γὰρ ἀγγέλοις ὑπέταξεν τὴν οἰκουμένην τὴν μέλλουσαν, περὶ ἧς λαλοῦμεν. Im Blick auf *diese* Aussage wird Ps 8.5-7 in V. 6-9 zitiert und ausgelegt!
[35] Das Verbum διαμαρτύρεσθαι 2.6 kennzeichnet die Psalmverse als *prophetisches* Zeugnis.
[36] Das in Ps 8.6a LXX modal gemeinte βραχύ τι wird vom auctor ad Hebraeos in temporalem Sinn verstanden. Vgl. dazu Tatian, Oratio ad Graecos 15.11.
[37] Der ὅπως-Satz V. 9b bezieht sich nicht auf ἐστεφανωμένον, sondern auf ἠλαττωμένον V. 9a.
[38] ὁ θρόνος σου ὁ θεὸς (!) εἰς τὸν αἰῶνα τοῦ αἰῶνος 1.8a (Ps 44.7a LXX); διὰ τοῦτο ἔχρισέν σε ὁ θεὸς (!) ὁ θεός σου 1.9b (= Ps 44.8b). Im hebräischen Text ist nur an der ersten Stelle der König als *'lhjm* angeredet: "Dein Thron, o Göttlicher, ist immer und ewig."
[39] Daß im Ernst der König Israels - und natürlich auch der Messias - nicht *'lhjm* genannt werden kann, spiegelt sich in der Übersetzung des Targum zu Ps 45.7a wider: "Der Thron deiner Herrlichkeit, Jahwe, bleibt bestehen in alle Ewigkeiten."
[40] V. 1: Hebr 1.13b (vgl. 1.3d; 8.1; 10.12-13; 12.2). - V. 4: Hebr 5.6b; 7.17,21 (vgl. 5.10; 6.20; 7.3,11,15).
[41] Das bedeutet zugleich: "*Throne* zu meiner Rechten!"

ἕως ἂν θῶ τοὺς ἐχθρούς σου ὑποπόδιον τῶν ποδῶν σου.)

Weil der auctor ad Hebraeos diesen Satz ganz wörtlich nimmt, bezieht er den Ausdruck ἐκ δεξιῶν μου auf den *himmlischen* Gottesthron.[42] Den Platz zur Rechten Gottes im Himmel aber vermag nicht einmal einer der Engel einzunehmen,[43] - wieviel weniger dann ein bloßer Mensch! Folgerichtig kann in Ps 110(109).1 nur von dem Sohn Gottes die Rede sein, der in der himmlischen Welt inthronisiert wurde und als Throngenosse Gottes über alle Engel erhöht ist (1.3d,4).[44] Ganz analog interpretiert der Verfasser den feierlichen Gottesschwur von Ps 110(109).4:

"Du bist Priester in Ewigkeit
nach der Ordnung Melchisedeks."

(σὺ ἱερεὺς εἰς τὸν αἰῶνα
κατὰ τὴν τάξιν Μελχισέδεκ.)

Wieder versteht er diesen Satz ganz wörtlich, so daß er in ihm einen Priester angeredet findet, dem ewiges und unzerstörbares Leben eignet und dessen Priestertum deshalb kein Ende nimmt.[45] Demnach kann hier grundsätzlich kein sterblicher Mensch und somit kein levitischer Priester oder Hoherpriester gemeint sein.[46] Angeredet ist vielmehr der Sohn Gottes, der "in der Kraft unzerstörbaren Lebens" Priester ist (7.16) und - weil *er* "in Ewigkeit bleibt"[47] - ein "unvergängliches Priestertum" hat (7.24).[48]

Blicken wir auf die besprochenen Psalmtexte zurück, so werden wir sagen müssen, daß diese Texte im Hebräerbrief zugleich mit ihrer Rezeption durchaus einen neuen Sinn gewonnen haben, ja, daß sie im Grunde sogar zu *neuen* Texten geworden sind. Die einzigartigen Hoheitsaussagen, die der Verfasser in den Texten wahrnimmt, lassen sich nach seinem Urteil einzig auf den ewigen Sohn Gottes beziehen, und nur wenn sie *ihn* meinen, können sie überhaupt als *wahre* Aussagen angesehen werden. Zu diesem Bild fügt sich, daß der Hebräerbrief umgekehrt solche Texte, die im Alten Testament exklusiv von Gott selbst

---

[42] S. dazu 1.3d; 8.1-2; 12.2.
[43] Dieser Gedanke ist in der Frage πρὸς τίνα δὲ τῶν ἀγγέλων εἴρηκέν ποτε 1.13a mit impliziert.
[44] Die Erhabenheit über die Engel, die in jüdischen Texten von Jahwe ausgesagt wird (s. dazu Hofius, *Christushymnus*, 87-88.133-134), ist Ausdruck der *göttlichen* Hoheit und Macht.
[45] S. dazu 7.15-17,23-25.
[46] Die levitischen Priester sind sterbliche Menschen: 5.1; 7.8,23,28.
[47] Der Ausdruck μένειν εἰς τὸν αἰῶνα 7.24 entspricht dem Ausdruck πάντοτε ζῆν V. 25.
[48] Das geheimnisvolle *Abbild* des Sohnes Gottes erkennt der Hebräerbrief deshalb in dem Priesterkönig Melchisedek (7.1-3), der ihm nicht als ein Mensch gilt, sondern als eine himmlische Gestalt, d.h. ein Engelwesen.

sprechen, ganz unbefangen auf *Christus* deuten kann. Das gilt zum einen für die beiden Psalmworte Ps 102(101).26-28 (zitiert in 1.10-12) und Ps 104(103).4 (zitiert in 1.7), in denen der Verfasser den Sohn Gottes als den Schöpfer der Welt bzw. als den Herrn über die Engel beschrieben sieht. Zum andern ist hier das Zitat von Dtn 32.43 LXX zu nennen, das wir in 1.6b an gewichtiger Stelle lesen:

"Es sollen ihn alle Engel Gottes anbeten."

(καὶ προσκυνησάτωσαν αὐτῷ πάντες ἄγγελοι θεοῦ.)[49]

Dem Sohn wird, weil er Gott gleich ist, *die* Anbetung zuteil, die nach dem Zeugnis der Schrift einzig und allein *Gott* gebührt. Die christologische Rezeption des alttestamentlichen Wortes dient somit dazu, die Dimension des "Sohn Gottes"-Begriffs in ihrer ganzen Tiefe aufzuzeigen: "Der Titel Sohn bedeutet . . ., daß Christus Gott ist und von aller Kreatur im Himmel und auf Erden als Gott angebetet sein will."[50]

### III

Wenden wir uns nunmehr den *soteriologischen* Aussagen des Hebräerbriefes zu, so tritt noch schärfer in den Blick, daß das Verhältnis des Briefes zum Alten Testament nicht nur durch Kontinuität, sondern gerade auch durch Diskontinuität gekennzeichnet ist.

In der grundsätzlichen Bestimmung dessen, was "*Heil*" ist, steht der Verfasser unseres Briefes ganz in der Kontinuität zum Zeugnis des Alten Testamentes. Weil Gottes Geschöpfe einzig in der Erkenntnis und im Lobpreis des Schöpfers das Leben haben, deshalb liegt das Heil des Menschen in der vollkommenen Gemeinschaft mit dem lebendigen Gott. In der näheren Kennzeichnung des Heils wird dann das priesterliche Denken des Verfassers sichtbar, das nachhaltig von den Kulttraditionen Israels geprägt ist. Alttestamentlichen Zeugnissen zufolge ist der Tempel der Ort, an dem Gott gegenwärtig ist und sein Volk ihm nahen, seine Herrlichkeit erkennen und ihn anbeten soll. Im Tempel allezeit bei Gott zu wohnen, das erscheint den Betern Israels als das höchste Glück, als die Fülle des Heils.[51] Der Verfasser des Hebräerbriefes teilt diese Auffassung, - allerdings mit einem ganz wesentlichen Unterschied: Nicht ein *irdischer* Tempel gilt ihm als die Wohnung Gottes, sondern das

---

[49] Vgl. neben Dtn 32.43 LXX auch Ps 96.7 LXX.
[50] Iwand, *Predigt-Meditationen I*, 120.
[51] Ps 23.6; 26.8; 27.4-5; 36.8-10; 63.2-5; 65.2-5; 84.2-5.

*wahre* Heiligtum, das sich in der *himmlischen* Welt befindet.[52] Dieses Heiligtum ist Gottes "Ruhestätte" (κατάπαυσις), und es soll nach seinem ewigen Heilswillen auch des Menschen "Ruhestätte" sein.[53] Im himmlischen Heiligtum in der unmittelbaren Nähe und Gegenwart Gottes zu wohnen, ihn *dort* zu schauen und ihm in Lobpreis und Anbetung priesterlich zu dienen, - *das* ist somit das "Heil", das Gott dem Menschen von Ewigkeit her zugedacht hat und das deshalb bereits im Reden Gottes "zu den Vätern" angekündigt und verheißen worden ist.[54] In Gottes Heiligtum kann nach dem Zeugnis des Alten Testamentes jedoch nur wohnen, wer "rein" und "heilig" ist.[55] Rein und heilig aber ist der von seinem Schöpfer abgefallene Mensch *nicht*. Seine *Sünde* steht zwischen ihm und Gott, und um ihretwillen bleibt ihm der Zutritt zu Gottes himmlischer Welt verwehrt.[56]

Daß die Sünde den Menschen abgrundtief von dem heiligen Gott scheidet und der sündige Mensch selbst vor diesem Gott nur vergehen kann, das weiß der Verfasser des Hebräerbriefes, wie schon die Zeugen des Alten Testamentes es wissen. Mit dem alttestamentlichen Zeugnis teilt der Verfasser jedoch nicht bloß die Erkenntnis, daß die Sünde den Zugang zu dem verheißenen Heil unmöglich macht und notwendig die Heillosigkeit zur Folge hat; ihn verbindet mit dem Alten Testament vielmehr zugleich auch das Wissen darum, was *nötig* ist, damit die Heillosigkeit überwunden und der Mensch trotz seiner Sünde des Heils teilhaftig wird. Die Sünde, die von Gott trennt, muß beseitigt, die Sünden-Wirklichkeit, die den Zutritt zur himmlischen Welt unmöglich macht, muß aufgehoben werden. Das aber kann nach der am Alten Testament orientierten Sicht des Hebräerbriefes nicht anders geschehen als durch "*heiligende Sühne*",[57] d.h. durch eine ganz umfassende "Reinigung",[58] durch die der Mensch in seinem Sein *neu* und *so* zur Gemeinschaft mit Gott fähig gemacht wird. *Daß* der gottferne Mensch solcher "Sühne" bedarf, das sieht der Verfasser in jenem Reden Gottes "zu den Vätern" angezeigt, für das er im Anschluß an Jer 31(38).31-34 den Ausdruck ἡ πρώτη διαθήκη geprägt hat.[59] Das Wort διαθήκη hat

---

[52] 8.1-2,5; 9.11-12,24; vgl. 12.22-23.
[53] 3.7-4.13. S. dazu im einzelnen: O. Hofius, *Katapausis. Die Vorstellung vom endzeitlichen Ruheort im Hebräerbrief*. WUNT 11 (Tübingen, 1970), 51-58.
[54] S. dazu vor allem 3.7-4.11; 6.12,13-20; 9.15; 11.8-16,39-40.
[55] Ps 15.1-5; 24.3-6; Jes 33.14-16.
[56] S. dazu wiederum 3.7-4.11; ferner 12.14.
[57] Dies ist mit dem Satz 9.22b gemeint: χωρὶς αἱματεκχυσίας οὐ γίνεται ἄφεσις.
[58] S. dazu den Begriff καθαρισμὸς τῶν ἁμαρτιῶν 1.3c; er bezeichnet die kultische Reinigung, die dem Menschen allererst erlaubt, dem heiligen Gott zu nahen und ihm priesterlich zu dienen (vgl. 9.14).
[59] Der volle Ausdruck erscheint 9.15; aber auch in 8.7,13; 9.1,18 ist zu ἡ πρώτη das Wort διαθήκη zu ergänzen. Um die πρώτη διαθήκη geht es ebenfalls in 9.20 (= Zitat von Ex 24.8). Daß der Begriff selbst aus Jer 31(38).31-34 (hier V. 32) gewonnen ist, zeigen die Ausführungen in Hebr 8.7-13.

hier nicht die Bedeutung "Bund",[60] sondern es heißt "Verfügung", "Ordnung" oder "Stiftung" und bezeichnet eine von Gott erlassene "*Setzung*", die das Verhältnis des Menschen zu Gott betrifft und regeln soll. Was mit der πρώτη διαθήκη konkret gemeint ist, kann nicht fraglich sein: Es ist das zur "Tora des Mose"[61] gehörende *Kultgesetz*, das Gott am Sinai verfügt hat.[62] Dieses Kultgesetz konstituiert das levitische Priestertum (die Λευιτικὴ ἱερωσύνη 7.11),[63] und es enthält die - im Hebräerbrief ausführlich referierten und kommentierten - Bestimmungen über das irdische Heiligtum[64] und die in ihm zu vollziehenden kultischen Riten.[65]

Ganz erstaunlich, ja vom Alten Testament her gesehen ganz unerhört ist nun das radikale Urteil, das der Verfasser des Hebräerbriefes über die *Wirkung* der im Kultgesetz angeordneten Sühneriten fällt. Alle diese Riten - und damit insbesondere auch der alljährlich am Versöhnungstag vom Hohenpriester selbst vollzogene große Sühneritus (Lev 16) - werden in entschiedener Eindeutigkeit als "Opfer" bezeichnet, "die niemals Sünden wegnehmen können".[66] Der durch die πρώτη διαθήκη verordnete Opferkult vermochte also den Israeliten die heiligende und reinigende Sühne *nicht* zu erwirken; er hatte *nicht* die Kraft, die Kultteilnehmer zu "vollenden", d.h. sie in jenen Zustand der Heiligkeit zu versetzen, in dem allein der Mensch Gott nahen kann und darf.[67] Im Blick auf dieses Unvermögen spricht der Hebräerbrief von der "Kraftlosigkeit und Nutzlosigkeit" des ganzen alttestamentlichen Kultgesetzes[68] und davon, daß die πρώτη διαθήκη schlechterdings "unzulänglich" war.[69]

Erstaunlicher noch als diese Urteile ist der Tatbestand, daß der auctor ad Hebraeos mit ihnen keineswegs ein sekundäres Defizit der Kult-Tora und der in ihr verfügten kultischen Institutionen behaupten möchte, sondern daß deren Kraft- und Nutzlosigkeit nach seiner Überzeugung von allem Anfang an gegeben ist, weil sie dem Willen Gottes *entspricht*. Nach Gottes eigener Verfügung hat das Kultgesetz "nur ein Schattenbild der zukünftigen Heilsgüter, nicht aber die wirkliche Gestalt der Dinge selbst" (10.1). Das meint: Die in der Tora vorgeschriebenen Sühneriten

---

[60] Gemeint ist mit der πρώτη διαθήκη also *nicht* der "Alte Bund"!
[61] Der Begriff νόμος Μωϋσέως erscheint in 10.28.
[62] S. dazu jeweils die Hinweise auf den νόμος bzw. die ἐντολή in 7.5,12,16,18-19,28; 8.4; 9.19-20,22; 10.1,8.
[63] Vgl. dazu 5.1-3 und 7.27-28.
[64] S. dazu 9.2-5.
[65] S. dazu 9.6-10; ferner auch 9.25; 10.1,11; 13.11.
[66] 10.11: θυσίαι, αἵτινες οὐδέποτε δύνανται περιελεῖν ἁμαρτίας.
[67] 7.11,19; 9.9-10; 10.1-2,4 (vgl. als indirektes Zeugnis auch 9.15).
[68] 7.18. Wie der Kontext zeigt, beziehen sich die Worte τὸ ἀσθενὲς καὶ ἀνωφελές auf die gesamte Kultgesetzgebung.
[69] Das ist der Sinn der Bemerkung von 8.7, daß die πρώτη διαθήκη nicht ἄμεμπτος ("untadelig") war.

*sollen* ausschließlich die *Notwendigkeit* der Sühne anzeigen. Sie sind der kräftige und unübersehbare Hinweis darauf, daß der sündige Mensch die "Reinigung von den Sünden" braucht, um zu Gott kommen zu können; daß es "ohne Blutvergießen keine Vergebung gibt" (9.22); daß es also eines Hohenpriesters bedarf und eines Sühne wirkenden Opfers, das dieser Hohepriester darbringt. *Hinweis* darauf ist die Kultgesetzgebung und der durch sie etablierte Opferkult, - mehr nicht! Die Sühneriten bringen deshalb wohl die Wahrheit zur Sprache, die bezeichnete Wirklichkeit aber haben sie nicht bei sich. In ihnen geschieht - immer neu - nur die ἀνάμνησις ἁμαρτιῶν (10.3): die Erinnerung an die Realität der Sünden und damit zugleich die Erinnerung daran, daß die Sünden aufgehoben werden *müssen*, wenn es für den sündigen Menschen einen Zugang zu Gott geben soll.[70]

Der Hinweis auf den Sinn und die Funktion der Sühneriten macht bereits deutlich, weshalb es für den Verfasser des Hebräerbriefes im Rahmen der alttestamentlichen Kultgesetzgebung keine Heilsverwirklichung geben kann. Der gleiche Sachverhalt wird lediglich von einer anderen Seite her beleuchtet, wenn der Verfasser in 10.4 kategorisch erklärt: "Es ist unmöglich, daß das Blut von Stieren und Böcken Sünden wegnehmen kann" (ἀδύνατον γὰρ αἷμα ταύρων καὶ τράγων ἀφαιρεῖν ἁμαρτίας). Wir würden diese Worte gründlich mißverstehen, wenn wir in ihnen eine Äußerung rationalistischer Kultkritik erkennen wollten. In dem Satz spricht sich vielmehr eine tiefe Einsicht in das Wesen der Sünde aus, wie sie auch sonst im Hebräerbrief greifbar wird.[71] Die Sünde ist für den Verfasser eine Größe, die buchstäblich zum Himmel schreit. Sie reicht bis vor den Thron Gottes! *Da* - vor Gott selbst - ist sie Realität und als solche festgehalten; *dort* verklagt sie den Sünder und trennt ihn von seinem Gott.[72] Soll die Sünde aufgehoben werden, so muß sie deshalb vor *Gott* aufgehoben werden; *dort* - vor seinem Thron - muß die Wendung erfolgen. "Sühne" kann demzufolge nur ein Sühnegeschehen bringen, das bis in den Himmel reicht und die Sünde *dort* tilgt, wo sie getilgt werden *muß*. Wie sollte da ein auf Erden vollzogener Sühneritus dieses heilsnotwendige Geschehen sein können, zumal noch dieser Ritus von einem Hohenpriester vollzogen wird, der selbst ein schwacher und sündiger Mensch und daher selbst und zuerst

---

[70] Vgl. dazu auch 9.8-9!
[71] Tiefgründig dazu: H.-J. Iwand, *Predigt-Meditationen I*, 485-492: 489-491 (zu Hebr 9.11-15); 675-684: 681-682 (zu Hebr 9.15,23-28).
[72] Dem *entspricht* die Aussage, daß die Sünde in der συνείδησις da ist: 9.9; 10.1-2; vgl. 10.22. Der Hebräerbrief denkt hier keineswegs an das subjektive Sündenbewußtsein oder an das "schlechte Gewissen". Es geht vielmehr um das objektive, durch den levitischen Kult ständig neu in Erinnerung gebrachte Wissen um die *Realität* der vom Menschen her unaufhebbaren Sünde, - also um das Wissen, daß die Sünde *objektiv* da ist, weil sie vor *Gott* da ist.

der Sühne bedürftig ist![73] Das wahrhaft heilvolle und heilschaffende, weil die Sünde vor Gott aufhebende Sühnegeschehen erblickt der Hebräerbrief in dem Selbstopfer des Hohenpriesters Jesus Christus.[74] Durch dieses sein Selbstopfer hat Christus "die Reinigung von den Sünden vollbracht",[75] die Sünden Vieler "gesühnt" und "aufgehoben"[76] und damit dem Volke Gottes eine "ewige Erlösung" erworben.[77] Das meint: Er hat die Erlösten durch seinen Sühnetod "geheiligt"[78] und "für immer vollendet",[79] so daß sie - als in ihrem Sein *neu* gewordene Menschen - am Tag der Heilsvollendung in das himmlische Allerheiligste und also in die unmittelbare Gottesgemeinschaft eingehen dürfen.[80]

Daß Christi Selbstopfer diese Kraft und Wirkung hat, das ist nach dem Hebräerbrief im Geheimnis seiner *Person* begründet.[81] Nur als der, der seinem Ursprung und Wesen nach Gott ist, konnte er der wahre, makellose Hohepriester und zugleich das wahre, makellose Opfer sein.[82] Das Sühnegeschehen selbst beschreibt der Hebräerbrief so, daß Christus vor den Toren Jerusalems am Kreuz stirbt (13.12) und hier seinen *Leib* opfert (10.10) und daß er dann in das himmlischen Allerheiligste eintritt, um dort sein *Blut* darzubringen (9.11-12,24-25). Was diese auf den ersten Blick recht merkwürdige Schilderung *theologisch* besagen will, liegt auf der Hand: Der Kreuzestod Jesu auf Golgatha ist ein Geschehen, "das in unserer Geschichte geschah, und doch Gottes Geschichte ist und bleibt".[83] In diesem Geschehen *ist* das Irdische das Himmlische, das geschichtliche "Einmal" als solches das eschatologische "Ein für allemal".[84] "Die Geschichte Jesu am Kreuz reicht in den Himmel, und in diesem Geschehen reicht der Himmel, reicht der ewige Wille des Vaters bis zur Erde. Gottes Wille wird hier Ereignis . . . und wirkt eine ewige Erlösung für uns."[85] Weil das so ist, deshalb *ist* das Reden Gottes

---

[73] 5.2-3; 7.27-28; 9.7.
[74] 2.5-18; 5.7-10; 8.1-10.18. Zum Begriff des "Selbstopfers" s. 7.27; 9.14,25-26,28.
[75] 1.3c; vgl. auch 9.14; 10.22.
[76] "Sühnung" (ἱλάσκεσθαι) der Sünden: 2.17; vgl. 10.12. - "Aufhebung" (ἀθέτησις) der Sünde: 9.26. - "Wegnahme" (ἀναφέρειν) der Sünden: 9.28. - "Erlösung" (ἀπολύτρωσις) von den Übertretungen: 9.15. - "Vergebung" (ἄφεσις): 10.18. - Stets ist gemeint, daß die Sünden vor *Gott* unwirksam, ja nicht mehr existent sind, weil *er* ihrer "nicht mehr gedenkt" (8.12; 10.17).
[77] 9.12; vgl. 5.9; 7.25.
[78] ἁγιάζειν: 10.10,14,29; 13.12 (vgl. auch 2.11).
[79] 10.14: μιᾷ ... προσφορᾷ τετελείωκεν εἰς τὸ διηνεκὲς τοὺς ἁγιαζομένους. Das Verbum τελειοῦν hat hier wie in 7.19; 9.9; 10.1 (vgl. τελείωσις 7.11) die Bedeutung: "zum hohenpriesterlichen Zutritt zu Gott fähig machen".
[80] S. dazu vor allem 10.19-25, aber auch 7.19 und indirekt 9.8-9.
[81] S. dazu bereits das 1. Kapitel des Briefes: Die Betonung der Gottgleichheit des Sohnes V. 3a.b hat ihren Bezugspunkt in der Sühnetod-Aussage V. 3c.
[82] 7.26-27 bzw. 9.14.
[83] Iwand, *Predigt-Meditationen I*, 683. Vgl. auch ebd., 676-677 sowie 486-487.
[84] Vgl. ebd., 676 bzw. 486.
[85] Ebd., 486.

"in dem Sohn" die Gewährung der heiligenden Sühne und somit die definitive Begründung und Eröffnung des von den Propheten verheißenen Heils.[86] Indem aber hier die *Wirklichkeit* der Sühne auf den Plan getreten ist, hat alles, was nur ihre *Notwendigkeit* anzeigen konnte, seinen Sinn verloren. Eben deshalb ist - wie wir im Hebräerbrief hören - die in der "Tora des Mose" verfügte πρώτη διαθήκη mit dem Kommen Christi annulliert und außer Kraft gesetzt[87] und der alttestamentliche Opferkult selbst aufgehoben.[88]

Alles, was der Verfasser des Hebräerbriefes über die Kraftlosigkeit und Nutzlosigkeit der alttestamentlichen Kultgesetzgebung und über ihre Aufhebung und Annullierung sagt, ist selbstverständlich von *Christus* her gesagt und damit als eine Konsequenz zu beurteilen, die sich dem Verfasser aus seiner Christologie und der in ihr begründeten Soteriologie ergeben hat. Als um so bemerkenswerter muß dann erscheinen, daß der Verfasser seine Sicht nicht einfach bloß dem alttestamentlichen Zeugnis entgegenstellt, sondern daß er sie auch inneralttestamentlich zu verifizieren sucht.

Es sind drei gewichtige Texte der Schrift, in denen er die Wirkungslosigkeit der πρώτη διαθήκη wie auch die zeitliche Begrenztheit ihrer Geltung deutlich angezeigt findet. In 7.11-28 argumentiert der Verfasser mit Ps 110(109).4, wobei ihm der Tatbestand wichtig ist, daß die mosaische Gesetzgebung dem "Psalm Davids" zeitlich vorausgeht (V.28). Wird nun aber in dem Psalm von der Einsetzung eines wahren und ewigen Priesters gesprochen, der dem levitischen Priestertum *nicht* angehört, so kann damit nur die völlige Unzulänglichkeit jenes Priestertums namhaft gemacht und seine Ablösung durch ein qualitativ anderes Priestertum angekündigt sein. - Der Abschnitt 8.7-13 enthält in seiner Mitte das volle Zitat des Textes Jer 31(38).31-34, der dann teilweise noch einmal im Kontext von 10.11-18 begegnet.[89] In diesem Gottesspruch sieht der Verfasser die "erste" διαθήκη durch Gott selbst als unzulänglich "getadelt" (V. 8) und "für veraltet erklärt" (V. 13) und eine "neue" διαθήκη angekündigt (V. 8), die das bringt, was die "erste" διαθήκη *nicht* zu bringen vermochte: die Sündenvergebung, die

---

[86] S. dazu besonders 2.3, aber auch 4.1-2 und 12.25-29. Weil das Kommen der σωτηρία durch das Reden Gottes "im Sohn" definitiv ins Werk gesetzt ist, deshalb können Unglaube und Ungehorsam *diesem* Reden gegenüber nur den definitiven Heilsverlust zur Folge haben: 2.1-4; 3.7-4.13; 10.26-31; 10.35-39; 12.25-29.

[87] 7.18 (ἀθέτησις - so präzise für das noch mehrdeutige μετάθεσις in 7.12); 8.13 (ἀφανισμός).

[88] 10.9b,18. - Der Sachverhalt ist *nicht* zutreffend beschrieben, wenn Gräßer bemerkt: "Christus ist das *Ende des Kults als Heilsweg*" (*Hebräer I*, 26); denn *Heilsweg* war der Kult nach dem Hebräerbrief *nie!* Ebenso problematisch ist es, wenn über den alttestamentlichen Kult gesagt wird: "Als heilskonstituierender Faktor kommt er nicht mehr (sic!) in Betracht" (ebd., 25).

[89] 10.16-17 = Jer 31(38).33-34.

vollkommene Gotteserkenntnis und die unmittelbare Gottesgemeinschaft (V. 10-12). Diese "*neue Setzung*" Gottes, die die "erste Setzung" ablöst, ist die heilvolle, weil Sühne bringende Christus-διαθήκη.[90] - Bei dem dritten alttestamentlichen Text handelt es sich um die Psalmworte Ps 40(39).7-9, die der Verfasser in 10.5-10 zitiert und kommentiert. Er versteht die Psalmverse als Worte des präexistenten Christus, die dieser unmittelbar vor seiner Inkarnation zum Vater gesprochen hat:

"Schlachtopfer und Speisopfer hast du nicht gewollt,
einen Leib aber hast du mir bereitet.
An Brandopfern und Sündopfern hast du kein Wohlgefallen gehabt;
da sprach ich: Siehe, ich komme
- in der Buchrolle steht es über mich geschrieben - ,
um zu tun, o Gott, deinen Willen."

In diesen Worten findet der Verfasser die Erklärung dafür, weshalb es "unmöglich" ist, "daß das Blut von Stieren und Böcken Sünden wegnehmen kann" (10.4)[91]: Die in der "Tora des Mose" vorgeschriebenen Opfer sind *nicht* die dem Heilswillen Gottes entsprechenden und deshalb das Heil wirkenden Opfer (10.8). Dem Heilswillen Gottes entspricht einzig das Selbstopfer dessen, der Mensch wurde, um sich selbst zur Sühnung der Sünden in den Tod zu geben (10.9-10).[92] Mit der Inkarnation und dem Opfertod Jesu aber ist - wie der Verfasser ausdrücklich bemerkt (10.9) - das "erste", d.h. die alttestamentliche Kultordnung, "aufgehoben" und das "zweite", d.h. die ewig gültige Christus-διαθήκη, "aufgerichtet" worden.[93]

Die drei alttestamentlichen Texte, die wir in aller Kürze in den Blick gefaßt haben, liefern dem Verfasser des Hebräerbriefes den Beweis dafür, daß sein christologisch begründetes Urteil über die mosaische Kultgesetzgebung durchaus auch dem Eigenzeugnis des Alten Testamentes entspricht. Im Alten Testament findet der Verfasser somit *nicht* bloß dies gesagt, daß der sündige Mensch der "Sühne" bedarf, wenn er des Heils teilhaftig werden soll; er sieht hier *zugleich* auch schon *den* angekündigt, der diese "Sühne" bringen und damit das Heil bereiten wird.

---

[90] Der Begriff der "neuen" διαθήκη (διαθήκη καινή 8.8,13; 9.15 bzw. διαθήκη νέα 12.24) ist direkt aus Jer 31(38).31-34 (hier V. 31) entnommen. In 8.7 wird sie als δευτέρα (sc. διαθήκη) bezeichnet. Von ihr ist auch in 7.22; 10.16,29; 13.20 die Rede.
[91] 10.5a schließt mit διό unmittelbar an 10.4 bzw. 10.1-4 an!
[92] Auf die *Inkarnation* deutet der Verfasser das Wort ἥκω Ps 40(39).8; den *Sühnetod* findet er in den Worten τοῦ ποιῆσαι ... τὸ θέλημά σου Ps 40(39).9a angesprochen.
[93] Der Ausdruck τὸ πρῶτον 10.9 entspricht dem Begriff ἡ πρώτη διαθήκη 9.15, der Ausdruck τὸ δεύτερον 10.9 dem Begriff der δευτέρα διαθήκη 8.7.

IV

Im Umgang mit dem Alten Testament, wie wir ihn im Hebräerbrief wahrnehmen konnten, dokumentiert sich ohne Frage eine erstaunliche hermeneutische Kühnheit. Das gilt insbesondere für die kritische Interpretation des Kultgesetzes und für die christologische Rezeption der Königspsalmen 2, 45 und 110. Daß die drei Psalmen durch die Übertragung auf Christus und die damit vollzogene Herauslösung aus der Konzeption eines menschlichen Königtums zu *anderen*, ja zu *neuen* Texten geworden sind, haben wir bereits gesehen.[94] Was sodann das Kultgesetz anlangt, so dürfte eine Ordnung, der "die wirkliche Gestalt der Dinge selbst" und damit jede Heilswirklichkeit radikal abgesprochen wird (10.1), ganz gewiß nicht mehr das Kultgesetz sein, wie es im Pentateuch begegnet und gemeint ist.[95] Daß im Schriftverständnis und entsprechend in der Schriftauslegung des auctor ad Hebraeos gravierende Verschiebungen und höchst gewichtige Uminterpretationen stattgefunden haben, kann also keinem Zweifel unterliegen.

Erwägen wir abschließend in aller Kürze, was der beschriebene Befund für die Frage einer "Biblischen Theologie" bedeutet, so ist zu sagen: Biblische Theologie, die den Spuren des Hebräerbriefes folgen wollte, wäre zweifellos eine dezidiert *kritische* Disziplin. Sie könnte und würde nicht einfach die Sacheinheit von Altem und Neuem Testament voraussetzen, sondern sie hätte allererst zu prüfen, *ob* solche Einheit gegeben ist und *wo* und *inwiefern* sie gegeben ist. Biblische Theologie wäre also in dem Sinn kritisch, daß sie das Verhältnis von Altem Testament und Neuem Testament nicht prinzipiell und ausschließlich unter der Prämisse der Kontinuität betrachtet, sondern sehr wohl auch mit Diskontinuität, ja sogar mit gewichtiger Diskontinuität rechnet. Als kritische Disziplin würde sich Biblische Theologie dann allerdings zugleich auch dadurch erweisen, daß sie nicht einfach umgekehrt von vornherein die Diskontinuität zu ihrer Prämisse erhebt. Hält Biblische Theologie - dem hermeneutischen Kanon von Hebr 1.1+2a folgend - im Blick auf das Alte und das Neue Testament grundsätzlich an der *Selbigkeit* Gottes fest,

---

[94] Ps 2 im Verständnis des Hebräerbriefes *ist* nicht mehr der zweite Psalm der Hebräischen Bibel oder der Septuaginta. Dieser analog für Ps 45 und Ps 110 geltende Tatbestand zeigt sich nicht zuletzt auch daran, daß die Königspsalmen im Rahmen einer christologischen Deutung nicht als Ganze, sondern nur *eklektisch* rezipierbar waren bzw. rezipiert worden sind. Ebenso konnte zwar 2 Sam 7.14a auf Christus bezogen werden (so Hebr 1.5b), keinesfalls aber die unmittelbare Fortsetzung 2 Sam 7.14b!

[95] Das Urteil des Hebräerbriefes über die mosaische Kultgesetzgebung ist etwas wesentlich anderes als das Wissen Israels um den "provisorischen" Charakter des mit jener Gesetzgebung etablierten Kultes. Zu diesem "provisorischen" Charakter s. H. Gese, "Die Sühne", in: ders., *Zur biblischen Theologie. Alttestamentliche Vorträge* (Tübingen, 1989³), 85-106: 105.

so wird sie auf der Grundlage des neutestamentlichen Christuszeugnisses gerade auch nach der Kontinuität im "Reden" Gottes fragen und hier insbesondere den Zusammenhang von *Verheißung und Erfüllung* und damit die Treue Gottes zu seinem Wort bedenken.[96]

Sollte - so ist zu fragen - Biblische Theologie eine in diesem Sinn *kritische* Disziplin sein? Ich denke: Sie sollte es in der Tat! Der Hebräerbrief weist, was den grundsätzlich-theologischen Weg anlangt, durchaus programmatisch die Richtung, auch wenn man in methodischer Hinsicht im einzelnen anders verfahren muß und wird, als er es tut. Wir müssen - im Unterschied zu ihm - von unseren historisch-kritischen Voraussetzungen her zunächst in sorgfältiger exegetischer Arbeit die Aussage der alttestamentlichen Texte selbst erheben und dann prüfen, wie dieser Befund im Lichte des neutestamentlichen Christuszeugnisses zu beurteilen und zu würdigen ist. Es dürfte sich dabei zeigen, daß es im Alten Testament sehr wohl *beides* gibt: zum einen Texte, die so, wie sie lauten, von Christus her zu bejahen und daher in ihrem *ursprünglichen* Sinn voll rezipierbar sind; zum anderen aber auch Texte, für die eben dies eindeutig *nicht* gelten kann.[97] Der 8. Psalm etwa wäre ein solcher in seinem ursprünglichen Sinn rezipierbarer Text, sind seine Aussagen über die Hoheit des von Gott geliebten Menschen doch durch Christi Einsatz *für* den Menschen endgültig in Kraft gesetzt und als wahr erwiesen. Der Psalm *muß* deshalb keineswegs in der Weise von Hebr 2.5-9 christologisch uminterpretiert werden. Anders steht es z.B. mit den Psalmen 2, 45 und 110, die in sehr erhöhtem Ton von dem davidischen König, von seiner weltweiten Herrschaft und von seinem Triumph über die Feinde reden. Diese Texte sind in ihrem ursprünglichen Sinn ganz gewiß *nicht* rezipierbar, sondern sie dürften in *dieser* Hinsicht nur religionsgeschichtlich oder traditionsgeschichtlich von Interesse sein. Denn christlich rezipierbar kann nur sein, was mit dem "Reden" Gottes "im Sohn" und also mit dem neutestamentlichen Christuszeugnis vereinbar ist.

---

[96] Zum Begriff der "Verheißung" im Hebräerbrief s. Chr. Rose, "Verheißung und Erfüllung. Zum Verständnis von ἐπαγγελία im Hebräerbrief", BZ 33 (1989), 60-80. 178-191.
[97] Ob solche alttestamentlichen Texte oder Aussagen, denen vom neutestamentlichen Christuszeugnis her zu widersprechen ist, nicht auch bereits durch *andere* Zeugnisse des *Alten Testamentes selbst* in ein kritisches Licht gerückt werden, wird jeweils genau zu prüfen sein. Ein Satz wie Hebr 10.4 ließe sich ja sehr wohl schon anhand von Aussagen alttestamentlicher Prophetie begründen!

CHAPTER EIGHT

# OLD TESTAMENT METAPHORS IN THE NEW TESTAMENT

Kirsten Nielsen, Århus

*I. Shepherd, Lamb, and Blood*

One of the main scenes in the Revelation to John is the sealing of the servants of God. John sees a great multitude that no man could number, standing before the throne and the Lamb, clothed in white robes. One of the elders asks him who they are, but John does not know until he is told that

> These are they who have come out of the great tribulation; they have washed their robes and made them white in the blood of the Lamb (Rev 7.14).

John is further informed that because they have made their robes white in the blood of the lamb, they are now part of the heavenly choir that serves God day and night. And they are under the protection of God.

> For the Lamb at the centre of the throne will be their shepherd, and he will guide them to springs of the water of life; and God will wipe away every tear from their eyes (Rev 7.17).

These verses are full of metaphors that must have been well known to the audience at the time, when Revelation was written. The author is not trying to hide anything; on the contrary he wants to give a clear and adequate description of what he has seen. If the reader is acquainted with the root metaphor of the text, nothing more needs to be said: the shepherd, and the way that it was used both in the Old Testament and in early Christian theology, was a familiar image.

We who read the text today however need some information in order to understand how red blood can make clothes white. In order to understand what may have been intended when the text was written down, we must try to discern what the author expected his audience to know about shepherds and lambs.

As exegetes we have to track the intertextuality of Rev 7.14-17 and to analyze the network of texts to which it belongs. A text always gets its meaning from a dialogue with other texts, and one of the "texts" in this dialogue is the actual reader.

In saying this I have already presupposed a number of ideas about interpreting metaphors, and I have involved myself in an ongoing debate about author, text, and reader.[1] Let us therefore leave the image of the shepherd and the lamb for a moment and take a look at my presuppositions and ideas about how to read a text full of metaphors.

## II. Personal background

Let me start with a confession: I am fascinated by metaphors and by the fact that metaphors can be used again and again and still say something of topical interest. I am fascinated now, and I have always been so. I was brought up in a Danish vicarage in a community that knew little about the Bible but was extremely fond of singing hymns. What I learned as a young child was, therefore, that the word of God is poetic, and that the word of God can be reused again and again and still be full of meaning.

I mention this personal background, because I find it typical for a lot of exegetes of my generation, who were educated in the German tradition. We actually began our study of scripture with a love for words and poetry, but during our education we became so "intellectual" that we repressed this first love and concentrated on theory and method: i.e. Textkritik, Literarkritik, Formgeschichte, Traditionsgeschichte, Redaktionsgeschichte.

What I have tried to reflect upon, therefore, is whether my own experience of God's words as poetry nevertheless has influenced my way of doing exegesis.

Another source of influence must be mentioned at the very outset. One of the main trends in modern exegesis is concerned with the intertextuality of texts. It is obvious that any text is part of a network of texts. But how do we study a text intertextually in a responsible way?

I am not the only one these days to call for "responsible reading".[2] But perhaps I have a special obligation to worry about the many problems concerning scholarly responsibility. For years I have worked with metaphors and tried to uncover the many possible meanings of

---

[1] Cf. Kirsten Nielsen, "Intertextuality and Biblical Scholarship", *SJOT* 2 (1990), 89-95, and Kirsten Nielsen, *Satan - den fortabte søn? Bibelske og pseudepigrafe forestillinger om Satan som en af Guds sønner* (København, 1991), 25-34.

[2] Cf. Werner G. Jeanrond, *Text und Interpretation als Kategorien theologischen Denkens* (Tübingen, 1986), 66 and 123; Anthony C. Thiselton, "Reader-Response Hermeneutics", in Roger Lundin, Anthony C. Thiselton, Clarence Walhout, *The Responsibility of Hermeneutics* (Exeter, 1985), 112-13; David Tracy, *Plurality and Ambiguity. Hermeneutics, Religion, Hope* (San Fransisco, 1987) IX.

metaphors. I have made it my task to demonstrate the openness of metaphors, to show how metaphors can be used and reused, interpreted and reinterpreted through generations, and I have argued that we must take the intertextuality of a text seriously.[3]

But is it then possible to ask for responsibility in exegesis? Would it be responsible at all to stop any time in the process of interpretation? And can we argue that one interpretation is better than another? I read a text in one intertextuality, which is the one I find most appropriate (appropriate for what purpose?) while my colleague reads the same text in her intertextuality. How do we decide which interpretation is worth listening to, and how do I defend mine against hers?

What I should like to present is, therefore, my own way of trying to be responsible when I interpret Biblical texts. I am not able to answer all the questions raised, but it is important for me to combine the fact that Biblical texts are historical texts with the fact that they are open to reuse. A responsible reader must therefore take the historical dimension of Biblical texts into consideration. Therefore I must respect the intertextuality that was intended by the Biblical authors when they wrote their texts. And I have to study the "Wirkungsgeschichte" of these texts as well. It may be that a certain text was reused later on by another author and interpreted by another audience. This reuse implies another intertextuality. New experiences have taken place, and new texts take part in the ongoing dialogue between author, text, and audience.

### III. Studies in Old Testament Metaphors

Before we go further into the question about the intertextuality of Rev 7 I should like to give a short summary of my ideas about metaphors. Some years ago I published my book on the tree as a metaphor in Isaiah 1-39.[4] Here I defended the four following theses concerning Old Testament metaphorical language

a) Metaphorical language functions in a concrete context by means of reciprocal interaction between two different statements.

b) One can derive from metaphorical language information in the form of new suggestions for understanding reality (informative function).

---

[3] Kirsten Nielsen, *There is Hope for a Tree. The Tree as Metaphor in Isaiah* (Sheffield, 1989), 66-67; Kirsten Nielsen, "Reinterpretation of Metaphors - Tree Metaphors in Isa: 1-39" in Matthias Augustin & Klaus-Dietrich Schunck (ed.), *"Wünschet Jerusalem Frieden." IOSOT Congress Jerusalem 1986* (Frankfurt am Main, 1988), 425-29; Kirsten Nielsen, "Shepherd, Lamb, and Blood. Imagery in the Old Testament - Use and Reuse", *StTh* 46 (1992), 121-132.

[4] Kirsten Nielsen (1989).

c) The purpose of metaphorical language is to engage the audience in such a way that by entering into the interpretation they adopt it as their own understanding of reality (performative function).

d) Metaphorical language can be reused in other contexts, which opens up for the possibility of reinterpretation.

First of all, I must stress that what I have done in this description is not to define what a metaphor *is*, but to describe how it *functions*.[5] The metaphorical function of a word is not part of the meaning of the word itself. No words are born as metaphors, but a word can in a concrete context be used as a metaphor. We therefore have to know the context in order to determine whether a word must be taken literally or metaphorically. And a word in its context is a word in function.

If a man begins to sing about a vineyard, we must consider the situation in which he sings and the whole cultural context behind the song in order to determine whether he is a winegrower, who sings about his favourite vineyard, or whether the song is some kind of parable, i.e. a love song, where the author praises his girlfriend by comparing her to a vineyard.

When we read about the vineyard in Isa 5, we face another possibility: the vineyard is used as a metaphor for Israel, the beloved of God. What is said about the vineyard must be understood as God's words about Israel. The audience already knows a great deal about the relationship between God and Israel. At the same time, something new is said in this metaphorical song, something that has to be heard in relation to what is already known about the covenant between the Lord and Israel.

This means that metaphorical language functions in a concrete context by means of a reciprocal interaction between two different statements: 1) the song itself and 2) what is elsewhere said about Israel's covenant with the Lord.

Second, I have taken note of the fact that metaphors are fit for reuse in new contexts. But when a metaphor is reused, it will always be reinterpreted. This means that if a metaphor can be interpreted differently by different audiences, the next question must be: What do we actually derive from metaphorical language? Can we get any kind of information through metaphors? My answer is yes. And the kind of information we can derive is what I would call new suggestions for understanding reality.

The person who uses a metaphor offers me a new way of seeing. I can accept these suggestions, or I can reject them as false. The intention of

---

[5] The above mentioned theses are presented in my book not as a definition, but as a *description of imagery's function* in the Old Testament. Kirsten Nielsen (1989), 65.

the speaker is of course to convince me that his or her way of interpreting reality is worth adopting.

We know that this is the case from daily life. If somebody has used a striking metaphor to characterize a certain member of our government or department, we are suddenly able to see this man with new eyes: we can see him as a rat or as a lion or as a sheep.

So far so good. But my characterisation of metaphorical language has some consequences. For if metaphors always function and must be interpreted in a concrete context, we must take seriously the fact that the reuse of a metaphor is reuse in a new context. The meaning of the metaphor will consequently change. Reuse always means reinterpretation. And it will therefore be of fundamental significance that we do not forget to state in which context we analyze a certain prophetic word, for instance. We must ask ourselves whether we are trying to get back to the first *Sitz-im-Leben* of Isa 5 (if that be possible at all), or whether we are preparing a sermon for our congregation and therefore see the actual Sunday service as the *Sitz-im-Leben* for the text.

So much for my ideas about metaphors. Now we turn to practical application and therefore to

## IV. Problems

When I began my work on the tree as metaphor, I felt rather confident that it should be possible to be more precise about the context than exegetes normally are.[6] But after a while I had second thoughts. I realized that the traditional question about dating a prophetic oracle had become even more difficult than before. Having noticed that metaphorical language is open for reinterpretation, I had to admit that it is extremely difficult to date a short text full of metaphors. Almost any date goes if the meaning of metaphors is totally dependent on their context.

But dating metaphorical language was not the only problem. When I analyzed the meaning of a metaphor and saw its many possible meanings, I had to admit that the possible contexts for a metaphor are so to speak limitless. Any text is part of a network of texts. In other words, any text should be interpreted in its intertextuality.

I could try to be precise and say that I was interested in knowing what the person Isaiah, the "author", actually meant when he created his lovesong about the vineyard and addressed it to his audience. But I might just as well ask what the audience actually heard on that day. Or I might try to look at the text "itself" to find the meaning of the text.

---
[6] Kirsten Nielsen (1989), 236-239.

## V. Redactional Criticism in a Postmodern Situation?

For some time I was not quite aware of how complex the situation actually is, thank God! I was convinced that the ambiguity of a metaphor and its fitness for reuse made it not only relevant but possible to analyze the history of the reuse of the tree as a metaphor in Isa 1-39. And to a certain extent, I still think that it is possible to do so. It is, for instance, obvious that Isa 5.1-7 has been reused in Isa 27.2-6, the song about the days to come, when "Jacob shall take root, Israel shall blossom and put forth shoots and fill the whole world with fruit" (27.6). The new text clearly quotes and transforms the old one.

If we try to follow the use and reuse of a metaphor like the vineyard in the Bible, what we are actually doing can be classified as a kind of redactional criticism, and what the redactors had on their minds must be seen from the texts and the way they combine them. We are then concerned about the intentions of the redactors. We see these redactors as theologians who have certain intentions, who wish to set forth a certain theology. They reuse older traditions, texts that belong to the culture of their society, in a new way to make their points. Another exegetical consequence is therefore that redactional activity should also be analyzed as the reinterpretation of metaphors.

But is it still possible to do redactional criticism in a postmodern society? Can we still talk about the author as a person with a clear intention, a person who says what he or she means, no more no less? And what do we know about the audience? Who were they, and how did they interpret the concrete metaphor? Many an exegete would therefore find it reasonable to declare that the text "itself" is the only object of our analysis. But is there *a text*? Every text is part of other texts, and the intertextuality of any text opens up for a number of possible interpretations, and *the text* seems to evaporate.

According to some critics it is of no use to try to talk about the author as a person who is capable of expressing his meaning clearly in a text so that his audience understands exactly what he intended to say (the intentional fallacy). The author is dead, it is said.[7] Nevertheless it seems that the reader is still considered a person with a mind, a person who interprets texts and creates new texts.

---

[7] See, for instance, Terry Eagleton's critic of E. D. Hirsch in Terry Eagleton, *Literary Theory. An Introduction* (Oxford, 1983), 67-70, or one of the classics in literary theory René Wellek & Austin Warren, *Theory of Literature* (3rd Ed. London, 1963), 41-42; 147-48. As to the term "intentional fallacy" cf. W.K. Wimsatt - M. C. Beardsley, "The Intentional Fallacy", in *Essays in Modern Criticism* (New York, 1952); David Jasper, *The Study of Literature and Religion*, an Introduction, 2nd ed. (London, 1992), 45-46.

But if such a person as a responsible reader exists, we might argue that the author of a text actually is such a responsible reader. The author of a text begins as reader of an earlier text. By his rereading of the older text the author creates a certain intertextuality. But how do we study a text in its intertextuality?

In order to find a starting point I turned to the American critic Harold Bloom. In his theory of poetry he gave the following statement:

> My concern is only with strong poets, major figures with the persistence to wrestle with their strong precursors even to the death.[8]

I have always felt that his way of looking upon the process of writing as a kind of wrestling with stronger precursors, or we might say, as a wrestling with other texts, is convincing. The fact that any text is part of a network of texts does not mean that these texts lie side by side in peaceful coexistence. I would therefore like to see the redactors of the Old Testament prophetic literature as theologians who have been wrestling with strong precursors. And I am sure that the widespread use of metaphors in prophetic preaching has made this continuous reinterpretation of the original message possible.

## VI. What is the context of a text?

As I have already mentioned, I find it important to respect *the historical context* of a certain text. But if the text in question is full of metaphors, I have to realize that the more I stress the openness and the ambiguity of metaphors, the more I have to stress the necessity of defining a precise context in order to interpret the metaphor. At the same time I have to accept the fact that it is almost impossible to find a precise date for the metaphor. Only *the redactional context* is there to help us. The metaphor itself, normally, gives little help as to the first and "original" *Sitz-im-Leben*.

But is it enough to say that Isa 5.1-7[9] is part of a redactional composition, where the song of the vineyard is put at the beginning, and the following woe-oracles can be seen as interpretations of what is meant by the metaphor of the wild grapes. The fruits of the vineyard turned out to

---

[8] Harold Bloom, *The Anxiety of Influence: A Theory of Poetry* (Oxford, 1973), 5.

[9] For the understanding of Isa 5.1-7 cf. J. Vermeylen, *Du Prophète Isaïe à l'Apocalyptique. Isaïe, I-XXXV, miroir d'un demi-millénaire d'expérience religieuse en Israël*, I-II (Paris, 1977-78), 159-68 and Anders Jørgen Bjørndalen, *Untersuchungen zur allegorischen Rede der Propheten Amos und Jesaja* (Berlin, 1986), 247-343.

be wild grapes instead of good grapes. What is meant by that is explained in Isa 5.8-24, where it is said that the people of Israel joined house to house, added field to field, ran after strong drink, and were inflamed by wine and did not regard the deeds of the Lord.

> Woe to those who drag iniquity along with cords of falsehood, who drag sin along as with cart ropes. Woe to those who call evil good, and good evil! (5.18,20a).

Isa 5.8-24 is, of course, the context of Isa 5.1-7. Nevertheless we must admit that the metaphor of the vineyard has a much broader context than these verses about the sin of Israel. But how do we handle this broader context, which is the intertextuality of the text? What about the context in the New Testament, where we have a number of parables about vineyards? Aren't they part of the intertextuality of the metaphor as well?[10]

In a stimulating article on critical exegesis Gary A. Phillips states that one of the modern presumptions that has been brought to light by Jacques Derrida is[11]

> ... that the text is somehow 'naturally' bound by the limits of the intentions of the voice of its 'author', or the responses of its original hearers/readers, or the history of the text's development.

This statement surely has some truth in it. The meaning of a text cannot be reduced to the author's intentions or to the understanding of the first audience, nor can it be reduced to the actual reinterpretation that has taken place up to this day. I may quote Terry Eagleton who in his introduction to literary theory puts it this way: "There is always more meaning where that came from".[12]

The fact that there is more meaning in a text than we immediately notice has to do with the intertextuality of texts. To use a metaphor we could say that a text is always part of an ongoing dialogue between older and younger texts. Our task as exegetes is therefore to try to trace this dialogue, this intertextuality, but to trace it through history. It is not just any intertextuality that I personally could find interesting that is the object of scholarly analysis, but the intertextuality that comes out of the historical situations in which the text was written, used and reused, as well as the historical situation in which I live as scholar and as person.

---

[10] Cf. Hans-Josef Klauck, *Allegorie und Allegorese in synoptischen Gleichnistexten* (Münster, 1978), 298-300.
[11] Gary A. Phillips, "Exegesis as Critical Praxis", *Semeia* 51 (1990), 29.
[12] Terry Eagleton, *Literary Theory* (Oxford, 1983), 128.

I must therefore challenge the tendency of some postmodern scholars[13] to argue that because all literary texts are woven out of other literary texts, because all literature is "intertextual", then any meaning is possible anytime. While I must reject such a position, how is it then possible to argue that a certain understanding of a text is more to the point, more correct, than another understanding? And what do we mean by "more to the point"? Which point? Whose point?

What I have learned from working with metaphors, and having been influenced to a certain extent by postmodern critics, is that a text is always open for reinterpretation, that it can be read in different ways, and that different interpretive communities will read the text differently, because they have different contexts. But this does not imply that we are unable to read and to interpret anything. Nor does it imply that the author of a text is unable to form his or her words and metaphors in such a way that he or she signals the intertextuality of his/her own text. Nobody would argue that Isa 5.1-7, the song of the vineyard, is not part of the intertextuality of Isa 27.2-6.

What could and should be debated is whether the words of Jesus in John 15, where Jesus calls himself the true vine in a text far later than Isa 27, belong to the intertextuality of Isa 27?

These considerations are necessary for studies in prophetic literature, because it is relevant to discuss whether the genre prophetic literature is a special kind of network where younger texts belong to the intertextuality of older texts and help to interpret the older texts. Could we argue that prophetic texts are texts that are read in a certain intertextuality, where it is meaningful to read older texts in the light of younger texts? The whole Old Testament could then be regarded as prophetic literature, seen from the point of view of the New Testament authors. Could we argue that what is called prophetic is not so much a genre, as it is something we, the readers or the redactors, do to texts? Is it just like reading love poems as poems written for me personally instead of trying to find out with whom the author was actually in love at that time (if he or she was in love at all).

---

[13] I see this tendency in the following argument by David J. A. Clines: "Nowadays we are recognizing that texts not only do not have determinate meanings, they do not 'have' meanings at all. More and more, we are coming to appreciate the role of the reader, or the hearer, in the making of meaning, and recognizing that, without a reader or a hearer, there is not a lot of 'meaning' to any text. The text means whatever it means to its various readers, and if their contexts are different, it is likely that it will mean different things to different readers. There is no one authentic meaning which we must all try to discover, no matter who we are or where we happen to be standing" ("Possibilities and Priorities of Biblical Interpretation in an International Perspective", *Biblical Interpretation* 1 (1993), 78). Cf. also Christopher Norris, *Deconstruction and the Interests of Theory* (New York, 1991); *Untying the Text: A Post-Structuralist Reader*, ed. Robert Young (London and New York, 1987).

In this article I am concerned with Old Testament metaphors in the New Testament. And one of the serious questions is, of course, how do we deal with the fact that the authors of the New Testament are convinced that their interpretation of an Old Testament metaphor, which is taken from an Old Testament prophetic oracle or from another Old Testament text that does not necessarily belong to the prophetic genre, is the only one that really says what was intended when the prophet formulated his message in quite another context. What are we actually doing, when we read Isa 53.7 in a Christian church on Good Friday? Are we reusing the text in a new context that allows us to understand more than the author in the 6th century B.C. Is that a responsible reading? Are we, as Harold Bloom puts it, wrestling with a strong precursor, creating a new text, even though we are reading word for word what is written in the Old Testament?

Let us now leave these theoretical considerations and take a look at some Biblical texts in order to answer some of the questions raised.

### VII. Root-Metaphors and Redactional Activity: The Shepherd as Metaphor in Hosea

The prophet Hosea, who lived in the 8th Century B.C., must have been fond of metaphors. His oracles are full of metaphors taken from daily life. Normally it is rather easy to understand what is meant by a certain metaphor, but now and then the redactors of his book combine them in a way that surprises and confuses a modern reader.

It is rather well-known that redactional activity often implies an effort to clarify the meaning of a metaphor. Metaphors have been supplied with interpretations that were not necessary, when the prophet and the audience met for the first time. The whole situation made it clear what the message was about, and the cultural background helped the audience to realize that the prophet was using metaphors.

In this connection it has now and then been argued that the redactors collected separate oracles and combined them with the help of catchwords.[14] That may occasionally be the case, but I would suggest that we look for other principles as well that have more to do with the metaphorical character of prophetic literature.

We all know that it is easier to remember a metaphor than an abstract expression. Therefore the whole process of tradition from one generation

---

[14] Cf. Georg Fohrer, *Das Alte Testament. Zweiter und dritter Teil* (Gütersloh, 1970), 30, or Bernhard Duhm, *Das Buch Jesaja*, 5th ed. (Göttingen, 1968), 12.

to another may very well have resulted in the preservation of metaphors instead of abstract words. And in order to keep the metaphors together we could imagine that the redactors combined metaphors which belong to the same "family", so to speak.

Let us illustrate this with an example, which brings us back to the theme of Rev 14.7, the blood of the lamb. In Hos 5.12-14 God proclaims that he is like cancer to Ephraim and like dry rot to the house of Judah. It is further said that Ephraim saw his sickness and Judah his wound. He sends to Assyria, but the great king is not able to cure Ephraim. In verse 14 God proclaims that he will be like a lion to Ephraim and like a young lion to the house of Judah, and nobody shall rescue anything the Lord has carried off. Israel now decides to return to the Lord

> ... for it is he who has torn, and he will heal us; he has struck down, and he will bind us up (Hos 6.1).

These oracles seem to be rather loosely connected by catchwords.[15] There is something about sickness and something about being torn and being in need of healing. But actually what binds these verses together is the root-metaphor that lies behind it all, namely God as a shepherd.[16] The shepherd is supposed to fight against the lion and save his flock from the wild beasts. And if it happens that a wild animal hurts one of his lambs, he will take care of it like a doctor and heal it.

The shepherd fights and he heals. But God is a very special shepherd: he turns himself into a wild beast, a lion, the enemy of the shepherd, and he hurts his own flock, but he heals his flock once he has hurt it.

### VIII. God as a Shepherd

In the book of Hosea God acts in a strange way. What is normally expected from an Israelite shepherd can be seen from the laws that make the shepherd responsible for the welfare of the flock. The shepherd must defend his sheep against thieves, and if one of the animals is torn by beasts, he must bring the sheep back as evidence. He has to enter the fight to protect the sheep and to prevent the beast from eating it (Exod 22.9-14). In Amos 3.12 the prophet warns the people that

---

[15] Cf. Hans Walter Wolff, *Dodekapropheton 1 Hosea*, 2nd ed. (Neukirchen-Vluyn, 1965), 149. According to Wolff the connection between Hos 5.12-15 and Hos 6.1-3 is based on catch-words.

[16] Cf. Paul A. Porter, *Metaphors and Monsters. A Literary-Critical Study of Daniel 7 and 8* (Toronto, 1985), 65, whose thesis is that the root metaphor 'shepherd' lies behind Daniel 7 and 8.

> As the shepherd rescues from the mouth of the lion two legs, or a piece of an ear, so shall the people of Israel who dwell in Samaria be rescued, with the corner of a couch and part of a bed.

And we suspect that the "good" shepherd also in this case acts both as shepherd and as beast. For who is able to rescue the sheep from the Lord himself? (Cf. Hos 5.14).

Both in the book of Hosea and in the book of Amos the double role of Yahweh is expressed through the metaphor of the flock that is attacked by a wild beast and only to some extent is defended by its shepherd. But in texts like Ps 23.1-2 the metaphor of God is solely positive.

> The Lord is my shepherd, I shall not want; he makes me lie down in green pastures. He leads me beside still waters; he restores my soul.

In an important chapter in the Book of Ezekiel (Ezek 34) the prophet is told to prophecy against the shepherds of Israel, who have been feeding themselves instead of feeding the sheep. The leaders are compared with evil shepherds, who slaughter the fatlings to eat their fat and to clothe themselves with their wool. They have not strengthened the weak, they have not healed the sick, the strayed they have not brought back, the lost they have not sought, and they have ruled them with force and harshness (cf. Ezek 34.2-6).

Therefore the Lord is against the shepherds, and he will require his sheep at their hand. He will rescue his sheep from the mouth of the shepherds, that they may not be food for them. God will make an end to the rule of the evil shepherds, the leaders of Israel.

> As a shepherd seeks out his flock when some of his sheep have been scattered abroad, so will I seek out my sheep...
> And you are my sheep, the sheep of my pasture, and I am your God, says the Lord God (Ezek 34.12,31).

In this chapter the roles are clear. The shepherds who have behaved like wild beasts and eaten their own flock shall be punished. A new shepherd shall take care of the sheep, a good shepherd, the Lord himself.[17] He shall rescue his flock and make an end to their suffering.

Yet another text from the Old Testament must be taken into consideration in this connection. In Second Isaiah a well-known theme is the

---

[17] Also in Deutero-Isaiah is God described as a shepherd, Isa 42.14-16; 49.8-12. Cf. Hans M. Barstad, *A Way in the Wilderness. The "Second Exodus" in the Message of Second Isaiah* (Manchester, 1989), 37-63.

suffering servant. In chapter 53 the author stresses that we have gone astray like sheep. Nevertheless the Lord has laid on the servant "the iniquity of us all". In the following description of the servant's suffering, Isa 53.7, the servant is compared with a lamb:

> He was oppressed, and he was afflicted, yet he opened not his mouth; like a lamb that is led to the slaughter, and like a sheep that before its shearers is silent, so he opened not his mouth.

Isa 53 has been interpreted again and again.[18] In the Old Testament context it is possible to understand the servant as metaphor either for the people or for an individual, a king, a prophet or somebody else, who played an important role at the time the text was written. Seen from a historical point of view, it is reasonable to argue that during the Babylonian Exile the main theological question was the problem of the suffering of the people. How was it possible for God to allow Jerusalem to be destroyed and his elected people to be exiled? One of the possible solutions to the problem was expressed by the metaphor of a lamb that is led to the slaughter and yet does not open its mouth. Could it be that the suffering of those exiled was a necessary sacrifice? Did they play the role of the suffering servant, the sacrificial lamb, on whom the Lord had laid the iniquity of all?

## IX. The Good Shepherd as Sacrificial Lamb

Not only the Jewish community reinterpreted the words of the prophet in order to understand the will and the righteousness of God. Some centuries later the Christian community tried to interpret the death of Jesus as part of God's plan for his people. Once again the metaphor of the lamb that had to be sacrificed became topical.

> Cleanse out the old leaven that you may be a new lump, as you really are unleavened. For Christ, our paschal lamb, has been sacrificed (1 Cor 5.7).

Christ is seen as a lamb, and the death of Christ is regarded as a sacrifice. The understanding of his death is not only a reinterpretation of the Old Testament paschal story, for it also reuses the theme from Isa 53 of the suffering servant who behaves like a sacrificial lamb.

---

[18] Cf. C. R. North, *The Suffering Servant in Deutero-Isaiah*, 2.nd ed. (Oxford, 1956).

This is not the only example of reuse in the New Testament. In John 10.11-12 the words of Jesus are clearly a reinterpretation of Ezekiel.

> I am the good shepherd. The good shepherd lays down his life for the sheep. The hired hand, who is not the shepherd, and does not own the sheep, sees the wolf coming and leaves the sheep and runs away - and the wolf snatches them and scatters them.

This text clearly reuses Ezek 34, but the metaphor of the good shepherd has been changed with regard to one, important point. In John 10 the shepherd gives his life for the sheep. He not only defends them against wild beasts, but he also dies for their sake. The good shepherd in John 10 is both shepherd and sacrificial lamb.

We have met a similar combination of roles in the Old Testament metaphor of God as shepherd and beast. In order to punish his people the Lord acts both ways. Now comes the positive variation, the metaphor of Christ as shepherd and lamb. In order to save his people the Lord acts both ways.

With this in mind we can return to the vision of those who stand before the throne of the Lord in Rev 7.14. Now the metaphor of the servants of God in their white robes, washed in the blood of the Lamb, is full of meaning. The Lamb is the good shepherd, who has given his life for his flock like a lamb that has been sacrificed for "the iniquities of us all". In a few words full of metaphors we read the whole story of salvation.

## X. Intertextuality in the Bible

What we have been doing on this short journey from metaphor to metaphor in the Old and New Testament is only to be taken as a rough sketch. My intention was to give a first impression of the importance of following a metaphor in its use and reuse in order to get a fuller understanding of the possible meanings of the metaphor and its openness for reinterpretation in new contexts.

We have acted as detectives, so to speak. We have tried to track who has been fighting with whom. Or to put it more strongly: who has been wrestling with whom in order to overcome the precursor and put his own text in place of the older one. The version in Rev 7.14 intends to overcome what has been previously said about shepherds and lambs. The final words shall be the words about Christ and his sacrifice.

The Revelation to John is the last book in the Bible. In the final chapters of the book we are back at the beginning. The first things and the last things meet. The last chapters of the Revelation are in dialogue with the first chapters of Genesis: metaphor talks to metaphor and reinterprets what was said before. The seer sees a new heaven and a new earth, and an angel shows him the river of the water of life, flowing not from the centre of Eden, but from the throne of God and the Lamb, through the middle of the new Jerusalem. And

> Blessed are those who wash their robes, that they may have the right to the tree of life and that they may enter the city by the gates (Rev 22.14).

## XI. Father-Son Metaphors

The shepherd and the lamb are well-known metaphors in the Bible. Another pair of metaphors that play an important role is father-son. The relationship between those two is often used to express love and intimacy. But if we analyze a text like Matt 4, we realize that the father-son relationship also makes it possible to express other feelings. What I shall be doing for the rest of this article is to trace some strong precursors to the author of the temptation narrative in the New Testament, Matt 4.1-11. And I shall do so by tracing its root-metaphor.[19]

Part of my analysis of the temptation narrative is based on the book of Birger Gerhardsson: "The Testing of God's Son".[20] Gerhardsson reads Matthew's temptation narrative as haggadic midrash and shows that Matt 4.1-11 is based on Deut 6-8. The three decisive replies in the dialogue between Jesus and the devil are all from this part of Deuteronomy, where the Deuteronomists wish to explain that God allowed his "son" Israel to wander in the wilderness so that he might discipline and test him. In the New Testament God's son, Jesus, is tested as well.

The fact that Matthew actually quotes word for word from Deuteronomy makes it of course easy to argue that the New Testament text has Deut 8 as part of its intertextuality. It is much more difficult when we try to claim that a theme or a metaphor is reused in a younger text. It may therefore be a good starting point for intertextual studies to begin with a text that quotes another text.

The temptation narrative in Matthew has the wilderness as its setting. The same setting is known from the traditions about the wilderness

---

[19] Cf. Kirsten Nielsen, *Satan - den fortabte søn?* (Satan - the Lost Son?); cf. n.1.
[20] Birger Gerhardsson, *The Testing of God's Son (Matt 4:1-11 & Par)* (Lund, 1966).

wandering in the Old Testament, and it is obvious that the author of Matt 4 actually wrestles with these traditions. He is not wrestling with all of these traditions but with those known especially from Deut 6-8, where the wilderness is regarded as the place where the elected people were humbled and tested for forty years by hunger, just like Jesus was humbled and tested in the wilderness after forty days of hunger.

> And you shall remember all the way which the Lord your God has led you these forty years in the wilderness, that he might humble you, testing you to know what was in your heart, whether you would keep his commandments, or not (Deut 8.2).

The elected people is in this tradition described as Son of God, which goes well with the tradition that Jesus was named Son of God after the baptism in Jordan and just before the temptation. Let me quote again from Deut 8:

> Know then in your heart that, as a man disciplines his son, the Lord your God disciplines you (Deut 8.5).

The main idea of the testing of Jesus is to test whether he trusts his father to take care of him just as God cared for his "son" Israel, when he was hungry in the wilderness. When Jesus answers Satan, he quotes directly from Deut 8.3:

> One does not live by bread alone, but by every word that comes from the mouth of the Lord.

Jesus behaves the way the elected people should have behaved then, but they demanded for better food instead.

An analysis of the two following temptations will lead us back to the same chapters in Deuteronomy and make it clear that the author is like the householder "which bringeth forth out of his treasure things new and old". And it will make clear as well that the key term in the temptation narrative is the term "Son of God". Birger Gerhardsson has shown how this term was used about the people in Deuteronomy. Yahweh is there compared with a father who disciplines his son, Deut 8.5, and paternal love is given as the reason why Yahweh chose this particular people to be his own possession, Deut 7.6.

Gerhardsson's analysis is convincing, but he has overlooked the fact that the temptation narrative is wrestling with yet another strong precursor. We may ask the question: Why is it exactly Satan who is testing Jesus? God himself might have done so as he did when his people were wandering in the wilderness. Or as God did when he tested Abraham in Gen 22. In Matt 4.1 we are told that Jesus was led up by the Spirit into the wilderness to be tempted by the Devil. This means that God is the initiator of the temptation, but God is not the agent. The agent is Satan.

If the term Son of God is the main term we may see a connection to yet another text in the Old Testament where a Son of God is active, i.e. the book of Job. Satan is one of the Sons of God (Job 1.6). Job is the favourite of God, a blameless and righteous man. He too is tested and proves faithful. And he is tested by the agent of God, Satan.[21]

If the story about Job too is a strong precursor we might supplement Gerhardsson's analysis with the following statement: the key term of the temptation narrative in the New Testament is actually the term "Son of God", but it is not pure coincidence that the one who is tempting the Son of God is himself considered a Son of God in the Old Testament. What is at stake is a wrestling between two Sons of God and the main test concerns the question: Which one of us is really the Son of God, or in more Biblical terms: Which one of us is the favourite Son of the father? This is why Satan formulates his temptation by repeating: If *you* are the Son of God.

And Jesus answers as the favourite son must answer to this kind of testing that he shall live by the words of God, that he shall not tempt God, and that he shall only worship God. Remembering the whole Old Testament tradition about the wilderness we know that being the favourite son does not only mean to be protected, but to be disciplined and tested by the father in order that he should know what is in the heart of his chosen son. Now the New Testament tells us that neither Israel, nor Satan is the favourite Son of God, but Jesus.

I shall not go into further details, but I hope that it has been enough to show that it is worth while asking Harold Bloom's question: "Who is wrestling with whom?" within Biblical texts instead of just using the term intertextuality and leaving it open as to whether we are looking for what was the intertextuality in which the text was once written and reused, or whether we as critics regard ourselves as producers of texts who can weave whatever kind of texture *we* like. To be a responsible reader implies a respect for the intertextuality that was intended and clearly signaled be the author, when he wrestled with his strong precursors and tried to rewrite their texts.

---

[21] See Kirsten Nielsen, "Intertextuality and Biblical Scholarship", 89-95.

CHAPTER NINE

DIE WEISHEIT IN MENSCHLICHER GESTALT

*Weisheitstheologie im Johannesprolog
als Paradigma einer Biblischen Theologie*

Hans Weder, Zürich

"Das Neue Testament an sich ist unverständlich, das Alte Testament an sich ist missverständlich".[1] Mit diesem seinerseits missverständlichen Satz untermauert Hartmut Gese die Notwendigkeit einer Biblischen Theologie. Unter Biblischer Theologie ist eine Theologie zu verstehen, die sich an der ganzen Heiligen Schrift Alten und Neuen Testaments orientiert.[2] Der Vorstoss zu einer solchen Theologie ist im Grunde kein historisches, sondern ein systematisch-theologisches, genauer: ein hermeneutisches Unternehmen. Es läge deshalb nahe, das Thema der Biblischen Theologie systematisch-theologisch anzugehen. Dies wird im folgenden nicht geschehen. Vielmehr wird versucht, die Thematik anhand eines Paradigmas zu klären. Dass dieses Paradigma ein neutestamentlicher Text ist, ist alles andere als Zufall. Denn gäbe es das Neue Testament nicht, gäbe es das Problem der Biblischen Theologie nicht. Erst das Neue Testament hält, weil es das Alte Testament in charakteristischer Weise rezipiert, die christliche Theologie dazu an, sich darüber klar zu werden, welche theologische Bedeutung sie dem Alten Testament zuschreiben will. Dieser Sachverhalt ist seinerseits schon ein grundlegender Hinweis dazu, wie eine Biblische Theologie inhaltlich zu entwerfen sei.

Gestellt wird das Problem durch ein historisches Phänomen, die Rezeption der hebräischen Bibel im urchristlichen Schrifttum, das Problem selbst ist ein systematisch-hermeneutisches, nämlich die Frage, was Altes angesichts des Neuen, des eschatologisch Neuen, für ein Gewicht haben könne. Deshalb ist es wohl sinnvoll, einen historischen

---

[1] Gese, "Erwägungen", 436. Darstellung und kritische Stellungnahme zur Position von Gese bei Oeming, *Gesamtbiblische Theologien*, 104-119.
[2] Vgl. Reventlow, *Hauptprobleme*, 138.

Text als Paradigma zu verwenden, um über das hermeneutische Problem einer Biblischen Theologie nachzudenken.

Der Johannesprolog, so lautet der weitgehende Konsens der neueren Exegese, ist religionsgeschichtlich gesehen im Rahmen der frühjüdischen Weisheitstheologie zu verstehen. Der missverständliche Satz von Gese erhält in dem Punkt recht, dass die Weisheitstheologie, ein zentrales Anliegen israelitischer und frühjüdischer Religion, im Johannesprolog herangezogen wird, um den Christus zu deuten. Er ist ein Anwendungsfall der neutestamentlichen Rezeption alttestamentlicher Theologie. Deshalb soll er im folgenden als Paradigma einer Biblischen Theologie dienen. Dieses Paradigma kann er freilich nur sein, wenn dieser Text nicht nur historisch beschrieben, sondern theologisch wahrgenommen wird. Bevor das Paradigma vorgeführt werden kann, sind einige charakteristische Momente des modernen Begriffs Biblischer Theologie zu nennen.

## I. Konturen der Biblischen Theologie

Gegenwärtig lassen sich drei Ansätze Biblischer Theologie unterscheiden.[3] Alle drei Ansätze enthalten einerseits wichtige Einsichten zur sachgemässen Durchführung der Biblischen Theologie, alle drei sind anderseits mit schwerwiegenden Aporien behaftet. Wir halten uns in einer knappen Skizze sowohl die Einsichten als auch die Aporien vor Augen. Die Beobachtungen werden es uns erlauben, gleichsam Minimalpostulate zu formulieren, die eine Biblische Theologie auf jeden Fall erfüllen muss. Mit einer dergestalt präzisierten Fragestellung werden wir uns hernach an die Bearbeitung des Paradigmas machen, um in einem dritten Teil den Ertrag für die Biblische Theologie zu formulieren.

Ein erster Ansatz[4] - er kann mit dem Stichwort "traditionsgeschichtlich" bezeichnet werden und hat in Hartmut Gese einen prominenten Vertreter gefunden - geht davon aus, dass der Weg vom Alten Testament ins Neue einen kontinuierlichen Traditionsprozess[5] darstellt: "das Neue Testament bildet den Abschluss eines Traditionsprozesses, der wesentlich eine Einheit, ein Kontinuum ist".[6] Wichtig an diesem Ansatz ist die Einsicht, dass die Texte des Neuen Testaments im Horizont ihres

---

[3] Im Anschluss an Reventlow, *Hauptprobleme*, 141-142.
[4] Zum Folgenden Reventlow, *Hauptprobleme*, 142-147.
[5] Sofern das heilsgeschichtliche Modell (vertreten durch den Pannenberg-Kreis und andere) einer vernünftigen Methodik folgt, kann es als eine Spielart des hier beschriebenen Ansatzes angesehen werden. Immerhin ist zu betonen, dass die geschichtsphilosophischen Probleme heilsgeschichtlicher Ansätze (trotz anderslautender Einschätzung von Oeming, *Gesamtbiblische Theologien*, 159) nach wie vor ungelöst sind.
[6] Gese, "Erwägungen", 420.

Werdegangs verstanden werden müssen. Sie stehen in einem Traditionsprozess, dessen Aufhellung für ihr Verständnis wichtig ist. Wichtig ist auch die Einsicht, dass der Traditionsprozess, der im Alten Testament beginnt, nach dem Selbstverständnis des Neuen Testaments in der Tat zu einem Abschluss kommt, sofern etwa Jesus Christus als die Erfüllung alttestamentlicher Verheissung verstanden wird.

Problematisch an diesem Ansatz ist die genauere ontologische Bestimmung des Traditionsprozesses selbst. Ist er darin ein Kontinuum, dass er organisch aus seinen Wurzeln im Alten Testament wächst, um in der Krone des Neuen Testaments seinen Abschluss zu finden? Wachstumsprozesse in der Natur verlaufen nach festgelegten genetischen Plänen. Soll das Neue Testament im selben Sinne das Ergebnis einer Traditionsgeschichte sein, wie der ausgewachsene Baum aus dem Schössling hervorgeht? Dies müsste zu einer traditionsgeschichtlichen Ableitung des Neuen Testaments führen und mithin zu einer Verflüchtigung des Novum als solchem. Das Neue Testament beruht auf einem Zufall, der sich jeder Herleitung aus dem Gegebenen entzieht. Wenn der Traditionsprozess im Neuen Testament seinen Abschluss findet, erhebt sich ferner die Frage, welchen Stellenwert das frühjüdische Schrifttum darin habe? Und es erhebt sich erst recht die Frage, wie bei diesem Ansatz der jüdische Umgang mit dem Alten Testament ernst genommen werden kann.

Ein zweiter Ansatz[7] ist dadurch zu charakterisieren, dass er einen Gedanken oder ein Phänomen als die systematische Mitte der ganzen Bibel zu erweisen sucht. So versucht etwa Peter Stuhlmacher zu zeigen, dass das Bekenntnis zur Auferweckung Jesu im Neuen Testament das israelitische Gottesbekenntnis im Alten Testament präzisiert.[8] Beide Testamente finden ihre systematische Einheit im Bekenntnis zu Gott, das deshalb dazu Anlass gibt, von dieser Mitte her eine Biblische Theologie zu entwerfen.[9] Wichtig an diesem Ansatz ist der Bezug beider Teile der Bibel auf dasselbe Thema der Wahrnehmung Gottes. Der Gottesgedanke schliesst notwendig den Gedanken der Selbigkeit dieses Gottes in sich.

---

[7] Zum Folgenden Reventlow, *Hauptprobleme*, 147-157.

[8] "Das christliche Auferweckungsbekenntnis ist eine christologische Präzisierung des in langer Traditionsarbeit ausgestalteten israelitischen Gottesbekenntnisses, und zwar im Blik auf Tod und Erscheinung Jesu" (Stuhlmacher, "Bekenntnis", 151). Hier erkennt man deutlich den auch von Reventlow namhaft gemachten Zusammenhang zum traditionsgeschichtlichen Ansatz Geses (Reventlow, *Hauptprobleme*, 147-148).

[9] Weil im Bekenntnis zur Auferweckung "israelitisches Gottesverständnis und Jesusgeschick fest aufeinander bezogen werden", ist die Theologie dazu verpflichtet, "die neutestamentlichen Glaubensgedanken aus eben dieser gegenseitigen Beziehung von israelitischem Gottesglauben und Jesusgeschick heraus nachzuvollziehen. Eine das urchristliche Auferweckungsbekenntnis in seinem historischen und theologischen Stellenwert systematisch ernstnehmende neutestamentliche Theologie muss also als eine zum Alten Testament hin offene Biblische Theologie des Neuen Testaments entworfen werden" (Stuhlmacher, "Bekenntnis", 151-152).

Altes und Neues Testament sind, wenn auch ganz erhebliche Brüche festzustellen sind, wenigstens darin verbunden, dass die Bekenntnisse zu Gott auf dieselbe Wahrheit Gottes ausgerichtet sind. Auch der Gedanke der Wahrheit impliziert ja, dass diese Wahrheit nicht aufgelöst wird in eine Pluralität von blossen Meinungen, sondern dass ihre Einheit mindestens als Postulat festgehalten wird. Eben diese Einheit Gottes oder der Wahrheit wird theologisch respektiert, wenn der Versuch unternommen wird, zu einem systematischen Zentrum des Alten und des Neuen Testaments vorzustossen.

Die Frage ist indessen, ob der Begriff der Mitte so beschränkt werden darf, wie dies bei diesem Ansatz der Fall ist. Erstreckt sich die Einheit Gottes oder der Wahrheit nur auf die Bibel? Auch der Gottesbegriff des Griechentums, vornehmlich der Stoa, muss doch nicht weniger auf jenes Zentrum bezogen werden als der Gott des Alten Testaments.[10] Gewiss kommt dem Alten Testament insofern eine Sonderstellung zu, als es durch Jesus und das Urchristentum in besonderer Weise rezipiert wurde. Gewiss kann man sagen, das Alte Testament komme im Bekenntnis zu Gott näher an die Wahrheit des christologisch gedachten Gottes heran. Aber daraus kann ein prinzipieller Ausschluss der nichtalttestamentlichen Gotteswahrnehmung nicht begründet werden. Problematisch ist an diesem Ansatz ferner, dass die Orientierung an einer systematischen Mitte der Bibel eine Neigung zur theoretischen Abstraktion hat. Von der Aussage, dass im Neuen Testament das alttestamentliche Bekenntnis zu Gott präzisiert worden sei, ist es nur ein kleiner Schritt bis zu dem Punkt, wo die Kontingenz des Seins Jesu Christi für das theologische Denken keine Rolle mehr spielt. Überdies erscheint es fraglich, die Christologie als blosse Präzisierung des alttestamentlichen Bekenntnisses zu Gott aufzufassen. Denn in einem solchen Konzept könnte die eschatologische Qualität des Christus verflüchtigt werden zu einem blossen Appendix alttestamentlicher Gotteswahrnehmung. Und wenn dies geschieht, wird die neutestamentliche Botschaft im Definitionsraum der (alttestamentlich gedachten) Mitte der Schrift aufgelöst; eine solche Biblische Theologie wäre dann eine alttestamentliche mit einem wirkungsgeschichtlichen Appendix. Wenn man sieht, wie die Interpretation des Gesetzes und der Gnade bei Paulus in weiten Kreisen der gegenwärtigen neutestamentlichen Wissenschaft aussieht, liegt der Gedanke der Auflösung des Evangeliums in den Definitionsraum des (jüdisch wahrgenommenen) Gesetzes jedenfalls nicht fern.

---

[10] Unverkennbar ist doch, dass das Urchristentum theologische Einsichten des hellenistischen Kulturraumes positiv rezipiert hat, was einerseits durch das hellenistische Judentum vermittelt war, andererseits in direktem Kontakt zur hellenistischen Welt geschah (als Beispiel sei 1 Kor 8.6 genannt; vgl. Conzelmann, *Korinther*, z.St.).

Der dritte Ansatz[11] ist charakterisiert durch den Bezug alt- und neutestamentlicher Botschaft hinsichtlich des Problems von (durch Gott geschaffener) Weltordnung (H. H. Schmid), beziehungsweise von Welterfahrung (U. Luck). Schöpfungsordnung oder Welterfahrung erweisen sich hier als Forum, auf das die Botschaft der gesamten Bibel bezogen wird. Wichtig an diesem Ansatz ist insbesondere die Einsicht, dass die Texte des Glaubens in eine Beziehung gesetzt werden zu elementaren Erfahrungsphänomenen, wenn sie eine Bedeutung haben sollen. Damit wird einem Dogmatismus entgegengesteuert, der nicht zuletzt im Unternehmen der Biblischen Theologie auf der Lauer liegt. Denn Biblische Theologie läuft Gefahr, dass sie die Aussagen beider Testamente in einer religiösen oder theologischen Theorie vereinigt, mit deren Hilfe über die Wirklichkeit dogmatistisch verfügt wird. Biblische Theologie kann zur biblizistischen verkommen, wenn sie nicht ständig der Evidenz der Erfahrung ausgesetzt wird. Man sollte den theologisch notwendigen Impuls des Erfahrungsbezugs nicht zu schnell mit dem Vorwurf natürlicher Theologie abweisen.[12]

Problematisch an diesem Ansatz ist die drohende Aufhebung besonderer, kontingenter, im Vordergrund der Welt zu machender Erfahrungen in die allgemeine Welterfahrung. So steht etwa die Einordnung Jesu in das Gerechtigkeitsthema in Gefahr, die Individualität und funktionale Unableitbarkeit Jesu aus dem Blick zu verlieren. Es kann geschehen, dass die Grundfragen die kreativen Impulse des Besonderen in sich verschlingen. Auf diese Weise entsteht ein nur scheinbarer Erfahrungsbezug Biblischer Theologie. Der Bezug auf allgemeine Erfahrung könnte die Tatsache aus dem Blick verlieren, dass auch die allgemeine Erfahrung in Wirklichkeit nur existiert als ein Konglomerat von mehr oder weniger vergleichbaren individuellen Erfahrungen. Während die Bibel Alten und Neuen Testaments prinzipiell auf das Erzählen angewiesen war, wenn sie die kontingenten Erfahrungen von Rettung und Verlassenheit oder das vielgestaltige Zukommen Gottes auf seine Geschöpfe vergegenwärtigen wollte, könnte die Einordnung des Besonderen in die Allgemeinheit der Welterfahrung oder -ordnung sich emanzipieren von der Sprachform der Erzählung und sich einer zeitinvarianten, theoretisch-definitorischen Sprache bedienen. Dann stünde die Biblische Theologie an der Schwelle einer denkerischen Ableitung der besonderen, kontingenten biblischen Botschaft, an einer Schwelle, die sie niemals überschreiten darf, will sie ihren Kontakt zur Bibel nicht verspielen.

---

[11] Zum Folgenden Reventlow, *Hauptprobleme*, 157-172.
[12] Vgl. Stuhlmacher, "Biblische Theologie", 59-60.

Die knappe Durchsicht dieser drei Ansätze führt zu Postulaten, die eine sachgemässe Biblische Theologie erfüllen muss. Diese sollen bei der im Hauptteil folgenden Betrachtung des Paradigmas richtungsweisend sein. (1) Biblische Theologie muss die historischen Texte, die ihr das systematische Problem aufgeben, in fundamentaltheologischer und hermeneutischer Ausrichtung auslegen. (2) Biblische Theologie muss den Werdegang vom Alten zum Neuen Testament als einen Zufall begreifen lernen, der ihr jede traditionsgeschichtliche Ableitung neutestamentlicher Theologie verbietet. Sie muss sich fundamental an der Kontingenz des Kommens Jesu Christi orientieren. (3) Eine Biblische Theologie muss die Tatsache respektieren, dass es eine frühjüdische und jüdische Interpretation der hebräischen Bibel gibt. (4) Eine Biblische Theologie kann das Neue Testament nicht als wirkungsgeschichtlichen Appendix des Alten betrachten. Sie hat deshalb besonders auf die Wechselwirkung zwischen Neuem und Altem Testament zu achten. (5) Eine Biblische Theologie, die an der Einheit der Wahrheit orientiert ist, darf sich nicht auf den Raum alttestamentlicher Religion beschränken, sondern sie muss die theologischen Impulse sowohl des hellenistischen und palästinensischen Frühjudentums als auch der hellenistischen Kultur rezipieren. (6) Eine Biblische Theologie muss gerade den Biblizismus vermeiden; sie ist deshalb fundamental an die Evidenz der Erfahrung zu binden. Der Bezug auf die Welterfahrung darf indessen die Kontingenz der Gotteserfahrung nicht antasten.

## II. Weisheit und Christus im Johannesprolog

Nachdem die gnostische Lokalisierung des Prologs falsifiziert worden ist[13] und als religionsgeschichtlicher Ort weder das Alte Testament[14],

---

[13] Dies gilt für Bultmanns Mandäerthese (Bultmann, *Johannes*, 5); nach Yamauchi ist erwiesen, dass der Mandäismus nicht vor dem 2.Jh. n.Chr. entstanden ist ("Jewish Gnosticism", 473). Die Hypothesen Rudolphs sind durch Quispel, Jacobsen und Green falsifiziert worden (a.a.O., 473-476). Zu der durch die Nag Hammadi-Texte evozierten Ableitung des Johannesevangeliums aus der Gnosis hält Koschorke zusammenfassend fest, dass erstens der Prolog häufig Gegenstand gnostischer Exegese gewesen und dass die Epistula Petri ad Philippum (NHC VIII/2) ein weiterer Beweis gnostischer Johannesrezeption ist (Koschorke, "Paraphrase", 388-389). Im Blick auf die Protennoia kommt Yamauchi (gegen die Thesen des Berliner Arbeitskreises) zum Schluss, dass die Annahme, die Protennoia habe christliches Material wie den Prolog bearbeitet, mehr Plausibilität für sich hat (Yamauchi, "Jewish Gnosticism", 484). Janssens führt die Gemeinsamkeiten von Joh und Protennoia auf einen gemeinsamen religionsgeschichtlichen Hintergrund zurück, obwohl sie feststellt, dass Ueberschneidungen dort am grössten sind, wo eventuell eine sekundäre Christianisierung anzunehmen ist (Janssens, "Protennoia", 242-243). Aehnlich entscheidet sich auch Hofrichter, der im hellenistischen Judentum den Urheber von (ungnostischem) Prolog und Gnosis sieht (Hofrichter, "Gnosis", 19-20).
[14] Eindrücklich vertritt Gese die Ansicht, der Prolog sei aus dem Gesamt der alttestamentlichen Tradition erwachsen und im Rahmen einer biblischen Theologie zu interpretieren. "Der Prolog knüpft nicht an irgendwelche Einzelheiten des Alten Testaments an, sondern steht mit der alttestamentlichen Tradition

noch das rabbinische Judentum,[15] noch die griechische Philosophie[16] in Frage kommt, geht die grosse Mehrheit der Arbeiten im zwanzigsten Jahrhundert religionsgeschichtlich von der hellenistisch-jüdischen Weisheit aus.[17] Diese Einordnung ist insofern gerechtfertigt, als sich in der Sophia-Theologie die meisten Parallelen zum johanneischen Prolog finden.[18] Im Vordergrund stehen Texte wie Spr 8 (besonders deutlich in der Septuaginta-Uebersetzung); Sir 24; Hiob 28; Weish 7.22-8.1; Bar 3.9-4.4; äthHen 42; Weish 18, Texte, in denen sich sehr ähnliche Aussagen finden wie im Johannesprolog.

Allerdings stehen auch dieser religionsgeschichtlichen Einordnung gewisse Schwierigkeiten entgegen. Zunächst ist festzuhalten, dass der λόγος-Begriff in den genannten Texten fehlt (mit der einzigen Ausnahme von Weish 18.15). Sie können also nicht erklären, wieso der Prolog vom λόγος und nicht von der σοφία spricht. In diesem Zusammenhang wird gewöhnlich auf Philo verwiesen, in dessen Schriften der Logos in der Tat eine grosse Rolle spielt. Doch Philos λόγος-Begriff steht dem hellenistisch-philosophischen Logosbegriff näher als dem Prolog. In den Weisheitstexten findet sich ferner keine Parallele zur johanneischen Inkarnationsaussage (1.14a). Am nächsten kommt die Aussage von Sir 24.23, wo die Weisheit mit dem Gesetz identifiziert wird. Allerdings ist gerade hier nicht von einer Fleischwerdung, sondern höchstens von einer Gesetzwerdung der Weisheit die Rede. Diese zwei Hauptdifferenzen des Prologs zur Weisheitstheologie machen klar, dass die Sophia-Theologie zwar eine wichtige Voraussetzung des Prologs ist, der Prolog selbst aber nur verständlich wird, wenn wir mit erheblichen Innovationen im Urchristentum rechnen. Gerade an diesem entscheidenden Punkt versagt eine traditionsgeschichtlich verfahrende Biblische Theologie.

Es wäre falsch, den Johannesprolog als ein Beispiel weisheitlicher Theologie zu betrachten und ihn in dieses theologische Unternehmen einzuordnen. Ihren Ausgangspunkt nimmt die johanneische Gemeinde nicht bei einer Theologie der Weisheit, sondern sie greift auf diese

---

selbst in Verbindung, die Gesamtkonzeption des Prologs ist aus dieser Tradition erwachsen" (Gese, "Johannesprolog", 201). Gese klammert ausdrücklich nachkanonische Schriften aus.

[15] So z.B. Bietenhard, "Logos-Theologie", 613-616; Hayward, "Holy Name", 28-31.
[16] Vgl. Schnackenburg, *Johannesevangelium* I, 258 (der eine Arbeit nennt, Anm. 3). Recht weit in der platonisch-hellenistischen Deutung geht Dodd (dazu Theobald, *Fleischwerdung*, 128-132), obwohl auch er nicht die griechische Philosophie als den geistigen Horizont des Hymnus annehmen will. Gegen eine monokausale Erklärung des Prologs nimmt Schnelle zu Recht Stellung und erinnert an Heraklit und die Stoa (Schnelle, *Antidoketische Christologie*, 234).
[17] Becker formuliert als Konsens, dass "sich Weltbild, Motivik und Sprache des Liedes der weitverzweigten jüdisch-hellenistischen Weisheitsspekulation verdanken" (Becker, *Johannes* I, 71). Vgl. im übrigen Haenchen, *Johannesevangelium*, 151-154; Schnackenburg, *Johannesevangelium* I, 205-207; Theobald, *Anfang*, 98-109; Schmithals, "Prolog", 34-35; Schoonenberg, "Sapiential reading", passim.
[18] Eine instruktive Zusammenstellung bietet z.B. Theobald, *Anfang*, 104-109; zu vergleichen sind auch die neueren Kommentare zur Stelle.

Theologie zurück, um ihr eigenes theologisches Problem zu bearbeiten. Ihr theologisches Problem ist ein christologisches, nämlich die Aufgabe, die δόξα des Menschen Jesus von Nazareth zum Ausdruck zu bringen. Der Höhepunkt des Hymnus, die Aussage von der Fleischwerdung des Logos, macht dies unverkennbar deutlich. Der Hymnus antwortet nicht auf die Frage, wie der Logos in die Welt gekommen ist, sondern auf die Frage, welches Gewicht den Erfahrungen von Gnade und Wahrheit[19] beizumessen ist, die mit Jesus Christus in der johanneischen Gemeinde zu machen waren. Um diesen Erfahrungen gerecht zu werden, greift die Gemeinde auf die Weisheitstheologie zurück. Sie erkennt im Menschen Jesus, der im Vordergrund der Welt existierte, die Weisheit wieder, die schon immer bei Gott existiert hat.

Die Weisheit, die unverkennbar hinter dem Logosbegriff des Prologs steht, erbringt also eine bestimmte Interpretationsleistung für die johanneische Christologie. Die Weisheit hat eine hermeneutische Funktion für die Christologie der Gemeinde. Und die Christologie der Gemeinde hat wiederum eine hermeneutische Funktion für die Erfahrungen, die mit Jesus Christus gemacht wurden. Indem die Christologie Jesus die δόξα des Einziggeborenen zuschreibt, macht sie auf die Tiefendimension der Erfahrung mit Jesus aufmerksam. Und indem die Weisheitstheologie den Christus als unvordenkliche[20] Zuwendung Gottes zur Welt verstehen lehrt, interpretiert sie die Doxa des Christus. Aus der Tatsache, dass die Weisheit hier eine Deutungsinstanz ist, darf indessen nicht auf ein einliniges Verhältnis von Weisheit und Jesus Christus geschlossen werden. Denn darin, dass die Weisheit den Christus deutet, wird sie ihrerseits neu gedeutet. Auf diese Wechselwirkung zwischen Weisheit und Christus werden wir besonders zu achten haben, wenn wir den vorliegenden Text als Paradigma Biblischer Theologie verstehen (vgl. das vierte Postulat).

Die Weisheit erlaubt der johanneischen Gemeinde, den Christus verstehen zu lernen (1) in seinem Verhältnis zu Gott (V.1-2), (2) in seinem Verhältnis zur Schöpfung (V.3-5) und (3) in seinem Verhältnis zu den Menschen (V.9-12). Es ist kein Zufall, dass der weisheitliche Hintergrund bei diesen Teilen des Prologs besonders deutlich ist, während er nachher merklich zurücktritt. Denn die Aussage von der Inkarnation[21] und der Erfahrung von Gnade benennen eben jenes Geschehen, zu dessen Deutung die Weisheit herangezogen wurde.

---

[19] Die Inkarnationsaussage und die Aussage über die Doxa des Einziggeborenen von V.14 werden in V.16 begründet mit der Erfahrung, von ihm Gnade und Wahrheit empfangen zu haben.
[20] Zum Begriff der Unvordenklichkeit vgl. Weder, "Mythos", 404-411.
[21] Für sie gibt es keine Analogie in der weisheitlichen Theologie.

## 1. Christus und Gott

Das Verhältnis von Christus zu Gott wird in dreifacher Hinsicht beschrieben. Im ersten Satzteil - er hat den Logos als Subjekt - wird die Aufmerksamkeit auf die ἀρχή, den unvordenklichen Anfang gelenkt.[22] Während in der Schöpfungstheologie vom Anfang nur gesprochen wird, um vom schöpferischen Tun Gottes zu sprechen, geht es dem Prolog um ein Sein vor aller Schöpfung. Um dieses Sein auszulegen, greift der Prolog auf weisheitliche Theologie zurück. Denn von der Weisheit wird gesagt, dass es sie vor allem Geschaffenen gab. Sie wird indes ausdrücklich als das erste Geschöpf Gottes bezeichnet.[23] Nicht so der Logos. Er ist nicht geschaffen worden, er ist seit unvordenklicher Zeit. In diesem Punkt geht der Prolog eindeutig über die Vorgaben der Weisheitstheologie hinaus.

Daraus folgt dann, dass es Gott nie ohne den Logos gab. Der Logos gehört unvordenklich zu Gott. Zwar ist auch die Weisheit die Personifikation des Zugehens Gottes auf die Welt, die Personifikation des redenden Gottes. Aber im Unterschied zur Weisheit, die Gottes erstes Geschöpf ist, ist Gott nicht mehr anders denkbar denn als der Redende. Und im Unterschied zur späteren Gnosis, wonach der Logos aus der σιγή, dem Schweigen, hervorgeht,[24] gibt es dieses Schweigen im Prolog nicht. Wenn Gottes Wort anfänglich aus dem Schweigen kommt, kann es jederzeit ins Schweigen zurückfallen. Im Prolog dagegen gehört Gottes Wort wesenhaft zu ihm.

Schon bei der Weisheit war zu beobachten, dass ihr anfängliches Sein auf ihre Massgeblichkeit verweist; als Erstling vor allem Geschaffenen ist sie massgeblicher als dies alles. Wenn in der rabbinischen Theologie von sieben Dingen[25] die Rede ist, die vor der Welt geschaffen wurden, so bedeutet es auch dort ihre Massgeblichkeit. Diese Massgeblichkeit wird beim Logos bis zum äussersten gesteigert, ist er doch nicht einmal als Erstgeschaffener, sondern überhaupt nicht zum Geschaffenen zu zählen.

---

[22] Zu betonen ist, dass der Logos "immer" schon war, nicht bloss seine Priorität vor dem Geschaffenen. Zur notwendigen Kritik am linearen Zeitverständnis, in dessen Rahmen das "im Anfang" gar nicht verständlich wäre, vgl. Ibuki, "Marginalien", 93-97. Ibuki weist zu Recht auf den Zusammenhang zwischen "Protologie und Eschatologie" hin: Die joh Theologie geht davon aus, dass in der endzeitlichen *Doxa* Jesu seine "anfängliche" Würde zum Ausdruck kommt.
[23] So in Spr 8.22 (MT: als 're'schijt', als erstes Erzeugnis seiner Wege; LXX: als ἀρχή, als Anfang seiner Wege zu seinen Werken); ähnlich Sir 24.3 ("hervorgegangen aus dem Munde des Höchsten").
[24] Zum Emanationsgedanken, der in der Gnosis eine überragende Rolle spielte, vgl. u.a. die Pistis Sophia, wo die Sophia als Emanation der Pistis vorgestellt wird, NHC II/ 5,145,24-146,11 (Rudolph, *Gnosis*, 81-82). Von der Protennoia heisst es, sie sei der Ruf, der seit Anbeginn im Schweigen existierte, vgl. NHC XIII 35,32-35 (Schenke, *Protennoia*, 26-27).
[25] Die "Tora, die Busse, der Gan Eden, der Gehinnom, der Thron der Herrlichkeit, das Heiligtum und der Name des Messias" (nicht der Messias selbst!), Pes 54a Bar (Bill II, 353).

Der zweite Satzteil bestimmt das Verhältnis des Logos zu Gott. Der Logos existiert in der Relation auf Gott hin. Im Uranfang strebt er so wenig von Gott weg wie im Eschaton. Die Einheitsaussagen von Joh 10.30; 17.10 bilden das eschatologische Gegenstück und die erkenntnismässige Grundlage zur protologischen Aussage der Einheit. Von der Weisheit heisst es in ähnlicher Weise, sie sei bei Gott gewesen, wobei die Richtung auf Gott hin nicht thematisiert wird.[26] Am nächsten kommt wohl Spr 8.30 (MT): "da war ich als Liebling ihm zur Seite ... und spielte vor ihm allezeit".[27] Hier könnte am ehesten an eine Aktivität der Weisheit gedacht sein, die auf Gott hin ausgerichtet ist. Der Aspekt der Relation zu Gott ist gegenüber der Weisheit, wo ihr Sein bei Gott im Vordergrund steht, hervorgehoben. Der Logos war immer schon auf Gott hin ausgerichtet; seine Relation zu Gott ist die Lebensbeziehung schlechthin.[28] Es ist dieselbe Lebensbeziehung, die - auf der Ebene der Menschen als "glauben" ($\pi\iota\sigma\tau\epsilon\acute{u}\epsilon\iota\nu$) präzisiert - die Menschen im Johannesevangelium zum Christus (3.15-16) und insofern zu Gott (5.14) haben, und die ihre Lebendigkeit ($\zeta\omega\acute{\eta}$) ausmacht.

Der dritte Satzteil bestimmt das Wesen des Logos in seinem Verhältnis zu Gott selbst. Subjekt ist der Logos, Prädikatsnomen ist das (artikellose) $\vartheta\epsilon\acute{o}\varsigma$. Wären Gott und der Logos gleichgesetzt, so müsste hier ein Identitätsurteil mit Artikel vor dem Prädikatsnomen vorliegen. Der vorliegende Satz ist ein Qualitätsurteil[29] und bedeutet, dass der Logos zwar nicht mit Gott identisch aber dennoch von demselben Wesen wie Gott ist. Dass dem Logos dasselbe Wesen wie Gott zugeschrieben wird, bedeutet wiederum eine Steigerung gegenüber der Weisheitstheologie. Von der Weisheit wird eine solche Qualität nicht ausgesagt.[30] Einige Aussagen von Philo kommen freilich in die Nähe, die den Logos als

---

[26] Vgl. Spr 8.27(LXX): "ich war bei ihm" ($\sigma\upsilon\mu\pi\acute{\alpha}\rho\epsilon\iota\mu\iota$ heisst "zusammen gegenwärtig sein", vgl. Liddell/Scott, Lexicon, 1681); 8.30(LXX): "ich war bei ihm" ($\mathring{\eta}\mu\eta\nu\ \pi\alpha\rho'\ \alpha\mathring{\upsilon}\tau\mathring{\omega}$); Weish 9.9 ("und mit dir ist die Weisheit, die deine Werke kennt, und die zugegen war, als du die Welt schufst"). Diese Differenz zwischen Logos und Weisheit wird verwischt, wenn man - etwa mit Schnackenburg, *Johannesevangelium* I, 210 - das $\pi\rho\acute{o}\varsigma$ mit dem $\pi\alpha\rho\acute{\alpha}$ gleichsetzt.

[27] Die Septuaginta gibt das hebräische 'amwn' (Pfleglung, Liebling, etwas, das gestützt, aufgezogen, getragen wird) mit $\acute{\alpha}\rho\mu\acute{o}\zeta o\upsilon\sigma\alpha$ (am ehesten: die Zusammenfügende, die die Teile aufeinander Passende) wieder. Damit wird der Akzent auf die Schöpfungsmittlerschaft gelegt.

[28] Die Präposition $\pi\rho\acute{o}\varsigma$ drückt nach Miller, "Logos", 75-76, eine "special, personal relation" zwischen Logos und Gott aus. Wichtig ist der Hinweis Millers auf 1.18, wo diese Relation mit "der an die Brust des Vaters ist" wiederholt wird.

[29] Dies bestreitet Miller, "Logos", 68-69.77, obwohl er dennoch einen Unterschied machen will zum Identitätsurteil: "It is true that the Logos was God, but it is not true that God was the Logos" (72). Genau dies besagt das Qualitätsurteil (Gott von Art).

[30] Reim, *Studien*, 158-160, will die Aussagen von Joh 1.1,18; 20.28 darauf zurückführen, dass die vorjoh Gemeinde den schon vorchristlich messianisch verstandenen Vers Ps 45.7 missverstanden habe und dass sie im Konflikt mit dem Judentum auf dem Gottesprädikat Jesu bestanden habe. Die erste These ist wenig plausibel, die zweite irreführend, da sie suggeriert, die Christologie sei aus dem Konflikt zum Judentum statt aus der Würdigung Christi hervorgegangen.

δεύτερος θεός bezeichnen.³¹ Allerdings wird gerade bei Philo das Wesen des Logos immer wieder vom Wesen Gottes prinzipiell unterschieden. Ferner darf man beim Prolog nie aus den Augen verlieren, dass hier nicht ein metaphysisches Zwischenwesen zwischen Gott und der Welt das Thema ist, sondern kein anderer als der Fleischgewordene, Jesus von Nazareth (1.14).³² Der Logoshymnus geht an die äusserste Grenze dessen, was von einem Wesen neben Gott (im Horizont des strengen jüdischen Monotheismus) noch sagbar ist. Die Wahrnehmung Gottes im Fleischgewordenen erreichte in der Zuschreibung der Wesensgleichheit von Logos und Gott ihren Höhepunkt. Sie nahm beim Handeln Jesu an der Stelle Gottes ihren Ursprung und führte - dank den Ostererfahrungen der Jünger - über Bekenntnisse wie Röm 1.3-4 zur Jungfrauengeburt und zu Hymnen wie Kol 1.1-15; 1 Tim 3.16 und Phil 2.6-11. In Joh 1.1 erreichte die christologische Reflexion, deren Anliegen es war, das Gewicht Jesu von Nazareth wahrzunehmen, ihr konsequentes Ende und ihren Gipfel.³³

Zu überlegen bleibt, wie es zum Logos-Begriff dieses Hymnus gekommen ist. Festzuhalten ist, dass Titel wie Menschensohn und Messias sich in dem Moment nicht eigneten, wo ein Rückgriff auf das Unvordenkliche, auf die Zeit vor aller Schöpfung getan wurde.³⁴ Allerdings hätte es in diesem Falle nahegelegen, Christus mit der Weisheit zu identifizieren.³⁵ Die Aussagen des Hymnus zeigen denn auch, dass der Logos ganz von der Weisheit her in den Blick genommen ist. Uebergänge von der Weisheit zum Logos lassen sich nur spärlich feststellen. Zu nennen ist einerseits Philo, bei dem Logos und Sophia in gleichem Sinne vorkommen.³⁶ Der Logos-Begriff Philos ist aber sehr weit vom Johannesprolog entfernt, da er im Grunde zur (theoretischen)

---

³¹ Philo, Leg All II.86 (ein Zweiter nach Gott); Leg All III.175 (über alle Dinge erhaben); Somn I.229-230 (der älteste Logos Gottes ist insofern θεός [ohne Artikel], als er nicht im eigentlichen Sinne Gott ist; vgl. Haenchen, *Johannesevangelium*, 116).
³² Will man Analogien zur Aussage des Prologs finden, so kommen neutestamentliche Texte am nächsten: Joh 20.28 (wo Thomas zum Auferstandenen sagt: "Mein Herr und mein Gott") und Phil 2.6 (ἐν μορφῇ θεοῦ ὑπάρχων und εἶναι ἴσα θεῷ).
³³ "Damit erst ist das deutliche Streben, den Anfang der Heilsgeschichte immer früher und schliesslich alles umfassend anzusetzen, zu sein endgültiges Ziel gekommen" (Haenchen, *Johannesevangelium*, 136). Man könnte sich höchstens fragen, ob im Zusammenhang so konsequent gedachter Universalität des Logos noch von "Heilsgeschichte" im alttestamentlichen Sinne gesprochen werden sollte.
³⁴ Mit Haenchen, *Johannesevangelium*, 116-117.
³⁵ Dies umso mehr, als schon in der synoptischen Christologie eine solche Identifikation sich angedeutet hat, vgl. Lk 7.35 par Mt 11.19; Lk 11.49-51; 13.34-35; Polag, *Christologie*, 137-138 (zurückhaltend).
³⁶ Philo, Rer div her 126 u.w., vgl. Colpe, "Logoslehre", 96-97. Mack, *Logos*, 141-154 zeigt, dass der Logos im Blick auf das Verhältnis zu Gott, zur Welt und zu den Menschen die gleiche Position wie die Weisheit einnimmt. "Im religiösen philosophischen System Philos hat also der Logos die Funktion der nahen Weisheit übernommen" (a.a.O., 153). Zu berücksichtigen ist freilich, dass der Logos eine Vielzahl von Namen (und damit von Funktionen) hat: Logos, Eikon, Anthropos, Nous, Logismos, Sophia, Pneuma, Phronesis, Kosmos noetos (Colpe, a.a.O., 97), weswegen er bei Philo ausdrücklich der "vielnamige" heisst (Conf ling 146; vgl. Hofrichter, *Anfang*, 337-338).

Vermittlung zwischen Gott und Welt dient. Mit Hilfe des Logos bewältigt Philo das (platonische) Problem des Uebergangs vom geistigen Gott zur materiellen Welt,[37] ein Gedanke, der dem Johannesprolog völlig fern liegt.[38] Zu nennen ist anderseits Weish 18, wo der Logos als soteriologische Gestalt auftritt.[39] Wohl unter ägyptischem Einfluss[40] ist hier von einem Logos die Rede, der gleichsam die Personifikation des göttlichen Eingriffs darstellt. Er springt vom Himmel, um helfend einzugreifen, mit seiner Gestalt Himmel und Erde verbindend. Rettung bringt er allerdings so, dass er den Tod um sich verbreitet (im Gegensatz zum johanneischen Christus, der nichts als Gnade und Wahrheit, das Leben austeilt). Vielleicht ist auch die alttestamentliche Rede vom Wort Gottes zu den Faktoren zu zählen, die eine Uebernahme des Logos-Begriffs durch Johannes erleichterten.[41] Allerdings lässt sich vom Wort Gottes nicht dieselbe Personalisierung feststellen, wie sie hier vorliegt.[42]

Grundsätzlich wird man also festhalten müssen, dass die religionsgeschichtlichen Gegebenheiten keine hinreichende Begründung für die Einführung des Logos-Begriffs im Prolog darstellen.

Eine hinreichende Begründung lässt sich meines Erachtens nur unter der Voraussetzung geben, dass der johanneischen Gemeinde eine theologische Innovation zugetraut wird. Sie stand ja gar nicht vor der Aufgabe, die Weisheits- oder Wort-Gottes-Theologie weiterzuentwickeln. Vielmehr ging es ihr elementar darum, ihren eigenen Glauben an Jesus Christus zu Ende zu denken. Der Rückgriff auf den Logos ist von allem Anfang an geleitet vom Menschgewordenen; abgesehen von der Menschwerdung ist der Logos kein Thema im Johannesevangelium. Der Rückgriff auf weisheitliche Theologie dient dazu, dem Christus das ihm zukommende Gewicht beizumessen. Er dient der Christologie.

---

[37] "Er (sc. der Logos) ist der allgemeinste Vermittler zwischen Gott und der Welt, die Weisheit und Vernunft Gottes, die Idee, welche alle Ideen, die Kraft, welche alle Kräfte umfasst, ..." (Colpe, "Logoslehre", 91).
[38] Zu weiteren Differenzen vgl. Hofrichter, *Anfang*, 337-347; Haenchen, *Johannesevangelium*, 152-153.
[39] "Denn als tiefes Schweigen alles umfasste und die Nacht in dem ihr eigenen Lauf bis zur Mitte fortgerückt war, da sprang dein allmächtiges Wort (ὁ παντοδύναμός σου λόγος) vom Himmel herab vom Königsthron aus wie ein grimmiger Krieger mitten hinein in das dem Verderben geweihte Land. Als scharfes Schwert trug er deinen unerbittlichen (ἀνυπόκριτον .. wörtlich: "ungeheuchelten") Befehl, und dastehend erfüllte er alles mit Tod; und er berührte (mit dem Haupt) zwar den Himmel, schritt aber auf der Erde einher" (Weish 18.14-16).
[40] Aegyptischen Einfluss stellt Mack schon für die älteren Wort-Gottes-Vorstellungen in Israel (Jes 45.23; 55.11; Ps 32(33).6; 106 (107).20 usw.) fest (Mack, *Logos*, 97-102). Auch der ägyptische Gott Thot (bei den Griechen als Hermes-Logos) hat ganz ähnliche kämpferische Seiten (vgl. Mack, a.a.O., 102-106).
[41] Besonders Jes 55.8-11 zeigt, dass das Wort Gottes als geschichtsbestimmende Macht betrachtet wird (mit Blank, *Johannes* 1a, 77).
[42] Weisheit, Wort Gottes und Anfang erscheinen unmittelbar beieinander im Targum Neophyti zu Gen 1.1 ("Vom Anfang her mit Weisheit brachte hervor [das Wort] Jahwes ..."), wobei die Aussagerichtung freilich anders als im Prolog ist (Schwarz, "Vergleich", 136-137). Schwarz rückt allerdings das Targum zu nahe an Joh 1.1 heran. Für die Ergänzung des 'memra' gibt es hingegen gute Gründe, insbesondere dass das Wort eine wichtige Rolle im Schöpfungsvorgang spielt, vgl. dasselbe Targum zu Gen 2.2a.

In diesem Zusammenhang lässt sich eine Reihe von Gründen angeben, die den Wechsel von der Weisheit zum Logos plausibel erscheinen lassen. (1) Dies mag - um mit dem äusserlichsten Grund zu beginnen - damit zusammenhängen, dass ein feminines Substantiv sich schlechter für die christologische Identifikation Jesu eignete.[43] (2) Vom Menschgewordenen her ist eine personalisierte Gestalt zu erwarten. Der Personalität Jesu entspricht der Rückgriff auf den hypostasierten Logos. (3) Der Logos-Begriff legte sich ferner aus dem Grund nahe, weil der Menschgewordene in eminenter Weise als Wort, als anredendes und zurechtbringendes Wort zur Erfahrung kam, sowohl seinen ersten Jüngern als auch der johanneischen Gemeinde.[44] Wenn der Menschgewordene nun ganz als der unvordenkliche Logos bekannt wird, dann spricht sich darin die Erfahrung aus, dass sein Wort absolut grundlegend, massgeblich und tragend ist. (4) Im Horizont der Christologie ging es der johanneischen Gemeinde darum, die durch den Menschgewordenen ausgeteilte Gnade und Wahrheit in ihrem ganzen Gewicht wahrzunehmen. Wollte sie dies tun, musste sie auf den Uranfang vor aller Schöpfung zurückgreifen. In allen anderen Fällen wäre die Gnade und Wahrheit partikulär oder sektoriell geblieben. Deshalb eigneten sich christologische Titel wie Messias oder Menschensohn nicht mehr.[45] (5) Schliesslich hatte die johanneische Gemeinde den Menschgewordenen als göttlichen Eingriff wahrgenommen, genauer: als rettenden Eingriff Gottes. Dieses Moment der rettenden Nähe Gottes hatte schon die Weisheit an sich gezogen, noch stärker verband es sich mit dem Logos.[46] Deshalb lag der Logos-Begriff nahe, um das Handeln Gottes im Vordergrund der Welt zur Sprache zu bringen. Im Begriff des Logos wurde einerseits das Kommen und Wirken Jesu ganz als göttlicher Eingriff erfasst und anderseits alles, was je an göttlichen Eingriffen wahrgenommen worden war, mit diesem Menschgewordenen in Verbindung gebracht. Alles, was je an Belehrung, Führung, Wohltat von seiten Gottes erfahren worden war, wurde nun als Erfahrung des Christus erschlossen.

---

[43] So z.B. Haenchen, *Johannesevangelium*, 152.
[44] Dem Wort Jesu glaubten verschiedene Menschen (2.22; 4.50; 4.41); wer es hört, erhält ewiges Leben (5.24; 8.51 vgl. 5.38); es ist das Wort des Vaters (8.55; 14.23-24; 17.14; 17.6); es wird sogar richten am Jüngsten Tag (12.48) (vgl. Hofrichter, *Anfang*, 85-86). Wer Jesus liebt, wird sein Wort halten (14.23-24).
[45] So zu Recht Haenchen, *Johannesevangelium*, 116.
[46] Die "nahe Weisheit" bietet den Menschen das "Heil" an (vgl. Spr 1.32-33; Weish 9.18; 10.1,4,5,6,9, 13,15; Mack, *Logos*, 31-32), der Logos tritt sowohl bei Philo als auch in Weish 18 an die Stelle der nahen Weisheit. Er steht besonders deutlich für den göttlichen Eingriff in Weish 18.14-15 (vgl. Anm. 39), wo er vom Himmel springt, um Israel aus der Bedrängnis zu retten (dieser Aspekt trat unter aegyptischem Einfluss in den Vordergrund, vgl. Mack, a.a.O., 102-106; weitere Stellen zum soteriologischen Charakter des Wortes Gottes: Mack, a.a.O., 97-102).

## 2. Christus und die Schöpfung

Das Verhältnis des Christus zur Schöpfung wird vornehmlich in den Versen 3-5 beschrieben. Die Auslegung von Vers 3 ist belastet durch das bekannte textkritische Problem, zu welchem Satz ὃ γέγονεν zu ziehen sei. Die von mir gewählte Lösung kann jetzt nicht begründet werden: Es ist meines Erachtens nach wie vor sinnvoller, den Punkt nach ὃ γέγονεν zu setzen.[47]

Die erste Satzhälfte von V.3 hält fest, dass alles[48] durch den Logos geworden sei. Dabei ist der Logos jedoch nicht Urheber,[49] sondern Vermittler der Schöpfung. Das Schaffen selbst wird (unausgesprochen) Gott überlassen, sein Schaffen jedoch vollzieht sich über die Vermittlung des Logos. Zum Vergleich wurde schon das Targum Neophyti herangezogen, wo allerdings das göttliche Wort (die '*memra*') nicht bloss Mittler ist, sondern als Subjekt des Schaffens erscheint.[50] Ebenfalls weit weg ist die alttestamentliche Vorstellung von der Schöpfung durch das Wort (Ps 33.6), wo das Wort weder personalisiert noch Schöpfungsmittler ist. Viel näher beim Joh sind wiederum Aussagen über die *Weisheit*: Gott hat durch die Weisheit (dativus instrumentalis) die Welt gegründet (Spr 3.19), sie fungiert als Schöpferin (γενέτις, Weish 7.12) und als Künstlerin (τεχνῖτις, Weish 8.6; 7.21), sie ist der Anfang der Wege Gottes zu seinen Werken (Spr 8.22). Bei der Gründung des Himmels und der Erschaffung des Lebensraums war die Weisheit dabei, als Liebling (MT) oder als "Zusammenfügende" (LXX) (Spr 8.27-30). Neben diesen direkten Aussagen finden sich in der Weisheitsliteratur Beschreibungen, wonach die Weisheit alle Räume des Himmels, der Erde und der Unterwelt schon bei der Schöpfung durchmessen habe (Sir 24.3-6; Spr 8.27-31) und das All durchwalte (Weish 8.1).

Das Thema dieser Schilderungen und der Aussagen zur Weisheit als Schöpfungsmittlerin ist noch nicht die Frage, wie es vom geistigen Gott zur materiellen Welt gekommen sei. Dies steht erst bei Philo im Vordergrund. Bei ihm bahnt sich - im Zuge seiner Rezeption des platonischen Denkens - bereits an, was im Neuplatonismus und in der

---

[47] Zum Problem vgl. Aland, "Bedeutung", 370-375. Beide Varianten als gleichwertig vorgeschlagen bei Bultmann, *Johannes*, 21. Schwerwiegend ist freilich, dass Bultmann vor ζωή so ohne weiteres den Artikel ergänzt. Zur weiteren Kritik vgl. Haenchen, *Johannesevangelium*, 122. Ein ähnliche Wiedergabe vertreten auch Becker, *Johannes* I, 73; Gese, "Johannesprolog", 163; Theobald, *Anfang*, 105. Dieselbe textkritische Entscheidung auch bei Schnackenburg, *Johannesevangelium* I, 217; Haenchen, *Johannesevangelium*, 122.

[48] Das πάντα ist im Sinne von "alles, was es gibt" zu verstehen und nicht auf die Menschenwelt einzuschränken (gegen Bultmann, *Johannes*, 20, der die kosmische Dimension ausschliessen möchte).

[49] Dies müsste mit der Präposition ὑπό ausgedrückt sein, nicht mit διά mit Genitiv, vgl. Blass / Debrunner, *Grammatik*, § 223, der allerdings für Röm 11.36 ein διά im Sinne der Urheberschaft annimmt (§ 223.3 mit Anm. 7).

[50] Dies hat Schwarz, "Vergleich", 136 (mit Anm. 3) übersehen, weshalb er von einer völligen inhaltlichen Aequivalenz zwischen dem Targum Neophyti zu Gen 2.2a und Joh 1.3 spricht.

Gnosis das entscheidende Problem sein wird: Die Diskrepanz zwischen der geistigen Erhabenheit Gottes und der materiellen Niedrigkeit der Welt verlangt nach einer Mittlergestalt.[51] Während bei Philo der Logos erklärt, wie es von Gott zur Welt gekommen sei, dient der Gedanke der Schöpfungsmittlerschaft in der jüngeren Weisheit zur Beantwortung der Frage, inwiefern die Welt die Signatur des Schöpfergottes trage. Die Frage ist nicht, wie es zur Welt gekommen sei, sondern die Frage ist, wie die Sinnhaftigkeit der Welt zu erkennen sei. Die Lebensräume des Menschen, ja selbst der Himmel und die Unterwelt sind durch die Weisheit gestaltet. Die Weisheit vermittelt die Ordnung der Welt. Sie sorgt für die Sinnhaftigkeit des Lebensraums. Die Weisheit freut sich am Geschaffenen, gleichsam als Platzhalterin der Menschen, denen aufgetragen ist, durch Erkenntnis zur Freude an der sinnhaften Ordnung der Welt durchzufinden.[52]

Die vorliegende Aussage wird noch besser verständlich im Zusammenhang neutestamentlicher Aussagen: Christus erscheint in 1 Kor 8.6 ebenfalls als Schöpfungsmittler, wobei sorgfältig zwischen dem Ursprung des Universums in Gott (ἐκ) und seiner Gestaltung durch Christus (διά) unterschieden wird. Dasselbe gilt für den Kolosserhymnus[53] und eingeschränkt auch für Hebr 1.2.[54] Diese neutestamentlichen Texte fragen ebensowenig wie die Weisheitsliteratur, wie es zur Materialität der Welt gekommen sei, sondern sie fragen primär, welches die Dimensionen des Christus seien. Genauso kommt es dem Logos-Hymnus darauf an, mit Hilfe der Vorstellung von der Schöpfungsmittlerschaft die kosmische Reichweite des inkarnierten Logos anzugeben. Dies wird im zweiten Satzteil ausdrücklich sichergestellt: Es gibt kein einziges geschaffenes Ding, das jenseits[55] von Christus entstanden wäre.[56] Damit dehnt der Hymnus die Präsenz Christi bis an die äussersten Grenzen der Welt aus.

---

[51] Die Weisheit ist jetzt nicht mehr nach dem Technikmodell die Mittlerin der Schöpfung, sondern die Mutter des κόσμου ζῶντος (Vater ist Gott selbst). Das Augenmerk wird bei Philo auf die Frage der Entstehung der Welt gerichtet, nicht mehr auf die Frage nach der Weisheit in den Dingen. Die Weisheit hat nichts mehr mit der Schöpfung zu tun. Sie wird vertreten durch den Logos, der als ὄργανον der Schöpfung für ihre Gestaltung sorgte; zum Ganzen vgl. Mack, *Logos*, 141-150 (mit vielen Belegen); weiteres bei Schnackenburg, *Johannesevangelium* I, 213; Theobald, *Anfang*, 104-105.

[52] Die Weisheit preist ihre Mittlerfunktion in Spr 8.30b,31, in der "Form des Spiels erscheint das Wirken der Weisheit" (Gese, "Johannesprolog", 178), sie ist Schöpfungslogos in Sir 24.3-6 (a.a.O., 179).

[53] Kol 1.16. Das ἐκ wird an keiner Stelle von Christus, wohl aber wird das διά an einer Stelle von Gott (statt von Christus) ausgesagt (Röm 11.36). Es dürfte sich hier um eine wichtige Asymmetrie im Gottesbegriff handeln.

[54] Es geht im Hebräerbrief um die Schaffung der Aeonen "durch ihn". Vgl. Schweizer, *Kolosser*, 60-61; Schnackenburg, *Johannesevanglium* I, 214.

[55] Das χωρίς meint einen Ort, der gänzlich von Christus abgeschnitten ist, einen Ort jenseits des Christus, der weder in positiver noch in negativer Weise auf Christus bezogen ist.

[56] Eine Parallele zu dieser Aussage ist 1QS XI.11: "... und durch sein Wissen ist alles entstanden. Alles, was ist, lenkt er nach seinem Plan, und ohne ihn geschieht nichts". Der Logos-Begriff kommt hier (wie überhaupt in Qumran) freilich nicht vor, vgl. Yamauchi, "Jewish Gnosticism", 476.

Kein Ding (οὐδὲ ἕν) von dem man sagen kann, es sei geschaffen worden, ist unberührt vom Logos.

Die Geschöpflichkeit der Dinge ist es, die das Gepräge des Logos trägt. Deshalb mag ein Mensch noch so weit gehen, er fällt nicht aus der Obhut des Christus heraus. Nie wird ein Mensch in Welten kommen, die vom Christus unberührt wären. Der Hymnus erklärt das, was im Inkarnierten in den Vordergrund der Welt getreten ist, die Lebensmacht von Gnade und Wahrheit, zur Prägung der Welt schlechthin. Der Sinn, der im Inkarnierten verkörpert zur Erfahrung gekommen ist, erfüllt die ganze Weite des Universums. Deshalb wäre es verfehlt, die Welt als fremd und unwirtlich zu diffamieren. Weil der Christus ihr das Gepräge gibt, ist sie das Zuhause derer, die an ihn glauben.

Man muss sich die eklatante Distanz klarmachen, die zwischen diesem Weltverständnis und dem (späteren) gnostischen liegt. Dies vermag gerade die gnostische Interpretation des vorliegenden Satzes zu zeigen: Herakleon versucht, den Logos aus dem Schöpfungsprozess herauszuhalten und stattdessen den Demiurgen zu belasten mit der Welt.[57] Die Naassener gar sagen, das Nichts, das ohne ihn geworden sei, sei die materielle Welt, vom Chaos und dem feurigen Gott El Schaddai geschaffen.[58] Sie wenden damit den johanneischen Satz in sein pures Gegenteil. Die Protennoia wird zwar als das "Abbild des unsichtbaren Geistes" bezeichnet, "und das All wurde abgebildet durch" sie,[59] aber die konkrete Welt wird nicht weniger als sonst in der Gnosis auf einen Demiurgen zurückgeführt, der die Licht-Menschen in der *Hyle* gefangenhält.[60] Dementsprechend ist die Erlösung gedacht als Befreiung der Menschen, in denen der Geist in der Schöpfung zurückgeblieben ist, aus den Banden der Materie.[61] Der Hymnus kennt demgegenüber keine widergöttlichen, ja nicht einmal logoslosen Dinge der Welt. Denn gerade die Geschöpflichkeit von Allem ist es, das die Verbindung mit dem Logos ausmacht.[62]

Dass der inkarnierte Logos dem ganzen Universum sein Gepräge gibt, ist eine kosmologische Aussage, die mit dem durchaus etwas zu tun hat,

---

[57] Bei Origenes, Comm in Joh II.14.
[58] Hipp V 8.5 (bei Haenchen, *Johannesevangelium*, 122).
[59] NHC XIII 38.11-12.
[60] NHC XIII 39.13-40.4 vgl. 40.4-19 (Kommentar bei Schenke, *Protennoia*, 117-120).
[61] "Wir allein sind [es, die du erlöst] [hast] a[us der si]chtbaren [Welt], wobei wir er[rettet sind hinsichtlich des] verborgenen [Menschen in unserem] Herzen [durch den] unaussprechlichen und [un]messbaren [Gedanken]" (NHC XIII 36.33-37.1; Schenke, *Protennoia*, 28-29). "Denn ich kam herab zur Welt [der] Sterblichen wegen des Geistes, der i[n ihr] zurückgelassen ist, dessen, der her[abgekommen] war, der hervorgegangen war a[us] der [arglosen] Sophia" (NHC XIII 47.31-34; Schenke, a.a.O., 46-47).
[62] "Es ist derselbe Logos, der bei der Schöpfung mitbeteiligt war, der dann als Offenbarer und Erlöser in die Welt kommt" (Blank, *Johannes* 1a, 85). Deshalb gehören Schöpfung und Heil nicht - wie in der Gnosis - "zwei völlig verschiedenen Dimensionen" an (ebd.).

was wir heute "Naturwissenschaft" nennen.⁶³ Zwar geht es hier nicht um naturwissenschaftliche Kenntnisse, sondern um die Wahrnehmung der Welt im Horizont des Christus. Der Glaube an Christus sieht die kreatürliche Welt als etwas an, das durch eben diesen Christus sein Gepräge hat. Wenn es dabei auch nicht um Welterklärung sondern um Weltwahrnehmung geht, verpflichtet diese Sicht des Glaubens trotzdem dazu, im Aufbau der Welt und des Lebens etwas von jener Gnade und Wahrheit aufzuspüren, die im Logos verkörpert sind.⁶⁴ Schon die Gabe des Geschaffenen als solche kann als gnädig Gegebenes verstanden werden, und vielleicht erscheint auch im Aufbau des Universums und in der Organisation des Lebendigen etwas von jener Wahrheit, die als inkarnierter Logos im Vordergrund der menschlichen Welt aufgetreten ist. Und es ist wiederum die Weisheitstheologie, die es dem Hymnus in Joh 1 möglich macht, den Glauben an die Verkörperung von Gnade und Wahrheit im Vordergrund der Welt zusammenzuhalten mit der Erkenntnis der Ordnungen, die den Aufbau des Universums bestimmen.

Im nächsten Vers (V. 4) werden Logos, Leben und Licht in eine bemerkenswerte Beziehung gesetzt. Im Logos war Lebendigkeit⁶⁵ gleichsam zuhause, und diese Lebendigkeit war das Licht für⁶⁶ die Menschen. Es steht also nicht einfach das Begriffspaar Licht und Leben dem Logos gegenüber.⁶⁷ Die Präposition ἐν ist von διά (V.3) zu unterscheiden: War dort der Logos Vermittler der Schöpfung, so ist er hier Raum⁶⁸ für Lebendigkeit. Das Leben ist in ihm beschlossen; Lebendigkeit hat ihren Daseinsraum dort, wo der Logos ist. Und nicht der Logos, sondern diese Lebendigkeit ist - so die metaphorische Prädikation in V.4b - das Licht der Menschen.

Wiederum steht die Weisheitstheologie im Hintergrund dieser Aussagen. Auch in der Weisheit ist Lebendigkeit zuhause. Denn wer die Weisheit findet, findet Leben, wer die Weisheit liebt, liebt das Leben.⁶⁹ Das Leben wird anderseits dem verheissen, der die göttlichen Gebote und prophetischen Mahnungen befolgt. Leben ist das Versprechen, das dem

---

⁶³ Gegen Blank, der zu schnell das Wirklichkeitsverständnis des Glaubens dissoziiert von der Naturwissenschaft (Blank, *Johannes* 1a, 85).
⁶⁴ Diese "naturwissenschaftliche" Komponente kommt ja schon den oben zitierten weisheitstheologischen Aussagen zu, vgl. von Rad, *Theologie* I, 438-441; II, 317-318.
⁶⁵ Wie im AT meint hier ζωή nicht bloss die biologische Tatsache des Lebens, sondern "die 'Lebendigkeit', die animalischen Wesen eigen, aber stets von Gott gegeben ist, ....insbesondere das wahre, heilvolle Leben des Menschen...." (Gese, "Johannesprolog", 193).
⁶⁶ So ist der Genitiv aufzulösen, nicht etwa im Sinne eines Genitivus subjectivus (das Licht, das den Menschen eignet), mit Bultmann, *Johannes*, 22.
⁶⁷ So etwas ungenau bei Schnackenburg, *Johannesevangelium* I, 219.
⁶⁸ Gewiss könnte das ἐν auch instrumental verstanden werden, jedoch ist es nicht notwendig, sofort an die Schaffung von Leben zu denken (anders Bultmann, *Johannes*, 21 Anm. 3).
⁶⁹ Spr 8.35; Sir 4.12 (Gese, "Johannesprolog", 193, mit dem Hinweis auf die "spirituelle Vertiefung bis hin zum transzendenten 'ewigen Leben'").

gilt, der das Gesetz tut.[70] In dem Augenblick, wo Gesetz und Weisheit gleichgesetzt werden, vereinigen sich die Lebens-Verheissungen beider zu einem grossen Lebensstrom.[71] So wie aber die Weisheit nicht identisch mit dem Leben ist, so ist auch der Logos nicht das Leben, sondern dessen Raum.[72] Und wie in der Weisheit insofern Leben ist, als sie Leben austeilt, so auch im Logos. Leben existiert immer nur in der Gestalt der Austeilung, so wie das Wort des Lebens grundsätzlich die Gestalt des Beziehungswortes hat.

In diese Aussage über den Logos sind alle Lebenserfahrungen eingegangen, die die johanneische Gemeinde mit dem Inkarnierten gemacht hat. Fraglich ist allerdings, ob die Gebote des Gesetzes das Leben noch in derselben Weise austeilen wie die Weisheit. Sie binden das Versprechen des Lebens an das Tun des Gebotenen. Demgegenüber begnügt sich der Hymnus mit der blossen Beziehung, genauso wie die Austeilung des Lebens im Evangelium in der Beziehung des Hörens, Glaubens, Empfangens zum Christus geschieht.

Diese Beziehung wird im zweiten Versteil durch eine Metapher beschrieben. Die Lebendigkeit, die im Logos wohnt, ist das Licht für die Menschen. Licht ist also weder die Weisheit, nach der es zu leben gilt, noch das Gesetz, das es zu tun gilt, um Leben zu erlangen, Licht ist die Lebendigkeit selbst, die im Logos als ausgeteiltes Leben ihren Raum hat. Das ausgeteilte Leben ist es, welches das Dasein des Menschen ins Licht stellt, erleuchtet, erhellt.[73] Die Metapher zielt auf das, was die Lebendigkeit an den Menschen wirkt: Sie erleuchtet die Menschen. Lebendigkeit kommt jedem Menschen zu, insofern ist das Erhellende jedem Menschen zugänglich.[74]

Licht ist ein religiöses Symbol von universaler Verbreitung. Es entstammt wohl der Erfahrung mit dem natürlichen Licht, das unabdingbare Voraussetzung für alles Leben ist.[75] Nicht nur dafür, dass man sich im Leben zurechtfindet, sondern - wie wir wissen - auch dafür, dass Leben überhaupt entstehen und erhalten werden kann. Das religiöse Symbol des Lichtes nimmt die Erfahrung mit dem natürlichen Licht auf, verleiht ihr Gewicht und macht sie für die Gotteserfahrung trans-

---

[70] So z.B. Lev 18.5 (Gese, "Johannesprolog", 193).
[71] Die Weisheit spendet Lebenslänge und Lebensglück (Bar 3.14). "Sie ist das Buch der Gebote Gottes, das Gesetz, das in Ewigkeit besteht: alle, die an ihr halten, gewinnen das Leben, die sie verlassen, verfallen dem Tode" (Bar 4.1). Nach Sir 24 ist die Weisheit am klarsten im Gesetz, nach Bar 3-4 nur im Gesetz gegenwärtig.
[72] Im Unterschied zum Evangelium, wo das Ich Jesu metaphorisch mit dem Leben identifiziert wird (Joh 14.6).
[73] Dazu Bultmann, *Johannes*, 22-26.
[74] Mit Haenchen, *Johannesevangelium*, 122.
[75] So noch in Ps 56.14; Hiob 3.20.

parent.⁷⁶ An dieser Erfahrung gilt es, das Moment der Kreativität des Lichtes festzuhalten. Nicht bloss um Beleuchtung geht es, die das Vorhandene sichtbar macht, sondern um Erleuchtung, die neue Dimensionen am Vorhandenen erschliesst. Im Hymnus wird nicht einfach menschliches Dasein beleuchtet und ans gleissende Licht der Unbarmherzigkeit gezerrt, sondern es fällt das Licht der gnädig gegebenen Lebendigkeit auf menschliches Dasein. Vom Logos wurde Gnade und Wahrheit ausgeteilt, eben dies ist die konkrete Gestalt, in welcher die in ihm wohnende Lebendigkeit Menschen erleuchtet.

Nicht auflösbar ist dabei das Moment der Beziehung. Schon die Metapher des Lichtes macht klar, dass Dasein immer nur in der Relation zum Licht erhellt wird. Es ist nicht selbst Licht, sondern bedarf des Erhellenden. Diese Relation vollzieht sich beim Menschen so, dass er nicht bloss Geschöpf ist, sondern um seine Geschöpflichkeit weiss.⁷⁷ Das Wissen um Geschöpflichkeit wiederum ist keine Theorie, keine Information über das Wesen der Menschen, sondern sie vollzieht sich als Anbetung des Schöpfers, als Dankbarkeit für das Gegebene und als Verantwortung für die Schöpfung. Erhellt wird das menschliche Dasein in der Beziehung zum Fleischgewordenen, der es zum Vollzug seiner Geschöpflichkeit geleitet. Aus dieser Lebensbeziehung kann sich der Mensch niemals emanzipieren wollen.

Im Unterschied dazu steht die *gnostische Anthropologie*. Dies wird besonders deutlich angesichts der vielen nahen Parallelen zu unserem Vers in der Protennoia.⁷⁸ Zwar wird hier die Protennoia ebenfalls als das Licht des Alls bezeichnet, zwar werden hier die Menschen "Kinder des Lichts" genannt,⁷⁹ aber die Protennoia ist zugleich die Lichtsubstanz, die in den Gnostikern erstrahlt.⁸⁰ Erleuchtung bedeutet hier nicht, ins Licht des Logos gestellt zu sein, sondern es bedeutet, die eigene Lichtnatur erkannt zu haben. Als Licht kommt der Logos in die Welt, um den (göttlichen) Keim des Menschen, seine Lichtsubstanz, zum Reifen zu bringen.⁸¹ Erkenntnis bedeutet im Rahmen dieser Anthropologie und Soteriologie gerade die Emanzipation von der Beziehung zum Erlöser, den Fortschritt zum Wissen um die Lichtnatur des Selbst.

---

⁷⁶ So in Ps 27.1, wo Gott geradezu mit dem Licht identifiziert wird.
⁷⁷ Mit Bultmann, *Johannes*, 25.
⁷⁸ Z.B. NHC XIII 35.12-13; 47.28-29, vgl. Robinson, "Gnosticism", 129-130.
⁷⁹ NHC XIII 41.1,16.
⁸⁰ Schenke hält dies für eine enge Parallele zu Joh 1.14, weist jedoch ihrerseits darauf hin, dass der Logos herabkommt, um das göttliche Element zu erlösen, das "den Gnostiker zum φύσει σῳζόμενος macht" (Schenke, *Protennoia*, 151, zu NHC XIII 47.28-34).
⁸¹ Schenke, *Protennoia*, 121 (zu NHC XIII 40.29-41.2). Interessant ist der Hinweis auf das Apokryphon Johannis (ebd. Anm.2), wonach der göttliche Geist aus der Lichtwelt herabkam, "um die Wesenheit zu erwecken, die ihm gleicht" (BG 63.18-64.1). Diese Wesenheit ist nach Schenke die im Menschen eingeschlossene Lichtsubstanz.

"Erleuchtung" ist hier die Information über die wahre Natur des Menschen, während gemäss dem Hymnus die im Logos beschlossene Lebendigkeit Licht für die Menschen nur insofern ist, als sie in der Beziehung zum Logos bleiben. Der Erkenntnis des Lichts im Selbst steht das Leben im Schein des fremden Lichts gegenüber.

Im nächsten Vers (V. 5) wird das Licht im Gegenüber zur Finsternis thematisiert. Am auffälligsten ist die Zeitstruktur dieses Satzes: Einem Präsens (das Licht scheint in der Finsternis) steht ein Aorist (und die Finsternis hat es nicht ergriffen, bzw. überwältigt) gegenüber.[82] Wahrscheinlich ist im Praesens der durative Aspekt zu sehen, im Aorist dagegen der momentane,[83] das Ereignishafte also. Das Scheinen des Lichtes ist seit der Schöpfung immerwährende Gegenwart,[84] das Nicht-Ergreifen des Lichts wird dagegen je und dann Ereignis. Schon diese Asymmetrie verbietet es, hier einen Dualismus im Stil von Qumran einzutragen.[85]

Hier geht es um das Licht, das Licht, das seit Urzeiten schien und deshalb auch jetzt scheint; dogmatisch gesprochen: Thema ist das

---

[82] Dies führt manche Ausleger dazu, die Gegenwart des Lichtes in Analogie zu 1 Joh 2.8 zu verstehen ("das Licht scheint schon"). Dann wäre der Satz auf die Inkarnation des Logos zu beziehen (so zum Beispiel Bultmann, *Johannes*, 26-27, übernommen von Käsemann, "Aufbau", 166, mit guten Argumenten abgewiesen dagegen von Haenchen, *Johannesevangelium*, 123-124), obwohl von dieser erst in 1.14 die Rede sein wird. Dann wäre Jesus das auch in der Zeit des Evangelisten noch scheinende Licht (so Schnackenburg, *Johannesevangelium* I, 221-222; Blank, *Johannes* 1a, 88), dessen Ablehnung durch die Welt durch den Aorist als vergangenes Geschehen gekennzeichnet würde. Doch müsste, wnn schon das Scheinen des Lichts in die Gegenwart hereinreicht, nicht auch die Ablehnung bis zur Gegenwart reichen?

[83] Dazu Blass / Debrunner, *Grammatik*, § 218.1.

[84] Nicht ganz adäquat wäre es, in diesem Zusammenhang von Zeitlosigkeit zu sprechen (abgelehnt von Käsemann, "Aufbau", 166; Schnackenburg, *Johannesevangelium* I, 222), da es vielmehr um die Fortdauer der Gegenwart geht. Die gleiche gegenwärtige Wirklichkeit wird in Weish 7.27-28 ausgesagt.

[85] Vgl. auch 3.19; 8.12; 12.35,46. Zu beachten sind jedoch die vielen Signale der Asymmetrie. Schon die Tempuswahl zeigt dies: Dem immer scheinenden Licht steht die jeweils aktuelle Ablehnung (bzw. der Ueberwältigungsversuch) gegenüber. Die aktuelle Ablehnung lebt vom ständig scheinenden Licht der göttlichen Zuwendung zur Welt. Ferner drückt sich im Verbum "scheinen" eine Bewegung aus, das Zugehen des Logos auf die Finsternis. Das Licht zeichnet sich durch Zuwendung aus, während sich die Finsternis in der Abwendung konstituiert. Trotz der Nähe zu Qumran ist hier der fundamentale Unterschied der johanneischen Theologie von jedem deterministischen Dualismus mit Händen zu greifen. Den "Söhnen der Finsternis" wird nach qumranischer Auffassung das Licht nicht angeboten, während es hier gerade in die Finsternis hinein scheint. Zu Qumran (mit den notwendigen Unterscheidungen gegenüber dem gnostischen Dualismus) vgl. Schnackenburg, *Johannesevangelium* I, 223-226. Aehnlich urteilt Becker, *Johannes* I, 74 (klare Abgrenzung vom gnostischen und qumranischen Dualismus). Richtig ist, dass in Qumran nicht von einem kosmischen Dualismus mit zwei selbständigen Prinzipien ausgegangen wird, da Gott über beiden steht. Zu fragen ist freilich, welche sachliche Bedeutung diese Ueberlegenheit Gottes noch hat, wenn Sezession und Kampf der einzige Umgang mit der Welt der Finsternis ist. Die Zuwendung der Lichtwelt zur Finsternis besteht nach qumranischer Auffassung im Kampf gegen die Finsternis, nicht im Leuchten des Lichtes ins Dunkel hinein. Bei Johannes geht es um die Zuwendung mit dem Angebot der Rettung, in Qumran um die Vernichtung im Kampf. Deutlich ist ferner, dass die Finsternis nur in der Negation des Lichtes ihre Existenz "gewinnt". Die Finsternis existiert nicht aus sich selbst, sie konstituiert sich als Ablehnung des Lichts. Damit ist die prinzipielle Asymmetrie zwischen Erschaffen und Zerstören zum Ausdruck gebracht. Von einem johanneischen Dualismus kann man im besten Falle dann sprechen, wenn damit dieses Ungleichgewicht zwischen dem leuchtenden Licht und der aus der Ablehnung entstehenden Finsternis gemeint ist.

Schöpfungslicht, nicht das Erlösungslicht.[86] Im Blick ist also nicht primär der Inkarnierte, sondern das Licht, das sich in ihm verkörpert hat. Dieses Verständnis des Satzes hat Konsequenzen im Blick auf das Exklusivitätsproblem. Einerseits könnte Exklusivität bedeuten, dass in keinem andern Licht ist als im Inkarnierten. Im Anschluss an den vorliegenden Vers müsste man anderseits sagen: In allem Licht, das seit Anbeginn der Welt leuchtet, leuchtet der Christus.

### 3. Christus und die Menschen

Ein dritter Aussagekreis konzentriert sich auf das Verhältnis des Christus zur Menschenwelt (V.9-12). Eine Klärung der grammatischen Probleme[87] von V.9 kann zeigen, dass der Satz heissen muss: "Das wahre Licht war das, welches jedem Menschen leuchtet, der zur Welt kommt."

Der Ton liegt zunächst auf der Echtheit[88] des Lichtes. Dies lässt auf eine zweifache Aussage schliessen. Einerseits geht es um das echte Licht im Unterschied zu allen Irrlichtern, die den Menschen bloss vermeintlich leuchten, um das Licht also, das seinem eigenen Wesen in wahrhaftiger Weise entspricht. Anderseits liegt der Akzent darauf, dass das Licht, das jedem Menschen leuchtet, der zur Welt kommt, kein unechtes oder uneigentliches Licht sei. In der Zeit der Erlösung leuchtet kein anderes Licht als in der Zeit der Schöpfung. Religionspsychologisch gesprochen:

---

[86] Dazu Bultmann, *Johannes*, 27, der sachgemäss auf die Kontinuität von Schöpfung und Erlösung hinweist.

[87] Zum Folgenden vgl. Bonsack, "Überlegungen". Als Subjekt des Satzes kommt (auch wenn der eingefügte Teil V.6-8 ausgeklammert würde) der Logos nicht in Frage. Subjekt ist am ehesten "das wahre Licht". Möglich wäre freilich auch, als Subjekt den Relativsatz anzunehmen, um dann "war das wahre Licht" als Kopula und Prädikatsnomen zu definieren (so offensichtlich Bonsack, "Überlegungen", 74). Der Bedeutungsunterschied dieser beiden Lösungen ist jedoch nicht gross. Prädikat ist demnach der Relativsatz. Schliesslich ist die Wendung ἐρχόμενον εἰς τὸν κόσμον nicht als conjugatio periphrastica zu verstehen, sondern attributiv zu ἄνθρωπον (vgl. die entscheidenden Einwände Bonsacks, "Überlegungen", 67-68). Neben der attributiven Beziehung des Partizips wäre auch eine kontributive möglich: "jedem Menschen, wenn er zur Welt kommt" (Bonsack, "Überlegungen", 69). Dann hiesse der Vers: Das wahre Licht leuchtet jedem Menschen in dem Vorgang seines Zur-Welt-Kommens, eine Annahme, die aus sachlichen und philologischen Gründen nicht wahrscheinlich ist. Zu beachten ist, dass der Ausdruck rabbinisch eine Umschreibung für "Mensch" darstellt; Bill II, 358. Die attributive Deutung entspricht der Grammatik am besten, keinesfalls verschlägt der Hinweis, man müsste einen Artikel vor dem Partizip erwarten; das Gegenteil ist der Fall (gegen Schnackenburg, *Johannesevangelium* I, 231 und Theobald, *Anfang*, 23). Von der Fügung πᾶς ὁ γεγεννημένος (3,8) ist strikte die "Fügung πᾶς + Substantiv + Partizip" zu unterscheiden, "die ganz gewöhnlich ohne Artikel gebildet wird, ja, gar nicht mit dem Artikel gebildet werden kann" (Bonsack, "Überlegungen", 64). Aus diesem Grund ist Bultmanns Versuch, ἄνθρωπον zu streichen, unsachgemäss (vgl. ebd. Anm. 34). Für eine ähnliche Lösung wie die im obigen Text gewählte entscheidet sich (ebenfalls im Anschluss an Bonsack) Theobald, *Fleischwerdung*, 191-193. Theobalds (im Anschluss an Borgen unternommener) Versuch, das ἐρχόμενον εἰς τὸν κόσμον als "adverbielles Partizip" zu ο[ zu verstehen, scheitert an grammatikalischen Schwierigkeiten und vor allem daran, dass ein duratives Partizip mit Sicherheit nicht auf das Kommen des Lichtes bei der Inkarnation bezogen werden darf (mit Bonsack, "Überlegungen", 69).

[88] Das Adjektiv ἀληθινόν bedeutet "wahrhaftig, echt, eigentlich" im Unterschied zu "unecht, vermeintlich, unwahrhaftig" (mit Bultmann, *Johannes*, 32).

Die religiöse Licht-Suche kann sich auf kein "wahreres" Licht richten als auf das, das jedem Menschen leuchtet. Das Licht vollzieht seine eigene Wahrheit gerade darin, dass es allen hell gibt.

Das Scheinen ($\phi\alpha\acute{\iota}\nu\epsilon\iota\nu$) des Lichts in V. 5 benennt die Tätigkeit, das Er- oder Beleuchten ($\phi\omega\tau\acute{\iota}\zeta\epsilon\iota\nu$[89]) im vorliegenden Vers dagegen die Wirkung dieser Tätigkeit auf die Menschen. Das Verbum $\phi\omega\tau\acute{\iota}\zeta\epsilon\iota\nu$ kommt im Neuen Testament (mit persönlichem Objekt) sowohl im Sinne von "jemanden ins Licht stellen" als auch im Sinne von "jemanden (innerlich) erleuchten" vor.[90] Beide Bedeutungen dürften hier anklingen. Gemäss V.4 ist die Lebendigkeit, welche im Logos beschlossen ist, das Licht für die Menschen. An dieser Lebendigkeit hat jeder Mensch teil, der geboren wird. Sie ist das wahre Licht, das jedem Menschen leuchtet, der das Licht der Welt erblickt. Und zwar leuchtet dieses Licht einerseits von aussen, in der Gestalt der Lebenswelt, und stellt so den Menschen und sein Dasein ins Licht. Und anderseits leuchtet es von innen, in der Gestalt der selbst erfahrenen Lebendigkeit, und erleuchtet so jeden Menschen. Die Lichtsymbolik erinnert wiederum an die Weisheitstheologie. Die Weisheit ist, sofern sie aus den Dingen heraustritt, das Licht, in dessen Schein das menschliche Leben erkennbar wird, und sie ist, sofern sie allen Dingen das Gepräge gibt, auch das Licht, das aus dem menschlichen Leben hervorleuchtet.[91] Das Licht der Lebendigkeit gibt einerseits Orientierung, sofern es die Welt und das menschliche Dasein beleuchtet, und es gibt Einblick in die Würde des Daseins, sofern es dieses ins Licht der göttlichen Kreativität stellt.

Festzuhalten ist schliesslich der universale Horizont dieses Satzes. Universal ist zunächst freilich nicht das Wirken des Offenbarers Jesus,[92] sondern das Licht der Lebendigkeit, die im Logos beschlossen ist. Man sollte diese Universalität nicht gegen die Exklusivität der johanneischen Christologie ausspielen. Richtig ist, dass der Christus das Licht der Welt ist (8.12). Richtig ist auch, dass das Joh die ganze Wahrheit exklusiv für den Christus in Anspruch nimmt (14.6). Jedoch ist auf den inneren Zusammenhang solcher Exklusivität mit der hier vorliegenden Univer-

---

[89] Das Verbum ist nicht sehr häufig im Neuen Testament (insgesamt 11 Belege) und kommt nur hier im johanneischen Schrifttum vor.
[90] Für die erste Bedeutung vgl. Lk 11.36, für die zweite Hebr 6.4; 10.32; Eph 1.18 (Bonsack, "Überlegungen" 63; Conzelmann, Art. $\phi\hat{\omega}\varsigma$, 344,10-12, legt die Bedeutung zu Unrecht auf die "Erleuchtung" fest).
[91] Zum weisheitlichen Hintergrund vgl. Conzelmann, Art. $\phi\hat{\omega}\varsigma$, 315,15-319,20; Schnackenburg, *Johannesevangelium* I, 229, Anm. 2. Wichtig ist der Hinweis darauf, dass die Lichtfunktion von der Weisheit auf die Tora überging.
[92] Gegen Theobald, der - beispielhaft für viele andere Ausleger das Licht sofort auf "Jesu Offenbarerwirken" einschränkt (Theobald, *Fleischwerdung*, 330). In gnostischen Texten wird dagegen der Ausdruck "jeder Mensch" auf den vollkommenen Menschen gedeutet, der selbst erleuchtet ist (Cl Al, Exc Theod 41.4). Hofrichter übersetzt den Vers mit "das (den) ganzen (...) Menschen erleuchtet", was grammatikalisch unmöglich ist (Hofrichter, *Anfang*, 153).

salität zu achten: Das wahre Licht, das jedem Menschen leuchtet,[93] ist verkörpert im Christus. Daraus könnte man nicht schliessen, nur wer im Licht des Christus lebe, sei erleuchtet. Vielmehr gilt das Umgekehrte: Wem immer das Lebenslicht leuchtete, dem leuchtete der Christus. Jeder Mensch wird hineingeboren in das Licht, das nun im Christus verkörpert ist. Niemand kann sagen, er sei im Dunkel geboren.[94] Denn jeder Mensch hat das Licht der Welt erblickt, bevor er sich für die Finsternis entschied. Diese Asymmetrie widerspiegelt eine Grundgegebenheit des Universums: Das Licht geht allem Dunkel prinzipiell voraus. Dies wiederholt sich sowohl im Licht der Lebendigkeit als auch im Kommen des Lichtes in die Welt.

Thema der folgenden drei Verse ist das Forum, wo das Licht (beziehungsweise der Logos)[95] wirkt.[96] Im durativischen Tempus der Vergangenheit wird vom Sein des Logos-Lichtes in der Welt gesprochen. Damit kann wohl nur die allgemeine, in Analogie zur Gegenwart der Weisheit[97] gedachte Präsenz des Logos gemeint sein.[98] Der Logos ist seit unvordenklicher Zeit in der Welt gegenwärtig als einer, der ihr das Gepräge gibt. Zu erwarten wäre, dass die Welt den erkennt, dem sie ihr eigenes Wesen verdankt. Dem ist nicht so. Die Finsternis konstituiert sich nach V.5 dadurch, dass sie das Licht ablehnt. Ebenso die (Menschen-)Welt: Sie verdankt ihr Sein dem Walten des Logos, und erkennt ihn dennoch nicht. Damit konstituiert sich Welt je und je[99] neu als eine von Gott abgewandte Welt. Sie ist beides zugleich: durch den Logos

---

[93] Man sollte diese unversale Wirklichkeit des Lichtes nicht verwandeln in eine universale Notwendigkeit für jeden Menschen (gegen Schnackenburg, *Johannesevangelium* I, 229). Dieser Satz spricht nicht davon, dass alle Menschen das wahre Licht nötig haben, sondern davon, dass das wahre Licht für alle Menschen die bestimmende Wirklichkeit ist, das grosse Zuvor ihres Lebens. In Umkehrung der hier vorliegenden Relationen wird in der Gnosis gerade der Mensch von 1.9 zum Erlöser, zum Erleuchter, statt dass er der Erlöste und Erleuchtete wäre (Belege bei Hofrichter, *Anfang*, 188-194).
[94] Ganz anders dagegen NHC XIII, 46,31-33, wo die zu Erleuchtenden gerade in der Finsternis wohnen.
[95] Unvermeidlich ist die Annahme, dass in V.10 ein nicht expliziter Wechsel des Subjekts vorliegt, da αὐτόν nur das maskuline λόγος meinen kann. Da in V.10 vom Licht ähnlich gesprochen wird, wie V.3 vom Logos sprach, ist die Annahme eines Subjektwechsels "nicht unverständlich" (mit Bonsack, "Überlegungen", 58).
[96] Mit Theobald, *Fleischwerdung*, 232.
[97] Die Weisheit ist seit Anbeginn der Welt in ihr gegenwärtig: Nach Sir 24.3-6 durchkreist die Weisheit alle Welt, nach Weish 8.1 durchwaltet sie das ganze All (Mack, *Logos*, 31). Daneben gäbe es auch die Möglichkeit, diesen Satz im Sinne der Gegenwart der Weisheit unter den Menschen zu verstehen (Sir 24.6-7; Prov 8.31; Bar 3.38; weitere Belege bei Mack, *Logos*, 31-32). Dann wäre die Welt schon im ersten Satzteil Menschenwelt, was sie im letzten ja ist.
[98] Gegen Theobald, der dies aufgrund der christologischen Konzentration des bisherigen Hymnus für ausgeschlossen hält (Theobald, *Fleischwerdung*, 232-233). Von christologischem Sinn der bisherigen Sätze kann jedoch nicht gesprochen werden. Vielmehr beziehen sich alle auf das Sein und Wirken des Logos *asarkos*.
[99] Auch hier ist der Wechsel vom durativischen ἦν zum aoristischen οὐκ ἔγνω konsequent wie schon in V.5. Allerdings wäre gemäss dieser Analogie hier auch ein durativisches Präsens möglich gewesen.

geprägtes Geschöpf Gottes und durch Nicht-Erkenntnis sich im Dunkel verlierende Abwendung.[100]

Im vorliegenden Zusammenhang wird überdies klar, dass die Nicht-Erkenntnis des Logos zugleich ein Verkennen des eigenen Daseins bedeutet. Indem die Welt den Logos verkennt, verkennt sie zugleich die eigenen Sinnstrukturen. Indem sie ihren Schöpfer nicht erkennt, verkennt sie ihre eigene Geschöpflichkeit. Indem sie das göttliche Wort banalisiert, wird sie selbst banal. Dieser paradoxe Satz von der den Logos und sich selbst verkennenden Welt wird hier - unerklärlich wie er ist! - ohne jede Erklärung festgehalten. Es wäre deshalb unsachgemäss, diese Unerklärlichkeit aufzulösen, sei es durch das Nicht-Können[101] oder das Nicht-Wollen.

Die Aoriste der Aussage in V. 11 bringen zum Ausdruck, dass das Kommen des Logos je und je Ereignisgestalt hatte, ebenso wie die Ablehnung aktuellen Charakter hat.[102] Dieser Vers spricht - wie vorher V. 10 - von der allgemeinen Präsenz des Logos in der Welt. Während dort durativisch vom dauernden Sein des Logos in der Welt die Rede war, wird diese Gegenwart hier präzisiert: Der Logos ist immer im Kommen, und sein Kommen ist je und dann ein Ereignis; seine Gegenwart hat die Gestalt seines Zugehens auf die Menschen. So hatte es schon von der Weisheit geheissen, sie gehe auf die Menschen zu, ihr Geist komme zum Menschen.[103] Schon in der Figur der Weisheit wurde der auf die Welt zugehende Gott, die göttliche Zuwendung persönlich vorgestellt. Mit Hilfe dieser weisheitlichen Vorstellung wird jetzt die universale Bedeutung des inkarnierten Logos begriffen. Was in der Person Jesu Fleisch geworden ist, ist die schon immer existierende Zuwendung Gottes zur Welt.

Es ist nicht ausgemacht, dass der Hymnus durch eine der Weisheit in Sir 24 vergleichbare Bewegung vom Universalen zum Partikularen geprägt ist. Ebenso denkbar wäre, dass sich nur die allgemeine Gegenwart des Logos in der Welt und dessen spezielle Inkarnation gegenüberstehen, so dass beide Pole einander interpretieren. Die allgemeine Rede vom Logos macht die Dimension des Inkarnierten deutlich, die spezielle Rede vom Inkarnierten macht die Qualität des Logos deutlich. Dies alles spricht dafür, in V.11 den universalen Horizont beizubehalten: "Das Seine" meint die Welt, sofern sie das Gepräge des Logos trägt, und "die

---

[100] Zu Recht betont Bultmann, *Johannes*, 33-34, dass der Kosmosbegriff bei Joh nicht in zwei verschiedene Begriffe aufgespalten werden darf.
[101] So etwa im gnostischen Text NHC VIII/2, 136.12-13 (Koschorke, "Paraphrase", 386), wo der nicht zur Erkenntnis befähigte Kosmos spezifiziert wird als die erkenntnisunfähigen Archonten, die nur die körperliche Wirklichkeit erkennen können, weil sie Schöpfer der Körperlichkeit sind.
[102] So zu Recht Schnackenburg, *Johannesevangelium* I, 234.
[103] Sir 24.6-7; Weish 7.7.

Seinen" meint die Menschen, die alle, kraft ihrer Geschöpflichkeit, zum Logos gehören.[104] Die Welt ist, weil sie auf diese Weise zum Logos gehört, immer schon als Stätte der Offenbarung bestimmt. Welterfahrung ist nicht bloss Entfremdung von Gott, sie ist erschliessbar als Gotteserfahrung. Unübersehbar ist die Differenz zu jeder gnostischen Weltvorstellung, wo der Logos gerade nicht in seine Heimat kommt, sondern wo er in die Fremde geht, um die Seinen, die in jener Fremde gefangen sind, in ihre himmlische Heimat zurückzuführen.[105]

Die Anknüpfung (in V. 12a) an den vorhergehenden Satz mit ὅσοι macht klar, dass das Aufnehmen das einzige Kriterium dafür ist, die Gabe der Gotteskindschaft zu erhalten.[106] Dass es wenige waren, die den Logos aufnahmen, kann höchstens aus dem Zusammenhang mit V.11[107] oder - religionsgeschichtlich - aus dem weisheitlichen Motiv der wenigen Gerechten gegenüber den vielen Ungerechten geschlossen werden. Doch den beiden Sätzen geht es gar nicht um Zahlenverhältnisse. Während V.11 den Widersinn dessen herausstreicht, dass die zum Logos gehörigen ihn nicht aufnehmen in ihrem Hause, spricht V.12ab vom Ertrag des Aufnehmens. Angesichts des Logos, des zur Welt kommenden Gottes, gibt es nur eine sachgemässe Einstellung: ihn kommen zu lassen, ihn zu empfangen. Auf diese menschliche Aktivität kommt alles an; es ist die Aktivität des Rezipierens. Der Logos kommt an, wo er auf Empfänglichkeit trifft.

Im Aufnehmen des Logos gestalten die Menschen ihr Verhältnis zu ihm. Nehmend sind sie auf den Logos eingestellt, dessen Wesen im Geben besteht. Er gibt eine ἐξουσία. Diese Vollmacht ist nicht zu verwechseln mit menschlicher δύναμις, Stosskraft, Vermögen, Eigen--Macht.[108] Es handelt sich um einen durch den Logos gewährten Freiraum des Daseins, nicht um eine Macht des Könnens. Der Freiraum des Daseins ist prinzipiell zu unterscheiden von der Macht des Tuns. Ferner existiert die Vollmacht nur in der Relation zum Logos; sie geht nicht

---

[104] Mit Blank, *Johannes* 1a, 94 (Welt, nicht Israel); Becker, *Johannes* I, 76; Bultmann, *Johannes*, 34 (fraglich ist freilich, ob schon τὰ ἴδια auf die Menschenwelt bezogen werden soll); Käsemann, "Aufbau", 161.
[105] Mit Blank, *Johannes* 1a, 94; Lindemann, "Gemeinde", 140 Anm. 46.
[106] Auch wo πάντες nicht steht, bedeutet ὅσοι "alle, welche" (Bauer, *Wörterbuch*, 1187) mit dem Akzent darauf, dass die Menge der "ihn Aufnehmenden" identisch ist mit der Menge derer, die die Vollmacht zur Gotteskindschaft erhalten.
[107] So Bultmann, *Johannes*, 35.
[108] Zum Unterschied von ἐξουσία und δύναμις vgl. Bultmann, *Johannes*, 36 Anm. 1. Der gemeingriechische Sprachgebrauch unterscheidet zwischen der Möglichkeit zu einem Handeln, sofern sich ihm keine Hindernisse in den Weg stellen (ἐξουσία), und der innewohnenden Möglichkeit zum Handeln (δύναμις). Das erstere bedeutet Recht, Vollmacht, Erlaubnis, Freiheit (so Foerster, Art. ἔξεστιν, 559,9-27). Diese Bedeutung ist sowohl in der Septuaginta als auch im neutestamentlichen Schrifttum noch breit belegt, obwohl sich in der Spätantike die Wortfelder beider Begriffe zu vermengen beginnen.

naturhaft auf den Menschen über,[109] noch ist sie das Produkt menschlichen Wissens.[110] Jede naturhafte Vorstellung wird durch das γενέσθαι unwahrscheinlich gemacht: Niemand muss werden, was er von Natur aus schon ist.

Das neue Sein wird präzisiert mit dem Ausdruck "Kinder Gottes". In unmittelbarer Nähe dazu befinden sich weisheitliche Texte. Dort ist von "Söhnen (υἱοί) der Weisheit" die Rede, die durch ihr Suchen der Weisheit zu solchen werden.[111] Wer die Weisheit sucht, richtet sich nach ihr, lässt sie für seine gesamte Lebensführung massgebend sein. Sohn der Weisheit sein bedeutet also, von und nach der Weisheit leben. Im Zuge der Theologisierung der Weisheit werden die Söhne der Weisheit zu Söhnen Gottes.[112] Söhne Gottes sind nicht einfach alle Menschen, sondern die Gerechten.[113] Und Gerechte sind die, die ihre Lebensführung nach der Weisheit, beziehungsweise nach dem Gesetz, in welches die Weisheit eingegangen ist (Sir 24; Bar 2), richten. In Weish 18, wo vom Kommen des Logos erzählt wird, gibt der Logos nicht die Vollmacht, Kinder Gottes zu sein, sondern zwingt die Feinde dazu, die Gottessohnschaft des Volkes oder der Gerechten anzuerkennen.[114] Zusammenfassend lässt sich für die Weisheitstheologie festhalten: Der "Sohn Gottes (oder der Weisheit)" bezeichnet eine lebenspraktische Einstellung des Menschen auf Weisheit und Gerechtigkeit hin. Sobald der

---

[109] Sowohl im CHerm (I 32) als Freiheit des inneren Menschen von den Einflüssen der Welt als auch - ohne den dualistischen Anschauungsrahmen - bei Epiktet ist die Vollmacht im Wesen des Menschen vorhanden (mit Foerster, Art. ἔξεστιν, 568,5-15).

[110] Wie etwa in NHC XIII, 37.18-20 (Schenke, Protennoia, 31), wo "denen, die existieren in der Finsternis" und "die existieren im Abgrund" und "die existieren in den verborgenen Gewölben", die Erkenntnis und Belehrung gebracht wird, wodurch sie zu "Kindern des Lichtes" wurden. Es kann keine Rede davon sein, dass diese Aussage im Sinne von Joh 1.12a interpretierbar ist (gegen Schenke, a.a.O., 108), da es erstens in Joh 1.12 gerade nicht um den Empfang einer Mitteilung geh, sondern um das existentielle Verhältnis der Rezeptivität zum Logos selbst, und da zweitens die Angeredeten im Joh nicht in der Finsternis wohnen, sondern - durch die Ablehnung des Lichts - selbst Finsternis sind. Während die Verbindung der Gnostiker mit dem Erlöser in der Protennoia substanziell ist (vgl. etwa NHC XIII 36.16,23-26), wird sie in Joh 1.12 zweifellos als Relation (Geben-Nehmen) gedacht. Aehnliches lässt sich auch in NHC VIII/2 beobachten: "Und ich gab ihm (sc. dem Meinigen, dem dank des in ihm vorhandenen Lichtfunkens erlösungsfähigen Menschen) Vollmacht (ἐξουσία), in das Erbe seiner Vaterschaft einzugehen" (Koschorke, "Paraphrase", 387). Der Uebergang zum Singular bedeutet eine Einschränkung auf den erlösungsfähigen Menschen, der substantiell analog zum Erlöser selbst als Zweiheit von vergänglichem Leib und erlösungsfähigem Funken verstanden wird.

[111] Sir 4.11; vgl. noch Lk 7.35 (Q; im Unterschied zur Mt-Parallele, wo die Söhne durch Werke ersetzt sind).

[112] Sir 4.10; Weish 2.13,16,18; vgl. Gese, "Johannesprolog", 198.

[113] Weish 2.18. Zur Weisheit vgl. Mack, Logos, 80-85. Sohn-Sein verbindet sich hier mit dem Herrschen (wohl nicht ohne ägyptischen Einfluss, vgl. Mack a.a.O., 82-83). Zu Philo und dem Zusammenhang "Logos als Sohn Gottes" und "Logos-Söhne" vgl. Culpepper, "Pivot", 20-21.

[114] Weish 18.13 vgl. 5.1-4.

Logos Christus im Rahmen der Weisheit verstanden wird, wird auch seine Gabe als die Vollmacht zur Gotteskindschaft verstanden.[115]

Dass im vorliegenden Vers τέκνα (nicht παῖδες oder υἱοί) gebraucht wird, hängt wohl damit zusammen, dass dieses Wort das Kind besonders unter dem Gesichtspunkt seiner Abkunft in den Blick nimmt.[116] Das Joh macht einen strikten Unterschied zwischen den τέκνα θεοῦ (den Menschen) und dem υἱός θεοῦ (dem Christus).[117] In Joh 1.12 bezeichnet τέκνα θεοῦ das Gottesverhältnis, das im Empfangen des Logos gewonnen wird. Inhaltlich wird im Hymnus das Empfangen des Logos bestimmt als Empfangen von "Gnade über Gnade" (V.16). Der Logos teilt weder Weisheit noch Gesetz aus, er verkörpert vielmehr die χάρις, das gnädige Geben Gottes. Ihn empfangen heisst deshalb die Gnade empfangen, die er verkörpert. Deshalb ist dieses Gottesverhältnis weder durch den Gehorsam gegenüber dem Gesetz noch durch die weisheitsgemässe Lebensführung, weder durch (heils-)geschichtliche Zugehörigkeit noch durch substantielle Verwandtschaft gegeben, sondern allein dadurch, dass diese im Logos verkörperte Gnade in Empfang genommen wird. Gnade ist der Inbegriff göttlicher Kreativität, ihr entspricht der Mensch in reiner Rezeptivität. Im Unterschied zum Gottesverhältnis, das etwa durch die Begriffe δοῦλος und κύριος umrissen wird und ein Arbeitsverhältnis darstellt, wird hier das Gottesverhältnis als Lebensverhältnis begriffen, als ein Verhältnis also, das mit dem Lebensvollzug selbst gegeben ist. Wer sich als δοῦλος θεοῦ versteht, tritt durch einen Vertrag ins Gottesverhältnis ein und gestaltet es durch immerwährende produktive Arbeit. Wer sich als τέκνον θεοῦ versteht, tritt mit der Geburt[118] ins Gottesverhältnis ein und gestaltet dies durch das Empfangen dessen, was der Vater zum Leben bereitgestellt hat. Entscheidender Punkt dieses Gottesverhältnisses ist es, dass der Mensch sich niemals vom Verhältnis zum Logos emanzipieren kann (indem er - wie etwa in der Gnosis - dessen Gabe, die Erkenntnis, selbständig besitzt). Denn es besteht ja im Empfangen selbst, weil es auf das göttliche Geben eingestellt ist (nicht auf eine allfällige Gabe).

---

[115] Auf der Ebene des Hymnus wird zwar der Logos stets von seiner Inkarnation her verstanden, aber dennoch gewährte er dieses Sein der Kinder Gottes schon vor der Inkarnation; diese Mehrschichtigkeit verkennt Culpepper, "Pivot", 15-17, der - ohne Begründung (vgl. a.a.O.) - vom jetzt vorliegenden Text ausgeht und mit Hilfe einer chiastischen Strukturanalyse V. 12b als "pivot" des Prologs herausstellt und die Kinder Gottes sofort mit der joh Gemeinde (oder vielleicht breiter: allen Christen) identifiziert.
[116] Oepke, Art. παῖς, 637,55-638,10.
[117] Zu dieser Unterscheidung vgl. Schweizer, Art. υἱός, 393,27-394,1.
[118] Zu Recht wird es deshalb in Joh 3.1-21 um die Wiedergeburt als Interpretament der Taufe gehen.

## III. Konsequenzen für die Biblische Theologie

Am Paradigma des Johannesprologs konnten wir beobachten, wie ein neutestamentlicher Text mit der Weisheitstheologie umgeht. Aus diesen Beobachtungen werden nun Schlüsse zu ziehen sein für eine Biblische Theologie. Schon auf den ersten Blick können wir im Prolog eine Wechselwirkung zwischen Christus und der Weisheit erkennen. Einerseits ist deutlich, dass die Weisheit herangezogen wird, um den Christus zu erschliessen. Anderseits ist nicht weniger klar, dass die Weisheit ihrerseits neu erschlossen wird durch den Christus, den sie interpretiert. Es ist zu vermuten, dass dies zu den fundamentalen Gegebenheiten einer vom Neuen Testament aus denkenden Biblischen Theologie gehört. Die Schrift wird zwar herangezogen, um den Christus auszulegen; zugleich aber wird dieselbe Schrift durch den Christus ihrerseits neu ausgelegt. Daraus muss der Schluss gezogen werden, dass es nicht nur alttestamentliche Voraussetzungen neutestamentlicher Theologie gibt, sondern auch neutestamentliche Voraussetzungen alttestamentlicher Theologie. Wir konzentrieren uns im Folgenden auf die Beschreibung der genannten Wechselwirkung zwischen Christus und der Weisheit.

### 1. Der Christus im Lichte der Weisheit

Die weisheitliche Theologie wird im Johannesprolog herangezogen, um die Wahrheit oder Würde des Christus zu erschliessen. Dies hat zur Folge, dass das theologische Problem der Weisheit bedeutsam wird für das Verständnis des Christus. Denn sofern die Weisheit den Christus erschliesst, muss dieser betrachtet werden als eine Antwort auf das theologische Problem der Weisheit. Dazu eine Skizze in knappen Strichen.

Ich erinnere zunächst an Bekanntes. In der älteren Weisheitsliteratur tritt die Weisheit nicht als eigenständige Person auf. Sie ist vielmehr erkennbar, indem man die Ordnung der Welt und der menschlichen Lebensvorgänge erkennt. Die Weisheit steht hier für die wunderbare Ordnung des Lebens, deren Sinn evident ist und die auf einen Schöpfer schliessen lässt, der sie geschaffen hat. Die Weisheit ist also in den Dingen anzutreffen, im Aufbau der Welt, in deren Ordnungen und Prozessen. Deshalb werden in der älteren Weisheit mit geradezu naturwissenschaftlichem Interesse Ordnungen aufgespürt, die das Leben tragen, Ordnungen, die zu kennen sich lohnt, weil es lebenswichtig ist, dass man sich an sie hält. Vielleicht ist es nicht unsinnig, auch in unserem Kontext daran zu erinnern, dass menschliches Leben sich nicht einfach foutieren kann um die Ordnungen, in die es eingelassen ist, eine Einsicht, die wir gegenwärtig recht schmerzlich zu spüren bekommen.

Aus Gründen, die jetzt nicht zu erörtern sind, kam es zur Krise des weisheitlichen Denkens. Auf einmal waren die Ordnungen der Welt und des Lebens nicht mehr einsichtig; alles schien gleichgültig zu werden. Die Welt drohte zu einem undurchschaubaren Gemenge zu werden, angesichts dessen nur noch die Skepsis des Predigers angebracht schien. In dieser Krise entwickelte sich ein neues weisheitliches Denken. Charakteristisch für diese jüngere Weisheit ist, dass sie den Weg der Skepsis nicht geht, sondern dass in ihren Texten die Weisheit als eine Person aufzutreten beginnt. Früher war die Weisheit in den Dingen anzutreffen; diese Anschauung hat ihre Evidenz verloren. Nun tritt die Weisheit aus den Dingen heraus. Sie tritt auf den Strassen und Marktplätzen an die Menschen heran, um sie auf die Ordnungen des Lebendigen hinzuweisen. Sie tritt als Person auf, ein Symbol dafür, dass an ihr festgehalten werden soll, gerade angesichts des Gemenges, das das Leben darstellt. Von dieser Person wird erzählt, sie habe Himmel, Erde und Unterwelt durchmessen; es gebe keine Räume, in denen sie nicht gewesen ist. So undurchschaubar es im Himmel zugehen mag, auch dort war die Weisheit; so chaotisch das Leben sein mag, es ist durch die Weisheit erschaffen; so gross das Durcheinander in der Unterwelt sein mag, auch dort war die Weisheit schon gewesen. Weil sie in den Dingen nicht mehr anzutreffen ist, tritt sie aus ihnen heraus, um so auf die Prägung der Dinge hinzuweisen. Die Person der Weisheit ist das Symbol dafür, dass an ihrer orientierenden Kraft festgehalten wird, auch angesichts des undurchschaubaren Gemenges. Und das wiederum bedeutet, dass festgehalten wird an der Erfahrungsdimension des Gottesgedankens. Es wird festgehalten an der Gegenwart Gottes inmitten der Erfahrungswelt.

Dies ist das theologische Problem der Weisheit. Und wenn der Hymnus in der Gestalt des Logos so intensiv die Personalität jener Weisheit aufnimmt, wäre es kein Vorteil, würde man das theologische Problem der Weisheit nicht auch mit dem Hymnus in Zusammenhang bringen. Der Prolog treibt die Personaliät auf die Spitze, lokalisiert er doch den Logos in einer menschlichen Person. Doch im Horizont der rezipierten Weisheit darf es keinesfalls dazu kommen, dass vom Logos nur noch exklusiv und in dieser Spitze die Rede ist. Wer den weisheitlichen Hintergrund des Hymnus im Blick behält, wird sofort erkennen, dass es ihm nicht nur auf die Lokalisierung der Weisheit in Jesus ankommt (und damit auf einen theologischen Besitzanspruch), sondern dass es ihm ebenso sehr darauf ankommt, die Erfahrungsdimension des Logos festzuhalten. Die Lebendigkeit, eine Erfahrung, die jeder Mensch an sich selbst machen kann, wird durch den Menschgewordenen neu erschlossen als etwas, dem auch eine Dimension der Gotteserfahrung zukommt. Das Licht, das jedem Menschen leuchtet, der das Licht der Welt erblickt, gehört zur Erfahrungsdimension, die die Gottesgegenwart hat. Dass dadurch die Rede von Gott nicht einfacher wird, wenn sie sich angesichts der Lebenserfahrung zu verantworten hat, darf niemanden von dieser Erfahrungsbezogenheit abhalten. Dass die Erfahrung dann nicht mehr nur als ein Bereich thematisch wird, der umzugestalten ist im Sinne Gottes, sondern als ein Bereich, der auch Offenbarungsqualität hat, ist eines der schönsten Geschenke der weisheitlichen Theologie an uns Spätgeborene, auch wenn dies unsere Theologie sehr viel schwieriger und verletzlicher macht als ein apokalyptisches oder gnostisches Modell, das sich auf die Welt nur noch negativ beziehen kann. Die Weisheit, die im Prolog rezipiert ist, verpflichtet die christliche Theologie in hermeneutischer Hinsicht. Sie verpflichtet dazu, den Christus in die Welterfahrung hinein auszulegen. Auf diese Weise sorgt die Weisheit dafür, dass eine Biblische Theologie des Neuen Testaments ferngehalten wird von jedem christologischen oder biblizistischen Dogmatismus. Was immer in Christus verkörpert ist, es muss ausgelegt werden im Blick auf die Evidenz der Lebenserfahrung.

So konkret der Logos im Fleischgewordenen anschaulich wird, so sehr muss er wieder ausgelegt werden in die weiten Räume, die einst die Weisheit durchmass und denen ja auch der Logos das Gepräge gibt. Der Christus verkörpert die göttliche Zuwendung, weil er als Gnade und Wahrheit zur Erfahrung kam. Eben diese Verkörperung ist - gleich der aus den Dingen heraustretenden Weisheit - ein Widerstand gegen die Herrschaft des weltlichen Gemenges von Gnade und Ungnade, von Wahrheit und Lüge. Denn der Christus verweist den Menschen an die Wahrheit, die er in jenem Gemenge auch erfährt, damit er sich an sie halte, und er verweist ihn an das gnädig Gewährte, das in jenem Gemenge auch vorkommt, damit er sein Leben darauf gründe.

Wenn der Christus ausgelegt wird in die weiten Räume der Weisheit, wird klar, dass es keine Welterkenntnis geben kann, die theologisch belanglos wäre. Denn in jeder Welterkenntnis erscheint etwas von jener Prägung, die dem Logos zu verdanken ist. Das Zusammenspiel etwa, auf dem alles Lebendige beruht, wird zur Auslegung des Beziehungsreichtums, den der Christus dem Leben zugrundelegte. Und es wird ebenso klar, dass es keine theologische Erkenntnis geben kann, die für die Welterkenntnis belanglos wäre. Theologische Erkenntnis wäre dann nicht bloss ethisch belangreich, sondern sie ist auch belangreich in dem Sinne, dass etwa die religiöse Wahrnehmung der Welt die Beschränkung aufbrechen kann, die sich in einer Welterkenntnis zeigt, die nur noch das

Funktionieren der Welt oder die Beherrschbarkeit ihrer Abläufe im Blick hat. Religiöse Wahrnehmung der Welt lässt die Würde und das Gewicht dessen erkennen, was in der Welterkenntnis erforscht wird.

So wie es zum theologischen Ertrag des weisheitlichen Denkens gehört, dass es keine weisheitsfernen Bereiche gibt und dass demzufolge an der Sinnhaftigkeit des Geschaffenen festzuhalten ist, genauso gehört es zur Auslegung des Johannesprologs, die Sinnhaftigkeit des Lebens des Menschgewordenen auszudehnen bis an die äussersten Grenzen. Dies hat zur Folge, dass die Welt einheitlich wahrgenommen wird, und diese Wahrnehmung wiederum unterläuft die Aufteilung der Welt in Welt und Gegenwelt, die Aufteilung der Menschen in Menschen und Unmenschen. Dass dadurch das Leiden, das Misslingen, das Tödliche zu einem viel grösseren Problem wird, darf niemanden davon abhalten, an der weisheitlichen Einheit der Welt festzuhalten, die auch im Logos-Hymnus aufgenommen ist.

Im Rahmen des weisheitlichen Nachdenkens über die Gottesgegenwart in der Welt wurde der Gedanke der Präexistenz der Weisheit vor aller Schöpfung entdeckt. Damit wird nicht nur die Massgeblichkeit weisheitlicher Lebensordnungen zum Ausdruck gebracht, sondern es wird zu verstehen gegeben, dass die Gottesgegenwart an den Anfang, ins Prinzip gehört. Denn die göttliche Zuwendung zur Welt wurde begriffen als Gottes erstes, grundlegendes Geschöpf, ein Geschöpf überdies, das von allen übrigen Geschöpfen darin unterschieden ist, dass es ihnen das Gepräge gibt. Die Weisheit steht für das, was Gott von sich zu verstehen gibt. Und dass sie Gottes erstes Geschöpf ist, macht klar, dass es nie eine Zeit des Schweigens und der Unkenntlichkeit Gottes gab. Auch an diesen Gedanken knüpft der Prolog an, um die Unvordenklichkeit des Kommens Jesu Christi denken zu können.

Wenn sein Kommen auszulegen ist als Gnade und Wahrheit, so ist es völlig konsequent, die Ewigkeit dieser Gnade festzuhalten. Denn Gnade ist stets das Überraschende, das aus keinen weltlichen Zusammenhängen abgeleitet werden kann. Im Zusammenhang der Welt lässt sich der Satz von der Erhaltung der Energie, religiös gesprochen also die Idee der Gerechtigkeit denken. Die Kreativität der Gnade hingegen muss auf den schöpferischen Ursprung zurückgehen, sie ist ein Widerschein jenes Geschehens, das das Universum überhaupt ins Sein rief. Die Eindeutigkeit, mit welcher das Kommen Christi als Erfahrung der Gnade begriffen worden war, führte dazu, dass der weisheitliche Gedanke von der Anfänglichkeit der Weisheit gesteigert wurde zur Unvordenklichkeit. Deshalb wird der Logos nicht mehr als Geschöpf Gottes gedacht. Denn nicht einmal der Gedanke der Schöpfung soll dazu verleiten, die Unvordenklichkeit der Gnade anzutasten. Diese kann nur noch gewürdigt werden, indem sie ganz zum Wesen Gottes selbst genommen wird. Dass Gott prinzipiell als Gnade, als Zuwendung, als Kreativität zu denken ist, verdankt sich einerseits der Vorgabe der Weisheit und anderseits der Klarheit dessen, was in Christus in den Vordergrund der Welt getreten war. Die ungeheuren Konsequenzen, die dieser Gedanke für das Gottesbild und die Gotteswahrnehmung der Menschen hat, warten noch immer darauf, zu Ende gedacht zu werden.

### 2. Die Weisheit im Licht des Christus

Am Ende des letzten Gedankengangs kam schon in den Blick, dass und in welcher Weise der Christus die Weisheit auslegt. Man könnte allgemein sagen, dass es zu einer Klärung der Weisheit kommt, wenn diese auf den Christus angewendet wird. Im Rahmen weisheitlicher Theologie wurde immer wieder versucht, die Offenbarungsqualität der Welterfahrung mit theoretischen Mitteln festzuhalten. Wenn schon die Dinge selbst ihre Prägung durch die Weisheit verbargen, musste man sie in den allgemeinen Zusammenhängen suchen. Dies führte zu einem Abstraktionsvorgang, in welchem man Grundordnungen zu benennen suchte, welche die göttliche Prägung erkennen lassen. In eine ganz andere Richtung führt der Gedanke der Inkarnation. Wenn die Weisheit in Jesus Christus verkörpert ist, so erscheint sie als das schlechthin Besondere, als eine besondere Gestalt im Vordergrund der Welt. Damit wird der theoretische Zug weisheitlichen Denkens durchbrochen; das Denken, das die göttliche Prägung zu erkennen sucht, wird an eine menschliche Gestalt im Vordergrund der Welt verwiesen. Offenbarungsqualität hat nicht die theoretisch abstrahierte Ordnung, sondern die Wahrheit Gottes erscheint in diesem besonderen Menschen, der mit Händen und Füssen der Rettung, der Gewährung von Leben verpflichtet war. Wer die göttliche Prägung der Welt sucht, wird hinfort nicht mehr beim Allgemeinen ansetzen, sondern er wird sich dem Besonderen zuwenden müssen, dem Fragment des Schöpferischen im weltlichen Gemenge, dem Blitz des Lichtes im Helldunkel der Welt, der helfenden Hand im Handgemenge des Lebens.

Je mehr die Welt als eine unwirtliche Fremde erfahren wurde, desto tiefer sank man in die apokalyptische Entfernung alles Göttlichen aus ihr. Je sinnloser die Welt zur Erfahrung kam, desto schneller entfernte sich die Weisheit aus der Erfahrungswelt. Die ferne Weisheit stellte den Menschen vor das Problem, ihre Gegenwart trotzdem zu denken. Lösungen dieses Problems wurden entwickelt, namentlich eine apokalyptische im äthiopischen Henoch und eine gesetzestheologische im Sirachbuch. Gemäss der apokalyptischen Lösung kehrt die Weisheit, nachdem sie nirgends eine Bleibe fand, in den Himmel zurück. In unerreichbare Ferne geht sie freilich erst, nachdem sie ihren Schatz an Wissen den Henochleuten überlassen hat. In dieser apokalyptischen Lösung hat die Gotteserkenntnis die Gestalt eines himmlisch vermittelten Wissens, das per definitionem nichts mit Welterfahrung zu tun hat. Die Weisheit existiert nicht mehr als Gepräge der Welt, sie existiert nur noch als Information über eine ganz andere Welt.

Der apokalyptischen Lösung steht die christologische diametral entgegen. Die ständige, omnipräsente Ablehnung beantwortet die Weisheit hier dadurch, dass sie in menschlicher Gestalt sich einmischt in die Geschäfte der Welt. Sie kommt als zerbrechlicher Mensch, sie begibt sich in die Hände der Menschen, verletzlich und angreifbar, und vielleicht kann die Härte der menschlichen Fäuste überhaupt nur so überwunden werden. Die Erfahrung der Abkehr beantwortet diese Weisheit mit der unwiderruflichen Zuwendung in der Inkarnation. Und damit wird eine Ambivalenz der Weisheit selbst, die Ambivalenz des Kommens und Gehens, der Zuwendung und der Abkehr, absolut überwunden. Die Unvordenklichkeit göttlicher Zuwendung zur Welt wird durchgehalten in der Menschwerdung des Logos, die ihn in die Hände der Henker führen wird. Die Unvordenklichkeit findet ihr Gegenstück in der Endgültigkeit, welche die Zuwendung in der Inkarnation gewinnt.

Gemäss der gesetzestheologischen Lösung erhält die Weisheit, nachdem sie nirgends Ruhe gefunden hat, ihre Wohnstatt im Gesetz (Sir 24.23). Der allgemeinen Gegenwart der Weisheit im Gefüge der Welt steht nun ihre konkrete Gegenwart im Gesetz des Mose gegenüber. Die Aussage von der Einkehr der Weisheit ins Gesetz gibt Gelegenheit, die Inkarnationsaussage von Joh 1.14 schärfer in den Blick zu bekommen. Wenn die Weisheit ins Gesetz einkehrt, so gelangt sie genau damit nicht bis ins Fleisch, bis in die geschöpfliche Wirklichkeit des Lebens selbst. Denn das Gesetz ist die Anweisung zum Leben, die Einweisung in richtige Gestaltung der Welt. Aus der Weisheit, die in Lebenserfahrungen an mich herantritt, ist eine geworden, die als Postulat auftritt. Die Weisheit gerät also gerade dadurch, dass sie im Gesetz in die Nähe kommt, in eine prinzipielle Distanz zum Fleisch. Wirklichkeit im Fleisch kann eine so in die Nähe gekommene Weisheit nur erhalten durch das, was die Menschen im Gehorsam gegenüber dem Gesetz tun. Die Weisheit wird nicht selbst Wirklichkeit, sondern sie wird in die Wirklichkeit umgesetzt durch das gesetzesgemässe Tun der Menschen. Auch hier begegnen wir einer Ambivalenz der Weisheit, die durch ihre Anwendung auf Jesus Christus überwunden wird. Nach dem Prolog ist die göttliche Weisheit selbst Fleisch geworden. Sie hat darin ihre eigene Wirklichkeit, und sie ist nicht angewiesen darauf, von menschlicher

Praxis verwirklicht zu werden. Der göttliche Logos ist nicht das Gebot, ein gnädiges und wahrhaftiges Leben zu führen, sondern er ist die Verkörperung jener Gnade und Wahrheit, die das menschliche Leben trägt. Eine Beziehung zu dieser Wahrheit entsteht dadurch, dass man sich von ihr tragen lässt, nicht etwa dadurch, dass man sie durch eigenes Tun in die Wirklichkeit umsetzt. Denn die Wirklichkeit, welche die Kreativität im Inkarnierten hat, macht jede Verwirklichung überflüssig. Genau hier liegt der entscheidende Unterschied zwischen Gesetz und Evangelium. Das Gesetz verspricht Leben denen, die es verwirklichen, das Evangelium verkörpert göttliche Wirklichkeit denen, die es wahrnehmen.

Angesichts der Einkehr der Weisheit ins Gesetz entsteht ein Grundproblem, das jede Theologie hat. Man könnte es das Grundproblem des Dogmatismus nennen. Denn jetzt entsteht die Frage, ob das Gesetz darüber bestimmt, was Weisheit genannt zu werden verdient. Es entsteht die Frage, ob das Gesetz zu definieren die Macht hat, was Weisheit ist, und zwar abgesehen von den Erfahrungsräumen, in denen die Weisheit einst zuhause war. Dies ist der Modellfall einer dogmatistischen Definition. Es liesse sich auch ein anderes Verhältnis von Gesetz und Weisheit denken. Dass das Gesetz und seine Auslegung der Ort sind, wo Weisheit wohnt, muss sich in dem erweisen, was das Gesetz zu verstehen gibt. Auch das Gesetz wäre dann also der Evidenz der Erfahrung untergeordnet, jenem Kriterium also, mit welchem die Empfänger erst in der Lage sind, über die Geltung des Gebotenen zu entscheiden. Ein analoges Problem besteht auch in der Inkarnationschristologie: Soll die Aussage, dass der Logos im Christus verkörpert ist, dogmatistisch dazu führen, dass es zur Behauptung der exklusiven Gegenwart des Göttlichen kommt, oder soll die Gegenwart des Göttlichen in diesem Menschgewordenen der Evidenz anheimgestellt werden, die sein Wort gewinnen kann, wenn es mit der Lebenserfahrung seiner Empfänger in Kontakt kommt. Die Interpretationsleistung der Weisheit ist es, wie wir gesehen haben, die exklusive Wahrheit des Christus auszulegen in die Weiten der Welterfahrung, sie preiszugeben an die Evidenz der Erfahrung. Darum bedeutet der von der Weisheit her verstandene Christus den entschiedenen Einspruch gegen jede Weisheit, die sich im Postulat des Gesetzes zu verflüchtigen droht. Und er bedeutet den entschiedenen Einspruch gegen jede göttliche Weisheit, die sich dem Dogmatismus des Gesetzes unterwirft. Dem missverständlichen Satz von Gese könnte darum entgegengehalten werden: Das Neue Testament wird dann verständlicher durch das Alte, wenn dieses eindeutiger geworden ist durch das Neue.

## Verzeichnis der zitierten Literatur

Aland Kurt, "Ueber die Bedeutung eines Punktes. Eine Untersuchung zu Joh 1,3.4", in: ders., *Neutestamentliche Entwürfe* (ThB 63), München 1979, 351-391.

Bauer Walter, *Griechisch-deutsches Wörterbuch* zu den Schriften des Neuen Testaments und der frühchristlichen Literatur, ed. K. Aland und B. Aland, Berlin/New York 1988[6].

Becker Jürgen, *Das Evangelium nach Johannes*, (ÖTK 4/1.2), Gütersloh/Würzburg, 1984[2]-1985.

Bietenhard Hans, "Logos-Theologie im Rabbinat. Ein Beitrag zur Lehre vom Worte Gottes im rabbinischen Schrifttum", in: ANRW II/19.2, 580-618.

Blank Josef, *Das Evangelium nach Johannes*, (GSL.NT 4/1a.1b.2.3), Düsseldorf 1977-1981.

Blass Friedrich/Debrunner Albert, *Grammatik des neutestamentlichen Griechisch*, bearbeitet von F. Rehkopf, Göttingen 1984[16].

Bonsack Bernhard, "Syntaktische Ueberlegungen zu Joh 1:9-10", in: J.K. Elliott (ed.), *Studies in New Testament Language and Text*. Essays in Honour of George D. Kilpatrick on the Occasion of his sixty-fifth Birthday, NovTest.S Leiden 1976, 52-79.

Bultmann Rudolf, *Das Evangelium des Johannes* (KEK II), Göttingen 1986[21].

Colpe Carsten, "Von der Logoslehre des Philon zu der des Clemens von Alexandrien", in: A.M. Ritter (ed.), *Kerygma und Logos. Beiträge zu den geistesgeschichtlichen Beziehungen zwischen Antike und Christentum*. Festschrift für Carl Andresen zum 70. Geburtstag, Göttingen 1979, 89-107.

Conzelmann Hans, Art. φῶς κτλ., in: ThWNT IX, 302,30-349,13.

Conzelmann Hans, *Der erste Brief an die Korinther* (KEK V), Göttingen 1981[12(2)].

Culpepper R. Alan, "The Pivot of John's Prologue", *NTS* 27 (1981), 1-31.

Foerster Werner, Art. ἔξεστιν κτλ., in: ThWNT II, 557,27-572,17.

Gese Hartmut, "Der Johannesprolog", in: ders., *Zur biblischen Theologie*. Alttestamentliche Vorträge (BEvTh 78), München 1977, 152-201.

Gese Hartmut, "Erwägungen zur Einheit der biblischen Theologie", *ZThK* 67 (1970), 417-436.

Haenchen Ernst, *Das Johannesevangelium. Ein Kommentar*. Aus den nachgelassenen Manuskripten herausgegeben von Ulrich Busse mit einem Vorwort von James M. Robinson, Tübingen 1980.

Hayward C.T.R., "The Holy Name of the God of Moses and the Prologue of St. John's Gospel", *NTS* 25 (1979), 16-32.

Hofrichter Peter, "Gnosis und Johannesevangelium", *BiKi* 41 (1986), 15-21.

Hofrichter Peter, *Im Anfang war der "Johannesprolog"*. Das urchristliche Logosbekenntnis - die Basis neutestamentlicher und gnostischer Theologie (BU 17), Regensburg 1986.

Ibuki Yu, "Marginalien zum Logoshymnus", in: Bulletin of Seikei University 22 (1985), 87-116.

Janssens Yvonne, "The Trimorphic Protennoia and the Fourth Gospel", in: A.H.B. Logan / A.J.M. Wedderburn (ed.), *The New Testament and Gnosis*. Essays in honour of Robert McL. Wilson, Edinburgh 1983, 229-244.

Käsemann Ernst, "Aufbau und Anliegen des johanneischen Prologs", in: ders., *Exegetische Versuche und Besinnungen* II, Göttingen $1968^3$, 155-180.

Koschorke Klaus, "Eine gnostische Paraphrase des johanneischen Prologs. Zur Interpretation von 'Epistula Petri ad Philippum'" (NHC VIII/2) 136,16-137,4, *VigChr* 33 (1979), 383-392.

Liddell Henry George / Scott Robert, *A Greek-English Lexicon*, ed. H. St. Jones, Oxford $1940^9$.

Lindemann Andreas, "Gemeinde und Welt im Johannesevangelium", in: D. Lührmann / G. Strecker (ed.), *Kirche*. Festschrift für Günther Bornkamm zum 75. Geburtstag, Tübingen 1980, 133-161.

Mack Burton L., *Logos und Sophia*. Untersuchungen zur Weisheitstheologie im hellenistischen Judentum (StUNT 10), Göttingen 1973.

Miller Ed.L., "The Logos was God", *EvQ* 53 (1981), 65-77.

Oeming Manfred, *Gesamtbiblische Theologien der Gegenwart. Das Verhältnis von AT und NT in der hermeneutischen Diskussion seit Gerhard von Rad*, Stuttgart/Berlin/-Köln/Mainz, 1985.

Oepke Albrecht, Art. παῖς κτλ., in: ThWNT V, 636,1-653,17.

Polag Athanasius, *Die Christologie der Logienquelle* (WMANT 45), Neukirchen-Vluyn 1977.

Rad Gerhard von, *Theologie des Alten Testaments*, I-II (KT NF 2.3), München $1987^9$.

Reim Günter, *Studien zum alttestamentlichen Hintergrund des Johannesevangeliums* (SNTS.MS 22), Cambridge 1974.

Reventlow Henning Graf, *Hauptprobleme der Biblischen Theologie im 20. Jahrhundert* (EdF 203), Darmstadt 1983.

Robinson James M., "Gnosticism and the New Testament", in: B. Aland (ed.), *Gnosis*. Festschrift für Hans Jonas, Göttingen 1978, 125-143.

Rudolph Kurt, *Die Gnosis. Wesen und Geschichte einer spätantiken Religion*, Göttingen 1980².

Schenke Gesine (ed.), *Die dreigestaltige Protennoia* (Nag-Hammadi-Codex XIII) (TU 132), Berlin 1984.

Schmithals Walter, "Der Prolog des Johannesevangeliums", ZNW 70 (1979), 16-43.

Schnackenburg Rudolf, *Das Johannesevangelium* (HThK IV/1-4), Freiburg, Basel, Wien 1965-1984.

Schnelle Udo, *Antidoketische Christologie im Johannesevangelium*. Eine Untersuchung zur Stellung des vierten Evangeliums in der johanneischen Schule (FRLANT 144), Göttingen 1987.

Schoonenberg P., "A sapiential reading of John's Prologue: some reflections on views of Reginald Fuller and James Dunn", ThD 33 (1986), 403-421.

Schwarz Günther, "Gen 1,1; 2,2a und Joh 1,1a.3a - ein Vergleich", ZNW 73 (1982), 136-137.

Schweizer Eduard, Art. υἱός κτλ. D. Neues Testament, in: ThWNT VIII, 364,1--395,16.

Schweizer Eduard, *Der Brief an die Kolosser* (EKK 12), Zürich, Neukirchen-Vluyn 1980².

Stuhlmacher Peter, "Das Bekenntnis zur Auferweckung Jesu von den Toten und die Biblische Theologie", in: ders., *Schriftauslegung auf dem Wege zur biblischen Theologie*, Göttingen 1975, 128-166.

Stuhlmacher Peter, "Zum Thema: Biblische Theologie des Neuen Testaments", in: K. Haacker u.a., *Biblische Theologie heute*. Einführung - Beispiele - Kontroversen (BThSt 1), Neukirchen-Vluyn 1977, 25-60.

Theobald Michael, *Im Anfang war das Wort*. Textlinguistische Studie zum Johannesprolog (SBS 106), Stuttgart 1983.

Theobald Michael, *Die Fleischwerdung des Logos*. Studien zum Verhältnis des Johannesprologs zum Corpus des Evangeliums und zu 1 Joh (NTA NF 20), Münster 1988.

Weder Hans, "Der Mythos vom Logos (Johannes 1). Überlegungen zur Sachproblematik der Entmythologisierung", in: ders., *Einblicke ins Evangelium. Exegetische Beiträge zur neutestamentlichen Hermeneutik*. Gesammelte Aufsätze aus den Jahren 1980-1991, Göttingen 1992, 401-434.

Yamauchi Edwin M., "Jewish Gnosticism? The Prologue of John, Mandaean Parallels, and the Trimorphic Protennoia", in: R. van den Broek / M.J. Vermaseren (ed.), *Studies in Gnosticism and Hellenistic Religions* presented to Gilles Quispel on the Occasion of his 65th Birthday (EPRO 91), Leiden 1981, 467-497.

CHAPTER TEN

# APOKALYPTIK ALS BIBELTHEOLOGISCHES THEMA

*Dargestellt an Dan 9 und Mk 13*

Aage Pilgaard, Århus

## I. Apokalyptik als biblische Theologie

Biblische Theologie ist ein umstrittenes Gebiet. Von einigen Exegeten wird es als dringende Aufgabe gesehen,[1] von anderen als Rückfall in unwissenschaftlichen Dogmatismus abgelehnt.[2] Es kann aber nicht übersehen werden, daß der zweiteilige Kanon eine historische Tatsache ist. Die Einheit des Alten und Neuen Testaments als biblischer Kanon der Kirche ist aber mehr als eine historische Tatsache, die auf Entscheidungen der alten Kirche beruht. Die alt- und neutestamentlichen Schriften als kanonische Einheit sind eine auch in der aktuellen Gegenwart der Kirche wirksame Tatsache.

Das hat die Diskussion um die vor kurzem abgeschlossene dänische Neuübersetzung der Bibel deutlich demonstriert. Und in ihrer Liturgie, ihrer Predigt und ihrem Unterricht, ja schon in ihrem Bekenntnis treibt die Kirche faktisch biblische Theologie. Das heißt: wollen die exegetischen Disziplinen nicht nur um ihrer selbst und um der Wissenschaft willen betrieben werden, sondern auch um der Kirche willen, dann kommen sie nicht umhin, auch die Frage einer biblischen Theologie zu berücksichtigen.[3]

Damit beabsichtige ich nicht eine Zweiteilung der exegetischen Aufgabe, so daß die exegetischen Disziplinen sowohl eine wissenschaftliche als auch eine "überwissenschaftliche", kirchliche Aufgabe

---

[1] B. Janowski, M. Welker, *JBTh* 1 (1986), 5-8.
[2] E. Grässer, "Offene Fragen im Umkreis einer biblischen Theologie", *ZThK* 77 (1980), 200-221. Dazu P. Stuhlmacher, "...in verrosteten Angeln", *ZThK* 77 (1980), 222-238. Siehe auch H. Hübner, "Biblische Theologie und Theologie des Neuen Testaments", *KuD* 27 (1981), 2-19.
[3] Zum Stand der Diskussion siehe K. Haacker u.a. (Hg.), *Biblische Theologie heute* (BThSt 1), Neukirchen, 1977; W. Zimmerli und O. Merk, *TRE* 6, 426-477; H. Graf Reventlow, *Hauptprobleme der Biblischen Theologie im 20. Jahrhundert* (EdF 203, Darmstadt, 1983), 138-172; ders., "Kritische Bilanz der Sicht des Alten Testaments in neueren christlichen Entwürfen einer Biblischen Theologie", in M. Klopfenstein u.a. (Hg.), *Mitte der Schrift* (Bern, Frankfurt a.M., New York, Paris, 1985), 9-27.

haben sollen.⁴ Nach meiner Ansicht ist es eben das strenge Festhalten an der Wissenschaftlichkeit der exegetischen Disziplinen - auch im Entfalten einer biblischen Theologie -, womit die exegetischen Disziplinen der Kirche dienen können.⁵

Bekanntlich bedeutet das Wort Theologie Lehre von Gott.⁶ Die Kernfrage einer biblischen Theologie ist demnach: wie wird Gott in den biblischen Schriften bezeugt? Sind die unterschiedlichen Zeugnisse von Gott in den biblischen Schriften miteinander vereinbar oder nicht?

Dabei muß die Geschichtlichkeit der biblischen Zeugnisse von Gott ernst genommen werden. Sie sind ja in historischen Kontexten gesprochen und gehört worden, und sie wirken selbst auf die Geschichte ein, so daß sie auf neue historische Kontexte mitschöpferisch einwirken. Denn die verschiedenen Zeugnisse von Gott in den biblischen Schriften sind nicht nur von außen her mitbestimmt, das heißt: nicht nur von neuen historischen Kontexten mitbedingt. Sie haben auch "innere" Bedingungen. Das heißt: die in der Tradition enthaltenen Zeugnisse von Gott wirken auf neue Kontexte ein als Verstehenshorizonte, die neue Zeugnisse von Gott mitprägen.

So wird die Frage nach der Vereinbarkeit der unterschiedlichen Zeugnisse von Gott in der Bibel zur Frage nach Kontinuität in Diskontinuität und umgekehrt. Gibt es trotz aller Diskontinuität eine grundsätzliche Kontinuität, die es ermöglicht, von *der Theologie der Bibel* zu reden? Es ist die Aufgabe für das Unternehmen "biblische Theologie", diese Frage zu beantworten.⁷

---

⁴ H. Graf Reventlow, *Hauptprobleme*, 160-172.
⁵ Mit Recht hebt C. Westermann die Überwindung der Spezialisierung der Theologie "in lauter kleine Fächer" als Aufgabe einer Biblischen Theologie hervor ("Zur Frage einer Biblischen Theologie", *JBTh* 1 (1986), 29); cf. "Aufgaben einer zukünftigen Biblischen Theologie", in *Erträge der Forschung am Alten Testament* (Ges. Studien III, München, 1984), 203-212.
⁶ Zum Begriff Theologie siehe G. Ebeling, "Was heißt 'Biblische Theologie'?", in ders., *Wort und Glaube* (Tübingen, 1967³), 69-89. Mit Recht kritisiert C. Westermann ("Frage", 16-19) G. Ebelings Versuch, den Begriff aus der Begegnung zwischen dem biblischen Offenbarungsverständnis und dem griechischen Denken zu erklären. Umgekehrt scheint mir aber Westermanns Hervorhebung des verbalen Sinnes im Begriff Theologie unter Berufung auf das hebräische Wort *dābār* als ein "primär einen Vorgang" bezeichnendes Wort, während das griechische Wort λόγος primär auf den Inhalt abzielt (14), die Kritik seitens James Barr (*The Semantics of Biblical Language*, Oxford, 1961) gegen ein solches Hervorgehen übersehen zu haben.
⁷ In diesem Zusammenhang ist es notwendig, die Begriffe Kontinuität und Diskontinuität sehr sorgfältig zu überlegen und zu definieren. Darauf kann hier leider nicht näher eingegangen werden. Nur soll darauf hingewiesen werden: 1. Geschichte ohne Diskontinuität gibt es meiner Meinung nach nicht. Das heißt: die Rede von Gott als Herr der Geschichte impliziert in gewissem Sinne Diskontinuität. 2. Das Bekenntnis zum Einssein Gottes schließt angesichts der Vielfältigkeit der Welt Diskontinuität nicht aus sondern ein.

In der apokalyptischen Literatur haben wir ein Gebiet, das eben diese Frage nach Kontinuität und Diskontinuität stellt.[8] Die Gattung Apokalypse - wenn man von einer solchen reden kann[9] - kommt nur am Rande der Bibel vor, aber sie ist doch eine Gattung, die in beiden Teilen des Kanons vorkommt. Im Alten Testament das Danielbuch und im Neuen Testament die Apokalypse des Johannes.

Meiner Meinung nach kann man mit gewissem Recht sagen, daß das Danielbuch, das die jüngste der alttestamentlichen Schriften ist, eine apokalyptische Deutung und Weiterführung von wichtigen alttestamentlichen Traditionen repräsentiert.[10] So steht an der Schwelle zwischen den beiden Teilen des Kanons eine Gedankenwelt, deren Bedeutung für das Neue Testament grundlegend ist.[11] Denn die apokalyptische Gedankenwelt macht sich im Neuen Testament durchgehend - und nicht nur in der Apokalypse des Johannes - geltend.[12]

Das Kernproblem der Apokalyptik (wie sie in der Bibel repräsentiert ist)[13] ist das Problem der Erkenntnis von Gottes Willen in und mit der Geschichte mit Bezug auf die Zeit, wenn Gott nach seinem Willen die Geschichte (als Unheilsgeschichte) zu Ende führt und endgültiges Heil schafft.

Im folgenden lasse ich die Fragen nach Ursprung, Entwicklung und Definition der Apokalyptik beiseite.[14] Stattdessen will ich die danieli-

---

[8] K. Koch: "Seit hundert Jahren steht die Frage im Raum, ob die apokalyptische Gedankenwelt nicht die Schaltstelle zwischen Altem und Neuem Testament darbietet, also jene religiöse Bewegung widerspiegelt, die unter dem Eindruck der Person Jesu und ihres Geschicks einen Teil des späten Israelitentums in das Urchristentum ausmünden liess" *(Ratlos vor der Apokalyptik* (Gütersloh, 1970), 118). Vgl. H. Gese, "Anfang und Ende der Apokalyptik, dargestellt am Sacharjabuch," *ZThK* 70 (1973), 20.

[9] Siehe J.J. Collins (Hg.), *Apocalypse. The Morphology of a Genre*, Semeia 14 (1979); ders., "The Genre Apocalypse in Hellenistic Judaism", i D. Hellholm (Hg.), *Apocalypticism in the Mediterranean World and the Near East* (Tübingen, 1983), 531-548; L. Hartman, "Survey of the Problem of Apocalyptic Genre", idem, 329-343; E.P. Sanders, "The Genre of Palestinian Jewish Apocalypses", idem, 447-459; H. Stegemann, "Die Bedeutung der Qumranfunde für die Erforschung der Apokalyptik", idem, 497-530.

[10] Das hat an Hand der Gattung Visionsbericht K. Koch klar gezeigt, ("Vom prophetischen zum apokalyptischen Visionsbericht", in D. Hellholm (Hg.), *Apocalypticism*, 413-446).

[11] Vgl. B. Otzen, *Judaism in Antiquity* (Sheffield, 1990), 221.

[12] Zur Beurteilung der Bedeutung der Apokalyptik für Das Neue Testament siehe K. Koch, *Ratlos*, 8; 115-119; R.E. Sturm, "Defining the Word 'Apocalyptic': A Problem in Biblical Criticism", in J. M. Marcus and M.L. Soards (Hg.), *Apocalyptic and The New Testament* (FS J.L. Martyn (JSNT.SS 24), Sheffield, 1989), 17-48; W. Zager, *Begriff und Wertung der Apokalyptik in der neutestamentlichen Forschung* (EHS.R 23, Theologie), Frankfurt a.M., Bern, New York, Paris, 1989.

[13] Ch. Rowland, *The Open Heaven* (London, 1985), passim, will das für die Apokalyptik Spezifische im Interesse für die obere Welt Gottes finden und lehnt eine wesenhafte Verbindung zwischen Apokalyptik und Eschatologie ab, ohne jedoch einen Zusammenhang zu verleugnen. Kritisch zu Rowland ist R.E. Sturm, "Defining", 1989, 36.

[14] Diese Fragen sind - wie bekannt - sehr umstritten, siehe H. Stegemann, "Bedeutung", in D. Hellholm, *Apocalypticism*, 498-501. M. Hengel erklärt: "'Den Apokalyptiker' und 'die Apokalyptik' im strengen Sinn gibt es noch weniger als 'die Gnosis' oder 'den Gnostiker'" ("Messianische Hoffnung und politischer 'Radikalismus' in der 'jüdisch-hellenistischen Diaspora'" in D. Hellholm (Hg.), *Apocalypticism*, 655).

sche Geschichtstheologie aufnehmen, wie sie in Dan 9 zum Ausdruck kommt. In diesem Kapitel wird ein Wort des Propheten Jeremia (Jer 25.12; 29.10) aufgenommen und neu interpretiert, und so die Frage der Kontinuität und Diskontinuität aktualisiert. Danach werde ich Mk 13 aufgreifen, um aufzuzeigen, wie die danielische Geschichtskonzeption hier aufgenommen und reinterpretiert wird.

## II. Daniel 9 als apokalyptische Geschichtstheologie

### 1. Die apokalyptische Deutung der Jeremia-Prophetie

Kap. 9 ist die Mitte des visionären Teils des Danielbuches,[15] nicht nur textlich, sondern auch sachlich.[16] In Kap. 9 geht es um die Interpretation einer Jeremia-Prophetie. Diese Interpretation schafft Raum für die Zeit der Weltreiche, die in Kap. 7-8 und 10-12 beschrieben wird.

Diese Bemühung, die Zeit der Weltreiche bis zum endzeitlichen Heil im prophetischen Wort Gottes zu verankern, zeigt, daß der Verfasser um Kontinuität in der Geschichte Israels bemüht ist. Die Jeremia-Aussage ist eine Aussage der Schriften[17] und somit autoritatives Wort Gottes (V. 2). Die Aussage hat jedoch eine entscheidende Wandlung erfahren, die darin besteht, daß das Verhältnis zwischen Ausdruck und Inhalt verschoben worden ist: Ausdruck und Inhalt decken einander nicht mehr. Aus dem offenen Ausdruck ist ein verschlüsselter geworden, dessen Sinn ebenso geheim ist wie die nicht entschlüsselten Visionen.

Die Wertschätzung des prophetischen Wortes ist damit entscheidend verändert. War das prophetische Wort im Jeremiabuch ein Ausdruck dafür, daß Gott sich in der Welt durch seinen Propheten offenbart, so ist das prophetische Wort im Danielbuch als göttlich qualifiziertes Wort ein zum himmlischen Bereich gehörendes Wort, dessen Sinn nur entschlüsselt

---

[15] Diese Beurteilung gilt der Endgestalt des aramäisch-hebräischen Danielbuches.- Zur Entstehungsgeschichte des Buches siehe J.J. Collins, *Daniel* (FOTL 20, Grand Rapids, 1984), 27-39; L.F. Hartman, A. Di Lella, *The Book of Daniel* (AB, New York, 1978), 9-18; J.-C. Lebram, *Das Buch Daniel* (ZBK, Zürich, 1984), 18-25; N.W. Porteous, *Daniel* (London, 1979²), 119-121.

[16] Die Bedeutung des Kapitels wird auch durch das eingefügte Gebet (V. 4b-19) hervorgehoben. Das Gebet ist meiner Meinung nach vom Verfasser des Kapitels und nicht erst von einem Redaktor eingefügt worden. Denn allen Unterschieden zum Trotz ist das Heil für Jerusalem das Anliegen des ganzen Kapitels, und sowohl im Gebet wie in der Antwort Gabriels geht es um Vertilgung der Sünden als Voraussetzung des Heils für Jerusalem (V. 16-18,24). Das Geschichtsverständnis des Gebets lässt sich nicht als ganz und gar deuteronomistisch charakterisieren (gegen J.J. Collins, *Daniel*, 95), denn das Heil ist nicht nur als eine Folge von Bußbereitschaft des Volkes gesehen, sondern vor allem als Ergebnis der Barmherzigkeit Gottes. In Übereinstimmung damit sind die 70 Jahrwochen (V. 24) nicht die Zeit für die Vollendung der Buße, sondern die Zeit, wo die Sünde sich steigert bis zur endzeitlichen Entsühnung, deren Zeitpunkt von Gott vorherbestimmt ist.

[17] Wörtlich "die Bücher" im technischen Sinne von den kanonischen Schriften - "the only occurrence in the Hebrew Bible of the use of the term in this sense" (Hartman, Di Lella, *Daniel*, 241).

werden kann, wenn der Mensch Einblick in den himmlischen Bereich bekommt (zum Beispiel durch eine Vision), und ihm der himmlische Sinn durch eine himmlische Gestalt geoffenbart wird.

Diese Betonung der Transzendenz des Gotteswortes und damit auch der Transzendenz Gottes entspricht aber der Hervorhebung der Gestalt Daniel: Daniel ist "Liebling" Gottes (9.23; 10.11,19), und in ihm wohnt der Geist der heiligen Götter (4.8,18; 5.11,14). In diesem Sinne ist Daniel mehr als ein Prophet. Er ist das Glied, das nicht nur die Kontinuität der Geschichte vom babylonischen Exil bis zum Ende der Geschichte, sondern auch die Verbindung zwischen der transzendenten Welt Gottes und der empirischen Welt der Menschen darstellt.

Es zeigt sich so, dass die apokalyptische Gedankenwelt die hermeneutischen Instrumente liefert, die es ermöglichen, den wahren Sinn des Jeremiawortes zu entziffern.

Die Deutung des Prophetenwortes durch den Engel bedeutet eine ungeheure Ausdehnung der Zeitspanne von 70 auf 490 Jahre.[18]

Diese Ausdehnung der Zeit ermöglicht jedoch eine aktualisierende Deutung des Prophetenwortes auf die Gegenwart des Verfassers hin. Im Lichte der aktualisierenden Auslegung des Prophetenwortes erkennen der Verfasser und seine Leser ihre eigene Situation sowohl qualitativ als die Zeit der Kulmination der widergöttlichen Weltreiche als auch quantitativ als die Zeit des nahen Endes. Diese Bestimmung der Zeit wird mit dem Ausdruck "Greuel der Verwüstung" signaliert, und dieser Ausdruck wird als Teil der himmlischen Auslegung des Prophetenwortes eingeführt. Auch darin zeigt sich die zentrale Bedeutung des 9. Kapitels im zweiten Teil des Buches, denn dieser Ausdruck weist auf 8.13 zurück und taucht danach zweimal wieder auf (11.31; 12.11).[19]

Mit diesen Überlegungen bewegen wir uns von der "erzählten Welt" in "die Erzählwelt" des Danielbuches.

Die "Erzählwelt" der Endredaktion des Danielbuches muß aller Wahrscheinlichkeit nach in der Zeit des Königs Antiochus IV gesucht werden, und die Endredaktion des Buches muß in Verbindung mit Antiochus' Prophanierung des Tempels gesehen werden.

Mit J. J. Collins[20] nehme ich an, daß der Kreis hinter dem Buch aus ehemahligen Diasporajuden, die theologisch als *chasidim* angesehen werden können, besteht.

---

[18] Zur Frage einer inkludierenden oder exkludierenden Deutung der 490 Jahre siehe K. Koch, "Die Bedeutung der Apokalyptik für die Interpretation der heiligen Schrift", in M. Klopfenstein, *Mitte*, 197-198.
[19] Zum Problem "Greuel der Verwüstung" siehe K. Koch, *Das Buch Daniel* (EdF 144, Darmstadt, 1980), 136-140.
[20] "Daniel and His Social World", *Int* 30 (1985), 131-143.

Für diesen Kreis lieferte die apokalyptische Gedankenwelt den entscheidenden hermeneutischen Schlüssel für seine aktualisierende Schriftinterpretation. Die apokalyptische Gedankenwelt ermöglicht es für diesen Kreis, den Sinn seiner aktuellen Geschichte zu erhellen und diesen Sinn im prophetischen Gotteswort der Schriften zu verankern.

Die Gestalt Daniel, die zeitlich in Verbindung mit Jeremia steht, dient dabei als Vermittler zwischen der alten prophetischen und der neuen apokalyptischen Gedankenwelt. Daniel ist die Gestalt, die die Kontinuität in der Diskontinuität gewährleistet.

## 2. Das Geschichtsverständnis des Danielbuches

Bekanntlich betonte G. von Rad den Unterschied zwischen dem prophetischen und dem apokalyptischen Geschichtsverständnis und ordnete religionsgeschichtlich die Apokalyptik der Weisheit zu.[21] Während die prophetische Geschichtsschau echt geschichtlich sei, sei die Geschichtsschau der Apokalyptik deterministisch und so in ihrem Kern ungeschichtlich.

G. von Rad hat damit etwas Wichtiges gesehen. Soll aber der Vergleich nicht schief werden, ist es notwendig, auf zwei Perspektiven des apokalyptischen Danielbuches aufmerksam zu sein. Es sind die Rückperspektive und die Universalperspektive. Das Danielbuch ist Geschichtsdeutung in Rückperspektive. Es gilt, das innerste Wesen der Geschichte zu enthüllen. Und dabei kommt es auf die Universalgeschichte an: Was ist das Wesen der Universalgeschichte? Es geht um die basale Struktur der Geschichte. Es ist das Wesen der Geschichte aus der Perspektive Gottes, worauf es ankommt. Und die Rück- und Universalperspektive dient dazu, den Sinn der Gegenwart und der nahen Zukunft im Lichte der Vergangenheit zu verstehen.[22]

In der Gegenwart ist aber nicht alles determiniert, wie J.J. Collins mit Recht betont hat: das Schicksal des Einzelnen hängt von seinem treuen Festhalten am Bunde ab. Eben dazu will das Danielbuch Menschen rufen, damit sie am Endheil teilhaftig werden können (11.33).[23] Der Aufruf scheint aber vor allem an den Kreis der Frommen gerichtet zu sein, und die universalgeschichtliche Perspektive ist an Jerusalem orientiert. Ihr Ausgangspunkt ist der Zug Nebukadnezars gegen Jerusalem, und ihr Ziel ist die letzte Freveltat gegen Jerusalem, die Signal zur Verleihung der

---

[21] *Theologie des Alten Testaments II* (München, 1968), 316-328; ders., *Weisheit in Israel* (Neukirchen, 1970), 337-363.
[22] Gegen von Rad: P. von der Osten-Sacken, *Die Apokalyptik in ihrem Verhältnis zu Prophetie und Weisheit* (ThExH 157), München 1969; Gese, "Anfang", 22-41.
[23] J.J. Collins, "Social World", 141-142.

universalen Herrschaft an das Volk Gottes in einem mit Jerusalem verknüpften Heilsgeschehen ist.

Diese Verknüpfung des Heils mit Jerusalem ist Weiterführung alttestamentlicher Tradition. Zwar wird von einer endzeitlichen Herrlichkeit des Tempels und der Stadt nicht direkt gesprochen; diese Erwartung liegt aber meiner Meinung nach implizit in der ganzen Zielrichtung von Kap. 9 und schimmert auch in 9.24 durch.

Die Universalgeschichte bis zum endzeitlichen Heil ist eine Zeit, die von immer größerem Unheil charakterisiert ist (9.24). Das hat zur Folge, daß der entscheidende Termin der empirischen Weltgeschichte auf die Kulmination des Aufruhrs der Weltmächte gegen Gott und sein Volk hin orientiert ist. Heil gibt es nur in der die Geschichte transzendierenden Zukunft, wenn Gott der Geschichte ein Ende setzt.

Dem transzendenten Charakter des Heils im Danielbuch entspricht dessen exklusive Realisierung durch göttliche Wundertat. Der Kreis hinter dem Danielbuch erwartet kein Heil durch politische und militärische Veranstaltungen.[24]

### 3. Die apokalyptische Auslegung als Prophetie

Daniels Reinterpretation des prophetischen Wortes setzt voraus, daß die Erfüllung des Wortes nicht mit dem Wiederaufbau des Tempels geschehen ist (9.25). Der eigentliche Inhalt des Wortes zielt auf einen endzeitlichen Wiederaufbau von kosmischem Ausmaß, der in der "Erzählwelt" als nahe bevorstehend erwartet wird. Diese Erwartung traf nicht zu: nicht die quietistische Erwartung des Danielkreises, sondern der makkabäische Aufruhr erbrachte die Befreiung für Israel, und diese war national, nicht kosmisch-universal. Das bedeutet aber nicht, daß die danielische Erwartung ihre Bedeutung verliert.

Mit der römischen Okkupation von Palästina ist eine neue Situation entstanden, die zu einer prophetischen Reinterpretation der danielischen Erwartung mitwirkt.[25] Daniel wird als Prophet angesehen, und das vierte Weltreich wird auf Rom bezogen, und später wird die Kulmination der Drangsal auf die römische Zerstörung Jerusalems im Jahre 70 bezogen. Das bedeutet, daß die apokalyptische Enthüllung des geheimnisvollen Jeremiawortes im Danielbuch selbst als ein geheimnisvolles Prophetenwort gelesen wird, das Enthüllung fordert. K. Koch, der auf diese Sachlage aufmerksam gemacht hat, hat sicher recht, wenn er

---

[24] J.J. Collins, "Social World", 140.
[25] Die Entwicklung läßt sich in den Danielhandschriften aus Qumran nachweisen, siehe K. Koch in Klopfenstein, *Mitte*, 211-213.

vermutet, daß es diese prophetische Lesung ist, die dem Danielbuch kanonischen Rang verliehen hat.[26]

So haben wir in der Entwicklung von Jeremia zu Daniel, und von Daniel zur Aufnahme des Danielbuches in den Kanon ein Beispiel dafür, wie die Nicht-Erfüllung eines Gotteswortes im wörtlichen Sinne nicht dessen Entfernung bewirkt, sondern - eben weil es als Gotteswort angesehen wird - sinngebend auf neue Situationen einwirkt durch aktualisierende Reinterpretation mittels hermeneutischer Instrumente, die aus Gedankenwelten geholt werden, die in der Situation sinnvoll sind.

Die Geschichte des Danielbuches und ihrer Interpretation zeigt zugleich, daß die Interpretation sich in verschiedenen Richtungen bewegen kann. Die politische Interpretation wurde schon im hasmonäischen Raum vollzogen, und diese Interpretation wurde wahrscheinlich von den jüdischen Zeloten weitergeführt.[27] Die politische Interpretation wird jedoch auch von Josephus aufgenommen und zwar in Beziehung auf die römische Herrschaft (B.J. 6,312-313).[28] Diese politische Interpretation hat zur Folge, daß die Transzendenz des Endheils, die für die Apokalyptik Daniels charakteristisch ist, verlorengeht. In Mk 13 finden wir eine Interpretation des apokalyptisch-transzendenten Endheils, die sowohl die politische Interpretation ablehnt als auch die Transzendenz überbrückt.

### III. Markus 13 als apokalyptische Geschichtstheologie

*1. Weissagung im Rahmen der danielischen Geschichtstheologie*
Wie in Dan 9 ist der Ausgangspunkt des Kapitels eine Weissagung (v. 2), und wie in Dan 9 wird nach dem Zeitpunkt für die Erfüllung der Weissagung gefragt (V. 3-4), und wie in Dan 9 wird die Frage beantwortet (V. 5-37). Ein weiteres gemeinsames Merkmal ist die Tatsache, daß Weissagung und Erklärung dem Tempel (und Jerusalem) gelten.[29]

---

[26] In M. Klopfenstein, *Mitte*, 215.
[27] Siehe H. Schwier, *Tempel und Tempelzerstörungen. Untersuchungen zu den theologischen und ideologischen Faktoren im ersten jüdisch-römischen Krieg (66-74 n.Chr.)*, (NTOA 11, Göttingen, 1989), 172. H. Schwier vermutet, daß die Zeloten sich auf Dan 9.24-27 berufen haben.
[28] Es ist jedoch sehr unsicher, an welche alttestamentlichen Stellen Josephus denkt. Siehe Schwier, *Tempel*, 240-250; vgl. aber F.F. Bruce, "Josephus and Daniel", *ASTI* 4 (1965), 148-162.
[29] Die folgenden Überlegungen beziehen sich auf die markinische Gestalt des Kapitels und sind insofern "synchronisch". Zur vieldiskutierten Frage der Traditions- und Redaktionsgeschichte des Kapitels siehe R. Pesch, *Naherwartungen. Tradition und Redaktion in Mark 13* (Düsseldorf, 1968); *Das Markusevangelium II* (HThK 2) (Freiburg, Basel, Wien, 1977), 264-318; "Markus 13", in J. Lambrecht (Hg.), *L'Apocalypse johannique et l'Apocalyptique dans le Nouveau Testament*, Paris-Gembloux (Leuven, 1980), 355-368; F. Neirynck, "Marc 13. Examen critique de l'interprétation de R. Pesch", idem, 369-401.

Im Unterschied zum Danieltext ist es aber dieselbe Person, die sowohl Weissagung als auch Erklärung gibt. Jesus vereint die Funktionen des Propheten (Jeremia) und des Deuteengels (Gabriel) in seiner Person, während die Position Daniels eher der Position der vier fragenden Jünger entspricht.

Diese Unterschiede bewirken, daß die Erklärung Jesu formal von der Erklärung in Dan 9 abweicht: sie geschieht nicht vom Himmel her in einer Vision. So genügt die Rede Jesu nicht den üblichen kommunikativen Kriterien der Gattung Apokalypse.[30] Der markinische Jesus kennt nicht nur das Schicksal des Tempels, sondern auch die Entwicklung der Geschichte kraft der ihm verliehenen Exusia.

Geht man aber vom Inhalt aus, zeigt sich viele apokalyptische Motive. Das gilt sowohl für die Fragerichtung auf das Ende hin (v. 3-4), wie für die stufenweise Realisierung der Weissagung in einer Reihe typisch apokalyptischer Ereignisse (v. 7-8,14-20,24-27).[31]

Die Erklärung der Weissagung in Mark 13 geschieht nicht mit explizitem Hinweis auf ein Schriftwort wie in Dan 9, und somit tritt die Erklärung nicht wie in Dan 9 als Schriftauslegung hervor. Dennoch gibt es viele Anspielungen auf alttestamentliche Schriftworte und vor allem auf das Danielbuch, was zu der Annahme geführt hat, das Kernstück der Rede sei ein Danielmidrasch.[32] Was mich aber in diesem Zusammenhang interessiert, sind zwei der Stellen, wo man von Zitaten aus dem Danielbuch reden kann.

Ich denke an V. 14, wo aus Dan 9.27; 11.31; 12.11 zitiert wird, und an V. 26, wo aus Dan 7.13-14 zitiert wird. Es zeigt sich also, daß sowohl die Kulmination der Krisenzeit als auch das Heilsereignis in der Sprache Daniels beschrieben werden.

Daniel wird somit in Übereinstimmung mit dem damaligen Judentum als Prophet angesehen. Direkt wird das in Mk 13 nicht gesagt. Das geschieht aber in dem parallelen Matthäustext (Mt 24.15). So scheint es mir deutlich, daß wir es in Mk 13 mit einer apokalyptischen Eschatologie zu tun haben, deren Problem die apokalyptische Geschichtsperspektive des als Propheten geschätzten Daniel ist.[33] Wie die jeremianische

---

[30] Als kommunikatives Merkmal der Gattung Apokalypse nennt J. J. Collins "...a narrative framework, in which a revelation is mediated by an otherworldly being to a human recipient,..." (*Semeia* 14, 9). Zum Fehlen diesen Merkmals in Mk 13 siehe A. Y. Collins, "The Early Christian Apocalypses" (*Semeia* 14, 96-97). Die Auffassung von L. Gaston (*No Stone On Another* (NovTest.S 23), Leiden, 1970), 41-46), Mark 13 parr. sei ursprünglich eine Rede des auferstandenen Jesus, halte ich für falsch.
[31] Siehe E. Brandenburger, *Markus 13 und die Apokalyptik* (FRLANT 134, Göttingen, 1984), 43-46.
[32] L. Hartman, *Prophecy Interpreted* (ConB.NTS 1, Lund, 1966). Siehe auch H.C. Kee, "The Function of Scriptural Quotations and Allusions in Mark 11-16", in E.E. Ellis, E. Grässer (Hg.), *Jesus und Paulus* (FS W.G. Kümmel, Göttingen, 1975), 165-188.
[33] Die Tendenz der Exegeten, den apokalyptischen Charakter des Kapitels abzulehnen, wird mit Recht von E. Brandenburger kritisiert (*Markus*, 9-12).

Weissagung Daniel Probleme bereitet, so bereitet die im Rahmen einer danielischen apokalyptischen Eschatologie verstandene Weissagung Jesu den Jüngern Probleme.

Im Rahmen des Danielbuches lag die Weissagung als Schriftwort vor, und ihr Rätsel wurde durch himmlische Enthüllung gelöst. Im Rahmen des Markusevangeliums wird die Weissagung mündlich formuliert, und ihr Rätsel liegt darin, daß sie im Sinne der Geschichtsperspektive der als Prophetie geschätzten Apokalyptik Daniels gehört wurde.

Das Hauptproblem Daniels war die Dauer der Zeit bis zum Wiederaufbau Jerusalems. Das Problem wird damit gelöst, daß nach einer zweiten Zerstörung Jerusalems das Heil in Bälde folgen wird. Eben diese Lösung ist aber in Mk 13 problematisch. Das zeigt die Formulierung der Fragen der Jünger in V. 4.

Bekanntlich bereitet die zweite Frage der Jünger Probleme.[34] Die Jünger fragen nach dem Zeichen ὅταν μέλλῃ ταῦτα συντελεῖσθαι πάντα (v. 4b). Wie ist aber die Beziehung dieser Frage zur ersten Frage nach dem Zeitpunkt der Zerstörung Jerusalems? Gilt die zweite Frage nur dem Zeichen, das den Zeitpunkt der Zerstörung signalisiert, oder gilt sie dem Zeichen, das das endzeitliche Heil signalisiert?

In Daniel 9 ist die zweite Zerstörung eng mit dem endzeitlichen Heil verknüpft. Diese Zerstörung bekommt eine Art Zeichencharakter, indem eben diese Zerstörung die Nähe des endzeitlichen Heils verbürgt.

In Dan 12.6-7 wird die Dauer der Zeit bis zum endzeitlichen Heil in Frage und Antwort behandelt, und die Formulierung der Antwort erinnert stark an die Formulierung der zweiten Jüngerfrage:

| Dan 12.7(LXX): | Mk 13.4b: |
|---|---|
|  | καὶ τί τὸ σημεῖον |
| καὶ συντελεσθήσεται | ὅταν μέλλῃ ταῦτα |
| ταῦτα πάντα | συντελεῖσθαι πάντα; |

Auf dem Hintergrund der danielischen Weissagung scheint es mir naheliegend, daß die zweite Frage der Jünger die danielische Konzeption der Endzeitereignisse voraussetzt. Die Frage wird auf dem Hintergrund des als prophetisch geschätzten Danielbuches gestellt. Gefragt wird also nach dem Zeichen, das die Zerstörung des Tempels und damit auch - auf dem Hintergrund der danielischen Konzeption der Endzeit - das endzeitliche Heil signalisiert. So löst sich die scheinbare Undurchsichtig-

---

[34] Hinter der Doppelfrage wird oft ein semitischer *parallelismus membrorum* gesehen, siehe L. Hartman, *Prophecy*, 221; W. L. Lane, *The Gospel of Mark* (NLC, London, 1974), 454. Das bedeutet aber nicht, daß die zwei Fragen semantisch identisch sind.

keit der zweiten Jüngerfrage, wenn sie im Kontext der danielischen Eschatologie gesehen wird.[35]

Jesu Beantwortung der Jüngerfragen zeichnet einen dreistufigen Verlauf bis zum endzeitlichen Heil: 1. Anfang der Wehen (V. 5-8), 2. Kulmination der Wehen (V. 14-23), 3. Erscheinung des Menschensohnes (V. 24-27).[36]

Es ist deutlich, daß eine enge Beziehung zwischen der ersten und der zweiten Phase besteht. Die zweite Phase wird mit dem danielischen Ausdruck "Greuel der Verwüstung" angekündigt (V. 14). Dieser als Weissagung verstandene Ausdruck ermöglicht es, die Kulminationsphase der Wehen festzulegen und damit auch die vorausgehenden Ereignisse (V. 5-8) als Anfang der Wehen zu bestimmen. Ebenso scheint es die durch Daniel gewonnene Bestimmung der Kulmination der Wehen zu sein, die es möglich macht, die dritte Phase als die Heilszeit zu bestimmen.

So scheint es mir naheliegend, daß die Frage nach dem Zeichen (V. 4b) mit V. 14a beantwortet wird.[37] Dann spielt der Prophet Daniel nicht nur für die Jünger, sondern auch für den markinischen Jesus eine wesentliche Rolle. Für den markinischen Jesus hat der danielische Ausdruck "Greuel der Verwüstung" eine Schlüsselrolle als das Zeichen, das die von ihm vorausgesagte völlige Zerstörung des Tempels signalisiert. Die Bedeutung des Ausdrucks wird durch den Zwischenbemerkung ὁ ἀναγινώσκων νοείτω hervorgehoben. Hier werden wir plötzlich und ganz unvermittelt aus der Welt des Redens in die Welt des Lesens geführt. Wahrscheinlich schimmert hier Markus' Benutzung einer schriftlichen Vorlage durch.[38] Was hier wichtig ist, ist die Funktion der Bemerkung im Kontext des Markusevangeliums. Mir scheint es naheliegend, daß die Bemerkung den Leser darauf aufmerksam machen soll, daß mit dem Ausdruck "Greuel der Verwüstung" auf den Propheten Daniel hingewiesen wird.[39]

---

[35] Wenn E. Brandenburger bemerkt: "Die Tempelzerstörung kann als Zeichen verstanden werden; aber nicht sie braucht ein Zeichen - wie man bei parallelem Verständnis von Frage 1 und 2 voraussetzen muss -, sondern die Wende der Äonen wird durch Zeichen angezeigt" (Markus, 97), dann wird nach meiner Ansicht der dichte Zusammenhang zwischen Tempelzerstörung und Äonenwende, der den Hintergrund der Doppelfrage bildet, übersehen. Die Pointe der Doppelfrage ist eben die, daß ein Zeichen der die Äonenwende signalisierenden Tempelzerstörung vorausgehen muß. Deshalb die Frage: Welches Zeichen?

[36] Vgl. G. Hallbäck, "Der anonyme Plan", LB 49, 1981, 38-52 (41-42).

[37] Darauf deutet auch das Verb ἴδητε (V. 14), denn die Frage nach dem Zeichen (V. 4) ist die Frage nach etwas, was gesehen werden kann.

[38] Zu den vielen Rekonstruktionsversuchen siehe E. Brandenburger, Markus, 21-42.

[39] Dagegen kann nicht eingewendet werden, "daß im Danielbuch nichts von Flucht steht," so daß "ein Verweis auf Daniel den Leser von Mk 13.14 in die Irre führen [würde]." Denn der Appell ist kognitiver Art, und danach wird die daraus resultierende Handlung direkt angegeben (gegen G. Theißen, Lokalkolorit und Zeitgeschichte (NTOA 8), Göttingen, 1989, 136-137). Zur Frage, welche der Daniel-Stellen (Dan 9.27; 11.31; 12.11) Markus zitiert, siehe L. Hartman, Prophecy, 162; J. Lambrecht, Die

Der Leser soll also verstehen, daß das Zeichen, wonach gefragt wurde, in der prophetischen Schrift Daniels angegeben ist.[40]

So wird die markinische Gemeinde dazu aufgefordert, im Schicksal Jerusalems die Erfüllung der Daniel-Jesus Prophetie zu erkennen.

Im Unterschied zum gewöhnlichen apokalyptischen Stil hat die Rede des markinischen Jesus einen ausgeprägten paränetischen Charakter, das sie in die Nähe der Testamentgattung rückt.[41] Die Paränese enthält teils polemische teils positiv warnende Elemente.

### 2. Ablehnung einer revolutionären Auslegung der danielischen Geschichtstheologie

Die polemischen Elemente der Paränese richten sich gegen Falschmessiasse und Falschpropheten, vor denen sowohl im ersten (V. 6) wie im zweiten Teil (V. 21-22) der Rede gewarnt wird.

Die "Erzählwelt" des Kapitels (die Zeit Markus' und seiner Gemeinde) ist eine Zeit, die von dem jüdischen Krieg gegen Rom geprägt ist; ob vor oder nach der römischen Eroberung des Tempels ist umstritten.[42] Ich ziehe eine Datierung nach der Eroberung vor.[43]

Eine Datierung nach der Zerstörung von Tempel und Stadt bedeutet aber nicht, daß die Erfahrungen während des Krieges gleichgültig werden. Die meisten Exegeten meinen, daß die Warnungen in V. 5-6 und V. 21-23 nur Sinn haben können, wenn sie die aktuelle Gegenwart des

---

*Redaktion der Markus-Apokalypse* (AnBib 28, Rom, 1967), 149; D. Ford, *The Abomination of Desolation in Biblical Eschatology* (Washington, 1979), 151-155.

[40] Zur Frage der Bedeutung des Ausdrucks "Greul der Verwüstung" in Daniel siehe Anm. 19. Schwieriger ist die Frage nach der Bedeutung des Ausdrucks in Mk 13.14, wo der Gebrauch von Maskulinum ἑστηκότα nach dem neutrischen βδέλυγμα besonders auffällig ist. Zu den verschiedenen Deutungen siehe D. Ford, *Abomination*, 158-172. H. Schwier bezieht den Ausdruck auf die römischen Siegesopfer im Tempel (*Tempel*, 358-360). G. Theißen sieht im Markusevangelium eine aktualisierende Interpretation, deren Anfang er in der Caligulakrise finden will. Markus erwarte nach der Zerstörung des Tempels "genau das, was man in der Caligulakrise befürchtet hatte, die Errichtung eines heidnischen anstelle des jüdischen Kultes". In diesem Zusammenhang will Theißen auch die Falschpropheten und Falschmessiasse einordnen, die nach Theißen Ausdruck für "die Usurpation religiöser Hoffnung durch die römischen Herrscher, die den Aufruhr niederwarfen," waren (*Lokalkolorit*, 272; 281). Mir scheint die These von H. Schwier die nächstliegende zu sein.
[41] Siehe E. Brandenburger, *Markus*, 75-83; 152-161; V. K. Robbins, *Jesus the Teacher* (Philadelphia, 1984), 171-179.
[42] Nach der Eroberung von Jerusalem u.a.: L. Schottroff, "Die Gegenwart in der Apokalyptik der synoptischen Evangelien", in D. Hellholm, *Apocalypticism*, 707-708; E. Brandenburger, *Markus*, 74-83; G. Theißen, *Lokalkolorit*, 284. Für eine Datierung vor der Eroberung hat M. Hengel ausführlich argumentiert *(Studies in the Gospel of Mark* (London, 1985), 14-28). Gegen M. Hengel: H. Schwier, *Tempel*, 359, Anm. 47.
[43] Für eine Datierung nach der Zerstörung Jerusalems scheint mir vor allem V. 23b zu sprechen, siehe E. Brandenburger, *Markus*, 80-81, vgl. aber 152. Dagegen kann ich E. Brandenburger nicht folgen, wenn er eine Beziehung zwischen V. 4 εἰπὸν ἡμῖν... und V. 23b προείρηκα ὑμῖν πάντα ablehnt (77-78). Daß die Behauptung einer solchen Beziehung auf rein assoziativem Hervorgehen beruhe, ist falsch. Textsemiotisch pragmatisch ist das, worum die Jünger bitten, ein *Sagen* Jesu, und der Inhalt dieses Sagens betrifft die Zukunft. In V. 23b weist Jesus darauf hin, daß er dieses Sagen jetzt gegeben hat. Als ein sich auf die Zukunft beziehendes Sagen, ist dieses Sagen notwendigerweise eine *Vorhersage*.

Evangelisten widerspiegeln. Dazu ist folgendes zu bemerken: Wenn Markus kurz nach der römischen Eroberung Jerusalems schreibt, zu einer Zeit, wo der Krieg noch nicht zu Ende ist, dann ist es ganz natürlich, daß Markus und seine Gemeinde sich auf ihre eigene Position im Verhältnis zum jüdischen Aufruhr besinnen müssen.[44] Sie verstehen die Katastrophe als Erfüllung der von Jesus vorausgesagten Zerstörung des Tempels,[45] die sie nur als Gericht verstehen können (vgl. Mk 11.15-17; 12.10-11; 15.38).[46] Das heißt, daß Markus und seine Gemeinde sich in einer radikalen Gegenposition zu den jüdischen Aufrührern befinden.

Aufgrund der Ausführungen von H. Schwier[47] bin ich der Meinung, daß die Theologie hinter dem Aufruhr sich als eine Weiterführung der die danielische Eschatologie aufnehmenden und ins Politische transformierenden Ideologie der Makkabäer verstehen läßt. Mit Daniel und den Makkabäern teilen sie die Orientierung des Heils auf Jerusalem, mit den Makkabäern - aber gegen Daniel - erwarten sie die Realisierung des Heils durch eine Synthese von Waffenmacht und göttlicher Hilfe, und auf dem Hintergrund des makkabäischen Sieges glauben sie - gegen Daniel - an die Unzerstörbarkeit des Tempels im Endkampf.

Auf diesem Hintergrund beziehen sich die Warnungen in V. 5-6 und in V. 21-23 nicht auf Gestalten innerhalb der Gemeinde sondern auf jüdische Messiasprätendenten und Propheten, die für den Krieg propagierten.[48]

Dann ist die Polemik gegen diese Gestalten sowohl am Anfang des ersten Teils wie am Abschluß des zweiten Teils der Rede sinnvoll: die Warnung in V. 5-6 bezieht sich gar nicht auf die "Wann"-Frage. Auf diese Frage wird erst mit V. 7 (ὅταν δὲ) eingegangen. Die Warnung in V. 5-6 ist prinzipiell. Sie bezieht sich auf Leute, die eine Zerstörung des Tempels schlechthin ablehnen.[49] Die Warnung in V. 21-23 bezieht sich

---

[44] Zum Abschluß des Krieges und seinen ideologischen Komponenten siehe H. Schwier, *Tempel*, 40-54; 308-337.

[45] Zur Frage: Echtheit oder vaticinium ex eventu des Tempelwortes siehe M. Hengel, *Mark*, 14-16 (Echtheit); G. Theißen, "Die Tempelweissagung Jesu", in *Studien zur Soziologie des Urchristentums* (WUNT 19, Tübingen, 1979), 142-159; *Lokalkolorit*, 206; 271 (eine ex eventu Variante des echten Tempelwortes). Vgl. D. Lührmann, "Markus 14.55-64. Christologie und Zerstörung des Tempels im Markusevangelium", *NTS* 27 (1981), 457-474. Zur Frage: Jesus und Tempel, siehe D. Juel, *Messiah and Temple. The Trial of Jesus in the Gospel of Mark* (SBL.DS 31), Missoula, 1977.

[46] Vgl. T.J. Geddert, *Watchwords. Mark 13 in Markan Eschatology* (JSNT.SS 26, Sheffield, 1989), 206-209.

[47] *Tempel*, 55-201.

[48] So auch W.L. Lane, "Theios aner Christology and the Gospel of Mark", in R.N. Longenecker, M.C. Tenney (Hg.), *New Dimensions in New Testament Study* (Grand Rapids, 1974), 156-158. Über Josephus siehe auch U. Mauser, *Christ in the Wilderness* (SBT 39, London, 1963), 56-58.

[49] Belege aus Josephus werden von R. Pesch angeführt (*Markus* II, 298-299). Der Ausdruck ἐπὶ τῷ ὀνόματί μου bezieht sich hier nicht auf Jesus als Person, sondern auf seine messianische Würde, was vom Kontext her klar ist, wenn man nicht Kap. 13 isoliert betrachtet (siehe 11.1-11,27-12.12,35-37). Die genannten Leute beanspruchen dann nicht, Jesus sondern der Messias zu sein.

auf dieselbe Gruppe, wird aber konkretisiert auf den Versuch von Repräsentanten dieser Gruppe, Menschen von der Flucht abzuhalten. Mit den scharfen Warnungen des markinischen Jesu gegen diese Leute markieren Markus und seine Gemeinde ihre Position dem jüdischen Aufruhr gegenüber. Diese Warnungen sind zugleich eine radikal verschärfte Weiterführung der danielischen Erwartung von einer exklusiv göttlichen Realisierung des Heils.

Die scharfe Ablehnung dieser Gestalten ist somit die Ablehnung - nicht einer falschen Naherwartung, sondern - einer an der Unzerstörbarkeit des Tempels orientierten politisch-nationalen Eschatologie.[50]

Nach der Ablehnung des politisch-nationalen Messianismus kann das in der zweiten Jüngerfrage - aufgrund der Daniel-Konzeption - enthaltene Problem über die Beziehung zwischen Tempelzerstörung und Endheil aufgenommen werden. Dieses Problem wird dadurch gelöst, daß der danielische "Greuel der Verwüstung" zwar Signal zur Zerstörung des Tempels war, aber - entgegen der danielischen Konzeption - nicht das entscheidende Kriterium der Nähe des Endheils ist.

Damit wird klar, daß Jesu Weissagung von der Zerstörung des Tempels die Weissagung einer endgültigen Zerstörung ist, und das bedeutet, daß die danielische Orientierung des Endheils auf Jerusalem hin aufgegeben wird. Jerusalem als Ort der universalen Herrschaft des Volkes Gottes wird abgelehnt. Das bedeutet aber auch eine grundsätzliche Wandlung der Geschichtsperspektive.

### 3. Die veränderte Geschichtsperspektive

In der danielischen Konzeption war die Geschichtsperspektive pessimistisch in dem Sinne, daß die Geschichte sich auf eine Kulmination der gottfeindlichen Mächte zubewegt. Diese Kulmination ist sozusagen die negative Voraussetzung der göttlichen Herbeiführung des Heils. Zwar hatte der fromme Jude eine missionarische Funktion den Weltmächten gegenüber zur Zeit der ersten Weltmächte, wie es beispielhaft an Daniel im erzählenden Teil des Danielbuches dargestellt wird; in der Endphase der Weltgeschichte gibt es eine solche Möglichkeit jedoch nicht. In der Rede des markinischen Jesu ist das aber anders. Das geht aus dem Abschnitt V. 9-13 hervor.

Es ist schon oft bemerkt worden, daß dieser Abschnitt den Zusammenhang der Rede unterbricht, und L. Hartman scheidet denn auch den ersten Teil (V. 9-11) dieses Abschnitts aus dem von ihm angenommenen

---

[50] Diese Ablehnung einer jüdisch-nationalen Eschatologie ist sehr verständlich, wenn das Markusevangelium in Rom geschrieben ist, (so M. Hengel, *Mark*, 28-30). Für eine (durchaus mögliche) Lokalisierung im syrischen Gebiet, siehe G. Theißen, *Lokalkolorit*, 246-261.

Danielmidrasch aus.⁵¹ Meiner Meinung nach ist es in diesem Abschnitt, wo wir die entscheidende Korrektur der danielischen Geschichtsperspektive finden.

Besonders wichtig ist vor allem V. 10. Hier wird oft hauptsächlich ein Indiz der Parusieverzögerung gefunden, indem das Wort πρῶτον hervorgehoben wird.⁵² Wichtiger scheint mir aber, daß hier nicht nur ein Kriterium für das "Wann" des Endtermins, sondern auch für das "Wie" der Zeit bis zum Endtermin gegeben wird. Das Letzte bedeutet eine entscheidende Änderung der Geschichtsperspektive Daniels: eine Änderung von einer Geschichtsperspektive, die an der Kulmination der Gottfeindlichkeit in der Geschichte orientiert ist, in eine Geschichtsperspektive, die an der universalen Verkündigung der Heilsbotschaft orientiert ist. Damit ändert sich die Geschichtsperspektive von der Perspektive einer in eine Klimax ausmündenden universalen Unheilsgeschichte zu der Perspektive einer in eine Klimax ausmündenden universalen Heilsgeschichte.

Es ist dabei wichtig zu erkennen, daß V. 10 die übergeordnete Perspektive für den ganzen Abschnitt V. 9-13 zeichnet und daß diese Perspektive insofern apokalyptisch ist, als die Verkündigung des Evangeliums für alle Völker ein im Willen Gottes determiniertes Geschehen ist und ein Geschehen, das bis zum Ende des jetzigen Äons andauert.⁵³ Die Verwendung von *passivum divinum* ist auch mit der apokalyptischen Perspektive vereinbar, denn darin kommt die Souveränität Gottes in der Geschichte zum Ausdruck: eigentlich ist es Gott selber, der sein Evangelium von Jesus Christus, dem Sohne Gottes (vgl. 1.1) verkünden läßt. Daraus ergibt sich ein sachlicher Zusammenhang zwischen V. 10 und 11. Denn daß der heilige Geist in Verhörssituationen für die Angeklagten reden will, zeigt, daß es Gott selber ist, der hinter dieser Verkündigung steht.

Die Christusgemeinde erhält somit in der Endphase der Weltmächte eine missionarisch heilsgeschichtliche Funktion, die mit der missionari-

---

⁵¹ L. Hartman, *Prophecy*, 172; 213-219; 235-236.
⁵² Kritisch dazu E. Brandenburger, *Markus*, 89-90.
⁵³ Daß in V. 10 eine apokalyptische Denkbewegung vorliegt, ist mit Recht von E. Brandenburger (*Markus*, 30) hervorgehoben worden.

Es scheint mir klar zu sein, daß im Markusevangelium eine enge Beziehung zwischen ἕνεκεν ἐμοῦ (13.9) und τὸ εὐαγγέλιον (13.10) besteht (vgl. 8.37; 10.29). Die Beziehung ist so dicht, daß sie einander interpretieren: ἕνεκεν ἐμοῦ heißt ἕνεκεν τοῦ εὐαγγελίου und umgekehrt. Die Erklärung dieser Beziehung liegt in 1.1, wo der Inhalt des Evangeliums angegeben wird: Ἰησοῦ Χριστοῦ υἱοῦ θεοῦ. Insofern ist R. Pesch' Hinweis auf 1.14-15 (*Markus* II, 285) nicht zutreffend, denn im Markusevangelium ist Jesu Evangelium vom Gottesreich (1.14-15) in (Gottes) Evangelium von Jesus Christus, dem Sohne Gottes eingeordnet. Das heißt: Wenn Markus das Wort εὐαγγέλιον absolut verwendet, dann schließt es immer Tod und Auferstehung ein. Denn diese Ereignisse sind die Jesus wahrhaft christologisch (Jesus als ὁ Χριστός) qualifizierenden Ereignisse (beachte die Verbindung zwischen 8.29-30,31-38). In diesem Sinne ist *das* Evangelium für Markus "das Evangelium von Jesus Christus, dem Sohne Gottes" (1.1).

schen Funktion Daniels in der Anfangsphase der Weltmächte verglichen werden kann. Wie Daniel den Willen Gottes den Weltmächten gegenüber verkündete, so verkündet die christliche Gemeinde mit dem Evangelium den Willen Gottes den Weltmächten gegenüber, und wie Daniel von Gott auf wunderbare Weise von Gott geholfen wurde, so wird der Gemeinde durch den Beistand des heiligen Geistes geholfen.

Die Voraussetzung dieser Interpretation hängt aber von der Eindordnung des Abschnitts (V. 9-13) in den apokalyptischen Geschichtsverlauf ab. Nach meiner Auffassung ist das πρῶτον (V. 10) auf das Ende hin orientiert und nicht auf den Zeitpunkt der Tempelzerstörung[54] und korrespondiert insofern mit dem εἰς τέλος (V. 13). Das heißt: die Einordnung des Abschnitts V. 9-13 soll nicht zeitlich als Einordnung in eine Reihe von Epochen, sondern sachlich verstanden werden. Die in V. 7-8 und V. 14-20 geschilderten Epochen sind mit der in V. 9-13 geschilderten Epoche gleichzeitig.[55] In V. 7-8,14-20 werden Ereignisse geschildert, die in Verbindung mit der Zerstörung des Tempels stehen, in V. 9-13 werden die Bedingungen für die Jünger als Jünger *Jesu* und damit als auf das Evangelium Verpflichtete geschildert.

Wird so die Zerstörung Jerusalems als das entscheidende Kriterium für den Termin des Endheils durch den Vollzug des Evangeliums modifiziert, so steht doch die Frage nach dem Übergang von V. 14-20 (21-23) zu V. 24-27 offen. Die doppelte Zeitangabe ἐν ἐκείναις ταῖς ἡμέραις μετὰ τὴν θλῖψιν ἐκείνην betont insofern nur, daß die Zerstörung des Tempels dem Ende sachlich vorausgehen muß.[56] Die Zerstörung des Tempels ist - wenn man so sagen darf - die negative Voraussetzung für das Ende, die positive Voraussetzung ist aber der Vollzug des Evangeliums.

So wird die danielische Geschichtsperspektive in der markinischen Apokalyptik auf zwei miteinander korrespondierenden Gebieten geändert: (a) die Orientierung auf die Kulmination des Unheils wird durch die

---

[54] So auch E. Brandenburger, *Markus*, 30; R. Pesch: "Der Evangelist gibt den Blick auf eine Epoche der Heidenmission vor dem Ende frei..." (*Markus* II, 267).

[55] Vgl. E. Brandenburger, *Markus*, 31. Vgl. Mt 24.14: καὶ τότε ἥξει τὸ τέλος.

[56] R. Pesch versteht die zweite Zeitangabe als Markierung eines scharfen Einschnitts zwischen Gegenwart (V. 5-23) und Zukunft (V. 24-27), womit Markus die Parusieschwärmer bekämpfen will (*Naherwartung*, 157-158). Ähnlich auch W. Schmithals, *Das Evangelium nach Markus* (ÖTK 2/2, Gütersloh, 1979), 577. Nach W.H. Kelber soll die zweite Zeitangabe sowohl die Nähe der Parusie als auch die notwendige Distanz zum Vorhergehenden betonen (*The Kingdom in Mark. A New Place and a New Time* (Philadelphia, 1974), 122f.). Nach H. Conzelmann hat die zweite Zeitangabe vor allem eine hermeneutische Funktion, indem sie das apokalyptische Schema, nach dem der Übergang in die Zukunft fließend ist, wobei Geschichtliches und Supranaturales zusammenfließen, entscheidend modifiziert ("Geschichte und Eschaton nach Mc. 13", *ZNW* 50 (1959), 210-221 (216)). Dagegen mit Recht L. Gaston, *Stone*, 50. Eine gewisse Zustimmung findet H. Conzelmann bei E. Brandenburger, der die Frage nach dem Zeichen in der Sicht Markus' in V. 24-25 finden will (*Markus*, 99-104). Nach T.J. Geddert will Markus eben die Unsicherheit hervorheben:"...he is saying we cannot be sure either that they are separated, or that they are connected" (*Watchwords*, 230).

Orientierung auf die Kulmination der Verkündigung des Evangelium modifiziert, und (b) die Orientierung auf Jerusalem wird durch eine Orientierung auf die Völker ersetzt.

Dann erhebt sich aber die Frage, ob die "positive" Paränese in V. 28-37 nicht ein anderes Bild der Terminfrage und der Funktion der Gemeinde zeichnet.

Die Sachhälfte des Gleichnisses vom reifenden Feigenbaume (V. 29) bezieht die aus dem Feigenbaume zu entnehmende Lehre auf das zeitliche Verhältnis von ὅταν ἴδητε ταῦτα γινόμετα und ὅτι ἐγγύς ἐστιν ἐπὶ θύραις. Hier scheint eine Belehrung über die Dauer des μετά in der zweiten Zeitangabe in V. 24 vorzuliegen.[57] Es ist deshalb naheliegend, ταῦτα γινόμενα in erster Linie auf das Zeichen in V. 14 und die damit beginnende große Drangsal zu beziehen. Wenn man aber den Hintergrund für die Anwendung des Feigenbaums überlegt, scheint es mir wahrscheinlicher, ταῦτα sowohl auf V. 14-23 als auch auf V. 9-13 zu beziehen.

Es ist ja bemerkenswert, daß die Zeit der großen Drangsal mit dem positiven Bilde der Entwicklung des Feigenbaums im Frühling gezeichnet wird (V. 18-20). Das entspricht aber genau der in V. 9-13 gezeichneten Geschichtsperspektive. Wird aber diese Geschichtsperspektive im Bilde des reifenden Feigenbaums gezeichnet, dann meldet sich als Kontrastbild der fruchtlose Feigenbaum als Bild des Tempelkults, dessen endgültige Auflösung das eine Thema der Jüngerrede Jesu war, deren zweites Thema das Evangelium für die Völkerwelt als Qualifikation der Geschichtsperspektive und als Kriterium des Endtermins war.[58] Beide Themen sind aber in der Perspektive einer apokalyptischen Eschatologie gesehen, insofern sowohl die epochenschaffenden Ereignisse wie die Zeitspanne unter göttlichem δεῖ steht.

Was aber unbekannt bleibt, ist der Zeitpunkt des Endheils (V. 32). Die Betonung, daß weder der Sohn noch die Engel diesen Zeitpunkt kennen, klingt wie eine Ablehnung von Dan 12.7-12.[59] Über diesen Zeitpunkt können auch Engel nicht informieren, ja auch der Sohn Gottes nicht. Das heißt: jede Hoffnung auf eine himmlische Enthüllung des Termins für das Endheil wird schlechthin abgelehnt. Deshalb muß auch ein dieses Endheil signalisierendes Zeichen abgelehnt werden. Stattdessen wird die Plötzlichkeit des Endheils betont (13.33-37). In diesem Sinne läßt sich sagen, daß die für die Apokalyptik charakteristische Betonung der Transzendenz

---

[57] ὅταν ἴδητε ταῦτα bezieht sich nicht auf V. 24-25 (gegen E. Brandenburger, *Markus*, 106-108).
[58] Vgl. T.J. Geddert, *Watchwords*, 247-253.
[59] Die Ausdehnung der Zeit im Danielbuch ist sicher ein Indiz dafür, daß der Kreis hinter dem Danielbuch die makkabäische Erneuerung als Erfüllung der Prophetie ablehnte und so an ihrer nicht-politischen Realisierung festhielt. Siehe auch J.J. Collins, *Daniel*, 104.

radikalisiert wird: der Termin des Endheils bleibt bei Gott verborgen. Wie ist aber die Funktion der Gemeinde nach V. 33-37?

Die Funktion der Gemeinde als der mit der Verkündigung des Evangeliums für alle Völker Beauftragten scheint durch V. 33-37 dementiert zu werden. Denn hier begegnet uns das Bild einer Gemeinde, die sich von der Welt abzugrenzen und sich exklusiv um die Türhüterfunktion zu kümmern scheint. Daß das nicht der Sinn sein kann, geht aber daraus hervor, daß die Türhüterfunktion nicht auf einbrechende Diebe, sondern auf den kommenden Menschensohn bezogen ist. Der betonte Aufruf zum Wachen in diesem Abschnitt steht nicht im Gegensatz zur missionarischen Funktion der Gemeinde, sondern wird eben darin wahrgenommen, wie es durch das Gleichnis vom Feigenbaum angedeutet wurde (vgl. auch 8.34-38).

Der eigentliche Grund der Veränderung der danielischen Geschichtsperspektive liegt in der Christologie. Das zeigt sich beispielhaft in der Parusieschilderung (V. 24-27), wo das zweite hier aufgenommene Zitat aus dem Danielbuch vorkommt.

*4. Die Christologie als Grundlage der Wandlung der Geschichtsperspektive*

Es scheint mir wichtig, wenn man sich mit dem Verhältnis zwischen der danielischen und der markinischen apokalyptischen Eschatologie beschäftigt, auf die Rolle des Menschensohnes im Danielbuch und im Markusevangelium achtzugeben.

Im Danielbuch ist die Menschensohngestalt Symbol des Gottesvolkes in der erneuerten Welt jenseits der jetzigen Geschichte (7.13-14,27),[60] im Markusevangelium ist die Menschensohngestalt die Gestalt, die die Transzendenz zwischen der Welt Gottes und der Welt der Menschen überbrückt, denn im Markusevangelium ist der Ausdruck "Menschensohn" Symbol der Präsenz Gottes in dem Menschen Jesus von Nazareth, in seiner Exusia (2.10,28), in seinem Leiden, Tod und Auferstehen (8.31; 9.31; 10.32-34), seiner Erhöhung und Parusie (8.38; 13.26; 14.62).[61]

---

[60] Vgl. M. Müller, *Der Ausdruck "Menschensohn" in den Evangelien* (AThD 17, København, 1984), 10-27; 39-44; B. Otzen, *Judaism*, 209-210; W.O. Walker, Jr., "Daniel 7:13-14", *Int* 39 (1985), 176-181. Diese Deutung ist zwar umstritten, siehe dazu K. Koch, *Daniel*, 216-239; P.R. Davies, *Daniel* (Sheffield, 1985), 100-108.

[61] Die Versuche, die Begriffsgeschichte des Ausdrucks "Menschensohn" zu erhellen, tragen zum Verstehen des Ausdrucks im Markusevangelium wenig bei. Im Markusevangelium werden alle Seiten des Wirkens Jesu auf Jesus als Menschensohn bezogen: Heilungen, Sündenvergebung (2.10), Herrschaft über den Sabbat (2.28), Tod und Auferstehung (8.31 (9.10; 14.21,41); 9.31; 10.32-34), stellvertretende Sühne (10.45), Erhöhung (14.62a) und Parusie (8.38; 13.26; 14.62b). Entscheidend für die Bedeutung des Ausdrucks im Markusevangelium ist es nicht, ob diese oder jene Seite seines Wirkens traditionsgeschichtlich mit einer Menschensohn-Konzeption verbunden war. Was aber wichtig ist, ist die Tatsache, daß

Hier liegt der entscheidende Unterschied zwischen der Gestalt Daniel und der Gestalt Jesus. Daniel ist Gottes Liebling, dem Gott Einblick ins Geheimnis der Geschichte von der ersten Zerstörung des Tempels bis zu seiner endzeitlichen Verherrlichung schenkt. Jesus ist der Menschensohn, durch den Gott sein Endheil in der Geschichte aktualisiert auf seine endzeitliche Realisierung hin. Wie diese Präsenz Gottes im geschichtlichen Wirken Jesu von Nazareth im diesseitigen, von den Weltmächten beherrschten Raum, Heil schafft, so schafft das Evangelium in der Zeit der Gemeinde Heil im diesseitigen Raum, denn im Evangelium ist die Exusia des abwesenden Menschensohnes präsent (Mk 3.15; 6.7; 13.34). So setzt sich die in "der erzählten Welt" des Markusevangeliums eigentümliche Doppelheit von schon/noch nicht in der Erzählwelt des Evangeliums fort.[62]

Während im Danielbuch Anfang und Ende der Universalgeschichte am Schicksal des Tempels orientiert waren, sind im Markusevangelium Anfang und Ende der Universalgeschichte am Schicksal Jesu orientiert: der Anfang der Universalgeschichte ist an der Zerstörung (Kreuzigung) Jesu orientiert (Mk 10.45; 14.24), die schon am Anfang des Evangeliums angedeutet ist (1.9-11,12-13)), und das Ende der Universalgeschichte ist an seiner Offenbarung als der himmlische Menschensohn orientiert (13.26-27). Das heißt: Jesus ersetzt den Tempel als Heils- und Hoffnungssymbol (12.10-11).

Nicht von ungefähr fängt Markus sein Evangelium mit dem Ausdruck "Anfang des Evangeliums von Jesus Christus, des Sohnes Gottes" an, und nicht von ungefähr nimmt er auf dieses Evangelium Bezug in der auf das Ende hin bezogenen apokalyptischen Geschichtsschau in Kap. 13: erst wenn das Evangelium allen Völker der Welt verkündet worden ist, ist das Evangelium zu Ende gekommen.

Darin tritt die Verbindung der transzendenten und der universalen Perspektive hervor: inhaltlich ist das Evangelium auf die Parusie des Menschensohnes als den endgültigen Durchbruch zur transzendenten Welt

---

Markus das ganze Wirken Jesu mit diesem Ausdruck verbindet. Wenn man synchronisch innerhalb des Markusevangeliums nach dem Ursprung dieses Ausdrucks fragt, dann liegt die Antwort im Taufereignis (1.9-11). Was das Taufereignis vor allem besagt, ist dies, daß Jesus der von Gott erwählte Mensch ist, der Antitypos zum ersten Adam (vgl. 1.12-13). Dann besagt der Ausdruck "Menschensohn" vor allem, daß Jesus der von Gott erwählte Mensch ist, und das heißt: Er ist der Ort, wo Gott präsent ist, und danach wird im erzählenden Verlauf des Markusevangeliums prädikativ entfaltet, wozu er erwählt ist. Dabei nutzt Markus die danielische Menschensohn-Konzeption aus.

[62] Diese Doppelheit wird in "der erzählten Welt" des Markusevangeliums durch das sogenannte "Messiasgeheimnis" ausgedrückt, das in dem Sinne apokalyptisch ist, das es den Dualismus zwischen der Welt Gottes und der Welt des Menschen thematisiert. In "der Erzählwelt" des Markusevangeliums setzt sich diese Doppelheit fort, insofern der Dagewesene und in der Zukunft Erwartete in der Gegenwart nur als der im Evangelium Verkündete präsent erfahrbar ist. In diesem Sinne ist das Markusevangelium die literarische Gestaltung des "Messiasgeheimnisses", denn das Markusevangelium als literarische Gattung ist zugleich Hervorhebung und Überbrückung der Transzendenz.

Gottes bezogen. Das geschieht aber erst, wenn dieses Evangelium der ganzen Welt (universal) verkündet worden ist. Das Heil ist aber nicht nur auf den Endtermin hin orientiert, sondern auch ein die Endzeitgeschichte qualifizierendes Geschehen, das sich in der Verkündigung des Evangeliums entfaltet. So wird die Letztphase der Universalgeschichte grundsätzlich evangelisch qualifiziert.

### IV. Biblische Theologie als apokalyptische Geschichtsdeutung

Am Anfang bezeichnete ich die Beantwortung der Frage nach einer grundsätzlichen Kontinuität in der Diskontinuität der biblischen Zeugnisse von Gott als die Aufgabe einer "biblischen Theologie". Diese Frage wird in der biblischen Apokalyptik als die Frage nach Gottes Willen in und mit der Geschichte thematisiert. Der Kreis hinter dem Danielbuch knüpfte dabei an die prophetische Tradition an, die unter Berufung auf göttliche Geheimoffenbarung in eine universalgeschichtliche und transzendente Perspektive hineininterpretiert wurde, ohne Jerusalem und Tempel als entscheidende Orte des Unheils und des Heils aufzugeben.

Für Markus ist die danielische Interpretation insofern bedeutsam, als er hier das vorausgesagte Zeichen für die Zerstörung des Tempels findet. Markus lehnt aber die Verknüpfung von Schicksal des Tempels und Endheil ab. Sie wird durch die Verkündigung des Evangeliums für die Völkerwelt ersetzt. Damit wird die Konzeption der Geschichte als eine bis auf das Endheil sich steigernde Unheilsgeschichte durch die Konzeption der Geschichte als eine nicht nur durch Leiden und Verfolgung sondern vor allem durch die Verkündigung des Evangeliums qualifizierte Geschichte ersetzt. Das hat zur Folge, daß jeder Versuch, den Termin des Endheils zu errechnen, abgelehnt wird.

Die Grundlage der Veränderung des danielischen Geschichtsbildes liefert die Christologie. Daniel ist der Liebling Gottes, dem Gott Einblick in seine Lenkung der Geschichte schenkt. Jesus ist der Menschensohn, durch den Gott Sühne für die Welt schafft (Mk 10.45) und an dem Gott die apokalyptische Hoffnung realisiert. War für Daniel die Sühne eng mit der Realisierung des endzeitlichen Heils verknüpft (vgl. Anm. 16), so verkündet Markus, daß diese Sühne durch Jesus realisiert ist (10.45; 14.22-24), und damit wird der Wille Gottes in und mit der Geschichte durch ihn als Heilsgeschichte geoffenbart, und Heil als ein sich zugleich gegenwärtig ereignendes und zukünftig sich realisierendes Geschehen verstanden.

So wird im Markusevangelium die apokalyptische Geschichtsschau auf Jesus bezogen und eben dadurch entscheidend transformiert, wie es

Markus' Interpretation des danielischen "Greuel der Verwüstung" und des danielischen "Menschensohnes" klar herausstellt. So ist die Christologie sowohl der Ort, wo die danielische Apokalyptik aufgegriffen wird, als auch die Grundlage für ihre Neuinterpretation.[63]

Die grundlegende Kontinuität zeigt sich aber in dem Zeugnis von Gottes True zu seiner Verheißung. Sowohl Daniel als auch Markus bezeugt Gott als der verheißende und auf sein Heil hin handelnde Gott in universaler Perspektive. Die Geschichte und alle die gottfeindlichen Mächte, die sie zu beherrschen scheinen, können Gottes auf sein Heil bezogenes Ziel mit der Geschichte nicht zerstören, egal ob das Ziel radikal zukünftig wie bei Daniel oder präsentisch-futurisch wie bei Markus gedacht ist. Dieses Zeugnis von Gottes Treue zu seiner Verheißung als der die Kontinuität der Geschichte sichernde Macht, wie sie so in der biblischen Apokalyptik hervortritt, ist ein Grundthema "biblischer Theologie" überhaupt sowohl in historischer als auch in aktueller Perspektive.

In diesem Sinne hat die biblische Apokalyptik auch ihren Beitrag zum Thema "Biblische Theologie" zu leisten.[64]

---

[63] P.D. Hanson, "Biblical Apocalypticism: The Theological Dimension", HBT 7, 1985, 8-9.
[64] Cf. P.D. Hanson "Apocalypticism", 14-15.

CHAPTER ELEVEN

# DIAKONIE ALS BIBELTHEOLOGISCHES THEMA

Helge Kjær Nielsen, Århus

In seinem Buch "Hauptprobleme der Biblischen Theologie im 20. Jahrhundert" unterteilt Henning Graf Reventlow die neuesten Versuche zur Wiedergewinnung einer gesamtbiblischen Theologie in drei Gruppen: 1. der traditionsgeschichtliche Ansatz; 2. der Versuch, einen bestimmten Begriff oder Zentralgedanken als Bindeglied zwischen den beiden Testamenten bzw. als deren "Mitte" herauszufinden; 3. der Ausgang vom Weltordnungsdenken.[1] Wenn mein Beitrag sich überhaupt einer dieser Gruppen zuordnen läßt, dann müßte es vermutlich die zweite sein - obwohl ich nicht behaupten möchte, Diakonie sei eine "Mitte", um die herum sich eine Biblische Theologie aufbauen ließe.

Ich finde es jedoch wertvoll und für die mögliche Erstellung einer Biblischen Theologie wünschenswert, daß möglichst viele Themen in einer gesamtbiblischen Perspektive untersucht werden. Insofern das Thema Diakonie das Verhältnis der Menschen zueinander im Lichte ihres Verhältnisses zu Gott betrifft, ist es in keinster Weise als unwichtig zu bewerten.[2] Deshalb - und weil dem Thema Diakonie in der Bibelwissenschaft nicht die gebührende Aufmerksamkeit erwiesen ist - ist es eine naheliegende Aufgabe, nach dem biblischen Verständnis der Diakonie zu fragen.

## I. Definition des Begriffes Diakonie

Zunächst möchte ich den im folgenden vorausgesetzten Bedeutungsgehalt des Begriffes Diakonie präzisieren. Zur Verdeutlichung möchte ich auf Mt 25.31-46 verweisen. In diesem Text, wo übrigens das Verb διακονεῖν vorkommt (V. 44),[3] finden wir eine schöne Exemplifikation des Begriffes Diakonie: den Hungrigen zu essen geben, den Durstigen zu

---

[1] H. Graf Reventlow, *Hauptprobleme der Biblischen Theologie im 20. Jahrhundert* (EdF 203; Darmstadt, 1983), 141-142.
[2] Vgl. u.a. Rudolf Weth, der in seinem Aufsatz "Der eine Gott der Diakonie. Diakonik als Problem und Aufgabe Biblischer Theologie", *JBTh* 2 (1987), 151-164, Diakonie als Problem und Aufgabe Biblischer Theologie bezeichnet.
[3] Die Sache der Diakonie ist natürlich nicht nur da bezeugt, wo die Wörter διακονία, διακονεῖν, und διάκονος zu finden sind.

trinken geben, den Nackten Kleidung geben, die Heimatlosen beherbergen, die Gefangenen und Kranken besuchen.[4]

"Alle sechs Werke", sagt Paul Philippi,[5]

> die im V. 44 im Worte διακονεῖν zusammengefaßt erscheinen, haben einen deutlichen Bezug auf irdische, zeitliche Lebensnöte: Hunger, Durst, Heimlosigkeit, Armut, Krankheit, Gefangenschaft. Sie heißen insofern mit Recht "leibliche" Werke der Barmherzigkeit. Doch darf diese "Leiblichkeit" nicht in zu engem Sinne verstanden werden. Das Schlußglied der ersten und dritten Dreiergruppe weitet das Verständnis auf "soziale" Nöte aus, die zwar selbstverständlich den Leib mitbetreffen, aber nicht zuerst an ihm erlitten werden.

Diakonie bezeichnet also die Hilfe und Fürsorge, die Menschen in konkreten und oft leiblichen Nöten erfahren.[6]

Zu dieser horizontalen Definition, die sozusagen das Gebiet der Diakonie umschreibt, kommt jedoch auch eine vertikale, die die Voraussetzung und Begründung der Diakonie angibt. Diese vertikale Definition verdeutlicht, daß Diakonie letzten Endes nicht eine menschliche Leistung ist - und letzten Endes nicht den Menschen zum Subjekt hat. Sie ist vielmehr als Wirkung des Verhältnisses zwischen Gott und Mensch zu verstehen, und zwar in dem Sinne, daß sowohl die Voraussetzung als auch die Begründung der Diakonie von Gott gegeben ist. Mit anderen Worten: Diakonie setzt ein göttliches πρῶτον voraus.

## II. Diakonie als gesamtbiblisches Thema

Traditionell ist Diakonie als ein neutestamentliches Thema angesehen und behandelt worden. Mit dem markanten und oft zitierten Satz: "Die Welt vor Christo ist eine Welt ohne Liebe", hat Gerhard Uhlhorn vor über hundert Jahren diese Auffassung deutlich zum Ausdruck gebracht.[7]

Natürlich bestreitet Uhlhorn nicht, daß der Gedanke des Dienens auch im Alten Testament bezeugt ist. Vor allem kennt auch er die vielen

---

[4] Vgl. z.B. Jes 58.6-7.
[5] Paul Philippi, *Christozentrische Diakonie. Ein theologischer Entwurf* (Stuttgart, 1975²), 154.
[6] Die Wörter διακονεῖν, διακονία und διάκονος können auch einen weiteren Bedeutungsgehalt haben. Siehe z.B. H. W. Beyer, "διακονέω, διακονία, διάκονος", ThWNT 2 (1935), 81-93. Vgl. C. E. B. Cranfield, "Diakonia in the New Testament", in: *Service in Christ. Essays presented to Karl Barth on his 80th Birthday* (Hrgg. James I. McCord und T. H. Parker, London 1966), insbes. 37-39. Obwohl es sachgerecht ist, Diakonie im Lichte von u.a. Mt 25.44 zu definieren, darf es also nicht vergessen werden, daß der so verstandene Dienst in tiefstem Sinne als Teil eines weiteren, sich auch in Worten entfaltenden Dienstes anzusehen ist. Siehe z.B. Mk 10.45 par.; Joh 12.26; Röm 11.13 und 1 Kor 3.5.
[7] Gerhard Uhlhorn, *Geschichte der Diakonie und Inneren Mission in der Neuzeit* (Berlin, 1983³), 11. Auf die anhaltende Wirkungsgeschichte der Beurteilung Uhlhorns macht Rudolf Weth aufmerksam ("Der eine Gott der Diakonie", 151-152.).

Ermahnungen, den Witwen, den Waisen, den Armen und den Fremden Hilfe zu leisten. Und doch will er dies nicht als Diakonie bezeichnen. Der im Alten Testament - und im Judentum - bezeugte Dienst an den Notleidenden unterscheidet sich nämlich - laut Uhlhorn - qualitativ von dem des Neuen Testaments, weil die Welt vor Christus eine Welt ohne Liebe war. Nur sehr ansatzweise vermag er in dieser vorchristlichen Welt die barmherzige Liebe zu spüren, die er als das Wahrzeichen echter Diakonie betrachtet. Die vertikale Dimension der Diakonie, die die barmherzige Liebe ermöglicht, ist erst in Christus gegeben.

Auch andere Auffassungen, die für das Verständnis der Diakonie entscheidend gewesen sind, haben dazu beigetragen, das Alte Testament im wesentlichen außer acht zu lassen, wenn es um das Thema Diakonie geht. So wird oft behauptet, im Alten Testament gehe es um Verdienst. Das ist zwar auch eine vertikale Dimension, aber eine vertikale Dimension in umgekehrter Richtung. Natürlich findet sich dieser Gedanke nicht selten im Alten Testament, aber das ist ja auch im Neuen Testament mehrmals der Fall.[8]

Ferner wird angenommen, die Unterscheidung zwischen Evangelium und Gesetz und - damit verbunden - das rechte Verständnis des Verhältnisses zwischen dem Werk Gottes und dem Tun des Menschen fänden wir nur im Neuen Testament, weil dies die Christusoffenbarung voraussetzt. Wieder ist zu fragen: Gibt es hier eine absolute Grenze zwischen den beiden Testamenten?[9] Ist es nicht eher so, daß viele Grenzen sich quer über beide Testamente erstrecken, anstatt sie zu trennen? Der pauschale Ausschluß des Alten Testaments, wenn es um das Verständis der Diakonie geht, kann meiner Meinung nach nicht sachgerecht sein.

Dies zu verdeutlichen ist die Absicht der folgenden Ausführungen, die jedoch bei weitem nicht alle Aspekte des Themas umfassen werden können. Ich muß mich darauf begrenzen, Diakonie im Lichte des Schöpfungsgedankens und im Lichte des Gottesgedankens zu behandeln. Die überaus wichtigen und oft behandelten christologischen Perspektiven sind nur dort berücksichtigt, wo sie einen engeren Bezug zu den oben erwähnten Perspektiven haben. Es ist mir auch nicht möglich, in diesem Aufsatz z.B. auf die ekklesiologische Perspektive einzugehen.[10]

Noch eine weitere Einschränkung muß vorausgeschickt werden. Ich diskutiere nicht das Alter, das gegenseitige Verhältnis und den re-

---

[8] Siehe z.B. Mt 6.3; 25.34-40; Lk 14.12-14; Röm 2.5-11; 2 Kor 5.10.
[9] Vgl. W.H. Schmidt, "Werk Gottes und Tun des Menschen. Ansätze zur Unterscheidung von "Gesetz und Evangelium" im Alten Testament", *JBTh* 4 (1989), 11-28.
[10] Eine eingehendere Darstellung der verschiedenen biblischen Begründungen der Diakonie findet sich in meinem Buch, *Han elskede os først [Er hat uns zuerst geliebt]*, Århus, 1994.

präsentativen Wert der erwähnten Texte. Es geht hier um die elementäre Frage: Wo in der biblischen Schriftsammlung finden wir Zeugnisse über Diakonie, und zwar im Lichte des Schöpfungs- und des Gottesgedankens? Es interessiert mich ganz besonders, Einblick in die theologische Begründung und damit auch in das theologische Verständnis der Diakonie zu gewinnen. Ich bin mir der Gefahr bewußt, daß das Gesamtbild der Untersuchung wegen dieser notwendigen Einschränkungen zu harmonisch wird. Hinweise auf Texte und Gesichtspunkte, die andere Aspekte hervorheben, beabsichtigen, diese Gefahr zu reduzieren.

### III. Diakonie im Lichte des Schöpfungsgedankens

Der biblische Schöpfungsgedanke ist u.a. ein Ausdruck des Unterschieds zwischen Gott und Mensch.[11] Dieser Unterschied - und damit die Begrenzung des Menschen - wird verdeutlicht z.B. mit dem Bild von Gott als Töpfer und dem Menschen als Ton in seiner Hand[12] und in der Gegenüberstellung von der Ewigkeit Gottes und der Flüchtigkeit des Menschenlebens.[13]

Der Schöpfungsgedanke umfaßt jedoch auch andere Aspekte im Hinblick auf das Menschenbild. Ich möchte im folgenden zwei Aspekte hervorheben, die beide für das Thema Diakonie von großer Bedeutung sind.

### 1. Die Würde des Menschen als Geschöpf Gottes
a) Das Alte Testament
In der Schilderung der Schöpfung im Alten Testament ist der Höhepunkt die Schöpfung des Menschen. Der Mensch wurde - wie aus Gen 1.26-27 hervorgeht - im Bilde Gottes geschaffen.[14] Bekanntlich ist es eine vieldiskutierte Frage, wie diese Verse zu deuten sind.[15] Es kann jedoch kaum bezweifelt werden, daß sie dazu beitragen, die Würde des

---

[11] Dieser Unterschied könnte als ontologisch charakterisiert werden.
[12] Siehe Jes 29.16; 45.9; Jer 18.1-6; Röm 9.20-21.
[13] Siehe z.B. Ps 90 und 103.13-17.
[14] Bezüglich der Gottebenbildlichkeit des Menschen siehe auch Gen 5.1; 9.6; Ps 8.6; Weish 2.23 und Sir 17.3. Vgl. Jak 3.9.
[15] Es gibt mehrere Übersichten über die Haupttypen der Deutungen. Siehe z.B. O. Loretz, *Die Gottebenbildlichkeit des Menschen* (Schriften des Deutschen Instituts für wissenschaftliche Pädagogik, München, 1967), 9-39; C. Westermann, *Genesis 1-11* (BKAT I/1, Neukirchen-Vluyn, 1974), 203-214; E. Schlink, "Die biblische Lehre vom Ebenbilde Gottes", in: *Pro Veritate. Ein theologischer Dialog. Festgabe für Erzbischof Dr. h.c. L. Jaeger und Bischof Prof. D.Dr. W. Stählin* (Hrgg. E. Schlink und H. Volk, Münster, Kassel, 1963), 1-8; L. Scheffczyk, "Die Frage nach der Gottebenbildlichkeit in der modernen Theologie", in: *Der Mensch als Bild Gottes* (Hrg. L Scheffczyk, WdF 124, Darmstadt, 1969), XXIII; B. Otzen, "Menneskesynet i Det gamle Testamente" ["Die Auffassung des Menschen im Alten Testament"], in: *Menneskesynet [Die Auffassung des Menschen]* (Hrg. S. Pedersen, København, 1989), 59-60.

Menschen zu betonen.[16] W. Zimmerli findet Anlaß zu der Behauptung, "die Ebenbildlichkeit" sei des Menschen "köstlichstes Schöpfungsgut", und kann deshalb sagen: "In der Abbildlichkeit besteht des Menschen Würde".[17] In der Rede von der Gottebenbildlichkeit spiegelt sich die Vorstellung von Gottes besonderem Verhältnis zum Menschen wider. "Gott setzt sich zum Menschen in ein solches Verhältnis, daß dieser sein Bild und seine Ehre auf der Erde wird".[18]

Das Verhältnis eines Menschen zu seinem Mitmenschen ist gleichzeitig ein Verhältnis zu seinem Schöpfer, denn er ist auch der Schöpfer des Mitmenschen. Ungeachtet der vielen und beachtlichen Unterschiede, die bei einem Vergleich zwischen den Menschen hervortreten, besteht die grundlegende Gleichheit, daß in jedem Mensch ein Geschöpf Gottes, ein Mitgeschöpf zu sehen ist. So heißt es denn auch in Gen 9.6:

Wer Menschenblut vergießt, dessen Blut wird durch Menschen vergossen. Denn: Als Abbild Gottes hat er den Menschen gemacht.[19]

Ferner geht aus Spr 17.5 und 14.31 hervor, daß das Verspotten des Armen und das Unterdrücken des Geringen ein Verhöhnen dessen ist, der den Armen und den Geringen geschaffen hat.[20]

Als Geschöpf Gottes hat der Mensch also eine Würde, die für das Verhältnis der Menschen zueinander bestimmend sein muß. So verstand es auch Hiob. Im Gedanken an den Mitmenschen, der seine Fürsorge brauchte, sagte er: "Hat nicht mein Schöpfer auch ihn im Mutterleib geschaffen, hat nicht der Eine uns im Mutterschoß gebildet?" (31.15). Hiob sah in seinem Mitmenschen ein Mitgeschöpf, einen anderen Menschen, der wie er selbst von Gott geschaffen war, und deshalb konnte er das Recht seines Knechtes oder seiner Magd nicht mißachten (V. 13), deshalb konnte er die Wünsche der Geringen nicht verweigern (V. 16), deshalb mußte er sich der Witwe annehmen (V. 16) und sein Brot mit dem Waisen teilen (V. 17-18), und deshalb mußte er den

---

[16] Ich habe überlegt, statt "Würde" das Wort "Wert" zu verwenden, um den Wertaspekt stärker hervortreten zu lassen. Dieser Aspekt ist also im folgenden in dem Wort "Würde" mitzuhören.
[17] *1. Mose 1-11. Die Urgeschichte* (ZBK, Zürich, 1967³), 332. Vgl. z.B. F. Mussner, *Traktat über die Juden* (München, 1979), 101; O. Hammelsbeck, "Die Würde des Menschen" in: *Libertas Christiana. F. Delekat zum 65. Geburtstag* (Hrgg. E. Wolf und W. Matthias, BEvTh 26, München, 1957), 63.
[18] Jürgen Moltmann, *Gott in der Schöpfung: ökologische Schöpfungslehre* (München, 1985), 226.
[19] Vgl. W.H. Schmidt, "Werk Gottes und Tun des Menschen", 21.
[20] Vgl. Sir 4.1-6; slHen 13.58-59.; TGad 5.5. "Der Mitmensch, dem der Fromme begegnet, ist ... nie der Mensch-an-sich, den es nicht gibt, sondern immer der Mensch-vor-Gott", sagt A. Nissen, *Gott und der Nächste im Antiken Judentum. Untersuchungen zum Doppelgebot der Liebe* (WUNT 15, Tübingen, 1974), 161.

Verlorenen und Verarmten mit Kleidung und Decken helfen (V. 19-20). Kurz gesagt: Deshalb mußte er Diakonie üben.

Mit diesem Bild von seinem notleidenden Mitmenschen wußte Hiob sich in Übereinstimmung mit dem Schöpfer. Von ihm gilt es nämlich, daß er nicht den Vornehmen vor dem Armen begünstigt, denn sie sind beide das Werk seiner Hände (34.19). Entsprechend heißt es in Spr 22.2: "Reiche und Arme begegnen einander, doch der Herr hat sie alle erschaffen." In 29.13 kommt dieses Grundverständnis folgendermaßen zum Ausdruck: "Der Arme und der Ausbeuter begegnen einander, der Herr gibt beiden das Augenlicht." Bei Maleachi finden wir in einem im übrigen auf manche Weise dunklen Abschnitt die Worte: "Haben wir nicht alle denselben Vater? Hat nicht der eine Gott uns alle erschaffen?" (2.10).

Das von Gott Geschaffensein verleiht dem Menschen eine Würde, die trotz aller menschlichen Beurteilungen fest steht, und diese Würde ist ein wesentliches Argument für Diakonie, da sie für das Verhältnis von Menschen zueinander als normativ aufgefaßt wird.[21]

b) Das Neue Testament

Das Verständnis, das in den erwähnten alttestamentlichen Texten zum Ausdruck kommt, wird meiner Auffassung nach in den neutestamentlichen Schriften vorausgesetzt.[22] Dies geht besonders deutlich aus der Schilderung von Jesu Umgang mit notleidenden und verachteten Menschen hervor. Dort, wo diesen Menschen ihre Würde abgesprochen war, wurde sie ihnen von Jesus wieder zugesprochen. Diese Würde des Menschen in seinen Augen ließ ihn seine Hilfe gegenüber Notleidenden mit den Worten begründen: "Der Sabbat ist für den Menschen da, nicht der Mensch für den Sabbat" (Mk 2.27). Hier wird nämlich genau von dem alttestamentlichen Schöpfungsgedanken her argumentiert. Und als er an einem Sabbat heilte, tat er dies unter Hinweis auf die Würde des Menschen (Mt 12.9-14). Weil Zöllner, Sünder und andere Ausgestoßene in seinen Augen einen Wert und eine Würde besaßen, nahm er sich ihrer an und nahm sie in seine Gemeinschaft auf.

In dieser Fürsorge für den Menschen sah man einen Zusammenhang mit Gottes Schöpferwerk, wie dies auch aus z.B. Mk 7.37 und Joh 5.17 hervorgeht. Der Chorschluß in Mk 7.37, "Alles hat er gut gemacht",

---

[21] Es läßt sich nicht leugnen, daß die Akzentuierung einer Reihe von Unterschieden (ausgewählt - nicht ausgewählt; gerecht - ungerecht; rein - unrein; reich - arm u.s.w.) die Erkenntnis der allen Menschen in der Schöpfung gegebenen Würde und das Festhalten an dieser Erkenntnis einer schöpfungsgegebenen Gleichheit erschwert hat.

[22] Meines Erachtens setzen die neutestamentlichen Autoren in höherem Grade als allgemein angenommen alttestamentliche Vorstellungen voraus. Methodisch ist es jedoch problematisch, im Neuen Testament alttestamentliche Vorstellungen vorauszusetzen, die nicht angedeutet sind.

erinnert an Gen 1.31[23] und in Joh 5.17 wird die Heilung des Lahmen als Beispiel für Jesu Gemeinschaft mit seinem Vater hinsichtlich des Erschaffens verstanden.

Als Gottes Geschöpf und als im Bilde Gottes geschaffenes Wesen besitzt der Mensch also eine besondere Würde. Dies ist das Verständnis sowohl des Alten als auch des Neuen Testamentes. Der Gedanke der Menschenwürde besitzt jedoch im Neuen Testament eine besondere Akzentuierung.

Zunächst einmal gibt es eine christologische Akzentuierung. In dem bereits erwähnten Bericht aus Mt 25 über das Weltgericht heißt es:

> Was Ihr für einen meiner geringsten Brüder getan / nicht getan habt, das habt Ihr auch mir getan / nicht getan (25.40,45).

Christus hat sich mit dem Mitmenschen identifiziert, der hilfsbedürftig ist.[24]

Eine andere Akzentuierung liegt in der Formulierung des doppelten Liebesgebotes oder richtiger in der *Zusammenstellung* von Dtn 6.4-5 und Lev 19.18. Obwohl es verschiedene Auffassungen davon gibt, inwieweit die Juden bereits vor Jesus eine ähnliche Zusammenstellung des Gesetzes kannten,[25] kann jedoch kaum bezweifelt werden, daß Jesus das doppelte Liebesgebot in einer Weise verabsolutierte, wie man es vorher nicht gekannt hatte, und damit die Würde des Mitmenschen betonte.

> In Mk 12.28-34 sehen wir Gott und den Menschen zusammen mit dessen Mitmenschen direkt einander gegenüber gestellt, wie am "Schöpfungsmorgen", d.h. am Sinai vorbei,

sagt Sigfred Pedersen.[26] Laut dieser Deutung ist das doppelte Liebesgebot eine sehr starke Markierung der Würde des Menschen als Gottes Geschöpf.

---

[23] "Und Gott sah alles, was er gemacht hatte und siehe, es war sehr gut".
[24] Siehe auch Mt 10.40 par. und Joh 13.20. Ein ähnliches Verständnis finden wir bei Paulus; und in Röm 14.15 und 1 Kor 8.11-12 dient dieses Verständnis als ein entscheidendes Argument in seinen Ermahnungen, wie Menschen sich einander gegenüber verhalten sollen, ohne daß dieses jedoch ausdrücklich in einen Bezug zur Diakonie gestellt ist. So wie jeder Mitmensch ein von Gott geschaffener Mensch ist (Aus 1 Kor 8.6 geht hervor, daß Paulus sich vorstellt, daß Christus bei der Schöpfung dabei war. Vgl. Joh 1.3,10 und Kol 1.16-17), so ist er auch ein Mensch, für den Christus in den Tod gegangen ist. Damit ist die Würde des Menschen angegeben. Daß dieses von grundlegender Bedeutung für das Menschenbild ist, das für das Verständnis von Diakonie und für die diakonale Praxis ausschlaggebend sein muß, ist einleuchtend.
[25] Siehe nicht zuletzt A. Nissen, *Gott und der Nächste*. Vgl. z.B. Franz Mussner, *Traktat über die Juden*, 194-198, wo auf weitere Literatur verwiesen wird (besonders 194-195, Anm. 65).
[26] "Det paulinske menneskesyn" ["Die paulinische Auffassung des Menschen"], 80.

Es ist außerdem eine Markierung dessen, daß der Begriff *Nächster* in der universellen Bedeutung zu verstehen ist, die eine Konsequenz der Verknüpfung mit dem Schöpfungsgedanken darstellt. Wird das doppelte Liebesgebot in dieser Weise als das größte, d.h. wichtigste Gebot angesehen, dann wird die Bedeutung der vielen Unterschiede zwischen den Menschen relativiert, und die schöpfungsgegebene Gleichheit wird als das wesentlichste gesehen. Die Hervorhebung des doppelten Liebesgebotes ist auch deshalb für den Diakoniegedanken sehr wichtig, weil das Dienen eine für die Liebe sehr charakteristische Ausdrucksweise ist.

*2. Die Verantwortung des Menschen als Gottes Geschöpf*
a) Das Alte Testament
Das biblische Schöpfungsverständnis umfaßt nicht nur die Vorstellung von der Würde des Menschen, sondern auch von dessen Verantwortung. Mit dem gleichen Recht, mit dem der Schöpfer Adam fragen konnte: "Wo bist du?" (Gen 3.9), konnte er auch Kain fragen: "Wo ist dein Bruder Abel?" (Gen 4.9). "In diesen beiden Wo-Fragen faßt sich all das zusammen, was der Mensch von Gott her gefragt wird und wofür er verantwortlich ist", sagt W. Zimmerli.[27] Hiob bekannte sich zu seiner Verantwortung:

> Wenn ich das Recht meines Knechts mißachtet und das meiner Magd im Streit mit mir, was könnt' ich tun, wenn Gott sich erhöbe, was ihm entgegnen, wenn er mich prüfte? Hat nicht mein Schöpfer auch ihn im Mutterleib geschaffen? (Hiob 31.13-15).[28]

Diese Verantwortung wird auch an den vielen Stellen bezeugt, wo betont wird, daß der Mensch vor Gott Rechenschaft ablegen muß über sein Verhältnis zu denen, die hilfsbedürftig sind. Wie der Schöpfer Abels Blut schreien hörte (Gen 4.9-10), so hört er auch das Schreien der Schwachen und Notleidenden[29] - das Schreien seiner schwachen und notleidenden Geschöpfe, die von ihren Mitgeschöpfen unterdrückt oder im Stich

---

[27] *1. Mose 1-11*, 216. Vgl. G. von Rad: "Die Verantwortung vor Gott ist die Verantwortung für den Bruder". *Das erste Buch Mose. Genesis* (ATD 2/4, Göttingen, 1961⁶), 86. Kain versuchte, sich der Verantwortung durch die Frage zu entziehen: "Bin ich der Hüter meines Bruders?", doch er wurde an seiner Verantwortung festgehalten mit den Worten: "Das Blut deines Bruders schreit zu mir vom Ackerboden!" (4.9-10).
[28] Vgl. H.W. Wolff, *Anthropologie des Alten Testaments* (München, 1973), 294.
[29] Siehe z.B. Ex 22.22-23,26-27. Über das Grundbild in Exodus schreibt W.H. Schmidt: "Als Empfangender wird der Mensch auf sein Handeln angesprochen". Siehe "Werk Gottes und Tun des Menschen", 27.

gelassen worden sind, weil diese sich nicht ihrer Verantwortung bekannt haben.

In dem Buch "Verantwortung" hebt Ernst Würthwein daher auch die Verantwortlichkeit als Grundelement des alttestamentlichen Menschenbildes hervor und zeigt anhand einer Reihe von Textbeispielen u.a. auf, was dies im Verhältnis zu Fremden, Witwen, Waisen und anderen Notleidenden bedeuten muß.[30] Als Mensch geschaffen zu sein bedeutet also mit einer Verantwortung geschaffen zu sein, und hierin liegt eine wesentliche Begründung der Diakonie.

Obwohl es in den alttestamentlichen Schriften kaum explizit zum Ausdruck kommt, ist es doch anzunehmen, daß man einen engen Zusammenhang zwischen der ethischen Verantwortung des Menschen und der Tatsache gesehen hat, daß er im Bilde Gottes geschaffen wurde. Gottes Verhältnis zu den Notleidenden muß nämlich als eine Norm für den Menschen aufgefaßt worden sein, der in seinem Bilde geschaffen wurde.[31] Als Argument hierfür sei u.a. auf die jüdische Literatur verwiesen, laut der die Gottebenbildlichkeit des Menschen für die prinzipielle Grundlegung des ethisch-religiösen Lebens wichtig ist.[32]

b) Das Neue Testament

Auch das Neue Testament zeugt von der Gottebenbildlichkeit des Menschen, und zwar auf eine Weise, die an das Verständnis im Alten Testament anknüpft und jedoch auch etwas Neues hinzufügt. Laut Röm 1.23 (vgl. 3.23) ist die Gottebenbildlichkeit des Menschen als eine Folge der Sünde verloren gegangen. Paulus ist jedoch davon überzeugt, daß sie wiederhergestellt werden kann. Das geht z.B. aus den eschatologisch geprägten Aussagen in Röm 8.29; 1 Kor 15.49 und Phil 3.21 hervor. Die Neuschöpfung der verlorenen Gottebenbildlichkeit ist jedoch nicht nur etwas Zukünftiges. Sie geschieht bereits jetzt, und dies ist von Bedeutung für das Verständnis von Diakonie.

In Kol 3.10 treffen wir die Vorstellung von der Gottebenbildlichkeit in der Aussage über *den neuen Menschen*,[33] der erneuert wird zur Erkenntnis und zur Ebenbildlichkeit seines Schöpfers. Wenn es heißt, daß der neue Mensch erneuert werden soll, um das Ebenbild seines *Schöpfers* zu werden, so liegt es nahe, darin die Markierung eines Zusammenhangs

---

[30] E. Würthwein und O. Merk, *Verantwortung* (Biblische Konfrontationen 1009, Stuttgart, 1982), insbes. 83-98.
[31] "Die Gottebenbildlichkeit besteht aus der Macht und der Verantwortung", sagt E. Nielsen in einem Kommentar zu Gen 1.26-28, wobei er allerdings nicht zuletzt die Verantwortung des Menschen für das ganze Schöpfungswerk betont. *Første Mosebog [Das erste Buch Mose]* (København, 1987), 42.
[32] J. Jervell, *Imago Dei. Gen 1,26f. im Spätjudentum, in der Gnosis und in den paulinischen Briefen* (FRLANT NF 58; Göttingen, 1960), 120.
[33] Hiermit ist der in der Taufe neugeschaffene Mensch gemeint. Vgl. z.B. Röm 6.4 und 2 Kor 5.17.

zwischen der Schöpfung des Menschen in Gottes Ebenbild am Schöpfungsmorgen und der Neuschöpfung in der Taufe zu sehen. Der Mensch wird darauf festgelegt, daß er nicht nur im Bilde Gottes geschaffen wurde, um nach seinem Willen in dieser Welt zu dienen, sondern daß die Erneuerung nach seinem Bilde auch auf das Leben in Gottes Schöpfungsordnung abzielt.

So auch R. Schnackenburg:

> Es ist ein grundsätzliches Ja zur Schöpfungsordnung, das sich in der Redeweise "neu nach dem Bild seines Schöpfers" oder "nach Gott geschaffen" ausspricht.[34]

Es zielt auf das Leben in Gottes Schöpfungsordnung und zwar insbesondere auf das Leben der Menschen miteinander. Deshalb geht es darum, Erbarmen, Güte, Demut, Milde, Geduld und vor allem die Liebe anzuziehen (Kol 3.12,14).[35] Dort, wo eine solche Erneuerung, eine Erneuerung nach dem Bilde Gottes stattfindet, dort wird Diakonie geübt.

Im Epheserbrief finden wir ein Verständnis der Gottebenbildlichkeit des Menschen, das demjenigen des Kolosserbriefes sehr ähnlich ist. Die Leser werden aufgefordert, den neuen Menschen anzuziehen, der nach dem Bild Gottes geschaffen ist (Eph 4.24). Auch hier wird auf die Neuschöpfung in der Taufe abgezielt.[36] Daß diese Neuschöpfung u.a. auf Diakonie abzielt, kommt im Epheserbrief expliziter zum Ausdruck als im Kolosserbrief. Zum einen heißt es in Eph 2.9-10:

> Seine Geschöpfe sind wir, in Christus Jesus dazu geschaffen, in unserem Leben die guten Werke zu tun, die Gott für uns im voraus bereitet hat.

Zum anderen ist es eindeutig, daß die Ermahnungen im Abschnitt 4.25-32 sozusagen ausschließlich das Verhältnis zum Mitmenschen betreffen, und daß die diakonale Perspektive vor allem in V. 28 und 32 zum Vorschein kommt.

An dieser Stelle sollte vielleicht auch 5.1-2 erwähnt werden, da in diesen Versen, die eindeutig eine christologische Begründung enthalten, die Vorstellung von der Gottebenbildlichkeit des Menschen noch mitklingt, wie aus folgender Ermahnung hervorgeht:

---

[34] "Der neue Mensch - Mitte christlichen Weltverständnisses. Kol. 3,9-11", in: *Schriften zum Neuen Testament, Exegese in Fortschritt und Wandel* (München, 1971), 402.
[35] Es ist bezeichnend, daß die erwähnten Worte oft Gott und/oder Christus charakterisieren. Siehe z.B. Mt 11.29; 18.26-27; Lk 6.36; Röm 2.4; 9.22; 11.22; 12.1; 2 Kor 1.3; 10.1; Eph 2.7; Phil 2.1,8; Tit 3.4 und 1 Petr 3.20.
[36] Diese Auffassung wird u.a. auch von J. Jervell vertreten. Siehe *Imago Dei*, 237.

Ahmt Gott nach als seine geliebten Kinder, und liebt einander, weil auch Christus uns geliebt und sich für uns hingegeben hat.

In einem Leben im Dienst für andere gewinnt der neue Mensch nach Gottes Ebenbild Gestalt.

Die Diakonie wird dadurch begründet und ermöglicht, daß Gott in der Taufe den Menschen nach seinem Bilde neugeschaffen hat. Ferner ist sie in der Tatsache begründet, daß der Mensch geschaffen wurde, um mit dem Ziel der Verwirklichung des Gottesbildes zu leben. "Gottebenbildlichkeit ist also Gabe und Aufgabe, Indikativ und Imperativ", heißt es zusammenfassend bei Jürgen Moltmann.[37] Und folgendes läßt sich hinzufügen: Je mehr das Wesen der Gottebenbildlichkeit als Gabe hervorgehoben wird, desto mehr wird die diakonale Verantwortung des in Gottes Ebenbild neugeschaffenen Menschen betont.

Der Gedankengang im Kolosser- und Epheserbrief ist deutlich christologisch geprägt. Das in unserem Zusammenhang entscheidende ist jedoch die positive Verknüpfung mit dem alttestamentlichen Schöpfungsgedanken. Der integrierte Zusammenhang zwischen Schöpfung und Neuschöpfung.

### IV. Diakonie im Lichte des Gottesgedankens

a. Das Alte Testament
"Barmherzig und gnädig ist der Herr ... ". Dieses Zitat aus Ps 103.8 hat Hermann Spieckermann als Überschrift über einen Artikel gewählt,[38] in dem er darstellt, daß es für das alttestamentliche Gottesbild charakteristischer ist als normalerweise angenommen, daß Gott als barmherzig und gnädig, als geduldig und von großer Güte aufgefaßt wird.[39] Ich bin der Meinung, daß dies eine richtige Erkenntnis ist. Die Aussagen über Gottes Barmherzigkeit sind nicht nur zahlreich,[40] sie gehen auch in zentrale Zusammenhänge ein. Das Letzte soll mit einigen Beispielen verdeutlicht werden.

Als Gott sich vor der Erneuerung des Bundes Mose vorstellte, geschah dies laut Ex 34.6-7 mit den Worten:

---

[37] *Gott in der Schöpfung*, 232.
[38] "Barmherzig und gnädig ist der Herr...", *ZAW* 102 (1990), 1-18.
[39] H. Spieckermann ist übrigens der Auffassung, daß dieses Gottesbild seinen Ursprung in vorexilischer Zeit hat ("Barmherzig und gnädig ist der Herr...", 3-4).
[40] Im Hinblick auf die Formulierung in Ps 103.8 bemerkt Spieckermann: "Dieser Satz ... kommt als ganzer mit Variationen siebenmal im Alten Testament vor, in Teilen und freien Anspielungen mehr als zwanzigmal" ("Barmherzig und gnädig ist der Herr...", 1).

> Jahwe ist ein barmherziger und gnädiger Gott, langmütig, reich an Huld und Treue: Er bewahrt Tausenden Huld, nimmt Schuld, Frevel und Sünde weg, läßt aber (den Sünder) nicht ungestraft; er verfolgt die Schuld der Väter an den Söhnen und Enkeln, an der dritten und vierten Generation.

Diese Aussage, die sich als eine Interpretation des in 3.14 offenbarten Namens "Ich bin, der ich bin" verstehen läßt,[41] ist natürlich wichtig, da sie als Gottes Vorstellung seiner selbst verstanden wird - eine Vorstellung, die ganz eindeutig die Barmherzigkeit betont.[42]

Es ist ein wichtiges Zeugnis vom Gottesbild der Menschen, d.h. von der Auffassung von Gott, die sich die Menschen gebildet haben, daß Gottes Barmherzigkeit in vielen Aussagen von bekenntnishaftem und doxologischem Charakter gepriesen und damit hervorgehoben wird. So heißt es in Neh 9.17:

> Doch du bist ein Gott, der verzeiht, du bist gnädig und barmherzig, langmütig und reich an Huld,

und in Ps 145.8-9:

> Der Herr ist gnädig und barmherzig, langmütig und reich an Gnade. Der Herr ist gütig zu allen, sein Erbarmen waltet über all seinen Werken.[43]

Auch in vielen Gebeten spiegelt sich das Bild von Gott als einem barmherzigen Gott wider.

> Denk an dein Erbarmen, Herr, und an die Taten deiner Huld, denn sie bestehen seit Ewigkeit (Ps 25.6). Erhöre mich, Herr, in deiner Huld und Güte, wende dich mir zu in deinem großen Erbarmen.[44]

---

[41] Vgl. G. von Rad, *Theologie des Alten Testaments*, I (München, 1962⁴), 194-195. Mit Hinweis auf Ex 34.14 bemerkt von Rad: "Es gab also eine Zeit, in der es offenstand, den Namen Jahwes nach dieser oder jener Seite hin theologisch zu interpretieren" (195).

[42] Insbesondere zu V. 6 bemerkt B. S. Childs: "The frequent use through the rest of the Old Testament of the formula in v. 6 by which the nature of God is portrayed (Num. 14.18; Neh. 9.17; Ps 86.15 etc.) is an eloquent testimony to the centrality of this understanding of God's person" (*Exodus. A Commentary* (OTL, London, 1974), 612).

[43] Zu diesen Versen bemerkt A. Weiser: "Vielleicht ist V. 8-9 als der die alte Kulttradition zusammenfassende Hymnus der Gemeinde zu verstehen (vgl. 2. Mose 34.6), der die Güte und Barmherzigkeit Gottes gegen alle seine Geschöpfe als den Grundzug seiner Wesensoffenbarung feiert" (*Die Psalmen* (ATD 14/15, Göttingen, 1963⁶), 572). Vgl. z.B. Dtn 4.31; Ps 111.4; 116.5 sowie die vielen Stellen, an denen wir die Formulierung, "denn seine Huld währt ewig", finden. LXX übersetzt *hæsæd* mit ἔλεος. Die Stämme *hsd, rhm, nhm* und *hnn* liegen oft der Übersetzung mit "barmherzig" zugrunde.

[44] Vgl. z.B. Ps 51.3; 79.8; 86.5,15; Dan 9.9 und Jon 4.2.

Ein Mensch in Not hat deshalb den Wunsch, dem Herrn - nicht den Menschen - in die Hände zu fallen, denn seine Barmherzigkeit ist groß (2 Sam 24.14).

Daß Barmherzigkeit ein herausragender Zug im Gottesbild ist, geht außerdem aus verschiedenen Aussagen hervor, in denen Gottes Barmherzigkeit in Relation zu seiner Eifersucht gesetzt wird, zu seinem Willen, Ungehorsam und Abfall zu strafen. Das Überwältigende an Gottes Barmherzigkeit wird u.a. durch die wiederholten Aussagen darüber verdeutlicht, daß er bis ins tausendste Glied Barmherzigkeit erweist, wohingegen er nur bis zum dritten und vierten Glied straft.[45] In Ps 30.5-6 heißt es:

> Singt und spielt dem Herrn, ihr seine Frommen, preist seinen heiligen Namen! Denn sein Zorn dauert nur einen Augenblick, doch seine Güte ein Leben lang.

Der Beter scheint die Erfahrung gemacht zu haben, daß Gottes Zorn seiner Barmherzigkeit und Güte dient. Sogar der Zorn kann also als Zeugnis der Barmherzigkeit aufgefaßt werden.[46]

Jes 54.7-8 sei auch erwähnt:

> Nur für eine kleine Weile habe ich dich verlassen, doch mit großem Erbarmen hole ich dich heim. Einen Augenblick nur verbarg ich vor dir mein Gesicht in aufwallendem Zorn; aber mit ewiger Huld habe ich Erbarmen mit dir, spricht dein Erlöser, der Herr.[47]

Die vielen Zeugnisse von Gottes Barmherzigkeit entspringen vor allem den Erfahrungen der Menschen. Sie sind ein Ausdruck dafür, daß Menschen erlebt haben, daß Gott aus Liebe und Barmherzigkeit handelt. Es ist in diesem Zusammenhang berechtigt, von einer Grunderfahrung zu sprechen. Diese kommt u.a. in Dtn 7.6-8 zum Ausdruck:

> Denn du bist ein Volk, das dem Herrn, deinem Gott, heilig ist. Dich hat der Herr, dein Gott, ausgewählt, damit du unter allen Völkern, die auf der Erde leben, das Volk wirst, das ihm persönlich gehört. Nicht weil ihr zahlreicher als die anderen Völker wäret, hat euch der Herr ins Herz geschlossen und ausgewählt; ihr seid das kleinste unter allen Völkern. Weil der Herr euch liebt und weil er auf den Schwur achtet, den er euren Vätern geleistet hat, deshalb hat der Herr euch mit starker

---

[45] Ex 20.5-6; 34.6-7; Dtn 5.9-10. Vgl. Dtn 7.9-10 und Jer 32.18.
[46] A. Weiser bezeichnet die Gnade als das eigentliche Motiv des Gotteszornes (*Die Psalmen*, 182).
[47] "Hier wird das Eigentliche gesagt; hier liegt die Mitte der Verkündigung Deuterojesajas", bemerkt C. Westermann, (*Das Buch Jesaja. Kapitel 40-66* (ATD 19, Göttingen, 1970²), 221).

Hand herausgeführt und euch aus dem Sklavenhaus freigekauft, aus der Hand des Pharao, des Königs von Ägypten.

Die zentrale Erlösungshandlung, die Befreiung des auserwählten Volkes ist durch Gottes Liebe und Barmherzigkeit begründet. Die entscheidende Bedeutung dieser Handlung spiegelt sich in dem oft beigefügten "Zunamen" Jahwes "der dich/euch aus dem Lande Ägypten herausgeführt hat" wider. Siehe z.B. Ex 20.2; Lev 11.45; 19.36; Dtn 5.6; Ps 81.11.[48]

Die grundlegende und bleibende Bedeutung dieser Handlung geht außerdem aus der Bestimmung hervor, daß sie jedes Jahr gefeiert werden soll, und daß bei dieser Gelegenheit ein Vater seinem Sohn erzählen soll, wie der Herr mit starker Hand das Volk aus Ägypten herausführte.

In jeder Generation ist jeder verpflichtet, sich als einer zu betrachten, der selbst aus Ägypten ausgezogen war,

sagt A. Simonsen.[49] Es kann also mit Recht von einer Grunderfahrung gesprochen werden, jedoch von einer Grunderfahrung, die dadurch bestätigt wird, daß Gottes weitere Geschichte mit seinem Volk hauptsächlich von der Liebe und Barmherzigkeit bestimmt ist, die sich in der grundlegenden Erwählung und Befreiung offenbarte.[50]

Für das Thema Diakonie ist es ferner wesentlich, daß die alttestamentlichen Schriften Gottes Barmherzigkeit als eine Barmherzigkeit bezeugen, die eindeutig Arme, Unterdrückte und Notleidende umfaßt. Am häufigsten werden wohl Witwen, Waisen und Fremde erwähnt.

Er verschafft Waisen und Witwen ihr Recht. Er liebt die Fremden und gibt ihnen Nahrung und Kleidung (Dtn 10.18). Er ist ein Vater der Waisen, ein Anwalt der Witwen (Ps 68.6). Er denkt an die Armen, und ihren Notschrei vergißt er nicht (Ps 9.13).[51]

Gottes Barmherzigkeit und Fürsorge gegenüber Witwen, Waisen, Fremden und anderen, die mit der Not als Realität oder als ständige

---

[48] Laut dem Neuen Testament ist die zentrale Erlösungshandlung die Auferweckung Christi, die entsprechend durch die Liebe und Barmherzigkeit Gottes begründet ist. Daß die Auferweckung als die neue Erlösungshandlung verstanden ist, spiegelt sich im neutestamentlichen Sprachgebrauch wider. Gott hat sozusagen einen neuen "Zunamen" bekommen. Siehe z.B. Röm 4.24; 8.11; 2 Kor 4.14; Gal 1.1; Kol 2.12.
[49] *Centrale tanker i jødedommens etik [Zentrale Gedanken in der Ethik des Judentums]* (København, 1983), 89.
[50] Siehe z.B. 2 Kön 13.23 und Ps 106.43-46.
[51] Vgl. z.B. Ex 22.22; Ps 10.12,14; 145.14 und 146.7-9.

Bedrohung lebten, zeigt sich außerdem in einer Reihe von Gesetzesbestimmungen, da diese als Ausdruck für Gottes guten Willen aufgefaßt werden. Es ist deshalb wesentlich, derartige Gesetzesbestimmungen in der Perspektive der Barmherzigkeit zu sehen.

> Du sollst das Recht von Fremden und Waisen[52] nicht beugen; du sollst das Kleid einer Witwe nicht als Pfand nehmen (Dtn 24.17).[53] Wenn bei dir ein Fremder in eurem Land lebt, sollt ihr ihn nicht unterdrücken. Der Fremde, der sich bei euch aufhält, soll euch wie ein Einheimischer gelten, und du sollst ihn lieben wie dich selbst (Lev 19.33).[54] Wenn ihr die Ernte eures Landes einbringt, sollt ihr das Feld nicht bis zum äußersten Rand abernten. Du sollst keine Nachlese von deiner Ernte halten. In deinem Weinberg sollst du keine Nachlese halten und abgefallene Beeren nicht einsammeln. Du sollst sie dem Armen und dem Fremden überlassen. Ich bin der Herr, euer Gott (Lev 19.9-10).[55]

Es ist ganz sicher ein idealistisches Bild, das sich in den zitierten Bestimmungen widerspiegelt. So hat z.B. Salomo die Fremden zu Zwangsarbeit gezwungen (2 Chr 2.17-18), und nicht zuletzt die vielen Reinheitsvorschriften waren für die Verwirklichung wahrer Fürsorge eine ernsthafte Hinderung. Dennoch ist es wichtig, daß das Alte Testament eindeutig die Verantwortung für Witwen, Waisen und Fremden hervorhebt. Auch in dieser Weise wird die grundlegende Barmherzigkeit Gottes bezeugt.

Die Auffassung, daß Gott Fürsorge für die Notleidenden trägt, kommt auch in Gerichtsworten bei mehreren der Propheten zum Ausdruck. Seine Mahnungen, Fürsorge zu zeigen, sind ernstgemeint. Ein Beispiel vom Propheten Jesaja:

> Wascht euch, reinigt euch! Laßt ab von eurem üblen Treiben! Hört auf, vor meinen Augen Böses zu tun! Lernt, Gutes zu tun! Sorgt für das Recht! Helft den Unterdrückten! Verschafft den Waisen Recht, tretet ein für die Witwen! (Jes 1.16-17).[56]

---

[52] Oder: "von Fremden, die Waisen sind".
[53] In Dtn 27.19 werden diejenigen verflucht, die das Recht der Fremden, Waisen und Witwen beugen.
[54] Vgl. Ex 22.21-23; 23.9. Es wird oft übersehen, wie stark die Fürsorge für die Fremden im Alten Testament betont wird. So heißt es in Num 15.16: "Gleiches Gesetz und gleiches Recht gilt für euch und für die Fremden, die bei euch leben". Vgl. z.B. J. Schreiner, "Gastfreundschaft im Zeugnis der Bibel", *TThZ* 89 (1980), 50-60.
[55] Vgl. Ex 22.20; Lev 23.22 und Dtn 24.19-21. Siehe ferner Rut 2.2. - Ex 22.20 kommentiert B. Mogensen u.a. mit den Worten: "Die Begründung spricht Menschen an, die um Jahwes Großtat, die Befreiung aus Ägypten, wissen", in: *Israelitiske leveregler og deres begrundelse [Israelitische Lebensregeln und ihre Begründung]* (København, 1983), 97.
[56] Siehe den ganzen Abschnitt Jes 1.10-31. Vgl. Jer 5.20-31; 7.1-15; Ez 22.23-31; Sach 7.8-14. Bei Jes 58.6-8 wird pointiert, daß Fürsorge für die Notleidenden ein Fasten nach Gottes Willen ist.

Es ist offensichtlich, daß Barmherzigkeit ein sehr markanter Zug des alttestamentlichen Gottesbildes ist,[57] wie dies auch beim neutestamentlichen Gottesbild der Fall ist - hier akzentuiert im Christusgeschehen. Dies ist von Bedeutung für das Thema Diakonie. Sowohl im Alten als auch im Neuen Testament herrscht nämlich die Auffassung, daß ein Zusammenhang zwischen Gottes Barmherzigkeit und der Barmherzigkeit besteht, die Menschen einander gegenüber ausüben sollen.[58]

Die Befreiung aus Ägypten wird, wie bereits erwähnt, als Gottes ganz zentrale Barmherzigkeitshandlung an seinem Volk verstanden. Umso interessanter ist es, daß die Ermahnung zur Barmherzigkeit mit einem Hinweis auf diese Handlung begründet werden kann. In Dtn 24.18 wird die Ermahnung zur Barmherzigkeit gegenüber dem Fremden, dem Waisen und der Witwe mit den Worten begründet:

> Denk daran: Als du in Ägypten Sklave warst. hat dich der Herr, dein Gott, dort freigekauft. Darum mache ich es dir zur Pflicht, diese Bestimmung einzuhalten.[59]

Es ist wichtig, zu beachten, daß die Befreiung aus Ägypten an vielen Stellen als Begründung mitgedacht ist, ohne explizit erwähnt zu sein. U.a. Lev 19 berechtigt nämlich zu der Annahme, daß die Aussagen "Ich bin der Herr" (z.B. V. 12, 14, 16 und 18) und "Ich bin der Herr, euer Gott" (z.B. V. 3, 4, 10 und 25) verkürzte Formulierungen sind, die der Aussage entsprechen: "Ich bin der Herr, euer Gott, der euch aus Ägypten geführt hat" (V. 36).[60] Dies bedeutet, daß auch die Ermahnungen zur Barmherzigkeit, die mit den Sätzen "Ich bin der Herr" und "Ich bin der Herr, euer Gott" begründet werden, in Wirklichkeit durch Gottes grundlegende Barmherzigkeitshandlung an seinem Volk motiviert sind.[61]

---

[57] Dieser Zug des Gottesbildes wird übrigens auch in der jüdischen Literatur der Periode kurz vor und während der neutestamentlichen Zeit vielfach bezeugt. Siehe z.B. A. Nissen, *Gott und der Nächste*.

[58] Dies wird allerdings - was das Alte Testament betrifft - von H. D. Preuss in seinem Beitrag zum Artikel "Barmherzigkeit" in der "Theologischen Realenzyklopädie" bestritten (*TRE* 5, 1980, 220), wohingegen G. Wingren im selben Artikel u.a. schreibt: "Gottes Barmherzigkeit ... erzeugt menschliches Barmherzigkeit" (236). Vgl. ferner F. Crüsemann: "Menschliches Handeln zugunsten der Elenden und ihrem Recht gründet im Tun Gottes selbst und hängt mit dem Gottesbegriff Israels in allen seinen Formen untrennbar zusammen" ("Das Alte Testament als Grundlage der Diakonie", *Diakonie - biblische Grundlagen und Orientierungen*. Veröffentlichungen des Diakoniewissenschaftlichen Instituts an der Universität Heidelberg - Band 2 (Hrgg. G. K. Schäfer und Th. Strohm; Heidelberg, 1990), 91. Siehe auch F. J. Helfmeyer, *Die Nachfolge Gottes im Alten Testament* (BBB 29; Bonn, 1968), insbes. 216-219.

[59] Vgl. z.B. Lev 19,32-37; Dtn 5,13-15; 15,12-15; Am 2,6-10.

[60] Vgl. Lev 25.38: "Ich bin der Herr, euer Gott, der euch aus Ägypten herausgeführt hat, um euch Kanaan zu geben und euer Gott zu sein." Ferner z.B. Lev 11.45; 22.32-33; 23.43; 25.55; 26.13,45; Ex 20.2; Ps 81.11; Mich 6.4.

[61] Siehe in bezug auf das Verhältnis zum Armen, Fremden, Nächsten, Tagelöhner, Tauben, Blinden, Geringen und Alten z.B. Lev 19.9-18,32-34; 23.22 und 24.22. Vgl. H.W. Schmidt, "Werk Gottes und Tun des Menschen", 27.

In diesem Zusammenhang darf auch die Ermahnung aus Lev. 19.2 nicht fehlen: "Seid heilig, denn ich, der Herr, euer Gott, bin heilig".[62] Erstens ist die Ermahnung zum Heiligsein u.a. eine Ermahnung zur Barmherzigkeit gegenüber Mitmenschen. M. Brocke behauptet zu Recht, daß das Gebot, den Nächsten zu lieben wie sich selbst, im Zentrum des Kapitels steht, das mit der Ermahnung zum Heiligsein eingeleitet wird.[63] Zweitens drückt die Ermahnung die Auffassung aus, daß Gott das Volk geheiligt und damit die Voraussetzung dafür geschaffen hat, daß es nun diese Heiligkeit im Leben verwirklichen kann - darunter auch im Leben miteinander. Mit F. Crüsemann:

> Die Heiligkeit ist also zuerst eine von Gott geschenkte Gabe. Israel soll diesem Status allerdings auch entsprechen, soll sein, was es bereits ist ... Nächsten- wie Fremdenliebe erwachsen also letztlich aus der Heiligkeit des in Israel anwesenden heiligen Gottes und dem von ihm seinem Volk gegebenen Status.[64]

Für das Verständnis von Diakonie ist deshalb auch Lev 19.2 eine wichtige Aussage.

b. Das Neue Testament

Die erwähnte *theo*logische Begründung für Diakonie ist dem Alten und dem neuen Testament gemeinsam. Das möchte ich anhand einiger weniger Beispiele verdeutlichen.

Die Tatsache, daß Gott in seiner Güte Menschen reichlich auch mit materiellen Gütern versorgen kann, kann als Argument dafür angeführt werden, mit anderen zu teilen. Dafür gibt es z.B. in 2 Kor 9.6-10 und 1 Tim 6.17-19 deutliche Beispiele.[65] Gottes Güte und Fürsorge sind auf diese Weise Voraussetzung und Muster für das Leben, das die Menschen leben sollen. Gottes Güte und Fürsorge bewirken Diakonie.

Bei Mt finden wir an zwei Stellen (9.13 und 12.7) den beim Propheten Hosea vorkommenden Ausdruck: "Barmherzigkeit will ich, nicht Opfer!" Mit dieser Aussage wird die Bedeutung des Verhältnisses zum notleidenden Mitmenschen stark betont. Die Worte "Barmherzigkeit will ich, nicht Opfer" sind in Mt 9.13 und 12.7 an Menschen gerichtet, die gegenüber

---

[62] Die Aussage wird in 1 Petr 1.16 zitiert.
[63] ""Nachahmung Gottes" im Judentum", in: *Drei Wege zu dem einen Gott. Glaubenserfahrungen in den monotheistischen Religionen* (Hrgg. A. Falaturi, J. J. Petuchowski und W. Strolz, Freiburg, 1980), 81. Vgl. F. Crüsemann, "Das Alte Testament als Grundlage der Diakonie", 89-90.
[64] F. Grüsemann, "Das Alte Testament als Grundlage der Diakonie", 89. Siehe z.B. Lev 20.8,26; 21.8; 22.32-33. Die Auffassung, daß Menschen gnädig und barmherzig wie Gott sein sollen, kommt oft in jüdischen Texten zum Ausdruck. Siehe A. Nissen, *Gott und der Nächste*, u.a. 69-76 und 267-277.
[65] Einen ähnlichen Gedanken finden wir im Alten Testament. Vgl. z.B. Dtn 15.6,14; 16.13-15; 26.9-11.

Verachteten und Hungrigen herzlos waren,[66] aber sie müssen sozusagen immer hinter den Ermahnungen zur Fürsorge gegenüber anderen mitgehört werden - sei es Fürsorge gegenüber Eltern (Mt 15.3-9 par.), Witwen (Mk 12.38-40 parr.), Kranken (Mt 12.9-14 parr.) oder anderen. Und sie müssen auch hinter den Weherufen über diejenigen gehört werden, die Recht, Barmherzigkeit und Treue außer acht lassen (Mt 23.23).

Wichtig in diesem Zusammenhang ist ferner das doppelte Liebesgebot. Es wurde bereits erwähnt als Ausdruck für den Wert des geschaffenen Menschen, doch es zeugt auch von der Gründung der Diakonie im Gottesgedanken und im Verhältnis zu Gott. Laut Markus lautete der erste Teil der Antwort Jesu an den Schriftgelehrten so: "Das erste ist: "Höre Israel, der Herr, unser Gott ist der einzige Herr"". Das Bekenntnis zu Israels Gott ging also der Ermahnung zum Lieben voraus. D.h. das Bekenntnis zu dem Gott, von dem Jesus laut Mk 10.18 sagte: "Niemand ist gut, außer Gott, dem Einen." In diesem Bekenntnis spiegelt sich die *theo*logische Begründung für das doppelte Liebesgebot wider.[67]

Die Grundhaltung, die die erwähnten Texte bezeugen, hat eine kurze und klare Ausdrucksform in Lk 6.36 in den Worten gefunden: "Seid barmherzig, wie es auch euer Vater ist!"[68] Die Ermahnung steht in einem Zusammenhang, in dem es um das Verhältnis zum Mitmenschen geht, und das Verständnis ist zweifellos, daß Gottes Barmherzigkeit Norm und Voraussetzung für das Leben ist, zu dem ermahnt wird. Dabei wird an die erfahrene Barmherzigkeit gedacht.[69] So ist es auch - wie J.Dupont betont - charakteristisch für Jesus, damit zu beginnen, von Gott und seinem Wesen zu verkünden.[70]

### V. Er hat uns zuerst geliebt

In 1 Joh 4.19 enthält die Aussage "Wir lieben, weil er (d.h. Gott) uns zuerst geliebt hat" ein Adjektiv mit einer sehr wichtigen Funktion. Es ist πρῶτος, das - plaziert in dem Satz, wo Gott das Subjekt ist, und zwar mit dem Wort Gott verbunden, - die Erkenntnis festhalten soll, daß die Möglichkeit des Menschen, Liebe zu zeigen, davon abhängt, daß er

---

[66] Zu 12.7 bemerkt P. Nepper-Christensen, *Matthæusevangeliet. En kommentar [Das Matthäusevangelium. Ein Kommentar]* (Aarhus, 1988), 151: "Wenn die Pharisäer verstanden hätten, daß Gottes Wesen ἔλεος (Barmherzigkeit) ist, wären ihre Deutungen der alttestamentlichen Gebote niemals so lebensfeindlich geworden, wie dies der Fall war".
[67] Obwohl diese Begründung explizit nur bei Markus angegeben wird, ist anzunehmen, daß das gleiche Verständnis in den anderen Evangelien vorliegt.
[68] Die Parallele bei Matthäus hat das Adjektiv "vollkommen", das sekundär zu sein scheint. Vgl. J. Dupont: "L'appel à imiter Dieu en Matthieu 5,48 et Luc 6,36", *RB* 14 (1966), 137-158.
[69] Die Konjunktion καθώς hat nicht nur vergleichende, sondern auch begründende Bedeutung.
[70] "L'appel à imiter Dieu en Mattieu 5,48 et Luc 6,36", 157-158.

selbst zuerst von Gottes Liebe umfaßt ist.[71] Entsprechend ist die Fähigkeit des Menschen, Diakonie zu üben, davon abhängig, daß Gott zuerst Barmherzigkeit erweist.

Dieses πρῶτος, das nicht nur ein zeitliches Proprium, sondern vielmehr eine sachliche Voraussetzung verdeutlichen soll, tritt im Neuen Testament stärker hervor als im Alten, und bei dem, was Gott "zuerst" getan hat, wird im Neuen Testament insbesondere an seine Handlung durch Christus gedacht. Hiermit sind wir bei der christologischen Begründung für Diakonie. Doch auch im Alten Testament ist dieses πρῶτος bezeugt. Im Schöpfungsverständnis gibt es ein πρῶτος, und ebenso im Gottesbild,[72] wie aus dem in diesem Aufsatz besprochenen Textmaterial ersichtlich worden ist. Diese Erkenntnis ist wesentlich für das rechte Verständnis von Diakonie und hierunter von deren Begründung, doch sie ist auch von Interesse als eines der vielen Zeugnisse von dem inhaltlichen Zusammenhang zwischen dem Alten und dem Neuen Testament.

---

[71] Die Diskussion, inwieweit an eine Liebe zu Gott oder eine Liebe zu anderen Menschen gedacht ist, halte ich für müßig, weil der Brief sich ja gerade gegen eine solche Alternative wendet. Auch das Doppelgebot der Liebe schließt diese Alternative aus.
[72] Vgl. F. Crüsemann: "An dem Zusammenhang des erfahrenen, bekannten und erhofften Handelns Gottes mit dem von Menschen geforderten Handeln läßt sich ein gutes Stück der Geschichte des theologischen Denkens wie der sozialen Entwicklung ablesen" ("Das Alte Testament als Grundlage der Diakonie", 85).

CHAPTER TWELVE

# JESUS, THE PEOPLE OF GOD, AND THE POOR

*The Social Embodiment of Biblical Faith*

Johannes Nissen, Århus

## I. Introduction: Biblical theology and social hermeneutics

Discussions within the last few decades have shown that biblical theology can be understood either as a historical or a systematic discipline. It could either be "a theology contained in the Bible", or "a theology in accordance with the Bible".[1] In the former case we have to do with a historical concept, and in the latter with a normative concept.[2] The easiest thing to do is to opt for one of these alternatives to the exclusion of the other. However, it is a more demanding task to recognize that there is a truth, or at least a potential truth in both ways of viewing biblical theology, and to attempt to achieve some kind of positive interaction between them.[3]

An increasing number of biblical scholars are trying to combine the historical and theological aspects by studying the connexion between the Old and the New Testaments and thus giving an account of their understanding of the Bible as a whole, that is, above all the theological problems that arise from the variety of the biblical witness considered in relation to its inner unity. The present article differs to some extent from this approach. I am sympathetic to the attempt to work out a biblical theology by studying the texts "from within" the two parts of the canon. However, I want to broaden the perspective by making two additions.

My first addition concerns the hermeneutical dimension. We must insist on the hermeneutical awareness that implies both the recognition of the difference between our horizon and that of the biblical writers and

---

[1] For this distinction see G. Ebeling, "Was heisst 'Biblische Theologie'.?", in: *Wort und Glaube* (Tübingen, 3. Aufl. 1967), 69-89.
[2] A modern advocate of this classical distinction is H. Räisänen, *Beyond New Testament Theology: A Story and a Program* (London 1990).
[3] Cf. also J.D.G. Dunn - J. Mackay, *New Testament Theology in Dialogue* (London, 1987), 2-3.

the conviction that the task of understanding is to enable a dialogue between the two.[4]

It is crucial to realize that this dialogue has already begun in the Bible itself.[5] The Bible is by definition an open book, that is, a book open to the ongoing process of transmission and interpretation. The transmission and interpretation of biblical traditions of faith which can be observed in the Bible remain normative. But this canonized interpretative process gives also freedom for new theological thinking and new prophetic action.[6]

The believing community is of central importance for this ongoing interpretation due to the fact that the Bible takes its origin from within the life of believing communities.

> It is interpreted within the continuing life of these communities; the standard of its religious interpretation is the structure of faith which these communities maintain; and it has the task of providing a challenge, a force of innovation and a source of purification to the life of these communities.[7]

The ongoing interpretation is characterized by a re-reading of the traditions of the past. New situations forced reexamination and recasting of tradition, and they provided the believing community with a dynamic and living traditional base upon which to build and in terms of which to understand its past in the light of its changing present and futures.[8]

The second addition has to do with the social dimension of biblical theology. In the past attention has been focused mainly on discovering the beliefs expressed in early Christian writings. What is proposed in this article is that we take seriously the continuous dialectic between ideas and social structure. Biblical theology has to be concerned with more than the logic of belief-systems, it also has to grasp the formation and reformation of the Christian community itself, the social embodiment of early Christian faith. The sociology of early Christianity wants to put

---

[4] For further reflections on this dialogue see A.C. Thiselton, *The Two Horizons: New Testament Hermeneutics and Philosophical Description* (Grand Rapids, 1980); S.M. Schneiders, *The Revelatory Text: Interpreting the New Testament as Sacred Scripture* (San Francisco, 1991).

[5] Cf. J.D.G. Dunn - J. Mackay, "The best example of a phrase which contains the dialogue within itself is 'the people of God'. Who are they? Israel, the seed of Abraham, the Jews, the Christians, only the Jews who believe in Jesus..?" (*New Testament Theology in Dialogue*, 7).

[6] H.-R. Weber, *Power: Focus for a Biblical Theology* (Geneva, 1989), 25-26. A theology which simply transmits and repeats biblical affirmations without any sensivity to new contexts of Christian obedience risks the danger of becoming unbiblical. Conversely, a theology which "reinvents" Christian faith only in response to challenge of its own time without being guided and corrected by Bible study cannot claim to be biblical.

[7] J. Barr, "The Bible as a Document of Believing Communities", in: H.D. Betz (ed.): *The Bible as a Document of the University* (Chico, Cal., 1981), 25-47, 25.

[8] Cf. P. Achtemeyer, *The Inspiration of Scripture: Problems and Proposals* (Philadelphia, 1980), 128.

body and soul together again.⁹ It is an attempt at understanding the early church more fully, more as it really was, a flesh-and-body reality. "If we want to understand its 'soul', what it means, we must find the 'body' it lived as".¹⁰ That is to say, we will not find the soul of early Christianity without finding the body.¹¹

It is not my intention to abandon biblical theology in favour of a pure sociology of the Bible. But I see sociological inquiry as making an invaluable contribution to traditional critical exegesis. The "meaning of the text" is much more than the verbal meaning. What the text "means" entails the competence to act, to use, to embody "a capacity realized only in some particular social setting".¹²

Given these two additions to a dominant trend within recent biblical theology, it is quite natural that the focus of this article is on the communal character of biblical faith. As stated by John L. McKenzie,

> the Bible is the story of God and man, but not of God and the individual man; it is the encounter of God and Israel which issues in the incarnation of Jesus, the new Israel, and His continued life in the new Israel, the Church.¹³

It should also be noticed that I am focusing primarily on the beginnings of Christianity, that is on the Synoptic gospels, since they most clearly reflect the basic aspects of the teaching and life of Jesus. From his life and teaching sprang a new group within Judaism. This group continued his practice of bringing into their fellowship people who had previously been excluded from Israel. This affected the very centre of Jewish understanding of God's actions towards his people. The rise of the Christians as a group with their own identity, separate from the synagogue, produced in the New Testament writings a re-examination of the relationship between God and Israel.¹⁴

---

[9] See R. Scroggs, "The Sociological Interpretation of the New Testament: The Present State of Research", *NTS* 26 (1980), 164-179, 165-166.

[10] B. Holmberg, *Sociology and the New Testament: An Appraisal* (Minneapolis, 1990), 3. See also 157.

[11] It is important to notice that this "sociological" broadening of the theological task of interpreting the Bible reflects the character of revelation itself. See, e.g., B. Holmberg, *Sociology and the New Testament*, 157.

[12] W.A. Meeks, "The Hermeneutics of Social Embodiment", in: G.W.E. Nickelsburg - G.W. MacRae (eds.), *Christians Among Jews and Gentiles*, FS K. Stendahl, (Philadelphia 1986), 176-186, 184.

[13] J.L. McKenzie, "The Social Character of Inspiration", *CBQ* 24 (1962), 115-124, 120. See also the preface to *JBTh* 7 (1992), V-VIII (B. Hamm & R. Weth); the volume is entitled "Volk Gottes, Gemeinde und Gesellschaft".

[14] Cf. H. Moxnes, *The Theology in Conflict: Studies in Paul's Understanding of God in Romans* (Leiden, 1980), 7.

## II. Jesus and the reconstitution of God's people

### 1. The struggle for identity in a period of crisis

A central and persistent theme of Scripture is that the people of Israel is to be a righteous people.[15] The source of righteousness is also clearly stated: "You shall be holy, for I the Lord your God am holy" (Lev 19.2). The people of Israel is a people belonging to God. This sense of being God's possession constitutes its identity, its vocation and its vision. The people of God is to be a "kingdom of priests and a holy nation" (Exod 19.6).

Although Exod 19.6 is only very rarely quoted in the literature of the first century C. E., the common ethos of life practice of Israel as the "kingdom of priests and a holy nation" determined all groups of first-century Judaism. All the Jewish groups were concerned with Israel's life and existence as God's holy people who were entrusted with the commandments of the whole covenants system of *mitzvot*, the revealed rules for salvation. Hence, temple and Torah were the key symbols of first century Judaism.[16]

All groups were united in the belief in one God, and the social correlate to this belief was the one people of God. There was, however, a diversity of Jewish identity at that time, so one may want to say that its oneness is only a mental construct. There was no single institution that embodied Israel. "Nevertheless it is not an empty paradox to say that the variety of attempts to embody Israel's uniqueness itself attests to the power of the symbol".[17]

The different groups answered the question of Jewish identity quite differently. The Sadducees seem to have been principally concerned with preserving the traditional form of temple worship, and they were ready to compromise politically with the ruling powers. The community of Qumran looked forward to the restoration of the true temple worship, but they withdrew into the desert into their separate community; where they could preserve the purity of the covenant and form a kind of living temple, a house of holiness. The Pharisees did not separate themselves from the people, but they sought to realize their vision of "a holy people of priests" by transferring cultic purity and priestly holiness to everyday

---

[15] See P.D. Hanson's important study of the biblical notion of community: *The People Called: The Growth of Community in the Bible* (San Francisco, 1986).
[16] See S.R. Isenberg, "Power through Temple and Torah in Greco-Roman Palestine", in: J. Neusner (ed.), *Christianity, Judaism and Other Cults*, Studies for M. Smith, Part II, (Leiden, 1975), 24-52; E. Schüssler Fiorenza, *In Memory of Her: A Feminist Reconstruction of Christian Origins* (London, 1983), 110.
[17] W.A. Meeks, *The Moral World of the First Christians* (London, 1987), 93.

life.[18] The Zealots seem to have been concerned with national and religious independence, but there is also evidence for their zeal for the sanctury and the laws of purity.

All these diverse Jewish renewal movements of the time were strongly concerned with how to realize in every aspect of life the obligations and hopes of Israel as the kingly and priestly people of God. They sought to hasten God's intervention on behalf of Israel by scrupulously doing the will of God as revealed in temple and Torah.[19] We can see how the different groups disagreed about how to understand cult and purity. This disagreement is not simply an academic liturgical point; it was a matter that went to the heart of Israel's struggle to find its identity, to find renewal and liberation.[20]

To summarize, the various Jewish groups were at odds with one another because each had a different view of what was requested of the people of God, but commen to all groups was an emphasis on the importance of the nation and of beeing the people of God. Furthermore, Jewish religion at that time seemed to be more concerned with doing than thinking, more with orthopraxy than with orthodoxy. As L. E. Keck states, "there were only two unquestionable beliefs: God is one, and Israel is his chosen people".[21]

## 2. The distinctiveness of the Jesus movement

How, then, did the movement started by Jesus fit into this picture? In which way did this group of people react to the crisis of identity? These questions have been addressed most emphatically by the sociology of early Christianity. Within the limits of this article, the answer must be limited to a few hints.

There is no full agreement about the sociological nature of the movement brought into being by Jesus. However, it is generally agreed that the movement should be interpreted as a millenarian movement - a community of the new age - that arises in a time of unrest and that promises decisive social change.[22]

---

[18] For a more detailed study of the beginnings of rabbinic Judaism, see J. Neusner, *The Pharisees: The Rabbinic Perspectives* (New York, 1985).
[19] Cf. E. Schüssler Fiorenza, *In Memory of Her*, 113.
[20] Cf. J.K. Riches, *Jesus and the Transformation of Judaism* (London, 1980), 117.
[21] L.E. Keck, *The New Testament Experience of Faith* (St. Louis, 1976), 28.
[22] E.g. J.G. Gager, *Kingdom and Community: The Social World of Early Christianity* (New Jersey, 1975) and R. Scroggs, "The Earliest Communities as Sectarian Movement", in: J. Neusner (ed.): *Christianity, Judaism and Other Cults*. Studies for M. Smith, II (Leiden, 1975), 1-23.

There is also a growing consensus for characterizing the Jesus group as a *renewal movement* within Judaism.[23] This movement can be seen as one of several responses to the deep-seated pluriform crisis that was troubling Jewish society. To describe it as a renewal movement has the merit of stressing the *continuity* of the work of Jesus with the religion of the Jews. It was in the Jewish context and very much from within Judaism that earliest Christianity grew.[24] But at the same time we must ask: In which way did the Jesus movement bring about a *transformation* of Judaism?

The central theological concern for Jesus and his group was the same as that of the other groups: The renewal of the people of Israel as God's holy elect in the midst of the nations. But there was a basic disagreement between the Jesus movement and the other movements as to what constituted the community.[25] The movement refused to define the holiness of God's elected people in cultic terms; instead, it redefined it as the wholeness intended in creation. It was a movement characterized by a praxis of inclusive wholeness.[26]

The implication of what has been said so far is that the "problem of the church" is not new. It existed in a certain sense already in first-century Judaism. Different groups were in competition as to the question of what it means to be the true "church" of God, the congregation (*qahal*) of Yahweh.[27] Seen in this perspective Jesus did not aim at creating a new religion. He did not found a new church, nor did he organize an institution. Instead, he aimed at a radical renewal of God's people, the "church" of God.[28]

---

[23] E.g. G. Theissen, *Soziologie der Jesusbewegung. Ein Beitrag zur Entstehungsgeschichte des Urchristentums* (München, 1977), and E. Schüssler Fiorenza, *In Memory of Her*, who speaks of the Jesus movement as "an alternative prophetic renewal movement within Israel" (100).

[24] Cf. D. Tidball, *An Introduction to the Sociology of the New Testament* (Exeter, 1983), 41.

[25] The Jewish scholar A. Segal, *Rebecca's Children: Judaism and Christianity in the Roman World* (Cambridge, Harv., 1986) in a similar way points out that community identity was the central concern of the Pharisees and that the conflict with Christians was over precisely this issue. The author argues that the differences and eventually antagonism between these two concurrent movements were not merely matters of theological concepts, but basic disagreements as to what constituted the covenant community.

[26] Cf. E. Schüssler Fiorenza, *In Memory of Her*, 113.

[27] Cf. also the following statement by A. Vögtle: "Im Judentum, in dem Jesus auftrat, existierte bereits das Kirchenproblem!" ("Das öffentliche Wirken Jesu auf dem Hintergrund der Qumranbewegung", in: *Freiburger Universitätsreden*. Veröffentlichung der Albert-Ludwigs-Universität und der wissenschaftlichen Gesellschaft in Freiburg, NF 27 (1958), 5-20), 17. For further reflections on this problem see R.N. Flew, *Jesus and the Church: A Study of the Idea of the Church in the New Testament* (London, 1938); K. Müller (ed.), *Die Aktion Jesu und die Re-Aktion der Kirche. Jesus von Nazareth und die Anfänge der Kirche* (Würzburg, 1972).

[28] Cf. H. Frankemölle, "Die Jesusbewegung als Basisgemeinde? Fakten und Impulse aus dem Neuen Testament", in: H. Frankemölle (ed.), *Kirche von Unten. Modelle, Erfahrungen, Reflektionen. Alternative Gemeinden* (München, 1981), 36-61, 46. According to G. Soares-Prabhu the Jesus movement was a community which emerged from the *abba*-experience of Jesus and it was marked by the following salient features: radical freedom, radical universalism (inclusiveness), radical sharing, radical service, and radical equality ("Radical Beginnings: The Jesus Community as the Archetype of the Church",

## 3. Kingdom, people and community

At the heart of Jesus' message was the announcement of God's new initiative, God's drawing near to establish his Kingdom. No single theme is more central to Jesus' message than this one. All scholars agree on this. But there is still disagreement on the crucial question: How is the Kingdom coming to human beeings? Is it coming to individual persons by entering their souls? Or is it coming publicly so that the people of God appears as a new society, as a new humanity?[29]

Although the second position is not new[30] it has gained strength from the insights of the sociology of early Christianity. Both the Kingdom of God and the reconstitution of God's people are the essential elements of Jesus' words and works.[31] It should be noticed that Jesus' way of speaking about the Kingdom is based upon a pictorial image of a house, a city, or a community. Thus, he speaks of people entering or not entering *into* the Kingdom (e.g. Mark 9.47; 10.15). They can sit *in* it and eat and drink *in* it (e.g. Mark 14.25; Matt 8.11-12). The Kingdom has a door or a gate (e.g. Matt 7.13) on which one can knock (Matt 7.7-8; 25.10-12). It is sometimes compared to a city or a house (Mark 3.23-27; Matt 12.25). There seems to be no doubt that the Kingdom is a socially structured society of people.[32]

Here we must ask how this is related to the central idea of the people of God. An increasing number of scholars are using the term "gather" to describe Jesus' particular activity with regard to Israel. This is a well-founded wiew, since the Synoptic gospels indicate that he addresses all Israel and wants to heal the deep breaches within Israel.[33] Unlike most of the other renewal movements, he does not create cadres of people to withdraw from the world. G. Lohfink has shown that a wide range of texts, including Jesus' threats, denunciations, parables of crisis, and

---

*Jeevadhara* 15 (1985), 307-325).

[29] See also N. Lohfink, "Die Sorge Gottes um die rechte Gesellschaft - eine gemeinsame Perspektive von Alten und Neuen Testament", in: M. Klopfenstein, U. Luz a. o. (eds.), *Mitte der Schrift? Ein jüdisch-christliches Gespräch* (Bern, 1987), 357-384, 362-363.

[30] See, e.g. N.A. Dahl, *Das Volk Gottes. Eine Untersuchung zum Kirchenbewusstsein des Urchristentums* (Oslo, 1941), 147.

[31] Cf. H.C. Kee, *Knowing the Truth: A Sociological Approach to New Testament Interpretation* (Minneapolis, 1989), 86.

[32] Cf. A. Nolan, *Jesus Before Christianity: The Gospel of Liberation* (London, 1977), 47. S. Aalen has shown that whereas the Kingdom language of Judaism generally points to a theophanic appearance of God's rule, Jesus tends to use spatial metaphors. "One enters (the kingdom), it is like a room in a house, a hall. The meal or feast...stresses the idea of community. This room or house is for men who are in fellowship with God, or with his representative Jesus, and with each other" ("'Reign'and 'House' in the Kingdom of God in the Gospels", *NTS* 8 (1962), 215-240, 228-229).

[33] R.N. Flew is correct in emphasizing that the concept of Messiahship inevitably implies the gathering of a new community: see *Jesus and His Church*, 14.

sayings against this generation, demonstrate how much Jesus was concerned with the gathering and restoring of God's people. But in Jesus' message there were no restorative national tendencies of any sort, no inclusion of the glorification of Jerusalem, no petition for liberation from the Romans in prayers like the Lord's Prayer. He rejected the efforts of the Zealots and avoided the Essene imagery of the holy war. Conflict with the restorative theology of the Sadducees brought him to his death.[34]

Jesus concentrated his mission on his disciples when the greater part of Israel rejected his call. However, his circle of disciples was anything but the holy remnant of Israel; still less was it a replacement for Israel. They represented an anticipation of what the full gathering one day should be.[35] Together with Jesus, the disciples constituted a contrast society, symbolically representing the new and renewed Israel. The number of the inner group was itself symbolic of the twelve tribes of Israel. The community of disciples with its exceptional style of life was intended to attract attention, like a city upon the mountaintop or a lantern in a dark place (cf. Matt 5.13-16). It had a mission to remind the rest of the people of the transcendent value of the kingdom of God.[36]

Two different forms of community seem to be in conflict: on the one hand the community of believers as an alternative society, on the other hand, the rest of humanity. In the Old Testament this conflict is solved by the concept of the pilgrimage of the Gentiles to the mountain of Zion - a concept which found its clearest expression in the book of Isaiah (Isa 2.2-3; 18.7; 45.18-25; 60.1-22). This concept is taken over by Jesus, but modified and transformed. The words of Jesus in Matt 5.14 must be seen as a reference to Isa 2. According to Matt 8.11 he says; "Many will come from east and west and will eat with Abraham, Isaac, and Jacob in the kingdom of heaven" (cf. Luke 13.28-29). And the symbolic cleansing of the temple can be seen as a preparation of the temple for this pilgrimage: cf. the quotation in Mark 11.17: "My house shall be called a house of prayer for *all the nations*".[37] The coming of many people to the fellowship with Jesus, then, can be seen as the fulfilment of the promise of the pilgrimage of the nations. It is the beginning of the eschaton.

---

[34] G. Lohfink, *Wie hat Jesus Gemeinde gewollt? Zur gesellschaftlichen Dimension des christlichen Glaubens* (Freiburg, 1982), 17-41.
[35] Jesus did not envision a purely spiritual and religious community. By contrast, "die Sammlungsbewegung ist etwas sehr Konkretes und Sichtbares" (G. Lohfink, *Wie hat Jesus Gemeinde gewollt?*, 40).
[36] Cf. A. Dulles, *Models of the Church* (New York, 1987), 209.
[37] Cf. N. Lohfink, *"Die Sorge um die rechte Gesellschaft"*, 379.

It should also be noticed that Matthew has a tradition about Jesus healing the blind and the lame in the temple court and about the children who continued to shout: "Hosanna to the Son of David" (Matt 21.14-16), incidents that caused the conflict with the temple authorities. This king, whose people consisted of children, forgiven sinners, and healed cripples, stood in the temple, the center of God's people, over against the high priests and scribes, who considered themselves to be the authorities in the temple and over the people of Israel.[38]

To summarize, we can say that Jesus worked in Israel, not in an ethnographic sense, but in a *heilsgeschichtliche* sense, calling the people of God to its real destiny, to be a blessing for the peoples of the earth (cf. Gen 12.3; Isa 49.6). "His immediate task was to create a new community within Israel to transform the life of this people, in the faith that a transformed Israel would transform the world".[39]

### 4. An inclusive view of the people of God

Jesus redefined community membership in a new inclusive way. When seen within its original first-century setting, this theme, addressing the old-age question - "Who belongs to the people of God?" - must be regarded as one of the most revolutionary in Jesus' teaching.[40] It is the Kingdom of God which creates the inclusiveness characteristic of the community of Jesus.[41] The idea that kingdom citizenship might be a prerogative of a cultural aristocracy, or of Israel as a "chosen race", is deliberately exploded by Jesus (e.g. Matt 21.43).[42] This inclusiveness of the Kingdom of God and the community around Jesus is reflected in Jesus' words and acts as can be seen from the following distinctive marks:

a) Jesus had *a special concern for the poor and disadvantaged.*[43]

---

[38] See H.-R. Weber, *The Invitation: Matthew on Mission* (New York, 1971), 67.

[39] D.T. Bosch, "'Jesus and the Gentiles' - a Review after Thirty Years", in: P. Beyerhaus-C.F. Hallencreutz (eds.), *The Church Crossing Frontiers. Essays in Honour of B. Sundkler* (Lund, 1969), 3-19, 10-11.

[40] Cf. P.D. Hanson, *The People Called*, 400.

[41] See also G. Forkman, *The Limits of the Religious Community: Expulsion from the Religious Community within the Qumran Sect, within Rabbinic Judaism and within Primitive Christianity* (Lund, 1972), 189-190.

[42] Cf. T. M. Taylor, "Kingdom, Family, Temple and Body: Implications from the Biblical Doctrine of the Church for the Christian Attitude Amid Cultural and Racial Tensions", *Int* 12 (1958), 174-193, 179.

[43] For a more detailed analysis see J. Nissen, *Poverty and Mission: New Testament Perspectives on a Contemporary Theme* (Leiden, 1984). In an interesting article entitled "Gruppenmessianismus. Überlieferungen zum Ursprung der Kirche im Jüngerkreis Jesu" (*JBTh* 7 (1992), 101-123) G. Theissen argues that Jesus shared his messianic charisma with other people. His movement reflects a group messianism. "Im bestehenden jüdischen Gemeinwesen herrschte Gott durch seine Gesetze und die im Synedrium organisierte Artistokratie. Jesus vertrat dagegen eine utopische theokratische Erwartung: Gottes Herrschaft ist im Kommen begriffen und nicht in den gegenwärtigen Institutionen schon realisiert.

Jesus directed a number of words to poor and deprived people (e.g. Luke 6.20-23 par.; 7.22-23 par.; 4.18) and he spoke on their behalf (Mark 10.21; 12.41-44; Luke 14.13-14; 16.19-31). He showed an open attitude to the despised Samaritans (e.g. Luke 10.30-37; 17.11-19; John 4.1-42). He freely associated with women, including them in the community of disciples, openly conversing with them, and publicly accepting their signs of affection and loyalty - actions that were taboo for a public religious teacher in the patriarchal society of Jesus' day (e.g. Luke 7.36-50; 8.1-3; John 4.27). His ministry therefore can be characterized as "a ministry of compassion to peripheral people".[44]

b) The inclusiveness of the Jesus community is also reflected in the attitude *toward foreigners and enemies*. Though members of a group, you must not react with an absence of love ("hate") towards those whose group loyalties and interests are divergent or opposed (e.g. Matt 5.38-48 par.). At Qumran, for example, group solidarity was fierce (cf. 1 QS 1.10; 9.20), while clan solidarity is a phenomenon common to many cultures. The group dynamics prompted by the Kingdom are very different: characterized not by exclusiveness or defensiveness, but by an openness to others that reflects the openness of God to his children (Matt 5.45). "The community must reach out to those who oppose it, and always seek to "overcome evil with good" (Rom 12.21)".[45]

c) Jesus' inclusive view of God's people is perhaps seen most clearly in his *table fellowship with tax collectors and sinners* (e.g. Mark 2.13-17; Luke 15.1-2). To understand the full meaning of this fellowship, we need to see that for the oriental, table-fellowship was a guarantee of peace, trust, and brotherhood. It was in a very real sense a sharing of life. As has already been noticed (note 18), the Pharisees as a group were especially concerned with the boundaries of the table fellowship, following the same rules as for those that were valid for the cultic purity of temple worship. Jesus threatened the sanctity of Jewish society as the people of God, breaking taboos by including unclean people, outsiders, in the table-fellowship. "More than other conflicts over the interpretation of the Law or keeping of rules, this was a conflict over the identity of the Jewish people as a group".[46] The primary function of meals, however, is not to provoke conflicts, but to start a new group around Jesus. "It threatens this (Jewish) society by being more open. Furthermore, it questions the very basis of distinctions between 'insiders',

---

Sie wird vielmehr von Menschen repräsentiert, die in der gegenwärtigen Gesellschaft Aussenseiter sind: von Armen, Kindern und den Nachfolgern Jesu" (118).

[44] Cf. D. Senior - C. Stuhlmueller, *The Biblical Foundations for Mission* (New York, 1983), 147.
[45] Cf. B. Chilton - J.I.H. McDonald, *Jesus and the Ethics of the Kingdom* (London, 1987), 102.
[46] H. Moxnes, "Meals and the new community in Luke", *SEÅ* 32 (1986-87), 158-167, 161. What is said here about Luke, applies also to the earliest tradition.

'righteous', on the one side, and 'outsiders', 'sinners and tax collectors' on the other side".[47]

d) This group round Jesus formed *a new social structure*. It was a group of disciples which, from the political and social point of view of that time, was a rather amazing group: men and women together, mostly from among the '*am ha'aretz*' in Galilee, some former disciples of John the Baptist, perhaps one or several former members of the Jewish resistance movements, John who had connections with the high priest in Jerusalem, a tax collector who collaborated with the Romans and later two Pharisees.[48] It is clear from the constitution of the community around Jesus that "he fully intended to create a group where all sorts and conditions of people could find a welcome".[49] This group hardly represented a natural or homogenous gathering of friends by first-century Jewish standards.

Although Jesus addressed the poor and the outcast and mixed socially with them, he did not break off contact with those in power. He also addressed the establishment, albeit in tones of warning and challenge. A clear example of this can be found in the parables that are a challenge to the establishment to change its atittude toward him and his defense of the poor. "The elder brother, the grumbling workers in the vineyard, the self-righteous Pharisee all represent the establishment who in effect say as Hillel was reputed to have said, 'No *am ha-aretz* fears sin'. Yet Jesus tries to keep the door open. The elder brother in the parable of the prodigal son is 'left' standing in the field. Whether he remains there or comes to the feast is still open".[50]

The openness of Jesus towards every individual, his capacity to communicate with people of every kind, privileged as well as disadvantaged, must probably be seen as a reflection of God's own freedom of love. God loves indiscriminately (cf. Matt 5.45).

Precisely because Jesus was a person for whom there was no favourite, he had a special concern for the disadvantaged. This does not mean that his love for these people was an exclusive love. Rather it is an indication that what Jesus valued was humanity, not status and prestige. The poor and disadvantaged had nothing to recommend them except their humanity and suffering. Jesus was also concerned about the privileged, not because they were particularly important people, but because they were people.

---

[47] H. Moxnes, "Meals and the new community", 163. On Jesus' rejection of the conventional purity rules and tight boundaries see also J. K. Riches, *Jesus and the Transformation of Judaism*, 112-144.
[48] Cf. H.-R. Weber, "Freedom Fighter or Prince of Peace?", *Study Encounter* vol 8. no. 2 (1972), 1-24, 23. See also J. Koenig, *New Testament Hospitality: Partnership with Strangers as Promise and Mission* (Philadelphia, 1985), 29-33.
[49] J. Koenig, *New Testament Hospitality*, 30.
[50] R. Scroggs, "*The Earliest Christian Communities*", 12.

But they had to give up their false values of wealth and prestige in order to become real people. Thus, "Jesus wished to replace the "worldly" value of prestige by the "godly" value of people as people" (cf. also 1 Cor 1.26-31).[51]

The Jesus-fellowship offered a welcoming place where people could feel themselves honoured as children of God apart from the niches they had fallen into at birth or carved out for themselves over the years.[52] This fellowship was the beginning of the new humanity, an anticipation of the messianic banquet.[53] It was a new family where they could "receive a hundredfold... houses and brothers and sisters and children and lands" (Mark 10.30; cf. Mark 3.31-35).

Jesus called into existence a community that was a challenge to the mental structures of his time, e.g. the use of power for domineering, the trust in money, and religious self-rightousness. Contrary to these abuses, Jesus preached and manifested in his life other structures, those of trust in God's coming Kingdom, self-giving service, etc. (Mark 10.41-45).

*5. The community of Jesus as an "alternative society"*

It is often asserted that the early Christians showed little or no interest in changing society as such. This assertion is based on the question: to what degree did Christians perform actions outside the community - actions that could change the social situation or even the structures of society?

This way of presenting the problem is open to criticism. The search for a just society was a central concern for the first Christians, but they did not try to achieve this goal by acting outside the community. Instead they aimed at constructing a community which in itself is an example of a just society.[54] As J. H. Yoder has put it,

> "the primary social structure through which the gospel works to change other structures is that of the Christian community".[55]

The church is a counter-community, where alternative norms and values are organized into a social grouping.[56]

---

[51] A. Nolan, *Jesus Before Christianity*, 57.
[52] Cf. J. Koenig, *New Testament Hospitality*, 29.
[53] S. Kappen, *Jesus and Freedom* (New York, 1977), 101. See also J. Roloff, "Heil als Gemeinschaft. Kommunikative Faktoren im urchristlichen Herrenmahl", in: P. Cornehl -H.E. Bahr (eds.), *Gottesdienst und Öffentlichkeit* (Hamburg, 1970), 88-117.
[54] See also N. Lohfink, *"Die Sorge um die rechte Gesellschaft"*, 380.
[55] J.H. Yoder, *The Politics of Jesus* (Grand Rapids, 1972), 157.
[56] Cf. S.C. Mott, *Biblical Ethics and Social Change* (New York/Oxford, 1982), 133.

The Christian community has as its standard none other than the example of God's impartial justice. "Be perfect, therefore, as your heavenly Father is perfect" (Matt 5.48; cf. v.45). These words of Jesus must be seen in the light of the Old Testament concept of the people of God, especially Lev 19.2. "To be God's people is" - in the words of P.D. Hanson - "by definition to be a people dedicated to righteousness in all areas and spheres of life".[57]

This understanding of God's people as being a righteous people is perhaps most clearly expressed in the Sermon on the Mount. Here we have a messianic ethics that reflects non-conformity with the values and norms of the world. This does not imply a negative view of the world. Rather, the followers of Jesus have the vocation to be the instruments of the Kingdom of God in the world in association with their Lord and under his leadership. "You are the light of the world" (Matt 5.14) is one clear expression of that calling. The subjects of the Kingdom fulfill this function as they live their lives in the world in all the variety of their earthly activities and relationships.[58]

The disciples are also characterized as the "salt of the earth" (Matt 5.13). This metaphor suggests that the people of God can carry out its task of bearing witness to God's alternative order only if it refuses to blend into habitations that have grown comfortable through refusal to question old values and assumptions. To be the "salt of the earth" a people must persist in radically reorienting life away from every idol and toward the one true God.[59]

It is worthwhile noticing what kind of people are addressed by these words. It is a group of poor and powerless people (cf. Matt 5.3-12) who have been given this task of witnessing. This is an indication that their power was not their own but that of the Spirit of God. "They were a community and they had work to do in the world. They were a small and seemingly insignificant group, but they were called the Light of the World".[60]

Thus, Jesus and his followers are forming a group that is now living in a new social order and, in this way as light and salt, has an impact on the lives of all nations. The purpose of this communial life is that Israel as a whole can be the light and the salt among the nations. Moreover, the Sermon on the Mount can be seen as unveiling the true meaning of the

---

[57] P.D. Hanson, *The People Called*, 508.
[58] Cf. G.R. Beasley-Murray, "Matthew 6:33: The Kingdom of God and the Ethics of Jesus", in: H. Merklein a.o. (eds.), *Neues Testament und Ethik*, FS R. Schnackenburg (Freiburg, 1989), 84-98, 96-97.
[59] Cf. P.D. Hanson, *The People Called*, 492. On the community as an alternative society see also G. Lohfink, *Wem gilt die Bergpredigt? Beiträge zu einer christlichen Ethik* (Freiburg, 1988), esp. part IV: "Weshalb verlangt die Bergpredigt notwendig eine Kontrastgesellschaft?".
[60] S.C. Mott, *Biblical Ethics and Social Change*, 141.

Torah. The Torah was given to Israel as an instruction to the people in order that the weak should be protected through proper institutions and through actions of solidarity. If those in power are failing to show this solidarity, then Israel is living in the same manner as other nations. However, the task given to Israel is that "there will be no poor among you" (Deut 15.4).[61] Although Deut 15.4 is not directly quoted in Matt 5-7, the ethos of the Sermon on the Mount can be seen as an attempt to fulfill the vision expressed in these words.[62] The same point can also be expressed by means of the metaphor of the household. Thus M. H. Crosby has characterized the Sermon on the Mount as "Building a House on the Rock of Justice".[63]

*6. The re-creation of a just society*

By attempting to recreate the just society Jesus is placing himself in line of the prophetic tradition in ancient Israel. Like Amos, Isaiah, and Jeremiah, as well as the post-exilic prophets, who followed them Jesus rebuked the people for turning away from God. The prophets attacked the exploitation of the poor by the rich because God demands not sacrifice but human justice; they condemned the people for turning the worship of God into a mechanical process divorced from the actions of justice. So too, Jesus criticized the leaders of the people for their hardheartedness, hypocrisy, and injustice. "Love of God, Jesus insisted, must involve the love for all peoples".[64]

---

[61] This passage is presupposed in Acts 2.44-45 and 4.35. Luke sees the radical sharing in the Jerusalem community as a fulfillment of the seventh year in Deut 15.4-5 and thus a sign that Christians were the true Israel. See also my analysis of Luke 4.16-30 in this article.

[62] See H. Gollwitzer, "Bergpredigt und Zwei-Reiche-Lehre", in: J. Moltmann (ed.), *Nachfolge und Bergpredigt* (München, 1981), 89-120. Cf. also R. Pesch, 32: "Jesu Wirken zielte in seiner Sammlungs- und Befreiungsbewegung in Israel auf die Rekonstruktion des 'Volkes Gottes' als einer eschatologischen neuen Gesellschaft - und die Entstehung der neutestamentlichen Gemeinde war die Geburt einer neuen Gesellschaft. Jesus ging es um die Erfüllung des 'Gesetzes' als der Sozialordnung Gottes für Gottes Volk in dem Versuch der Wiedererweckung dieses Volkes, das er nicht mehr für eine göttliche Gegengesellschaft halten konnte!"...(36): "Das Ethos der Bergpredigt zielt auf eine neue, versöhnte Gesellschaft und eine neue, versöhnte Welt - in allen Bereichen, die die Welt konstituieren" ("Neues Testament - kein Ethos der Weltgestaltung?", in: N. Lohfink-R. Pesch, *Weltgestaltung und Gewaltlosigkeit. Ethische Aspekte des Alten und Neuen Testaments in ihrer Einheit und ihrem Gegensatz* (Düsseldorf, 1978)).

[63] M.H. Crosby, *House of Disciples: Church, Economics and Justice in Matthew* (New York, 1988). The author argues that both the concept of house and that of justice can be found throughout the entire Old Testament. On the concept of God as divine householder he says: "As Psalm 24 indicates, the Hebrew envisioned God's role in creating the world to be like that of a builder of a house (see Ps. 127:1) in possession of the entire world (Ex. 19:5; Ps. 89:12; 95:5), which contained all households" (171).

[64] Rabbi Dan Cohn-Sherbok, *On Earth as It Is in Heaven: Jews, Christians, and Liberation Theology* (New York, 1987), 50. The author points to a common ground between the ancient Hebrew prophetic demand for social justice and the concerns of contemporary Christian liberation theology. Cf. also the following statement: "The vision of Jesus as a prophet of Israel calling the people back to true worship of God is at the heart of Christian liberation theology. Certainly for the liberation theologian, Jesus is

This prophetic understanding is emphasized most clearly in the gospel of Luke. Here God is conceived of as a benefactor who wants to make Israel into a just community. That can only happen through a total reversal of the present situation of wrongdoings by an elite towards the large mass of the people; that means by creating a totally new situation. On the other hand, this new situation in many ways means a return to the old ideals of Israel. E. g., behind Jesus' inaugural speech in Nazareth (Luke 4.16-30) lies the notion of the Jubilee year. That was a year of re-creation of a just society, based on the right of every Israelite to a secure living on his land.[65]

Luke 4 is of special interest since it shows how the Jubilee language can function as a powerful metaphor in a new situation. In her analysis of the concept of the Jubilee, S. Ringe shows that the concrete language of Israel continues to have transformative and subversive power when used in new contexts. At the same time, she shows that the old conventional way of law-gospel, promise-fulfilment, or typology does not take into account the primal power of textual language itself. The Jubilee laws (e.g. Lev 25; Exod 21.2-6; 23.10-11; Deut 15.1-18; see also Jer 34.8-22; Isa 61.1-2) are significant in that, in the very midst of the Holiness Code with its emphasis on cultic matter, these laws bear witness to the continuing power of the image of God as sovereign over Israel, and to the fact that such an image of God has ethical consequences. To confess God as sovereign includes caring for the poor and granting freedom to those trapped in a continuing cycle of indebtedness.[66]

In Luke 4.16-30 Jesus is presented as reading Scripture in a way that is quite different from that of his contemporaries.[67] This is seen from the striking change that takes place. For Jesus' audience it was a stumbling block that he announced the good news not only to the privileged but also to the disadvantaged. He invited every one to have a share in his kingdom - even enemies and foreigners. That is probably the reason why he did not quote the whole passage of Isa 61 but omitted the last part of v.2 with reference to the "day of the vengeance of our God". The fact that Jesus only read the portion on grace and not the one on vengeance is of great importance since in his days the preaching of the synagogue used to put the whole emphasis precisely on these latter

---

more than a prophet" (51).
[65] Cf. H. Moxnes, *"Meals and the new community"*, 159; R. B. Sloyan, *The Favorable Year of the Lord: A Study of the Jubilary Theology in the Gospel of Luke* (Austin, 1977).
[66] S. H. Ringe, *Jesus, Liberation, and the Biblical Jubilee: Images for Ethics and Christology* (Philadelphia, 1985), 28.
[67] Although Luke 4 is of central importance in Lucan theology, it is based on a historical tradition. See also J. Nissen, *Poverty and Mission*, 74-75.

words. "God's compassion on the poor and outcast has superseded divine vengeance".[68]

The important thing in Luke 4 is the combination of two issues: the announcement of the good news to the poor (the Jubilee-theme) and the opening of the new age to foreigners. Between the two issues there is a "negative" correlation, since the undercutting of social egoism by the second issue prevented the former from being taken in a nationalistic sense. Thus, the prophetic reference to the poor and the oppressed cannot refer to Israel or Judaism at large as collectively oppressed. The liberation intended is too wide for that. The new age is for all human beings![69]

It is instructive to compare Jesus' reading of the Old Testament with that of the community at Qumran. Among the Essenes, there is a tendency to interpret the Old Testament in a manner that is favourable to the sect itself. As noted by J.A. Sanders:

Every blessing is seen as flowing toward themselves in the End time and every possible curse on their enemies... .[70]

The method used by the Dead See community can be labeled in-group-exegesis, because the community fails to perceive the Old Testament as a challenge to the in-group. Instead the traditions are understood as confirming the in-group. An alternative way of reading the Old Testament can be described as prophetic critical hermeneutics. This is an approach that challenges the in-group, and it is employed by Jesus himself.

In spite of that difference there is common ground between the community at Qumran and Jesus. They were both convinced that the Kingdom of God had come near and that the words of Scripture are fulfilled in the present time. Thus, they shared the "eschatological axiom". Where they differed was in the understanding of a second axiom. While the Essenes gave this axiom a constitutive character (confirming the in-group), Jesus employed prophetic criticism of the in-group. In doing so, he "turned the very popular Isa 61 passage into a judgment and a challenge to the definitions of Israel of his day".[71]

---

[68] D.J. Bosch, *Witness to the World: The Christian Mission in Theological Perspective* (London, 1980), 56. See also J. Jeremias, *Neutestamentliche Theologie 1: Die Verkündigung Jesu* (Gütersloh, 1971), 200.
[69] Cf. J.H. Yoder, *The Politics of Jesus*, 39-40.
[70] J.A. Sanders, "The Ethic of Election in Luke's Great Banquet Parable", in: J.L. Crenshaw - J.T. Willis (eds.), *Essays in Old Testament Ethics*, J.P. Hyatt in Memoriam, New York, 1974, 247-271, 253.
[71] J.A. Sanders, "From Isaiah 61 to Luke 4", in: J. Neusner (ed.), *Christianity, Judaism and other Greco-Roman Cults*, FS M. Smith, Part 1, (Leiden, 1975), 75-106, 99.

This reversal of values and circumstances is accentuated when one compares the lists in Luke 4.18; Matt 11.5/Luke 7.22; Matt 5.3-6 and Luke 14.13,21 with other lists in the literature of Second Temple Judaism and in the Hebrew Scriptures that deal with people excluded from special roles in the religious life of the community. Those excluded from the Aaronic priesthood (Lev 21.17-23), those denied membership in the Qumran community (1QS 2.2-5) and those not allowed to take part in the holy war (1QM 2.4-6) include all the categories found in the Gospel lists noted above except "the poor". In other words, Jesus includes those people who are otherwise excluded. In doing so, he challenges the identity of those who consider themselves to be "called".

> Like the classical prophets of the Old Testament Jesus precisely raises the question of the identity of Israel and challenges the assumptions concerning election...God has a kind of bias for those in apparent disfavor.[72]

There were probably two motives for Luke in recording the sermon of Jesus in chapter 4 and the two parables in chap. 14 (14.12-14; 14.16-24). First, he wanted to stress the proclamation of the good news for all the dispossessed. Second, he wanted to say that these stories contained a call to the Christian communities of his own day to be open communities. Christians of the second and third generation could easily become closed groups, reading the Bible in a way similar to the Qumran community. In other words, Luke wanted to prevent Christians from subverting the prophetic in-group critique of Jesus into a constitutive axiom.

The parables in Luke 14 contain a subversion of the Deuteronomic ethic of election (see Deut 20.5-8), and there is always a risk that Christian communities forget this subversion and make use of a "constitutive" hermeneutic concerning the privileged position of the church receiving the promised blessing. Perhaps this occured in the community for which Luke wrote.[73] Even if the readers of the Gospel of Luke understood themselves as the heirs of the outcasts to whom Jesus' message was brought, and consequently read chap. 14 as a new basis on which to assume their election, the bite of the original teaching and parable is still felt.

---

[72] J. A. Sanders, *"The Ethic of Election"*, 264 and 265. See also J. Jeremias, *Neutestamentliche Theologie*, 173.

[73] Sanders discusses whether Luke was really turning prophetic criticism into a constitutive axiom: Was Luke, in structuring this parabolic tradition (i.e. Luke 14) in the way he did, attempting to say, "The Jew opted out and Gentiles must be urged to come in"? It is quite possible, indeed, that such was his purpose (*"The Ethic of Election"*, 266).

Such presumption is always overturned in the drama of the parable itself, for as soon as such an assumption is made, the guest list is changed: "the poor" are always those who have nothing on which to presume.[74]

In addition to Luke 4 and Luke 14 there are a number of other texts in the Gospels that must be seen in a similar way in the light of the Jubilee and sabbath-year traditions of Hebrew Scriptures.[75] The language is primarily a language of ethics, dealing with values, social relationships, and the establishment or restoration of justice. But in the Gospels a new dimension is added, that of Christology. As noted by S.H. Ringe, in the Gospels the images of the Jubilee traditions highlight the fact that in Christ people are met by the healing, freeing, redeeming presence of God at their points of greatest pain. The redemptive work of Christ is depicted as touching all of human life. A new more open and more just community is created, the basis of which can be characterized by the words "in Christ we are set free" (cf. Gal 5.1).[76]

## III. Hermeneutical Perspectives

In a concluding paragraph, I shall summarize the findings of this article with a specific view to their hermeneutic relevance (cf. my remarks in the introduction). Due to the limits of an article of this kind, I shall limit myself to the following points:

a. The quest for a just society
We have seen that there is a correlation between the Kingdom of God and the people of God.[77] Jesus did not found the church[78] (in a way the church already existed before him as God's people). But the church in question is simply the sum of those who responded positively to Jesus' appeal to Israel. The *subject* supposed by Jesus' ethical teaching now comes into view. This subject is not the isolated individual person. It is a restored Israel, a community of disciples.[79] This attempt to restore Israel must be seen as the quest for a just society. Jesus established

---

[74] S.H. Ringe, *Jesus, Liberation and the Biblical Jubilee*, 59.
[75] These include among others: Matt 11.2-6 par.; Matt 5.3-6 par.; Mark 10.17-22 par.; Luke 19.1-10; Mark 14.3-9 par.; Luke 7.36-50; Matt 18.23-35; Matt 6.12 par. and Luke 16.1-8.
[76] S.H. Ringe, *Jesus, Liberation and the Biblical Jubilee*, 91-98.
[77] See also G. Lohfink, "Die Korrelation von Reich Gottes und Volk Gottes bei Jesus", *ThQ* 165 (1985), 175-183.
[78] Even if Matt 16.18 can be traced back to the historical Jesus, the best translation probably would be "assembly" or "people of God". See also T.M. Taylor, "Kingdom, Family, Temple, and Body", 179.
[79] Cf. B. Wiebe, "Messianic Ethics: Response to the Kingdom of God", *Int* 45 (1991), 29-42, 30-31.

fellowship with all those who were at the margins of society. By doing so he placed himself in the line of the prophetic tradition of the Old Testament. The recognition of this should play a role in the ongoing Jewish-Christian dialogue.[80]

b. Particularism and universalism

To speak of the people of God raises a question: Is it not an arbitrary claim to special privilege on the part of one people at the expense of all the others? Is it not a prime example of chauvinism and group egoism? Although this protest may often be justified, it springs from a misconception of the true force of the phrase "of God". This means that the accent must fall on God who creates this society as his people by his choice of them.[81] Election is not a kind of privilege. It is for service. If this is not realized, those who are chosen develop a kind of "elitism". And the covenant is turned into a contract.[82]

It is in this light we must understand the two foci of Jesus. He focused almost exclusively on Israel and within this framework particularly on marginalized people (cf. also the expression "the lost sheep of the house of Israel"; Matt 15.24). Elsewhere I have expressed this in the following way.

> Obviously, the life project of Israel was to gather all Israel, nobody excluded. It is *on the basis* of this vision of brotherhood among all Israelites Jesus had to show a special concern for the poor and disadvantaged precisely because they were excluded from Israelite fellowship. Furthermore, Jesus seemed to be convinced that God wanted the Jews to make the great change which would bring salvation and solidarity to all men. Just as he concentrated on the lost sheep of the house of Israel for the sake of Israel, so he concentrated on Israel for the sake of all men.[83]

God's action in and through history is linked to the scandal of particularity: the election of Israel (Old Testament); the preferential option for the poor (New Testament). But the particular is chosen for the sake of the universal. Therefore, the option for the poor is for the sake of all humanity.[84]

---

[80] See also D. Cohn-Sherbok, *On Earth as it is in Heaven* (cf. note 64) and N. Lohfink, "*Die Sorge um die rechte Gesellschaft*" (with references to modern Jewish theologians).

[81] Cf. P. S. Minear, *Images of the Church in the New Testament* (London, 1960), 68-69.

[82] For a more detailed discussion of the issue of particularism and universalism see my book *Poverty and Mission*, esp. 169-171 and 19-21.

[83] J. Nissen, *Poverty and Mission*, 20.

[84] On Jesus' special concern for the poor, A. Nolan, says: "Solidarity with the 'nobodies' of this world, the 'discarded people' is the only concrete way of living out a solidarity with mankind" (*Jesus Before Christianity*, 65).

c. The re-reading of Scripture

The first Christians were faced with a fundamental question: What does it really mean to be God's people *now*? As was argued in the introduction to this article, the first believers interpreted and renewed their traditions (the Old Testament) in the light of their own experiences.

This approach to Scripture is also characteristic of liberation theology[85] and feminist exegesis. Rosemary Ruether, for instance, finds the core of the biblical message of liberation in the prophetic-messianic tradition. By this tradition she means not simply a particular body of texts that would be understood as a canon within the canon. Rather, she would define this tradition as

> a *critical perspective and process* through which the biblical tradition constantly reevaluates, in new contexts, what is truly the liberating Word of God, over against sinful deformations of contemporary society and also the limitations of past biblical traditions... .[86]

As exemplified in Luke 4, Jesus reinterpreted Isa 61.1-2 in the light of the new situation created by the Kingdom of God. In his reinterpretation he widened the circle of those who belong to the people of God. Today we must reinterpret the text once more, otherwise we could easily read Jesus' reinterpretation of Isaiah as a triumphalist justification of Gentile Christianity over against the inferior particularism of Judaism. Today the text must be reinterpreted to proclaim the inclusion of women and poor people over against patriarchy.

> The feminist interpretation of prophetic critique as feminist critique thus continues the process of scriptural hermeneutic itself, whereby the text is reinterpreted in the context of new communities of critical consciousness.[87]

If the people of God shall remain inclusive - also of women it is necessary to understand the Bible as an open book, open to the ongoing process of transmission and interpretation. In this process there is a need for a theological criterion that can be formulated as follows:

---

[85] See, e.g., C. Rowland - M. Corner, *Liberating Exegesis: The Challenge of Liberation Theology to Biblical Studies* (London, 1990).

[86] R.R. Ruther, "Feminist Interpretation: A Method of Correlation", in: L. M. Russell (ed.), *Feminine Interpretation of the Bible* (Oxford, 1985), 111-124, 117 (italics added). Her method is that of correlation (cf. Schillebeeckx).

[87] R.R. Ruether, "*Feminist Interpretation*", 122.

Early Christian history and theology has to become ecumenical, i. e. inclusive of all Christian groups. All early Christian groups and texts have to be tested as to how much they preserve and transmit the apostolic inclusivity and equality of early Christian beginnings and revelation.[88]

d. "Decentering of perspective"
An important feature of the primitive Gospel tradition is that the disadvantaged - the women, the poor person, the stranger etc. - suddenly take center stage. The poor and the needy came into this world not as mere recipients of gifts from the wealthy, but as those upon whom the future of the world is dependent. A "sinful woman", a tax collector, and an outsider represent the signs of the "economy of the Kingdom". This is a "decentering of perspective" and a reversal of the world as it is presently known and legitimized.[89]

This "decentering of perspective" is highlighted by biblical sociology and even more by liberation theology. It challenges us to see the world from the viewpoint of the poor. We are also challenged to see biblical theology in a broader perspective as usual. For instance, redaction criticism tends to concentrate on ideas and concepts, on "the theology" of the author as found in his redactional statements and redactional arrangements. e.g. his statments about the issue of "the people". Sociology of early Christianity reminds us of the importance of seeing the "social world" of the people. And liberation theology insists on seeing the people as subjects of their own history.[90]

e. From the people of God to the body of Christ
In the Synoptic material analysed above a certain development takes place: from the people of God to the community of disciples, which is forming an "alternative society" with its own rules and way of life. It would not be correct to speak of a Christology in connection with this community. On the other hand, it is clear that Jesus played a unique role. He was the person in whom the usual group solidarity was transcended. And he was the person in whom people are met by the healing and redeeming presence of God.

---

[88] E. Schüssler Fiorenza, "Feminist Theology and New Testament", *JSOT* 22 (1982), 32-46, 42.
[89] Cf. H. Moxnes, *The Economy of the Kingdom: Social Conflict and Economic Relations in Luke's Gospel* (Philadelphia, 1988), 168. In this book attention is devoted not to the historical Jesus but to the social world of the gospel narrative in Luke. However, what the author says can in my opinion also be applied to the earliest traditions of the gospels. Here the poor are seen as "agents of the dawning Kingdom" (Nissen, *Poverty and Mission*, 171-173.)
[90] E.g. Ahn Byung Mu, "Jesus and the Minjung in the Gospel of Mark", in: Kim Yong Bock (ed.), *Minjung Theology: People as the Subjects of History* (Singapore, 1981), 136-151.

In the years after Easter, the Christological aspects of Ecclesiology become more evident. The church is still understood as the people of God, but the project of gathering people takes on a new dimension.[91] It is seen in the use of the word *ekklesia*.[92] It means both the actual process of gathering and the gathered community itself. The former should not be overlooked. "*Ekklesia* is not something that is formed and founded once and for all and remains unchanged; it becomes an *ekklesia* by the fact of a repeated concrete event, people coming together and congregating, in particular congregating for the purpose of worshipping God".[93]

Another forceful metaphor of the church is "body of Christ". It is interesting to see how it can be combined with "people of God". This occurs in Eph 2.11-18 where the alienation from "the commonwealth of Israel" has been overcome by the reconciliation "in one body through the cross".[94] Since the body of Christ has many features in common with the community around Jesus, it is important to see how the two pictures "the people of God" and "the body of Christ" can profit from each other.[95]

The strength of the body of Christ image is that it underlines the intended inclusiveness of the people of God. No longer can the image of the people of God be considered narrowly as it had been considered by many at the time of Jesus. The people of God can no longer be defined by a collective law, but only by the corporate law of Christ, the law of Christ's body which is love.

---

[91] However, the common goal of Jesus and Paul should not be overlooked. G. Lohfink, states: "Beiden, Jesus wie Paulus, geht es um die Sammlung beziehungsweise um den Bau des einen Gottesvolkes, das jetzt, in der Endzeit, nach dem unabänderlichen Willen Gottes endgültig errichtet wird" (*Wie hat Jesus Gemeinde gewollt?*, 119).

[92] On the use of this word in the Pauline letters see for instance, W.A. Meeks, *The First Urban Christians: The Social World of the Apostle Paul* (New Haven and London, 1983), 107-110, and R. Banks, *Paul's Idea of Community: The Early House Churches and their Historical Setting* (Exeter, 1980), 33-42. It should be noticed that the word has two roots. In Jewish circles, as the Septuagint shows, *ekklesia* is generally used to translate the Hebrew word for "assembly" of the people of Israel before God. This word then is a reminder to the Christians of their 'election' by God as the new Israel of God. But the word is also used in common Greek to refer to the town meeting of free male citizens of a city. In the New Testament, however, the term is used in a broader sense. Christian fellowship encompasses not only the free male citizens, but all sorts of people, including slaves and women! As is noticed by G. Decke, a seemingly socially irrelevant group of Jews and Greeks, free and slave, children and women, of socially an religiously marginalized people calls itself *ekklesia*, which is the term for the assembly of free men who are capable of enacting business and engaging in war ("Trinity, Church and Community", *LW* 23 (1976), 41-46, 44).

[93] H. Küng, *The Church* (New York, 1968), 84.

[94] On Ephesians see M. Barth, *The Broken Wall* (Chicago, 1959). See also *The People of God* (Sheffield, 1983), 45-49.

[95] On the relationship between "the people of God" and "the body of Christ" see also the interesting article by J. Hainz, "Vom 'Volk Gottes' zum 'Leib Christi' - Biblisch-theologische Perspektiven paulinischer Ekklesiologie", *JBTh* 7 (1992), 145-164.

Thus we can say that association with the body image produced a Christological definition of the people image that made the latter image more explicitly universal, more corporate, more personal, more existential, and more spiritual.[96]

If the uniqueness of the Christian church is better conveyed by the image "body of Christ" than by "people of God", the latter image has the advantage of emphasizing the *theo*-logical aspect of the church. The people of God are called to be a blessing for all nations (Gen 12.1-3) and to be the light of the world and the salt of the earth (Matt 5.13-16). This image also insists on the church as an "exodus community" pioneering the future of the world.

The people of God must be a righteous people with a special concern for all those who are lowly and oppressed, for all the "nobodies" of this world, for the "discarded people".[97] It is the task of the church to continue the Jesus' ministry of compassion to the peripheral people. But after his death and resurrection this *process of no-people becoming people* (cf. Hos 1.9-10) has to take on a new dimension. This was realized by Paul in his specific use of the image of the body of Christ: "If one member suffers, all suffer together" (1 Cor 12.26). Today we must continue the same process when we try to embody the Christian faith.

---

[96] P. S. Minear, *Images of the Church in the New Testament*, 229-230.

[97] As P.D. Hanson points out: "As God had acted to deliver precisely those who had been excluded from the privileges of the Egyptian social system, so too Israel was to act on behalf of the vulnerable and dispossessed around it, giving rise to the quality of *compassion* as another cardinal characteristic of her notion of community" (*The People Called*, 470).

CHAPTER THIRTEEN

# THE CONCEPT OF GOD AS THEME OF BIBLICAL THEOLOGY

Sigfred Pedersen, Århus

*I. Methodological Perspective*

We are now present at a conference where we have been celebrating the 50th anniversary of the official beginning of the scientific study of the New Testament here in Århus. But in the context of international Biblical scholarship it is an important anniversary indeed, only in this connexion it is a 100th anniversary.

In 1892 Johannes Weiss' little book appeared in Göttingen with the title *Die Predigt Jesu vom Reiche Gottes*, which, together with works by Hermann Gunkel and Wilhelm Bousset, helped the New Testament texts increasingly to be read as an integral part of the Jewish and Near Eastern religious history of the Greco-Roman period. The goal of Weiss' work was to ensure that the concept of the "Kingdom of God" in the New Testament, one of the fundamental concepts of the Jesuanic tradition, did not become filled with a modern religio-philosophical content which would have been alien to the sphere of religious ideas within which Jesus historically made his proclamation.[1]

The struggle to protect the study of the New Testament texts from illegitimate, "foreign" influence from without is still on-going, in spite of the fact that the danger can also come from the opposite side. This is made concrete by the fact that after a century of research it is above all the religio-historical approach, which was originally intended hermeneutically to uncover and emphasise the New Testament texts in their historical context, and which is now in danger of erasing or undermining the understanding of the formation of the historical specific nature of the formation of the New Testament tradition in the first

---

[1] J. Weiss, *Die Predigt Jesu vom Reiche Gottes* (Göttingen, 1892), 13-22, 61-67 (in extracts published as an appendix to the 2nd ed. edited by F. Hahn, Göttingen, 1964). A. Schweitzer compared the main point of the work with the views of both H.S. Reimarus and D.F. Strauss: "Es wirkt wie eine Erlösung, wie der Abschluss eines Alten und der Anfang eines Neuen" (*Geschichte der Leben-Jesu-Forschung*, 6th ed. (Tübingen, 1951), 233). See additionally W.G. Kümmel, *Das Neue Testament*, 2nd ed. (München, 1970), 286-92, and the actualising remarks of G. Lohfink, "Der Not der Exegese mit der Reich-Gottes-Verkündigung Jesu", *Studien zum Neuen Testament* (Stuttgart, 1989), 383-402.

century. The antidote against this is, with Johannes Weiss' pioneering study, to read the texts yet again as the independent writings they in fact are, and to do so with a view to developing an ever more genuine evaluation of their respective forms and contents in their literary and religious manifestations.

Thus it would be possible to claim that the New Testament texts are "Hellenistic" texts and that Christianity is a "syncretistic" religion, and, as such, a reflection of the richly-facetted Hellenistic religiosity which we are learning more and more about these days.[2] However, because of its pluralistic contents this characterization would not say very much, except the major concession that the artist is using a broad brush here, which implicitly reinforces the tendency inherent in our analogous processes of analysis and ratiocination, at the expense of the unique, to put all phenomena on the same level.

That which above all requires our fundamental interest, not only as a theological need, but also as a requirement of historical science, is: what does it mean, both generally and concretely, for our exegesis of the New Testament texts, that it is precisely on the basis of their specific character that they may be regarded as *Jesuanic-christological* — also according to their own self-understanding? Two hermeneutical delimitations are contained in this question, as, from both a literary and an historical point of view, the New Testament context will be the primary, if not the sole, indicator as to (a) which traditio-historical investigations ought to be undertaken, and (b) what content is to be assigned to the traditio-historical elements chosen for study. This is still a question of broad delimitations which are nevertheless vital and relevant with respect to both the religio-historical approach and to the methodological approaches deriving from other sciences which scholars have attempted to exploit for New Testament research in recent decades.

It is not least from the perspective of this theoretical question that it might be relevant to test the possibilities inherent in a renewed "Biblical-theological" approach[3] to the New Testament texts conducted on the

---

[2] See K. Rudolph, "Early Christianity as a Religious-Historical Phenomenon", in B.A. Pearson (ed.), *The Future of Early Christianity* (= FS H. Koester) (Minneapolis, 1991), 9-19. Or, with H. Koester himself: "Thus, early Christianity is just one of several Hellenistic propaganda religions, competing with others who seriously believed in their god and who also imposed moral standards on their followers" (Pearson, 1991, 473). Against this, see, among others, L.W. Hurtado, *One God, One Lord* (London, 1988), 1-15, 129-30.

[3] See the problematic as defined by, among others, P. Stuhlmacher, *Schriftauslegung auf dem Wege zur biblischen Theologie* (Göttingen, 1975), 126-27, 137-39, 175-78. And see the criticisms of M. Kalusche, "Das Gesetz als Thema biblischer Theologie"?, *ZNW* 77 (1986), 180-205.

terms of present-day Biblical study.⁴ In my view, the primary goal must be to arrive at a more coherent understanding of the New Testament tradition in its first century. In this connexion it may be supposed that the tradition about Jesus of Nazareth entailed a new-reading of the Biblical tradition as a more or less established canonical collection of writings,⁵ a reading which had the character of a rediscovery of the writing behind the dominant interpretations of the time (John 2.22; 12.16, etc.).⁶

*II. The Understanding of God as the Dividing-line between Jews and Christians*

The texts of the New Testament represent a religious tradition which was rooted in the Jewish religion and in the ancient Jewish background; nevertheless, it has been preserved and transmitted to us in a radically different linguistic garment, namely a Greek-Hellenistic one. The expression "linguistic garment" here goes far beyond purely philological matters. The texts' present form describes, in both positive and negative highlights, the "reciprocal" encounter between the conceptual realm of the Jesuanic-Christian and the cultural-religious ideas of the rest of the Hellenistic world.⁷ During this encounter with a generally cosmospolitan world which, broadly speaking, was characterized by (at least) two distinct diasporas, one Greek and the other Jewish, the Christians understood themselves to be and presented themselves as "*the third people*".⁸

The anonymous author of the treatise "*Ad Diognetum*" (ca. 190-200 CE) refers by way of introduction to the Christians as the "new people

---

⁴ H. Hübner offers the following definition: "Biblische Theologie ist also heute ein neues Postulat... das Postulat einer Theologie, die das *Alte Testament* und das *Neue Testament* als *theologische Einheit* zu begreifen sucht" (*Biblische Theologie des Neuen Testaments*, Band 1: *Prolegomena* (Göttingen, 1990), 14). See further the bibliographies in *JBTh* 1 (1986), 210-44 (B. Janowski); 4 (1989), 301-47 (D.R. Daniels/B. Janowski); *VF* 27 (1982), 28-45 (H. Seebass); 33 (1988), 19-40 (O. Merk).
⁵ Cf. Sir Prol.; Philo, *Vit Cont* 3.25; Luke 24.27; Josephus, *C Ap* 1.37-41; cf. B.S. Childs, "Biblische Theologie und christliche Kanon", *JBTh* 3 (1988), 13-27.
⁶ When E. Grässer asks (with W. Wrede) whether then-contemporary Judaism is not the religio-historical basis of Christianity instead of the Old Testament ("Offene Fragen im Umkreis einer Biblischen Theologie", *ZThK* 77 (1980), 217), the answer is both yes and no. The increased attention being paid to the intertestamental literature is absolutely important (cf. J.H. Charlesworth, "Biblical Interpretation: The Crucible of the Pseudepigrapha", in T. Baarda et al. (eds.), *Text and Testimony* (= FS A.F.J. Klijn) (Kampen, 1988), 66-78). On the other hand, Mark (like the other evangelists) presumably reflects factual reality when he depicts the tradition about Jesus of Nazareth as taking its beginning in both Judaism and the Old Testament (Mark 1.2-8).
⁷ See, in more detail, B. Noack, "A Jewish Gospel in a Hellenistic World", *StTh* 32 (1978), 45-55.
⁸ In conjunction with LXX of Ps 18.5 (Rom 10.18; cf. Acts 2.9-11), Tertullian depicts the "world-embracing" propagation of the Church (Adv Jud 7) in phrases reminiscent of Philo's and Josephus' references to the Jewish diaspora (respectively Leg 281-284 and BJ 2, 398; Ant 14, 114-115; C Ap 2, 282).

or way of life" (1.1; καινὸν τοῦτο γένος ἢ ἐπιτήδευμα).[9] More concretely, he says that the Christians are not different from other peoples socially. Thus they do not live in ghetto-like special parts of the city, nor do they distinguish themselves from their environment in point of language, clothing or nourishment. Nevertheless, the personal conduct (πολιτεία) of this third diasporan group, whose real home is in heaven (Phil 1.27; 3.20; cf. 1 Pet 1.17; 2.11), is so different from both the Hellenic and the Jewish that they are met with hatred, contempt and persecution: "They are combated by the Jews as foreigners (ὡς ἀλλόφυλοι), and the Greeks persecute them, and yet those who hate them are unable to give any reason for their hatred" (ch. 5).

Furthermore, the actual origin of this religio-social confrontation lay in the strongly divergent views of God of the three groups, which people of the time apparently were able to divide into Hellenes, Jews and Christians (chs. 2 and 3). And the adversative role of the concept of God seems to have been quite general. "Show me your God!" (Δειξόν μοι τὸν θεόν σου) was the provocative challenge directed to anyone who bore the title of Christian (Theophilus, *Ad Autolycum*, 1.2,14).[10]

Moreover, in the introduction to *Ad Diognetum* this is formulated more precisely by stating that the Christians do not reckon the gods of the Greeks to be gods, nor do they practise Jewish forms of worship, which they characterise as superstition. This opposition can be traced back to the "*Kerygma Petri*", dating from the beginning of the 2nd century, where we find the Christians characterized as "the third kin", those who worship the "one" (εἷς) God of Creation "in a new way" (ὑμεῖς δὲ οἱ καινῶς αὐτὸν τρίτῳ γένει σεβόμενοι Χριστιανοί).[11] And this characterisation is accompanied by stress on the fact that the worship which the Christians require differs from both the Hellenes' worship of their self-made deities or diverse animal species, in their ignorance (cf. Acts 17.29-30), and from the Jews' worship of angels and elemental spirits, and in spite of the claim by the latter group to possess the true

---

[9] Alexandria has been proposed as the site where the work was composed; see R. Brändle, *Die Ethik der "Schrift an Diognet"* (AThANT 64) (Zürich, 1975), 12.230-231. The text is in Bihlmeyer / Schneemelcher, *Die Apostolischen Väter* (Tübingen, 1956), 141.

[10] R.M. Grant, *Theophilus of Antioch, Ad Autolycum. Text and Translation by...*, (Oxford, 1970), 2 and 20.

[11] Fragments in Clement of Alexandria, Strom VI 5.39-41; cf. Origen, In John XIII, 17. Text in E. Preuschen, *Antilegomena*, 2nd ed. (Gieszen, 1905), 88-91 (192-96). W. Schneemelcher holds that the writing came into being in Egypt; he characterises its contents as a middle-ground between the early Christian missionary sermon attested to in Acts and Greek apologetic (Schneemelcher, *Neutestamentliche Apokryphen*, Band II, 5th ed., (Tübingen, 1989), 35-37).

knowledge of God.[12] Scriptural witness for this is found in Jer 31.31-34, the expectation of the "new covenant" which is to replace the one which was concluded with the fathers on Horeb.

The Christian rejection of the conceptions of God inherent in the Greco-Roman/Near Eastern religious sphere, with its attendant types of cult can hardly surprise us, especially inasmuch as the Christian proclamation which was directed to non-Jews seems from the very beginning to have battened onto that Jewish apocalyptic which was centred around the concept of God, with its Biblical roots (1 Thess 1.9; Gal 4.8-9; 1 Cor 12.2; Rom 1.23; cf. Acts 14.11-18). It should be emphasised much more than has hitherto been the case, that these contemporary ancient texts help to clarify the fact that the separation between ways of understanding God also applied to Jews and Christians; and they did so in a way that was no less fundamental. The background for some basic theological divergences and some decisive traditio-historical differences with respect to the relationship between Old Testament and New Testament tradition also resides in this decisive distinction between the Jewish and Christian conceptions of God. What was central in this controversy around the understanding of God in the earliest Christian era was namely not the (later) trinitarian concept-formation from the Christian side (as we know it from the Jewish-Christian polemic of later centuries), but rather the Jesuanic-messianic interpretation of the Jewish *credo* in Deut 6.4: "Hear, O Israel, the Lord your God is one!"

This is formulated polemically by *Ignatius* when he explains the fact that the Christian Jews no longer celebrated the Sabbath, but rather Sunday: "the most divine prophets lived in agreement with Jesus Christ. Therefore they were also persecuted, inspired as they were by his grace so that they might fully convince the disobedient that God is one (εἷς), he who revealed himself through his son Jesus Christ, who is his word..." (Ign Magn 8,2).

It is this Jesuanic-Christologically difference in the conception of God which will be analysed in what follows.

First, however, it must be pointed out that this important divergence between Jewish and Christian faith was of a schismatic nature: the break may definitely not be designated as accidental. The differentiated evolution of the Biblical understanding of God was by no means without precedent. Indeed, the new development in the New Testament may even

---

[12] The accusation is also to be found in Origen as quotation from Celsus, who, however, rejects it as indicating lack of knowledge of the Jews (*C Cel* 5,6). L.W. Hurtado regards it as a polemical interpretation of the Jewish cult (cf. Gal 4.1-11; Col 2.8-23) instead of being a factual description of it (*One God, One Lord*, 33-35).

be seen as continuation of a process which had been going on during the first phases of the formation of the Biblical traditions.[13] After all, the conception of God is in reality the most delicate topic of all from a theological and existential point of view.[14] It is not least in the New Testament that this historical mutability of the conception of God comes to expression through a number of predicative re-formulations, and it does so as a Biblical inheritance which is also familiar to us thanks to the intertestamental literature.[15] Our analysis is therefore to be concentrated around three central fundamental divine predicates.

*III. Biblical-theological Divine Predicates*

1. *God as the one who does not distinguish between people*
Acts 10.34-43 is a text which is exceptionally pertinent to our problem. Luke relates his theoretical theological foundation for the Biblical-theological extent of the epoch-making transition to proclaiming for the Hellenes as well in a note in Acts 11.19-26.[16] Through the speech by Peter in Caesarea he redactionally allows his readers to understand the conception of God that is implicit in the tradition about Jesus of Nazareth. In this connexion, Luke does not obscure the fact that we have to do with a radical new perception: "Truly I perceive (ἐπ' ἀληθείας καταλαμβάνομαι...) that God shows no partiality (οὐκ ἐστιν προσωπολήμπτης ὁ θεός); but in every people anyone who fears him and does righteously may be received by him" (v.35).[17] Furthermore, Luke has this new conception of God appear sharply defined with a creation-theological foundation through the previous account of Peter's vision of

---

[13] H. Gese has regarded the connexion between OT and NT as one of successive tradition ("Erwägungen zur Einheit der biblischen Theologie"; and now: *Vom Sinai zum Zion*, (*BEvTh* 64) (München, 1974), esp. 16-17). Gese's argument is discussed by, among others, H.-J. Kraus, "Theologie als Traditionsbildung?" *EvTh* 36 (1976), 498-507.

[14] This delicate openness in the circumlocutory definition of the understanding of God may receive a prophetic-Christological accent when, in John, Jesus refers to God "the one who has sent me" (John 5.30,38; 6.29; 7.28; 8.16,29; 12.44; cf. Luke 10.16 par.). Or an existential accent, as when Paul, employing Biblical phraseology, refers to God as "the one who called me / you" (1 Thess 5.24; Gal 1.6 (15); 5.8; Rom 9.12; cf. 1 Pet 1.15; 2.9; 2 Pet 1.3).

[15] Naturally, this may be related to the fact that the same is true of the NT as H.Hübner has determined in connexion with the OT, namely that we have to do with a "Gotteserkenntnis aus der Geschichte" (*Biblische Theologie*, 109, cf. 217). In complete agreement with this is, among others, N. Lohfink (n. 35), 112-13; J. Schlosser, *Le Dieu de Jésus* (*LD 129*) (Paris, 1987), 27-28.

[16] On the entire question of this tradition see, among others, K. Löning, "Die Korneliustradition", *BZ* (1974), 1-19 ("die Petrusvision paßt nicht nur in den Kontext der Korneliustradition, sondern ist konstitutives Element ihrer Struktur als Erzähleinheit", 6); K. Haacker, "Dibelius und Cornelius", *BZ* 24 (1980), 234-51.

[17] On the interpretation of this statement see W.C. van Unnik, "The Background and Significance of Acts X 4 and 35", in: *Sparsa Collecta*, Vol. I (Leiden, 1973), esp. 246-56; F. Bovon, "Le Dieu de Luc", in: "L'oeuvre de Luc" (*LD 130*) (Paris, 1987), esp. 237-39.

the descending sheet which is laden with all the animals in creation, and which is let down from heaven three times. The auditive interpretation of this vision lies in its polemical formulation: "What God had cleansed you must not regard as profane!" (10.15; 11.9). This vision/audition, which is referred to no less than four times (10.3-6,22,29b-33; 11.33-34) reveals that it is God himself who is behind the distinctive knowledge and praxis.[18]

In other words, we are here confronted with the Creator's (!) own break with the Jewish, Biblically-grounded dietary precepts and that tradition's concomitant distinction between clean and unclean people.[19] In its historical context the understanding of God contained in the passage in question is as absolute and unconditional as one could imagine, in Caesarea, Antioch, Corinth (1 Cor 8.8), Rome (Rom 14.14) and elsewhere throughout the Roman empire (Col 2.16-3.11) the Jesuanic interpretation of the Biblical conception of God was imported during these decades, with all their sociological tensions between Hellenes and Jews.

Word for word, however, the divine predicate in question is not unique. Indeed, in traditio-historical terms it occurs frequently. As is so often the case, we do not have to do with new tradition here, but rather with a fundamentally different interpretation of an already extant and interpreted tradition. Furthermore, the new interpretation has even been undertaken with the aid of other Biblical traditions. In particular: the idea of Creation figures as the ground of the concept of holiness, rather than vice versa.[20]

The divine predicate "that God is no respecter of persons" occurs, in terms of Biblical theology, for the first time in a credo-like context in Deuteronomy (10.12-22). Here the theo-logy is monotheistic (v.17) while the ethno-logy ("ecclesiology") is particularistic (v.15). It is probable that the predicate in this connexion has polemical force directed against the "gods" and "lords" of the non-Israelite peoples. What is remarkable, however, is that the local sociological concretisation of the fundamental divine predicate (*imitatio Dei*) contains a socio-ethical opening towards the stranger in the country/among the people. This is, in part, explained by the claim that God himself loves the stranger (*ger*), and in part by the fact that Israel itself is supposed to have been a stranger in Egypt (v. 18-19; cf. Exod 23.9), i.e., emphasising that Israel had not only had

---

[18] See, correspondingly, S.G. Wilson, *The Gentiles and the Gentile Mission in Luke-Acts* (*SNTS.MS* 23) (Cambridge, 1973), 176-78.
[19] See additionally F. Bovon, "Tradition et rédaction en Actes 10,1-11,18" in *L'oeuvre de Luc*, 97-120.
[20] See, in greater detail, my article "Det gamle Testamente i Ny Testamente" in (ed.) S. Pedersen, *Skriftsyn og metode* (*DKNT* 1) (Århus, 1989), 39.

experience of the situation of the stranger, but also of God's liberating love (cf. Deut 7.6-8; 10.20-11.7).[21]

The predicate in question is also susceptible of transferral to the Israelites' internal reciprocal relationships.[22] Thus, for example, in 2 Chron 19.7 the predicate motivates the warning to the judges, as one phase in the establishment of a disinterested administration of justice in which bribery plays no part (cf. Deut 1.17; 16.19). Behind all this is the fundamental idea of God's impartial relationship to people, who are his creatures (Job 34.19) — also as the future eschatological judge (Sir 4.22; 35.13; Jub 5.16; Ps Sal 2.18; 1 Esra LXX 4.39).[23]

What is important for our purposes is, however, the fact that in Rom 2.11 Paul transfers this predicate to the relationship obtaining between Jews and gentiles when he stresses that they will be "equal" (although in accordance with the revelation-theological principle of "first the Jew, and then the Greek") in the eyes of an impartial God who will judge them by their works alone (the positive soteriological counterpart to this is Rom 10.12). By his choice of address in Rom 2.1 (ὦ, ἄνθρωπε πᾶς; plus 2.3: ὦ, ἄνθρωπε), Paul allows his readers to understand that it is human existence as such, both before and after Christ, that is, the Creator's relationship to his creatures (1.25), that he analyses in Rom 1.18-3.20,21-31. In the course of this analysis the differing statuses of Jew and non-Jew, from the point of view of the history of revelation, are partial aspects, and not only here! From the vantage of Biblical theology one becomes aware that, as Paul understands matters, we receive human existence in the form of two main currents which run more or less parallel through the whole of the letter to the Romans. One of these is

---

[21] Here we find at least the forerunners of that which we later know as the twofold love-commandment in Mk 12.28-34 parr. and Lk 6.36, including the use of the verb 'āhab in Exod 10.12,15,18,19. This is rendered in the LXX by ἀγαπᾶν and is related to the proselyte, as in Lev 19.33-34 (for a close analysis of the content and range of this verb see G. Wallis, ThWAT Vol.I, col. 109-15; 124-28). See also C. van Houten, *The Alien in Israelitic Law* (JSOT 107) (Sheffield, 1991), 106-08; 155-57; 179-83; C. Bultmann, *Der Fremde im antiken Juda* (FRLANT 153) (Göttingen, 1992), 121-34; 213-19.

[22] Examples of religious/social exploitation of this Biblical-theological predicate are likewise common in the Christian tradition: Gal 2.6; Eph 6.9; Col 3.25; Jas 2.1,9; 1 Pet 1.17; Did 4.3,10; Barn 19.4,7; Pol Phil 6.1. Moreover, it is possible for teachers to be urged to learn the truth without respect for persons (Mark 12.14 parr.). In antiquity, this may have been directed against the Sophists (1 Thess 2.3-6).

[23] On the use of this predicate in the intertestamental literature, see J.M. Bassler, *Divine Impartiality. Paul and a Theological Axiom* (SBL.DS 59) (Chico, CA, 1982), conclusion on 43-44 ("it is clear that divine impartiality was regarded in this period as an axiomatic attribute of God"; but God's impartiality in this respect never canceled the distinction between Jews and Gentiles). A similar conclusion was the case with Philo (104, 118-19) and the rabbinical materials (65-66). However, it is argued that universalistic tendencies, characterised as "unique among Jewish writings", are present in the much later midrash, "Tanna debe Eliahu" (66), with respect to equality before God's judgement for both Jew and Greek (and, for that matter, for man and woman). This is derived from the divine predicate itself, and it is the case without presupposing Paul's Christian concept of grace and missionary fervour in Rom 2.11 (76). Further on Paul, see 164-69 ("Paul has taken a familiar Jewish axiom, infused it with a new content...").

creation-theological, while the other is salvation-historical.[24] Of these two, it is the creation-theological line, symbolised by the term "man" ('Αδάμ/ἄνθρωπος) which is the supra-ordinate category,[25] rather than the revelation-theological line which is signalled by the phrase "the Jew first and then the Greek" ('Ιουδαῖος τε πρῶτον καὶ ῞Ελλην; 2.9-10). This remains the case even though scholars have been primarily preoccupied with the latter aspect. In other words, the last-mentioned phrase is in the centre to the extent that it points up in a way that is striking for its own time the fact that the dominant revelation-theological distinction between Jews and Hellenes (heathens) does not apply to the God of the Creation, whose attitude towards men is impartial, as the predicate in 2.11 indicates.[26]

In Paul's follow-up it is made clear that what is eschatologically crucial in relation to God is the personal and concrete life that one lives together with others, independent of the revelation-historical differences which apply to Jew and non-Jew, as symbolized by the Mosaic Law, represented by the Decalogue, and by circumcision, as sign of the Covenant. One is not a Jew, that is, to be subject to God's election, by virtue of ethnic or revelation-historical considerations, but through the concrete life that one lives together with others (2.25-29; cf. Matt 3.8-9). Paul's argument for this is based precisely on the concept of God (2.1-5,29). And the demands which are levied on the individual are not derived from casuistically determined laws (2.20), but from the created life which one must live together with other creatures. This is developed in 1.18-32 with specific address to the Hellenes; and in 2.17-24 with address to the Jews. Or, more precisely: here, too, the Law has been interpreted in terms of creation theology, so that God's will as expressed in the Law is identified with the will of the Creator (τὸ θέλημα τοῦ θεοῦ; 1.19; 2.18; cf. 12.2). The question is not whether works are to be done, but rather to determine which works: those based on law-existence, or those based on existence in grace.[27] We have to do with one and the same truth, that of the Creator of all (ἡ ἀλήθεια τοῦ θεοῦ; 1.18,25; 2.8,20). Otherwise, how would it be possible for the heathen to perform it (2.14-15)?

---

[24] According to G. Lohfink it is possible to find a corresponding duality in Jesus' view of God and his proclamation of the Kingdom of God ("Gott in der Verkündigung Jesu", in *Studien zum Neuen Testament*, esp. 37-42).
[25] See additionally Rom 1.18,23; 2.9,16; 3.4,28; 4.6; 5.12,18-19; 7.24; 12.18.
[26] See the analysis of J.M. Bassler, "Divine Impartiality in Paul's Letter to the Romans", *NovTest* 26 (1984), 43-58; further, J.-M. Cambier, "Le jugement de tous hommes par Dieu seul, selon son vérité, dans Rom 2,1-3,20", *ZNW* 67 (1976), 186-213; N.A. Dahl, "The Missionary Theology in the Epistle to the Romans", in *Studies in Paul* (Minneapolis, 1977), 77-80.
[27] I cannot detect any awareness of this problematic in K.R. Snodgrass, "Justification by Grace — to the Doers: An Analysis of the Place of Romans 2 in the Theology of Paul", *NTS* 32 (1986), 72-93.

The reference to God's eschatological "judgement after works" (2.6-8) is intended precisely to serve to point to the demands and possibilities of actual life as the criterion of that which is for all people irrespective of their status the truth about the Creator's will towards his creature (2.12-13). It is therefore possible for Paul to concentrate his attack on the second tablet of the Law (2.21-22), in order to turn back to it positively in 13.9. In my opinion there is no basis for doubting that we are confronted here by Biblical-theological conceptions like those found in Matt 5.17-48.[28]

In terms of scriptural theology, this brings us all the way back to the very first chapters in the Bible, as Paul himself repeatedly indicates in succeeding sections. Thus, for example, in Rom 5.12-19, in order to suggest the universality of the righteousness by faith which he has developed in ch.4 on the basis of Gen 15.6, Paul harks back to the description of the Fall of the first man in Gen 3 which, as he says, has been actual in all men's lives ever since (ἐφ' ᾧ πάντες ἥμαρτον, v. 12c; cf. 3.23).[29]

The christological use of the creation-theological designation "man", as is expressed by the characterisation of the one man, Jesus Christ (Rom 5.15), as obedient Adam, suggests by virtue of its implicit collective dimension the cosmic horizon through which Paul basically views Jesus' death and resurrection (Gal 6.14-15; 2 Cor 5.14-19). In a corresponding fashion, the depiction of man's general emergency situation before Christ in Rom 7.7-24 alludes to the Biblical Creation/fall depiction in Gen 1-3.

The Biblical-theological conception of God which underlies the Biblical theologoumenon that God is not "a respecter of persons" is thus grounded, in its New Testament usage, in creation theology. This means that creation theology and revelation theology are not to be played off against one another. To assume this would be to operate with false alternatives. In the Jesuanic-messianic interpretation of the Biblical tradition, it is creation theology that gives revelation theology its content and horizon. This may also be derived from the Pauline use of the revelation-theological expression "God's glory" (ἡ δόξα τοῦ θεοῦ) in the ethical context as a reflection of the Biblical idea that man has been created in the image of God (Rom 1.22-23; 3.22; 8.21; 15.6,7).

Therefore, as the apostle to the gentiles, Paul is able in Rom 9-11 to confirm the Biblical witness of Israel's privileges, which are vouched for by revelation theology. It is truly the case that God does not rescind

---

[28] Cf. C.H. Dodd, "Matthew and Paul", in *New Testament Studies* (Manchester, 1953), 62-65.

[29] See further K. Kertelge, "Adam und Christus: Die Sünde Adams im Lichte der Erlösungstat Christi nach Röm 5,12-21", in (eds.) C. Breytenbach and H. Paulsen, *Anfänge der Christologie* (= FS F. Hahn) (Göttingen, 1991), esp. 146-51.

either the evidences of his grace or the call he has sent out. Hence that Israel which at the time rejected Christ remains by virtue of God's election his "beloved" (ἀγαπητοί; 11.2,28-29). On the other hand, Paul is unable to allow God, as the God of Creation, to reserve his shows of grace and his calling *exclusively* for Israel.[30] Nor can the God of Creation reserve the divine love, out of which the proofs of grace and the calling proceed, *exclusively* for the Christian church.

The Jesuanic-messianic expression for this is the confession that the historical Jesus, being the crucified man, has been exalted by God to be, not (merely) the Lord of the church, but of Creation. And in this connexion, as is well known, "the lord of all" means "the servant of all" (Phil 2.6-11; Rom 10.8-12), as Paul to superfluity makes clear in his summarising statement of the "truth about God" (15.3-4,8-9).

For this reason the letter to the Romans cannot end on the eschatological vision in ch.8. In a Christian context the Biblical-theological concept of idolatry could be defined as not to expect or miss the remaining chapters of the epistle, if they were not there or, alternatively, to ignore these chapters for many centuries! Following on ch. 9-11 we find a creation-theological concretisation of Christian ethics (see the designation "all men" in 12.17-18) which is succeeded by a clarification of what "lord" (κύριος) signifies within the Christian fellowship (14.1-23). It is there where observations of the Law are not determined in their essence by human desire back to the Biblical account of the Fall (13.14), but by that love which found earthly form in Jesus as Christ and Lord in the fulfilment of the commandment to love one's neighbour as oneself (13.8-10).

Finally, in the "travel section", in a continuation of 1.14 we find the creation-theological crystallisation of Christian missiology which is the concrete topic of the letter to the Romans. As Christians, Paul and the congregation in Rome shared an "indebtedness" to make good for that part of God's creation which otherwise lay outside of the revelation-theological diasporas of the time (15.24).[31]

The actual background for all this is a divine predicate of even more fundamental character.

---

[30] For this reason, already in his first letter Paul transfers such Biblical-theological honorifics as "chosen" and "beloved" on to non-Jews (1 Thess 1.4). See additionally J. Becker, "Die Erwählung der Völker durch das Evangelium", in (ed.) W. Schrage, *Studien zum Text und zur Ethik des Neuen Testaments* (= FS H. Greeven) (Berlin-New York, 1986), 82-101; and M.A. Getty, "Paul and the Salvation of Israel: A Perspective on Romans 9-11", *CBQ* 50 (1988), esp. 458-60; 468.
[31] See the argumentation for this view in my article, "Theologische Überlegungen zur Isagogik des Römerbriefes", *ZNW* 76 (1985), 47-67.

*2. "The Lord your God is one!"*

In Old Testament research it is, briefly put, usually assumed that southern traditions about a mountain-god called Yahweh[32] have merged with patriarchal traditions dealing with a "god of the fathers" called Yahweh to comprise the notion of "Israel's" Yahweh, who thus has absorbed a number of local conceptions of deity into himself (Deut 26.16-19).[33] The final redaction of the Biblical tradition will have existed in New Testament times; it must have represented a conception of God which was foreign to the originally mutually independent but later combined traditions.

The original monolatry may still be discerned, if in radicalised form, in the struggle of the prophet Elijah to purify the Israelite cult of original Baal-elements. Its historical consequence was monotheism, which was specific for Israel's faith.[34] However, this first took place in exilic-post-exilic times. Even the confession of God's unity in Deut 6.4-5 is to be understood as a reflection of monolatry (Micah 4.5), provided that we not read it together with the preceding ch.4 within the scope of the final Deuteronomistic redaction. It is namely the case that, alongside of reference to the covenant between Yahweh and Israel, we also find a number of polemical and strongly derogatory statements about other peoples and their deities, while at the same time Israel's Yahweh is depicted as the universal supreme God (v.13,19,28-29,31,35,39; cf. ch.7).[35]

This evolution will not be touched on further here, as our task is to determine the New Testament conception of God, as that conception is expressed in a number of statements which are based on the form possessed by the Biblical traditions when they were available to the authors of the New Testament. However, I should mention that there are two aspects of scholarship's past understanding of the role of the "credo"

---

[32] Judg 5.4: from Mount Seir; in Deut 33.2 we find mention of Sinai, Seir and Paran.

[33] See the brief exposition of this, with bibliography and discussion, in H. Hübner, *Biblische Theologie*, 242-51.

[34] On this, see F. Stolz, "Monotheismus in Israel" in (ed.) O. Keel, *Monotheismus im Alten Testament und seiner Umwelt* (*BibB* 14) (Fribourg, 1980), 154-84; W.H. Schmidt, *Alttestamentlicher Glaube in seiner Geschichte*, 6th ed., (Neukirchen-Vluyn, 1987), 63-88.

[35] Cf. Hos 13.4; Isa 44.6; 45.5,21-22; Ps 82.6-7; 96.5. For discussion see M. Peter, "Dtn 6,4 — ein monotheistischer Text?" *BZ* 24 (1980), 252-62; P. Höffken, "Eine Bemerkung zum religionsgeschichtlichen Hintergrund von Dtn 6,4", *BZ* 28 (1984), 88-93; N. Lohfink, "Gott im Buch Deuteronomium", in (ed.) J. Coppens, "La Notion biblique de Dieu" (*BETL* 41) (Gembloux-Leuven, 1976), 101-26; the same, "Kennt das Alte Testament einen Unterschied von "Gebot" und "Gesetz"? Zur bibeltheologischen Einstufung des Dekalogs", *JBTh* 4 (1989), esp. 78; G. Braulik, "Das Deuteronomium und die Geburt des Monotheismus", in *Studien zur Theologie des Deuteronomiums* (Stuttgart, 1988), 259-64; 280-95; (ed.) E. Haag, *Gott, der Einzige. Zur Entstehung des Monotheismus in Israel* (*QD* 104) (Freiburg-Basel-Wien, 1985); F.-L. Hossfeld, "Der Pentateuch", in (ed.) E. Sitarz, *Höre, Israel! Jahwe ist einzig* (Stuttgart, 1987), 52; the same, "Einheit und Einzigkeit Gottes im frühen Jahwismus", in (ed.) M. Böhnke-H. Heinz, *Im Gespräch mit dem dreieinen Gott* (= FS W. Breuning) (Düsseldorf, 1985), 57-74.

(i.e., the Shemah) of the Jewish faith which I regard as historically and theologically untenable. In the first place, it has often been claimed that this "credo" did not play any significant role at all;[36] and in the second, it has been held that the confessions of God's unity, as manifested in the New Testament, are addressed to then-contemporary non-Jewish worship as idolatry (in continuation of Jewish apologetic).

But already general sociology-of-religions considerations suggest a completely different point of view. The Jewish "credo" and the Biblical passages associated with it, including the Decalogue, as this tradition of liturgical prayer has now been confirmed through the discovery of phylacteries from Qumran,[37] formed the theological and existential horizon for every (male) Jew's concrete existence to an extent which it would be very difficult for us today to grasp the full intimacy and intensity of (Philo, Spec Leg 4.137-142; cf. 1QS 10.13-16).[38] And it is precisely this concept of God, as well as the role played by the Mosaic Law as both personal and social hermeneutical horizon, to which the Deuteronomistic confession of God's unity provides ideal expression.[39]

The Jesuanic-messianic understanding of God with its accompanying interpretation of existence did not entail the surrender of this close Biblical-theological framework for one's daily existence. Rather, it meant an even more absolute understanding of what it means to affirm that God is one, with (a) all the thereby implied anthropological consequences and (b) the corresponding scriptural-theological / traditio-historical consequences. It may be that it was such an insistence that lies behind the repeated New Testament claims that the Christian understanding of God and interpretation of the Scriptures did not represent the abolishment of the Law, but a completing realisation of it (Rom 3.31; 8.4; 13.10; Matt 5.17). Rather than experiencing their theological and existential interpretation of the shared Biblical conception of God as threatening to

---

[36] The positive exception to this rule is, above all others, B. Gerhardsson; see most recently "The Shema' in Early Christianity", in (ed.) F. Van Segbroeck et al., *The Four Gospels* (= FS F. Neirynck) (Leuven, 1992), 275-93 (his own contribution is found in the notes). However, Gerhardsson's studies concentrate on v. 5, rather than v. 4, and certainly not on the connexion between 4 and 5 in Deut 6. See, however, F. Hahn, "The Confession of the One God in the New Testament", *HBT* 2 (1980), 69-84; J.Gnilka, "Zum Gottesgedanken in der Jesusüberlieferung", in (ed.) H.-J.Klauck, *Monotheismus und Christologie*, FS K.Kertelge (*QD* 138) (Freiburg-Basel-Wien, 1992), 144-62.

[37] See, among others, K. G. Kuhn, *Phylakterien aus Höhle 4 von Qumran* (Heidelberg, 1957), esp. 24-31.

[38] See I. Heinemann, *Prayer in the Talmud* (*StJ* 9) (Berlin-New York, 1977), 218-24; T. Zahavy, *The Mishnaic Law of Blessings and Prayers, Tractate Berakoth* (Atlanta, 1987), 2-4; S. Dean McBride, "The Yoke of the Kingdom", *Int* 27 (1973), esp. 273-304; P. Navè, "Höre Israel", in (ed.) M. Brocke et al., *Das Vaterunser. Gemeinsames Beten von Juden und Christen* (Freiburg-Basel-Wien, 1974), 56-76. See also n. 35, above.

[39] It is possible to understand the recital of Deut 6.4-5 as a daily reanimation of the giving of the covenant on Sinai. See further S.S. Cohon, "The Unity of God", *HUCA* 26 (1955), 438-41; F.-L. Hossfeld, *Der Pentateuch*, 44-54.

God's unity, they experienced it as a further development of the confession deriving from the fathers. The God of father Abraham was also the God of both the Gentiles and the Jews (Rom 4.9-12).[40]

The confession of God's unity also underlies a number of both theologically significant and traditio-historically fundamental texts in the New Testament.[41] This applies to the direct quotation of Deut 6.4 in the fashioning of the twofold love-commandment in Mark 12.29,32 (ἐπ' ἀληθείας εἶπες...), which manifests itself as the very hermeneutical masterkey to the New Testament tradition.[42] In addition to this are such central passages in Mark's gospel as 2.7 and 10.18.

The last-mentioned reference to the Jewish "credo" has its parallel in Matt 19.17 (and Luke 18.19). There is, admittedly, no corresponding reference in Matt 22.37. On the other hand, we find an urgent statement of God's unity in v.9 of that ch.23 which, like an extensive specialised composition, reflects the evangelist's own polemical situation with respect to the Jewish tradition, which will probably have been the official Jewish synagogue at Antioch.[43]

There are a few entirely central texts for our purposes within the Pauline corpus, all of which display a pronounced emphasis on God's unity. Paul's actual intentions in Gal 3.20 are admittedly controversial.[44] However, it is at least clear that the reference to God's unquestioned unity in relation to the Biblical tradition about Moses as the middleman in conjunction with the law-giving on Sinai is intended to deny the Mosaic legislation the character of immediate divine revelation.[45] One

---

[40] This very problematic is discussed by L.W. Hurtado, *One God, One Lord*, 2 and esp. by H. Moxnes, *Theology in Conflict. Studies in Paul's Understanding of God in Romans*, *(NovTest.S 53)*, (Leiden, 1980), Part Two. Note further the examination of the futuric-universalistic dimension of the concept of God on the basis of, among other texts, Zech 14.9, by M. Wyschogrod, "Der eine Gott Abrahams und die Einheit des Gottes der jüdischen Philosophie", in *Das Reden vom einen Gott bei Juden und Christen*, (JeC 7), (Bern-Frankfurt-New York, 1984), 39-46.

[41] For the "God alone" (Μόνος θεός) statements in the doxologies in 1 Tim 1.17; 6.15-16 and Rom 16.27 I must confine myself to mentioning E. Stauffer, *ThWANT* 3, 98-99, and G. Delling, *Studien zum Neuen Testament und zum hellenistischen Judentum* (Göttingen, 1970), 391-400.

[42] See more extensively in "Det paulinske menneskesyn", in (ed.) S. Pedersen, *Menneskesynet* (København, 1989), esp. 75-78.

[43] See, for the present, my article "Antijudaisme og antisemitisme i evangelierne?" in (ed.) T. Kronholm, *Judendom och kristendom under de första århundradena*, (Stavanger, 1986), esp. 198-204.

[44] See U. Mauser, "Gal. III.20: Die Universalität des Heils", *NTS* 13 (1966-67), 258-70, where Gal 3.20 is interpreted on the basis of 3.29; H. Risesenfeld, "The Misinterpreted Mediator in Gal 3.19-20" in (ed.) W.C. Weinrich, *The New Testament Age* (= FS B. Reicke), Vol. II, (Macon, GA, 1984), 405-12, where the "mediator" in Gal 3.20a is identified with Moses, who is mentioned in 3.19.

[45] See T.Callan, "Pauline Midrash: The Exegetical Background of Gal 3:19b", *JBL* 99 (1980), 549-67. - Of course, one might then naturally ask whether this polemic against Moses' role in the history of revelation could not at least in theory apply equally well to 1 Tim 2.5, where the confession of the unity of God is followed by a speech about the man Jesus Christ as the only mediator between God and man (εἷς καὶ μεσίτης θεοῦ καὶ ἀνθρώπων)? One should note that in Heb 8.6; 9.15 and 12.24 this Christian language is even attached to the giving of the covenant.

might also consider whether Paul is not here on his way to transferring the Biblical tradition about the Ten Commandments having been pronounced directly by God's own mouth, while the more detailed laws were mediated through Moses (Exod 20.1-22; Deut 5.4-31), onto the divine statement to Abraham in Gen 15.6 and 12.3, which is quoted in Gal 3.6-9.[46] This could be seen in an extension of the fact that in the previous chapters Paul has energetically stressed the canonical character of his own call through God's own direct revelation, in contradistinction to insight which has been mediated through people (1.1,11-12,15-16).[47] This is to say that the Law of Moses not only arrived on the scene historically much later (Gal 3.15-18), but in terms of revelation theology it is also of subordinate rank with respect to the word of promise ("added"), so that in what follows Paul is forced to confirm that it nevertheless does not conflict with this word, but is subordinated to it with respect to both function and the chronological framework (3.21-22).[48]

1 Cor 8.6 is significant for several reasons. We see here how the confession of God's unity as father (εἷς θεὸς ὁ πατὴρ) leads to the confession of the unity of the lordship of Jesus Christ (εἷς κύριος 'Ιησοῦς Χριστός). And, as the historically manifested definition of what God's love (ἀγάπη) covers in its creation-theological content (8.1; cf. Rom 5.6-8),[49] this lordship has received its most pregnant expression in Jesus' death also on behalf of the "weak" in the congregation in Corinth. In other words, the designation "lord" (κύριος) has here a revelation-theological function with respect to God as Father, as we read in Phil 2.11: "and every tongue shall confess that Jesus Christ is Lord, to the glory of God the Father" (cf. Mark 2.27-28; 12.35-37).[50] Thus the

---

[46] Cf. Gen R 49.10; cited in S. Sandmel, "Philo's Place in Judaism: A Study of Conceptions of Abraham in Jewish Literature", *HUCA* 26 (1955), 200.

[47] Just as the Lord God had written the all of the pronounced commandments by himself on the two tablets of the Law (Exod 31.18; 32.15-16; 34.1; Deut 4.12-15; 9.9-11; 18.16-18). The actuality of the tradition in question is attested to by Philo (Decal 18-19; 175; Spec Leg 2.189; 3,7; 4.132). Moses' role is here described as that of prophet and interpreter. See also Josephus (Ant 3.83-94,101), who also emphatically points to the fact that, in spite of Moses' august role, it is not a question in this instance of human words; see also Mek Exod 15.11.

[48] On the other hand, N.T. Wright interprets Gal 3.20a (ἑνός) on the basis of 3.16 (ἑνός) and Rom 3.30, so that the inadequacies of the Mosaic law are of a specifically ecclesiological nature with respect to the Church's type of both Jew and heathen-Christian (*The Climax of the Covenant* (Edinburgh, 1991), 157-74). However, Gal 3.19-22 deals specifically with the soteriological function of the Mosaic law, understood as the basis for its ecclesiological consequences.

[49] See also C. Demke, "'Ein Gott und viele Herren'. Die Verkündigung des einen Gottes in den Briefen des Paulus", *EvTh* 36 (1976), esp. 478-83 ("ist hier Gott als Gott für die Liebe ausgelegt so dass das Bekenntnis zu seinem Einzigsein das Bekenntnis zu seiner Einzigkeit einschliesst").

[50] This fundamentally hermeneutical side of Christ's activity is also traceable in Matt 23, where the confession in v 9 of the unity of the heavenly Father is followed, in v 10, by a confession of the unity of Christ as teacher. This parallelism suggests that the previous confession of the one teacher in v 8 likewise refers to Christ.

Biblical confession of the unity of God is regarded as the relevant expression of the idea that the lordship of Christ means that the cosmic ecclesiology of the sibling relationship is founded on the universality of the Father-relationship.[51]

We note in this text that the creation-theological interpretation leads to an understanding of the conception of God's unity the anthropological consequences of which do not entail reduction to particularity, but rather expansion to universalism. Its background lies in the hermeneutical reworking of the creation-theological insight for which the Jesuanic-messianic determination of the supreme concept of *agape* is the expression. The introductory expression in 8.1-3 and the concluding statement in 11.1 make up, respectively, the "prologue" and "epilogue" of an integral work the Christological centre of which is in 8.11-12, while its anthropological concretisation is in 9.19-23, and the fundamental understanding of God is in 8.3.

The emphasis on the anthropological "everyone" ($\pi\acute{\alpha}\nu\tau\epsilon\varsigma$; 9.19-23) which is implicit in the Jesuanic-messianic confession of God's unity in its creation-theological development, which in the context of 1 Cor 8.1-11.1 primarily enjoys an internal ecclesiological address, receives universal revelation-historical perspective in Rom 3.30. The confession of God's unity is grounded argumentatively in Paul's understanding of Christian soteriology (3.28; cf. Gal 2.16), as the latter is developed in terms of theology of scripture and theology of creation in what follows (4.1-25; 5.12-19). This makes it clear that the real controversy about the unity of God had to do with its anthropological implications.[52] It is important to note that in this connexion Paul argues controversially on the basis of the known and accepted thesis that God is also the God of the heathen.[53]

The struggle, then, is not primarily about the confession of God's unity in a polemical relationship to other varieties of hellenistic worship,[54] but about the anthropological content of the Biblical confession of God's unity as the common presupposition in a polemical relationship

---

[51] See, additionally, N.T. Wright, "...v.6 functions as a Christian redefinition of the Jewish confession of faith, the *Shema*" (*The Climax of the Covenant*, 121; cf. 127-29). See also C.H. Giblin, "Three Monotheistic Texts in Paul", *CBQ* 37 (1975), 527-47.

[52] See also E. Grässer, "Ein einziger ist Gott" (Rom. 3,30); now in *Der Alte Bund im Neuen* (*WUNT* 35) (Tübingen, 1985), esp. 254-58, n. 99 which refers to U. Wilckens, *Der Brief an die Römer* (*EKK*) (Köln and Neukirchen-Vluyn, 1978), 248-49, where it is likewise pointed out that Paul is here interpreting the daily Jewish confession of faith "gezielt provokativ ...: Gott hat seine Einzigkeit *darin* erwiesen, dass er als der Eine alle rechtfertigt".

[53] As pointed out by N.A. Dahl, "The One God of Jews and Gentiles", in *Studies in Paul*, 178-91, including the conclusion. Instructive material has been collected by W.D. Davies in *Paul and Rabbinic Judaism* (London, (1948) 1965), ch. 3-4.

[54] On this see G. Schneider, "Urchristliche Gottesverkündigung in hellenistischer Umwelt"; now in: *Lukas, Theologe der Heilsgeschichte* (*BBB* 59) (Bonn, 1985), 280-96.

to the Judaism of the time (εἴπερ εἰς ὁ θεὸς ὅς...). The religio-sociological battlefront positions in this controversy between Jews and non-Jews, as is to superfluity expressed in the other ancient sources, is not smoothed over or nullified by the fact that it is possible today by means of tradition history to demonstrate the presence of universal elements in the preceding Biblical and the later rabbinical tradition.[55] However, their historical actuality meant that the struggle over the anthropology led to a struggle about the understanding of God, that is, to a struggle about the understanding of the God of the common Biblical revelation as the God of the common Biblical concept of creation (1 Cor 8.6; 15.28; 2 Cor 4.6; Rom 15.6).

The result in a Christian context is that the accentuated reference to the unity of the Biblical God leads to an universal soteriology, the consequences of which are not merely an ethics which defies all confines, but above all an universal missiology which, despite related tendencies within ancient Judaism and the ancient mystery religions, seems to be unique within the Hellenistic context because of its theoretical nature and its practical intensity.

What is the background for the fact that the Christians manifested themselves as the outwardly-orientated mission *par excellence* of the Hellenistic world? To me, this question seems to be of a more profound nature than is, for example, the currently lively discussion as to the understanding of the Law in the New Testament writings. Or, perhaps more accurately: the two stand to each other in a relation of cause and effect.

### 3. The Jewish Exodus tradition and the Christian resurrection proclamation

There is naturally room for discussion as to which is the most fundamental divine predicate in the *Old Testament*. To those schooled in the modern philosophy of religions, the divine self-presentation in Exod 3.14 is the most immediately striking example.[56] However, one should note that already in its own context this predicate is defined in an "historifying" way such that the God of the fathers, the God of Abraham, Isaac and Jacob, is also the God who acknowledged Israel as his own people

---

[55] On this see O. Schmitt, *Du sollst keinen Frieden schliessen mit den Bewohnern des Landes* (BWANT 11) (Stuttgart, 1970), esp. 154-63.
[56] For a survey of Jewish interpretations see C. Thoma, "Der eine Gott Israels als Kraft und Ziel der Geschichte", *Judaica* 39 (1983), 85-97.

(Exod 4.22) by liberating it from Egyptian slavery under the leadership of Moses.[57]

This salvation-historical theme also recurs in many such credo-like formulations of considerable traditio-historical antiquity as Deut 26.5-9; 6.20-24; Jos 24.2-13 (cf. 1 Sam 12.6,8; 1 Kgs 8.51,53; Jer 2.6; 11.4; Ezek 20.5-10; Ps 80.9).[58] In numerous individual statements we find that the content of the conception of God has simply been determined by this liberation of Israel from Egypt.[59] Thus, for example, in Hos 12.10 and 13.4, after it has already been made clear (11.1) that this liberation is an expression of God's love "for his son". Or, with a view to establishing a covenant, in Lev 11.45: "For I am Yahweh who brought you up out of the land of Egypt, to be your God; you shall be holy, because I am holy" (cf. 19.36; 22.33). Or, in Ps 81.11: "I am Yahweh, your God, who led you up from Egypt; open your mouth, and I will fill it". Israel is elsewhere characterised as a people through this very liberation (Exod 19.4-5; Deut 4.20,34; 7.6-8). In 2 Sam 7.22-24 it is furthermore emphasised that the greatness of the name of the Lord is attached to the fate of Israel, to "the people you liberated from Egypt". And in Jer 16.14-15 we note that the predicate is not only part of an oath formula, but that it also forms a model for the expectation that, though in exile, the Israelites will one day return to the land of their fathers.

In this connexion, scholars have maintained that the Sinai tradition and the Exodus tradition originally belonged to independent circles of tradition.[60] However, in the present state of the text these two traditions have been conjoined, as is indicated by the fact that the divine predicate "I am Yahweh your God, who led you out of Egypt, out of the house of bondage" has been used as an explanatory introduction to the Decalogue, which is itself a prologue to the two great Horeb-Sinai complexes of laws which specify the contents of the covenant (Deut 5.6; 6.21; Exod 20.2). In subsequent rabbinical tradition it was possible for the liberation from Egypt, the giving of the Law on Sinai and the conquest of the Promised Land in its entirety to be seen as the fulfilment of God's fundamental promises to Abraham in Gen 12.2-3 (Num R 11.2). Thus it is established also as a matter of principle within the Old Testament understanding of

---

[57] This supra-ordinate Exodus perspective was also continued in Qumran; cf. A. Strothmann, *Mein Vater bist du! (Sir. 51,10) (FrThSt* 39) (Frankfurt am Main, 1991), 330-36. And the Palestinian targums rendered the divine predicate in Exod 3.14 by "I am He who was with you in the bondage of Egypt and who will be with you in every bondage" (cf. A.F. Segal, *Two Powers in Heaven (SJLA* 25) (Leiden, 1977), 51).

[58] Cf. G. von Rad, *Das erste Buch Mose (ATD)*, 6th ed., (Göttingen, 1961), 7-16.

[59] By the same token, note M. Buber's universal interpretation of the predicate in Amos 9.7 on the basis of Isa 2.3, in contradistinction to Micah 4.5 and Dan 8.25, in O. Betz, et al. (eds.), *Abraham unser Vater* (= *FS* O. Michel) (Leiden, 1963), esp. 52-53.

[60] See H. Gese, "Bemerkungen zur Sinaitradition", in *Vom Sinai zum Zion*, 31-48.

God that God's intervening new-creation for the salvation of the people makes and determines the content of the covenant prior to God's commandments to Israel,[61] just as the election was based solely on God's love for Israel.[62]

But this God's love for Israel can naturally be seen in relation to the Creation, which enables us to say that God created the world out of love, or, concretely, that he created the world for Israel's sake. The God of Israel was therefore the Creator, the same who later liberated Israel from Egypt and gave her the law on Sinai, with Moses as its interpreter. This provides the basic theological structure in the liturgical prayers (Neh 9.5-37, and, later, the morning and evening liturgies).[63] There developed from this a conception (associated with Prov 8.22-36; Sir 1.1,4; 24.9; Wis 9.9; Ab 3.18) that the Creation took place on the basis of that law which was with God prior to the Creation (Gen R 1.1), a conception which is also applicable to Israel herself. It implies that insight into the Creation is achieved through knowledge of the Torah.[64]

In the actual context of the 1st century, this means that the Biblical picture of the God of Israel as the powerful liberator of his chosen people[65] who humiliates their oppressors becomes a present reality among the people not only in connexion with the annual celebration of Passover (Deut 6.21; 16.1), but also through the daily recitation of the Shemah together with the Biblical texts associated with it (Deut 6.4-9; 11.13-21; Num 15.37-41).[66] Moreover, this daily concession of the

---

[61] Cf. among other examples the Mekilta tradition by B. Ego, "Eine Untersuchung zur Rezeption der Königsmetapher in der Mekhilta de R. Yishma'el", in M. Hengel and A.M. Schwemer (eds.), *Königsherrschaft Gottes und himmlischer Kult im Judentum, Urchristentum und in der hellenistischen Welt* (WUNT 55) (Tübingen, 1991), 277-81. Note also M. Kadushim, "Aspects of the Rabbinic Concept of Israel. A Study in the Mekiltah", *HUCA* 19 (1945-46), esp. 71-80; L.J. Liebreich, "The Benediction immediately Following and the One Preceeding the Recital of the Shema'", *REJ* 126 (1966), esp. 154-64.
[62] Cf. H.H. Rowley, *The Biblical Doctrine of Election*, 2nd ed., (London, 1964), 18; 41-44; W.H. Schmidt, "Werk Gottes und Tun des Menschen", *JBTh* 4 (1989), 11-28.
[63] J.J. Liebreich, "The Impact of Nehemiah 9.5-37 on the Liturgy of the Synagogue", *HUCA* 32 (1961), 227-37.
[64] Cf. R.T. Herford, *Pirke Aboth. The Ethics of the Talmud: Sayings of the Fathers*, 3rd ed., (New York, (1945) 1966), 87-88; A.M. Goldberg, "Schöpfung und Geschichte", *Judaica* 24 (1968), 27-44; E.E. Urbach, *The Sages. Their Concepts and Beliefs*, Vol.1, (Jerusalem, 1975), 527-34; E. Stiegman, *Rabbinic Anthropology* (ANRW II, 19,2) (Berlin, 1979), 498-99; J. Maier; "Torah und Schöpfung", JBTh 5 (1990), 139-150.
[65] This intimate connexion between the concept of God and the popular self-understanding presumably underlies R. Akiba's daring identification of Israel's liberation from Egypt with God's own liberation from there (Mek Ex 12.41); J.Z. Lauterbach, *Mekilta de-Rabbi Ishmael* (Philadelphia, 1976), Vol.I, 114; and S Num § 84, with reference to 2 Sam 7.23; K.G. Kuhn, *Sifre zu Numeri (Tannaitische Midraschim III)* (Stuttgart, 1959), 226). See also W. Bacher, *Die Agada der Tannaiten*, Vol. I, 2nd ed., (Strassburg, 1903), 280-81.
[66] Cf. Ber 1.4-5; Tamid 5.1 and Josephus, *Ant* 4.212-213. Further T. Lehnardt, "Zur Vorstellung von der Königsherrschaft Gottes im Shema und seinen Benediktionen" (in M. Hengel and A.M. Schwemer (eds.), *Königsherrschaft Gottes und himmlischer Kult...*, esp. 292-299); and note Lehnardt's important conclusion (306): "Im Rückblick auf die beim Auszug aus Ägypten widerfahrene Erlösung wird der

unity of the God of Israel has the careful observance of his divine "Saviour's" commandments as its existentially obligating practice throughout the ancient Mediterranean region.

The religio-sociological reaction of varying surroundings to this included, from the 3rd century BCE, the widely-flung anti-Jewish polemic originating in Egypt, the basic theme of which was "the impure and human-threatening Jews' outrageous expulsion" of the Egyptian people.[67]

We find within the *New Testament* numerous divine predicates of a fundamental nature. Here the constitutive "Exodus"-event is Jesus' life, death and resurrection, as a culminating unity.[68] Therefore the Jesuanic-Christological divine predicate *par excellence* takes the form of a confession-like expression stating that God is "the one who woke Jesus Christ from the dead" (1 Cor 6.14; 15.15; 2 Cor 1.9; 4.14; Gal 1.1; Rom 8.11; cf. Acts 4.10; 5.30 ("the God of our fathers raised Jesus...");  13.30,37; Col 2.12; Eph 1.20).[69] Similarly, to be a Christian is defined as "believing in the God who raised Jesus" (Rom 4.24; 10.9; 1 Pet 1.21)[70] — a faith which was presumably articulated with the help of loans from the language of the Jewish Eighteen-Prayer (2 Cor 1.9), which Paul traced back from the vantagepoint of scriptural theology to Abraham as the "father of the faith" (Rom 4.16-22; Gal 3.6-9).[71] It is

---

Schlußsatz des Meerliedes (Ex 15,18), in dem die Berakha nach dem Shema endet, als erstmalige Proklamation der Königsherrschaft Gottes verstanden... Das Erleben der königlichen Machttaten Gottes in der vergangenen Erlösung beim Auszug aus Ägypten wird damit zum Grundmodell aller künftigen Erlösung im kommenden Königreich Gottes". See also R. Kimelman, "The Šema' and its Blessings. The Realization of God's Kingship" in (ed.) L.I. Levine, *The Synagogue in Late Antiquity* (Philadelphia, PA, 1987), esp. 76-78 ("God's past conduct serves as a warranty for the future").

[67] On this see, among others, J.L. Derry, "Anti-Semitism in the Hellenistic-Roman Period", *JBL* 98 (1979), 45-65; L.H. Feldman, "Anti-Semitism in the Ancient World" in D. Berger (ed.), *History and Hate. The Dimensions of Anti-Semitism* (Philadelphia et al., 1986), 15-41.

[68] According to U. Luz, the following is true of Matthew: "Im Unterschied zu biblischen und nachbiblischen Neuerzählungen der alten Heilsgeschichte erzählt Matthäus eine neue Grundgeschichte des Heils... Das Bekenntnis zu dem einen Gott ist eine interpretationsbedürftige Formel... Nur wenn man ernst nimmt, dass der alttestamentliche und jüdische Gott für Matthäus voll und ganz durch das Evangelium Jesu definiert wird, wird man auch von der Identität Gottes sprechen dürfen, dessen Wesen gerade seine im Sinn von Ex 3,14 verstandene Freiheit, neu zu handeln und sich neu zu definieren, ist" ("Das Matthäusevangelium und die Perspektive einer biblischen Theologie", *JBTh* 4 (1989), 240). But one might equally well claim that Luz' observation applies generally throughout the linguistic/theological variations of the New Testament tradition as a whole.

[69] See further J. Moltmann, *Der gekreuzigte Gott. Das Kreuz Christi als Grund und Kritik christlicher Theologie* (München, 1972), 175-77; B. Rigaux, *Dieu l'a ressuscité* (Gembloux, 1963), esp. 317-19; G. Lohfink, "Der Ablauf der Ostereignisse und die Anfänge der Urgemeinde", in *Studien zum Neuen Testament*, 167.

[70] See also J. Becker, "Das Gottesbild Jesu und die älteste Auslegung von Ostern" in (ed.), G. Strecker, *Jesus Christus in Historie und Theologie* (FS H. Conzelmann) (Tübingen, 1975), 105-126; W. Schrage, "Theologie und Christologie bei Paulus und Jesus auf dem Hintergrund der modernen Gottesfrage", *EvTh* 36 (1976), 129-35.

[71] See additionally D.-A. Koch, *Schriftauslegung als Zeuge des Evangeliums* (BHTh 69) (Tübingen, 1986), 348-53.

also possible to speak of Christ predicatively, as the one who "was awakened from the dead" (1 Thess 1.10; 2 Cor 5.15; Rom 7.4; 8.34; cf. 2 Tim 2.8).[72]

In this connexion, it is essential to understand that here the apocalyptic concept of the *resurrection* has been interpreted in terms of Creation-theology, as a result of the present-future character of the Christian eschatology (2 Cor 5.17-19). This has three consequences for the New Testament conception of God:

a) God is the single active subject of the new-creation (its $δύναμις$), i.e., he is "the one who makes the ungodly righteous" (Rom 4.5); "who gives life to the dead and calls into existence things that do not exist" (4.17);[73]

b) it is the concrete life-together-with-one-another within the framework of the Creation (6.4-7,11) which, in new creation, is liberated from death's oppression. After all, sin is not sin against particular laws, but against that which God has created (8.19-22).

c) As the liberation ("Exodus") brought about by the Creator himself, this necessarily applies to the entire Creation.[74] In that Letter to the Romans which can be determined as Genesis II this includes both the Jewish nay-sayers and the barbarians outside of the governing diasporas (15.1-13). To an astonishingly great degree, the collective ($πάντες$) is the main goal behind this letter.

---

[72] This new fundamental event did not prevent the relating of the OT exodus narrative typologically to Jesus Christ in Matt 2.15. And Melito was able to use it as the metaphorical model for his Christian Easter sermon (*Peri Pascha* 1-45); Irenaeus was able to interpret it typologically of the liberation of the Christians from heathendom (*Adv haer* 4.30,4; cf. 1 Cor 10.1-11; Heb 3.11-19). Justin Martyr even found it possible to write that the Christian god was the self-same God who had led the fathers out of Egypt (*Dial* 11.1). According to M. Hengel, the motif of the exodus also underlies Jn 5.1-9 ("Die Schriftauslegung des 4. Evangeliums auf dem Hintergrund der urchristlichen Exegese", *JBTh* 4 (1989), 286-87).

[73] On this usage see O. Hofius, "Rechtfertigung des Gottlosen als Thema biblischer Theologie", *JBTh* 2 (1987), 79 and 86 (now: Paulusstudien (WUNT 51), Tübingen 1989).

[74] See additionally U. Mell, *Neue Schöpfung* (BZNW 56) (Berlin et al., 1989), 314-22; 390-97. G. Delling made the central difference between these two fundamental divine predicates more clear in the following manner: "Erinnert das in der Tat an die alttestamentliche partizipiale Bezeichnung Jahwes als dessen, der Israel aus Ägypten geführt hat, so ist die neutestamentliche Wendung doch nicht ausdrücklich auf die Heilsgemeinde bezogen...gerade das ist für die Urchristenheit bedeutsam: der Auferweckte ist der Anfänger einer neuen Menschheit" ("Geprägte partizipiale Gottesaussagen in der urchristlichen Verkündigung", in *Studien zum Neuen Testament und zum hellenistischen Judentum*, 408).

In all three perspectives, the Christian resurrection-proclamation is to be seen as a perfection-conferring adherence to the Biblical confession of God's unity *sui generis*.[75]

From the point of view of *anthropology* this conception of God has some fundamental, table-turning consequences. The *(primarily) narrow "exodus" of the people has received the depth and nature of a (primarily) generally anthropological one.* Man is brought into the centre as the creation-theological object, since God is the single new-creating subject. And the unity of the conception of God has its counterpart in the single commandment in Lev 19.18 which summarizes all the commandments: "you shall love your neighbour as yourself" (Rom 13.9).[76] According to the Jesuanic-Christological understanding of the unity of God it is also the case that the question of who is one's neighbour is solved by the multiplicity of Creation, as an indirect description of "the third people".

From a *traditio-historical* point of view, this conception of God has some fundamental selective consequences. Thus, with the Shemah and the Decalogue as interpretive summarizing passkeys to the Mosaic complexes of tradition, the first part pertaining to worship drops out.[77] Also in this respect the Jesuanic-messianic conception of God denotes a third position with respect to both Hellenic and Jewish worship.

For this reason we find everywhere in the New Testament only the second table of the Decalogue.[78] Of the Shemah, we find that the confession of the unity of God figures in intensified form in central, significant contexts. The subsequent commandment to love God with all

---

[75] See U. Mauser's view of the purpose of a "biblical theology" in "Εἷς Θεός und Μόνος Θεός in Biblischer Theologie", *JBTh* 1 (1986), esp. 83-87 ("Biblische Theologie ist die Aufgabe gestellt, die Christologie des Neuen Testaments so zu interpretieren, dass sich in ihr die Einzigartigkeit, Ausschliesslichkeit und Einheitlichkeit Gottes letzthin überzeugend durchgesetzt hat und noch durchsetzt"). See also H. Merklein, "Die Einzigkeit Gottes als die sachliche Grundlage der Botschaft Jesu", *JBTh* 2 (1987), esp. 24-32.

[76] In *Neophyti* one finds the explanatory comparison for the statute in Lev 19.18, "...who is like to yourselves" (A. Diez Macho, *Neophyti*, I, Vol. III, (Madrid and Barcelona, 1971), 131, commentary on 379). Nor is there any lack of tentative beginnings of creation-theological explanations in rabbinical contexts, since, among other things, the prohibition against murder was seen in relation to Gen 9.6 (Mek Ex 20.16; Gen R 34). R. Ben Azzai's reference to the idea that the neighbour has been created in the image of God, as an exploration of R. Akiba's characterisation of Lev 19.18 as "a great commandment in the Law" (*S Lev* 19.18), has been controversial. See A. Nissen, *Gott und der Nächste im antiken Judentum* (WUNT 13) (Tübingen, 1974), 288-308; 400-07; P. Lenhardt - P. von der Osten-Sacken, *Rabbi Akiva* (Berlin 1987), 175-192.

[77] As far as the Decalogue is concerned, this central concern does not seem to play any significant role for R.M. Grant, "The Decalogue in Early Christianity", *HThR* 40 (1947), 1-17; B. Reicke, *Die zehn Worte in Geschichte und Gegenwart* (Tübingen, 1973), 51-52; W. Harrelson, *The Ten Commandments and Human Rights* (Philadelphia, 1980), 157-72; R.H. Fuller, "The Decalogue in the New Testament", *Int* 43 (1989), 243-55.

[78] In Theophilus' *Ad Autolycum* (3,9), only the third and fourth commandment have been omitted (cf. R.M. Grant, "The Decalogue in Early Christianity", 110-13). See the survey by F.E. Vokes, (ed.F.L. Cross) *The Ten Commandments in the New Testament and in First Century Judaism* (TU 103) (Berlin, 1968), 146-54.

one's heart, soul and mind is retained in Mark 12.30, but its theological-existential status has been altered by combining it with the commandment to love one's neighbour as one's self (Mark 12.31). We find it after this in Rom 5.6-8 (cf. 1 Jn 4.10), where it directly emphasizes the fact that the coming of Jesus of Nazareth has turned the subject-object relation inside-out in the understanding of the Biblical confession of faith in Deut 6.5, so that here it is God who is the subject, and man who is the object (cf. note 42).

In traditio-historical terms the Christian confession of the unity of God functions not only selectively, but also expansively. For this reason it is possible to run into ethical formulations familiar to us from both Jewish ethics and Hellenism's generally philosophically orientated behavioural patterns (Phil 4.8; Eph 5.21-6.9) in the actual parenesis in the New Testament texts. Also with respect to tradition history the Christian interpretation of life manifests itself theologically and existentially as the "third way".[79]

In its New Testament form of *the twofold commandment of love*, the Biblical confession is subsequently to be found everywhere serving as a hermeneutical key to the New Testament tradition in its entirety. This is the case with Paul, from his first letter (1 Thess 4.9) to his last (Rom 3.30; 5.8; 13.9). And it takes place traditio-historically with the replacement of the *Shemah* and the Decalogue in their previous Jewish forms by the same Biblical confession. What tradition history reveals on the periphery in other contexts occupies the centre of the Christian tradition-formation with the twofold commandment of love, in all its unchangeable and inalienable unity.

## IV. Perspective

This creation-theological analysis of the Jesuanic concentration on the unity of God implies the possibility historically and contemporarily to build a bridge to 1) an dialogue with contemporary Jewish tradition[80] 2) a dialogue with the other world religions[81] 3) a dialogue with people

---

[79] See further E. Lohse, "Kirche im Alltag. Erwägungen zur theologischen Begründung der Ethik im Neuen Testament", in D. Lührmann and G. Strecker (eds.), *Kirche* (= FS G. Bornkamm) (Tübingen, 1980), esp. 406-14.
[80] Cf. J.J. Petuchowski, "Der werdende Gott?", in J.J. Petuchowski et al. (eds.), *Gott Alles in Allem* (Freiburg-Basel-Wien, 1985), 13-39; J. Neusner, *Telling Tales: Making Sense of Christian and Judaic Nonsense - The Urgency and Basis for a Judaic-Christian Dialogue* (Louisville, Kent. 1993), 5-6; 19-23; 104 ("...Dialogue will begin with the recognition of difference, with a search for some grounds of form for communication, rather than with the search for commonalities"); 106; 161-164.
[81] See additionally, J. Lähnemann, "Jesu Rede von Gott - als christlicher Beitrag im Gespräch mit Menschen anderen Glaubens" in D.-A. Koch, et al. (eds.) *Jesu Rede von Gott und ihre Nachgeschichte im frühen Christentum* (= FS W. Marxsen) (Gütersloh, 1989), 443-56.

whose "world-experiences" (H. Weder) are non-religious about, not one and the same God, but one and the same world.[82]

The sequence here expresses both a priority and a context in which the last two points are contained in the first one.[83]

---

[82] To the extent that God and the world can be thought of independently of one another. As far as Christian theology is concerned, every conception of God implies not only an anthropology, but also a cosmology, both of which are existentially experienced. Cf. U. Luck, "In der Erwartung der Gottesherrschaft ist Gottes- und Welterfahrung nicht von einander zu trennen. Gotteserfahrung ist nicht nur eine Betroffenheit vom Worte Gottes her, sie setzt immer auch eine Weise der Welterfahrung voraus" ("Der Anfang der Christologie, die Sache Jesu und die Gottesherrschaft", in *Jesu Rede von Gott und ihre Nachgeschichte im frühen Christentum*, 37).

[83] Cf. M. Wyschogrod: "Die Grundsolidarität zwischen Juden und Nichtjuden wurzelt darin, daß der Mensch als Bild Gottes geschaffen ist (Gen 1,26) - vielleicht die wichtigste Einzelaussage der Hebräischen Bibel. Und diese Aussage bezieht sich auf Adam, sie liegt vor der Erwählung Abrahams" ("Zugang zu einer biblischen Ethik im gegenwärtigen Judentum", in W. Breuning-H.P. Heinz (eds), *Damit die Erde menschlich bleibt. Gemeinsame Verantworung von Juden und Christen für die Zukunft* (Freiburg, et al., 1985), 82).

# INDEX OF AUTHORS

Aalen, S.  226
Achtemeyer, P.  221
Aland, K.  156, 177
Alexander, L.  78, 84
Alexander, G.  2
Ashton, J.  94
Bacher, W.  261
Badenas, R.  36, 37
Banks, R.  80, 241
Barr, J.  106, 181, 221
Barrett, C.K.  100
Barstad, H.M.  137
Barth, K.  19, 109
Barth, M.  241
Barton, J.  43, 44
Bassler, J.M.  250, 251
Bauer, W.  167, 177
Beardsley, M.C.  131
Beasley-Murray, G.R.  232
Becker, J.  103, 149, 156, 162, 167, 177, 253, 262
Berger, K.  80
Beyer, H.W.  202
Bietenhard, H.  149, 177
Bihlmeyer-Schneemelcher,  246
Bjørndalen, A.J.  132
Blank, J.  154, 158, 159, 162, 167, 177
Blass, F./Debrunner, A.  156, 162, 177
Bloom, H.  132
Bock, D.L.  81
Boerts, H.  25
Bonsack, B.  163, 164, 165, 177
Borgen, P.  98
Bosch, D.J.  235
Bosch, D.T.  228
Bovon, F.  79, 84, 85, 248, 249
Brandenburger, E.  188, 190, 191, 194, 195
Brändle, R.  246
Braulik, G.  254
Braun, H.  85
Brocke, M.  217

Bruce, F.F.  187
Buber, M.  260
Bultmann, C.  250
Bultmann, R.  2, 15, 18, 93, 105, 148, 156, 159, 160, 161, 162, 163, 166, 167, 177
Burger, C.  87
Byung Mu, A.  240
Cadbury, H.J.  78
Callan, T.  256
Cambier, J.M.  251
Cerri, G. - Gentili, B.  79
Charlesworth, J.H.  245
Childs, B.S.  93, 212, 245
Chilton, B. - McDonald, J.I.H.  229
Clines, D.J.A.  134
Cohn-Sherbok, D.  233-234, 238
Cohon, S.S.  255
Collins, A.Y.  188
Collins, A.  2
Collins, J.J.  182, 183, 184, 185, 186, 188, 196
Colpe, C.  153, 154, 177
Conzelmann, H.  65, 66, 78, 80, 85, 89, 146, 164, 177, 195
Cranfield, C.E.B.  35, 37, 202
Crosby, M.H.  233
Crüsemann, F.  216, 217, 219
Cullmann, O.  87, 93, 104
Culpepper, R.A.  168, 169, 177
Dahl, N.A.  37, 99, 100, 226, 251, 258
Daniels, D.R.  245
Danker, F.W.  89
Davies, P.R.  197
Davies, W.D.  258
Decke, G.  241
Delling, G.  256, 263
Demke, C.  257
Derry, J.L.  262
Di Lella, D.  183
Dibelius, M.  77
Dietzfelbinger, C.  29
Dodd, C.H.  252

Dugandzic, I.   31, 35, 37, 41, 45, 46
Duhm, B.   135
Dulles, A.   227
Dunn, J.D.G.   25, 27, 34, 35, 36, 220, 221
Dupont, J.   218
Eagleton, T.   131, 133
Ebeling, G.   25, 26, 30, 47, 58, 181, 220
Ego, B.   261
Feldman, L.H.   262
Fitzmyer, J.A.   37, 84, 85, 87, 89
Flacius, M.   1
Flew, R.N.   225, 226
Foerster, W.   167, 177
Fohrer, G.   135
Ford, D.   191
Forkman, G.   228
Frankemölle, H.   225
Franklin, E.   87
Frei, H.   25
Fuller, R.H.   264
Gager, J.G.   224
Gärtner, B.   79
Gasque, H.   77
Gaston, L.   188, 195
Geddert, T.J.   192, 195, 196
Geldsetzer, L.   1
Gentili, B. - Cerri, G.   79
Gerhardsson, B.   140, 255
Gese, H.   42, 58, 95, 98, 105, 124, 143, 144, 148-149, 156, 157, 159, 160, 168, 177, 182, 185, 248, 260
Getty, M.A.   253
Giblin, C.H.   258
Glöckner, R.   90
Gnilka, J.   255
Goldberg, A.   102
Goldberg, A.M.   261
Gollwitzer, H.   233
Goulder, M.   70
Grant, R.M.   246, 264
Grässer, E.   36, 40, 106, 108, 108, 122, 180, 245, 258
Grotius, H.   1
Gunneweg, A.H.J.   28, 44
Haacker, K.   81, 180, 248

Haenchen, E.   31, 36, 41, 42, 59, 77, 149, 153, 154, 155, 156, 158, 160, 162, 177
Hahn, F.   87, 243, 255
Hainz, J.   241
Hallbäck, G.   190
Hamm, B.   222
Hammelsbeck, O.   205
Hanson, A.T.   94
Hanson, P.D.   200, 223, 228, 232, 242
Harnack, A. von   2
Harrelson, W.   264
Hartman, L.   182, 188
Hartman, L.F.   183, 188, 189, 190, 193-194
Hayward, C.T.R.   149, 177
Heidegger, M.   13, 15, 22
Heinemann, I.   255
Helfmeyer, F.J.   216
Hengel, M.   27, 77, 93, 103, 104, 182, 191, 192, 193, 263
Herford, R.T.   261
Hirsch, E.   2
Höffken, P.   254
Hofius, O.   6, 7, 54, 108, 109, 110, 114, 116, 118, 263
Hofrichter, P.   148, 153, 154, 155, 164, 165, 178
Holmberg, B.   222
Holtz, T.   81
Hossfeld, F.-L.   254, 255
Houten, C. van   250
Hübner, H.   2, 3, 10, 16, 22, 25, 28-29, 32-33, 34, 36, 37, 38, 43, 54, 58, 63, 80, 180, 245, 248, 254
Hurtado, L.W.   244, 247, 256
Ibuki, Y.   151, 178
Isenberg, S.R.   223
Iwand, H.-J.   109, 110, 111, 112, 117, 120, 121
Janowski, B.   180, 245
Janssens, Y.   148, 178
Jasper, D.   131
Jeanrod, W.G.   127
Jeremias, J.   235, 236
Jervell, J.   5, 77, 78, 81, 82, 87, 209, 210
Johnson, M.D.   87-88
Johnson, G.   86
Juel, D.   192

# INDEX OF AUTHERS

Jüngel, E.   40
Kadushim, M.   261
Kalusche, M.   244
Kappen, S.   231
Käsemann, E.   18, 36, 68, 93, 162, 167, 178
Keck, L.E.   224
Kee, H.C.   188, 226
Kelber, W.H.   195
Keller, R.   1
Kertelge, K.   4, 47, 50, 252
Kieffer, R.   63
Kimelman, R.   262
Kingsbury, J.D.   65, 66, 68, 85
Klauck, H.-J.   133
Klein, H.   3
Klinghardt, M.   80
Koch, D.-A.   28, 30, 36, 38, 41, 42, 262
Kock, K.   182, 184, 186, 187, 197
Koenig, J.   230, 231
Koester, H.   244
Koet, B.J.   81
Koschorke, K.   148, 166, 168, 178
Kramer, W.   28
Kraus, H.-J.   2, 47, 248
Kuhn, K.G.   255, 261
Kühschelm, R.   95, 96
Kümmel, W.G.   46, 80, 243
Küng, H.   241
Lähnemann, J.   265
Lambrecht, J.   190-191
Lane, W.L.   189, 192
Lang, F.   109
Lauterbach, J.Z.   261
Lebram, J.-C.   183
Lehnardt, T.   261-262
Lenhardt, P.   264
Liddell, H.G./Scott R.   178
Liebreich, L.J.   261
Lieu, J.M.   6, 7, 93, 95, 96, 97, 99
Lindemann, A.   35, 167, 178
Ljungman, H.   63, 64
Lohfink, N.   226, 227, 231, 238, 254
Lohfink, G.   226, 227, 232, 237, 241, 243, 248, 250, 262
Lohse, E.   265
Löning, K.   248

Loretz, O.   204
Luck, U.   3, 147, 266
Lührmann, D.   192
Luz, U.   28, 29, 30, 31, 32, 39, 42, 49, 56, 60, 63, 67, 262
Macho, A. Diez   264
Mack, B.L.   153, 154, 155, 157, 165, 168, 178
Mackay, J.   220, 221
Maddox, R.   78
Maier, F.W.   54
Maier, J.   261
Marsh, J.   93
Marshall, I.H.   77
Mauser, U.   192, 256, 264
McBride, S. Dean   255
McKenzie, J.L.   222
Meeks, W.A.   222, 223, 241
Meier, J.P.   66, 73, 75
Mell, U.   263
Merk, O.   40, 47, 57, 180, 209, 245
Merklein, H.   264
Miller, E.L.   152, 178
Minear, P.   89, 238, 242
Moberly, R.W.L.   42
Mogensen, B.   215
Moltmann, J.   205, 211, 262
Mott, S.C.   231, 232
Moxnes, H.   222, 229, 230, 234, 240, 256
Müller, M.   5, 6, 9, 58, 64, 72, 73, 197
Müller, K.   225
Müller, P.-G.   2, 86
Munck, J.   27
Mussner, F.   205, 207
Navè, P.   255
Neirynck, F.   187
Nepper-Christensen, P.   218
Neusner, J.   75, 224, 265
Nielsen, H.K.   8, 201, 203
Nielsen, K.   7, 126, 127, 128, 129, 130, 140, 142
Nielsen, E.   209
Nissen, J.   9, 220, 228, 234, 238, 240
Nissen, A.   205, 207, 216, 217, 264
Nixon, R.   80
Noack, B.   245
Nolan, A.   226, 231, 238

Norris, C.   134
North, C.R.   138
Oeming, M.   143, 144, 178
Oepke, A.   169, 178
Osten-Sacken, P. von der
   3, 185, 264
Otzen, B.   182, 197, 204
Overbeck, Fr.   66
Pannenberg, W.   43
Pedersen, S.   9, 207, 243, 249, 253, 256
Pegeant, R.   64
Pervo, R.I.   78
Pesch, R.   187, 192, 194, 195, 233
Peter, M.   254
Petuchowski, J.J.   265
Philippi, P.   202
Phillips, G.A.   133
Pilgaard, Aa.   8, 180
Plümacher, E.   77, 79
Polag, A.   153, 178
Porter, P.A.   136
Porteus, N.W.   183
Potterie, I. de la   87
Preuschen, E.   246
Preuss, H.D.   216
Probst, H.   55
Pryor, J.W.   105
Rad, G. von   42, 159, 178, 185, 208, 212, 260
Rahner, K.   13, 14, 15, 16
Räisänen, H.   24, 27, 32, 39, 44, 45, 54, 55, 70, 220
Reicke, B.   264
Reim, G.   103, 152, 178
Reimarus, H.S.   2
Rese, M.   37, 81
Reventlow, H. Graf   2, 26, 31, 32, 95, 143, 144, 145, 147, 178, 180, 181, 201
Riches, J.K.   224, 230
Riesenfeld, H.   256
Rigaux, B.   262
Ringe, S.   234, 237
Robbins, V.K.   191
Robinson, J.M.   161, 178
Roloff, J.   231
Rose, C.   125
Rowland, C. - Corner, M.   239
Rowland, C.   182
Rowley, H.H.   261

Rudolph, K.   148, 151, 179, 244
Ruether, R.R.   239
Salo, K.   80
Sand, A.   61
Sanders, E.P.   45, 182
Sanders, J.A.   235, 236
Sandmel, S.   257
Scheffczyk, L.   204
Schenke, G.   151, 158, 161, 168, 179
Schlink, E.   204
Schlosser, J.   248
Schmid, H.H.   147
Schmidt, W.H.   203, 205, 208, 216, 254
Schmithals, W.   149, 179, 195
Schmitt, O.   259
Schnackenburg, R.   96, 149, 152, 156, 157, 159, 162, 163, 164, 165, 166, 179, 210
Schneemelcher, W.   246
Schneider, G.   258
Schneiders, S.M.   221
Schnelle, U.   149, 179
Scholem, G.   31
Schoonenberg, P.   149, 179
Schottroff, L.   191
Schrage, W.   262
Schreiner, J.   215
Schröger, F.   112
Schubert, P.   81
Schüssler-Fiorenza, E.   223, 224, 225, 240
Schwarz, G.   154, 156, 179
Schweitzer, A.   243
Schweizer, E.   157, 169, 179
Schwier, H.   187, 191, 192
Scobie, C.H.H.   25
Scroggs, R.   222, 230
Seckler, M.   23
Seebass, H.   245
Segal, A.   225, 260
Seifrid, M.A.   80
Senior, D. - Stuhlmueller, C.   229
Siegert, F.   37, 38
Simon, R.   2
Simonsen, A.   214
Sloyan, R.B.   234
Smend, R.   40
Snodgrass, K.R.   251
Soares-Prabhu, G.   225
Spieckermann, H.   211

# INDEX OF AUTHERS

Stanton, G.   61, 62
Stauffer, E.   256
Stegemann, H.   182
Stemmer, P.   2
Stiegman, E.   261
Stolz, F.   254
Strecker, G.   65, 71, 74
Strothmann, A.   260
Stuhlmacher, P.   3, 24, 50, 58, 106, 145, 147, 179, 180, 244
Sturm, R.E.   182
Syreeni, M.   80
Talbert, C.   78, 89
Taylor, T.M.   228, 237
Theissen, G.   43, 44, 190, 191, 192, 193, 225, 228-229
Theobald, M.   149, 156, 157, 163, 165, 179
Thiselton, A.C.   127, 221
Thoma, C.   259
Thornton, J.   77, 79
Tidball, D.   225
Tracy, D.   127
Trocmé, É.   78
Uhlhorn, G.   202
Unnik, W.C. van   248
Urbach, E.E.   261
Vermes, G.   95, 100
Vermeylen, J.   132
Vielhauer, Ph.   28, 29, 36, 41, 77, 66
Vögtle, A.   225
Vokes, F.E.   264
Vos, J.S.   35, 37
Voss, G.   87, 89
Walker, R.   65, 66, 67, 69, 71, 72, 74, 75

Walker, W.O.   197
Wallis, G.   250
Walter, N.   33, 54
Warren, A. - Wellek, R.   131
Weber, H.-R.   221, 228, 230
Wedderburn, A.J.M.   4, 24, 27, 32
Weder, H.   7, 143, 150, 179
Weinrich, M.   3
Weiser, A.   212, 213
Weiss, J.   243-244
Weiss, B.   71
Welker, M.   180
Wellek, R. - Warren, A.   131
Wellhausen, J.   40
Westermann, C.   181, 204, 213
Weth, R.   201, 222
Wiebe, B.   237
Wilckens, U.   38, 258
Wilkens, W.   104
Wilson, S.   80, 249
Wimsatt, W.K.   131
Windisch, H.   98, 110
Wingren, G.   216
Wolff, H.W.   136, 208
Wright, N.T.   257, 258
Würthwein, E.   209
Wyschogrod, M.   256, 266
Yamauchi, E.M.   148, 157, 179
Yoder, J.H.   231, 235
Young, R.   134
Zager, W.   182
Zahavy, T.   255
Zerwick, M.   111
Zimmerli, W.   31, 40, 42, 106, 180, 205, 208

# INDEX OF PASSAGES

A. OLD TESTAMENT

*Gen*

| | | | |
|---|---|---|---|
| 1 | 15 | 23.10-11 | 234 |
| 1.1 Tg Neoph | 154 | 25 | 55 |
| 1.27 | 75 | 27.12,21,22 | 97 |
| 1.26 | 266 | | |
| 1.26-27 | 204 | *Exod/Ex* | |
| 1.26-28 | 209 | 3.6,7 | 9 |
| 1.31 | 207 | 3.14 | 31, 212, 259, 261 |
| 1-3 | 252 | 3.14 pal Targ | 260 |
| 1-4 | 105 | 4.22 | 9, 260 |
| 2 | 15 | 10.12,15,18,19 | 250 |
| 2.2a Tg Neoph | 154, 156 | 19 | 20 |
| 2.24 | 75 | 19.4-5 | 260 |
| 3 | 252 | 19.5 | 48, 233 |
| 3.9 | 200 | 19.6 | 223 |
| 3.15 | 99 | 20.1-22 | 257 |
| 3-4 | 101 | 20.2 | 213, 216, 260 |
| 4 | 6, 98 | 20.5-6 | 213 |
| 4.1 Ps Jon | 99 | 22.9-14 | 136 |
| 4.7 Ps Jon | 100 | 22.20 | 215 |
| 4.8 MT | 99 | 22.21-23 | 215 |
| 4.9 | 208 | 22.22 | 214 |
| 4.9-10 | 208 | 22.22-23,26-27 | 208 |
| 4.10 | 100 | 23.9 | 215, 249 |
| 4.25 | 99 | 24.8 | 118 |
| 5.1 | 204 | 24.9-11 | 17 |
| 5.3 Ps Jon | 99 | 30.13-14 | 68 |
| 9.6 | 204, 205, 264 | 31.18 | 257 |
| 12 | 10 | 32.15-16 | 257 |
| 12.1-3 | 4, 242 | 33.18-23 | 110 |
| 12.2-3 | 260 | 34.1 | 257 |
| 12.3 | 228, 257 | 34.6 | 212 |
| 12.7 | 11 | 34.6-7 | 211-212, 213 |
| 15.6 | 48, 51, 52, 252, 257 | 34.14 | 212 |
| 15.18 | 262 | *Lev* | |
| 17.5 | 51 | 9.4,6 | 110 |
| 17.5-6 | 62 | 9.23b,24 | 110 |
| 18 | 55 | 11.45 | 214, 216, 260 |
| 18.18 | 62 | 16 | 119 |
| 21.2-6 | 234 | 18.5 | 35, 160 |
| 21 | 55 | 19.2 | 217, 223, 232 |
| 22 | 142 | 19.3,4,10 | 216 |
| | | 19.9-10 | 215 |
| | | 19.9-18,32.34 | 216 |
| | | 19.12,14,16,18 | 216 |

| | | | |
|---|---|---|---|
| 19.18 | 207, 264 | 8.3 | 141 |
| 19.18 Targ N | 264 | 8.5 | 141 |
| 19.32-36 | 216 | 9.9-11 | 257 |
| 19.33 | 215 | 10.12-22 | 249 |
| 19.33-34 | 250 | 10.15 | 249 |
| 19.36 | 214, 216, 260 | 18.16-18 | 257 |
| 20.8,26 | 217 | 10.17 | 249 |
| 21.8 | 217 | 10.18 | 214 |
| 21.17-23 | 236 | 10.18-19 | 249 |
| 22.20 | 215 | 10.20-11.7 | 250 |
| 22.23 | 215 | 11.13-21 | 261 |
| 22.32-33 | 216, 217 | 15.1-18 | 234 |
| 22.33 | 260 | 15.4 | 233 |
| 23,22 | 216 | 15.4-5 | 233 |
| 23.43 | 216 | 15.6,14 | 217 |
| 24.22 | 216 | 15.12-15 | 216 |
| 25 | 234 | 16.1 | 261 |
| 25.38 | 216 | 16.13-15 | 217 |
| 25.55 | 216 | 16.19 | 250 |
| 26.13,45 | 216 | 20.5-8 | 236 |
| | | 21.23 | 36 |
| *Num* | | 24.17 | 215 |
| 14.18 | 212 | 24.18 | 215 |
| 15.16 | 215 | 24.19-21 | 215 |
| 15.37-41 | 261 | 26.5-9 | 260 |
| | | 26.9-11 | 217 |
| *Deut/Dtn* | | 26.16-19 | 254 |
| 1.17 | 250 | 27.19 | 215 |
| 4 | 254 | 28.29 | 97 |
| 4.12-15 | 257 | 29.4 | 55, 95 |
| 4.13,19,28-29,31, | | 30.11-14 | 36 |
| 35,39 | 254 | 30.12-14 | 36 |
| 4.20,34 | 260 | 32.18 | 100 |
| 4.31 | 212 | 32.43 LXX | 112, 117 |
| 5.4-31 | 257 | 33.2 | 254 |
| 5.6 | 214, 260 | | |
| 5.9-10 | 213 | *Josh/Jos* | |
| 5.13-15 | 216 | 24.2-13 | 260 |
| 6.4 | 247, 255, 256 | | |
| 6.4-5 | 207, 254, 255 | *Judg/Ri* | |
| 6.4-9 | 261 | 5.4 | 254 |
| 6.5 | 254, 265 | | |
| 6.20-24 | 260 | *Ruth/Rut* | |
| 6.21 | 260, 261 | 2.2 | 215 |
| 6-8 | 140 | | |
| 7 | 254 | *1 Sam* | |
| 7.6 | 141 | 12.6,8 | 260 |
| 7.6-8 | 213-214, 250, 260 | *2 Sam* | |
| 7.9-10 | 213 | 7.12-16 | 62 |
| 8 | 141 | 7.14 | 112, 113 |
| 8.2 | 141 | 7.14a | 124 |

274                INDEX OF PASSAGES

| | | | |
|---|---|---|---|
| 7.14b | 124 | 23.1-2 | 137 |
| 7.22-24 | 260 | 23.6 | 117 |
| 7.23 | 261 | 24 | 233 |
| 24.14 | 213 | 24.3-6 | 118 |
| | | 25.6 | 212 |
| *1 Kings/1 Kön* | | 26.8 | 117 |
| 8.51,53 | 260 | 27.1 | 161 |
| | | 27.4-5 | 117 |
| *2 Kings/2 Kön* | | 30.5-6 | 213 |
| 13.23 | 214 | 32.1-2 | 51 |
| | | 32 (33) | 154 |
| *2 Chron/2 Kön* | | 33.6 | 156 |
| 2.17-18 | 215 | 35.8 | 55 |
| 19.7 | 250 | 36.8-10 | 117 |
| | | 40.7-9 | 6 |
| *1 Esra* LXX | | 40(39).7-9 | 112, 123 |
| 4.39 | 250 | 40(39).8 | 123 |
| | | 40(39)9a | 123 |
| *Neh* | | 44.7a LXX | 115 |
| 9.5-37 | 261 | 44.8b | 115 |
| 9.17 | 212 | 45 | 124, 125 |
| | | 45.7 | 152 |
| *Job/Hiob* | | 45.7a Targ | 115 |
| 1.6 | 142 | 45.7-8 | 6 |
| 3.20 | 160 | 45(44).7-8 | 112, 113, 115 |
| 5.14 | 97 | 51.3 | 212 |
| 12.25 | 97 | 56.14 | 160 |
| 28 | 149 | 63.2-5 | 117 |
| 31.13 | 205 | 65.2-5 | 117 |
| 31.13-15 | 208 | 68.6 | 214 |
| 31.15 | 205 | 69.22-23 | 55 |
| 31.16 | 205 | 79.8 | 212 |
| 31.17-18 | 205 | 80.9 | 260 |
| 31.19-20 | 206 | 81.11 | 214, 216, 260 |
| 34.19 | 206, 250 | 82.6-7 | 254 |
| | | 84.2-5 | 117 |
| *Ps* | | 86.5,15 | 212 |
| 2 | 124, 125 | 86.15 | 212 |
| 2.7 | 112, 113-114, 114 | 89.12 | 233 |
| | | 90 | 204 |
| 2.7-8 | 6 | 95.5 | 233 |
| 2.8 | 114 | 95(94).7-11 | 112 |
| 8 | 125 | 96.5 | 254 |
| 8.5-7 | 112, 113, 114-115, 115 | 96.7 LXX | 112, 117 |
| | | 101.26 LXX | 110 |
| 8.6 | 204 | 102(101).26-28 | 112, 117 |
| 8.6a LXX | 115 | 103.6 | 51 |
| 9.13 | 214 | 103.8 | 211 |
| 10.12,14 | 214 | 103.13-17 | 204 |
| 15.1-5 | 118 | 104(103).4 | 112, 117 |
| 18.5 LXX | 245 | 106(107).20 | 154 |
| 22(21).23 | 112 | 106.43-46 | 214 |

# INDEX OF PASSAGES

| | | | |
|---|---|---|---|
| 110 | 124, 125 | 8.14 | 36, 97 |
| 110(109).1 | 112, 113, 115-116, 116 | 8.17-18 | 112 |
| | | 18.7 | 227 |
| 110.1,4 | 6 | 26.20 | 112 |
| 110.4 | 6, 115 | 27 | 124 |
| 110(109).4 | 112, 113, 116, 122 | 27.2-6 | 131, 134 |
| | | 27.6 | 131 |
| 111.4 | 212 | 27.9 | 56 |
| 116.5 | 212 | 28.16 | 36 |
| 118.22-23 | 70 | 29.16 | 204 |
| 127.1 | 233 | 29.18 | 95, 96 |
| 145.8-9 | 212 | 29.18-19 | 95 |
| 145.14 | 214 | 33.14-16 | 118 |
| 146.7-9 | 214 | 42.6-7 | 95 |
| | | 42.14-16 | 137 |
| *Prov/Spr* | | 43.8-10 | 95, 97 |
| 1.32-33 | 155 | 44.6 | 254 |
| 3.19 | 156 | 45.5,21-22 | 254 |
| 8 | 149 | 45.9 | 204 |
| 8.22 | 150, 156 | 45.18-25 | 227 |
| 8.22-36 | 261 | 45.23 | 154 |
| 8.27 LXX | 152 | 45.24 | 51 |
| 8.27-30 | 156 | 49.6 | 228 |
| 8.27-31 | 156 | 49.8-12 | 137 |
| 8.30 MT | 152 | 51 | 37 |
| 8.30 LXX | 152 | 53 | 1, 138 |
| 8.30b,31 | 157 | 53.1 | 97 |
| 8.31 | 165 | 53.7 | 135, 138 |
| 8.35 | 159 | 54.7-8 | 213 |
| 14.31 | 205 | 55.11 | 154 |
| 17.5 | 205 | 58.6-7 | 202 |
| 22.2 | 206 | 58.6-8 | 215 |
| 29.13 | 206 | 59.9-10 | 95, 96, 97 |
| | | 59.10 | 55, 95, 97 |
| *Isa/Jes* | | 59.10 MT | 95 |
| 1.10-31 | 215 | 59,20-21 | 56 |
| 1.16-17 | 214 | 60.1-3 | 12 |
| 1-39 | 128, 131 | 60.1-22 | 227 |
| 2 | 227 | 61 | 234, 235 |
| 2.2-3 | 227 | 61.1-2 | 234, 239 |
| 2.3 | 260 | 61,2 | 234 |
| 5 | 129, 130 | 66.18 | 12 |
| 5.1-7 | 131, 132, 133, 134 | | |
| | | *Jer* | |
| 5.8-24 | 133 | 2.6 | 260 |
| 6 | 11, 12, 17 | 5.21 | 95 |
| 6.5-7 | 4 | 5.21-31 | 215 |
| 6.6-7 | 12 | 7.1-15 | 215 |
| 6.9 | 96 | 11.4 | 260 |
| 6.9-10 | 6, 95, 97 | 16.14-15 | 260 |
| 6.10 | 97 | 18.1-6 | 204 |
| 7 | 1 | 25.12 | 183 |

| | | | |
|---|---|---|---|
| 29.10 | 183 | 1.10 | 55 |
| 31 | 64 | 2.25 | 55 |
| 31.31-34 | 6, 112, 247 | 5.12-14 | 136 |
| 31(38).31-34 | 118, 122 | 5.12-15 | 136 |
| 31(38).32 | 118 | 5.14 | 136, 137 |
| 31(38).33-34 | 122 | 6.1 | 136 |
| 32 | 64 | 6.1-3 | 136 |
| 32.18 | 213 | 12.10 | 260 |
| 34.8-22 | 234 | 13.4 | 254, 260 |

*Ezek/Ez*  
*Amos/Am*

| | | | |
|---|---|---|---|
| 11 | 64 | 2.6-10 | 216 |
| 22.23-31 | 215 | 3.12 | 136-137 |
| 20.5-10 | 260 | 9.7 | 260 |
| 34 | 137, 138 | | |
| 34.2-6 | 137 | *Jonah/Jon* | |
| 34.12,31 | 137 | 4.2 | 212 |
| 36 | 54 | | |

*Micah/Mich*

*Dan*

| | | | |
|---|---|---|---|
| 2.34,44-45 | 71 | 4.5 | 254, 260 |
| 4.8,18 | 184 | 6.4 | 216 |
| 5.11,14 | 184 | | |
| 7 | 136 | *Hab* | |
| 7.13-14 | 188 | 2.4 | 50, 51, 53 |
| 7.13-14,27 | 197 | 2.3-4 | 112 |
| 7-8 | 183 | | |
| 8 | 136 | *Zech/Sach* | |
| 8.13 | 184 | 7.8-14 | 215 |
| 8.25 | 260 | 14.9 | 256 |
| 9 | 8, 180, 183, 184, 186, 187, 188, 189 | *Mal* | |
| | | 2.10 | 206 |
| 9.2 | 183 | | |
| 9.4b-19 | 183 | **B. THE INTERTESTAMENTAL LITERATURE** | |
| 9.9 | 210 | | |
| 9.16-18,24 | 183 | | |
| 9.23 | 184 | *Ecclus/Sir* | |
| 9.24 | 183, 186, 187 | Prol | 245 |
| 9.24-27 | 8 | 1.1,4 | 261 |
| 9.25 | 186 | 4.1-6 | 205 |
| 9.27 | 188 | 4.10 | 168 |
| 10.11,19 | 184 | 4.11 | 168 |
| 10-12 | 183 | 4.12 | 159 |
| 11.31 | 184, 188 | 4.22 | 250 |
| 11.33 | 185 | 14.3 | 150 |
| 12.6-7 LXX | 189 | 17.3 | 204 |
| 12.7-12 | 196 | 24 | 149, 160, 166, 168 |
| 12.11 | 184, 188 | 24.3-6 | 156, 157, 165 |
| *Hos* | | 24.6-7 | 165, 166 |
| 1.9-10 | 242 | | |

| | | | |
|---|---|---|---|
| 24.9 | 261 | 2.2-5 | 236 |
| 24.23 | 149, 175 | 4.11 | 95 |
| 35.13 | 250 | 9.11 | 157 |
| | | 9.20 | 229 |
| *Wis/Weish* | | 10.13-16 | 255 |
| 2.13,16,18 | 168 | | |
| 2,18 | 168 | 1QM | |
| 2.23 | 204 | 2.4-6 | 236 |
| 5.1-4 | 168 | | |
| 7.7 | 166 | *Bar* | |
| 7.12 | 156 | 2 | 168 |
| 7.21 | 156 | 3.9-4.4 | 149 |
| 7.22-8.1 | 149 | 3.14 | 160 |
| 7.27-28 | 162 | 3-4 | 160 |
| 8.1 | 156, 165 | 3.38 | 165 |
| 8.6 | 155 | 4.1 | 160 |
| 9.9 | 152, 261 | | |
| 9.18 | 155 | *Ps Sal* | |
| 10.1,4,5,6,9,13,15 | 155 | 2.18 | 250 |
| 18 | 149, 154, 155, 168 | *4 Macc* | |
| | | 18.9 | 99 |
| 18.13 | 168 | | |
| 18.14-15 | 154 | slHen | |
| 18.14-16 | 154 | 13.58-59 | 205 |
| 18.15 | 149 | | |
| | | *Vita Adae et Evae* | |
| *12 Patriarkers Testamenter* | | 20-21 | 21 |
| TJudah | | | |
| 18.6 | 96 | *Philo* | |
| | | Leg All | |
| TGad | | II.86 | 153 |
| 3.3 | 96 | III.175 | 153 |
| 5.5 | 205 | | |
| | | Deus imm | |
| TSim | | 61 | 37 |
| 2.7 | 96 | 62 | 37 |
| TBenj | | Conf ling | |
| 7-8 | 101 | 146 | 153 |
| *äthHen* | | Rer div her | |
| 42 | 149 | 126 | 153 |
| *Jub* | | Somn | |
| 5.16 | 250 | I.229-230 | 153 |
| *Qumran* | | Decal | |
| CD | | 18-19 | 257 |
| 1.9 | 95 | | |
| | | Spec Leg | |
| 1QS | | 2.189 | 257 |
| 1.10 | 229 | | |

| | | | |
|---|---|---|---|
| 3.7 | 257 | 5.38-48 | 229 |
| 4.132 | 257 | 5.45 | 229, 230, 232 |
| 4.137-142 | 255 | 5.48 | 232 |
| | | 5-7 | 233 |
| Vit.Cont. | | 6.3 | 203 |
| 3.25 | 245 | 6.12 | 237 |
| | | 7.7-8 | 226 |
| Leg | | 7.13 | 226 |
| 281-284 | 245 | 7.23 | 72 |
| | | 8.10 | 73 |
| Quaest. in Gen. | | 8.11 | 69, 227 |
| I.59 | 99 | 8.11-12 | 226 |
| | | 8.29 | 67 |
| *Josephus* | | 9.13 | 217 |
| BJ | | 9.34 | 67 |
| 2.398 | 245 | 10 | 5, 67 |
| 6.312-313 | 187 | 10.18 | 67 |
| | | 10.22-23 | 67 |
| Ant | | 10.40 | 207 |
| 1,2.1 (§.53) | 99 | 11.2-6 | 237 |
| 4.212-213 | 261 | 11.5 | 236 |
| 3.83-94,101 | 257 | 11.12 | 62 |
| 14.114-115 | 245 | 11.13 | 62 |
| | | 11.19 | 153 |
| C Ap | | 11.25-30 | 68 |
| 1.37-41 | 245 | 11.29 | 210 |
| 2.282 | 245 | 12.6 | 63 |
| | | 12.7 | 217, 218 |
| | | 12.9-14 | 206, 218 |
| | | 12.25 | 226 |
| C. NEW TESTAMENT | | 12.34 | 67 |
| | | 12.41,42 | 63 |
| | | 13.13-15 | 74, 96 |
| *Matt/Mt* | | 13.37-38 | 73 |
| 1.23 | 76 | 13.39,40,49 | 75 |
| 2.15 | 67, 263 | 14.33 | 68 |
| 3.2 | 62 | 15 | 73 |
| 3.8-9 | 251 | 15.3-9 | 218 |
| 3.9 | 69 | 15.24 | 238 |
| 3.15 | 63, 64, 67 | 15.28 | 73 |
| 4 | 140 | 16.16 | 68 |
| 4.1 | 142 | 16.18 | 237 |
| 4.1-11 | 7, 140 | 16.19 | 67 |
| 4.3,6 | 67 | 17.5 | 67 |
| 5,3-6 | 236, 237 | 17.9 | 66 |
| 5.3-12 | 232 | 17.24-26 | 68 |
| 5.13 | 232 | 18.18 | 67 |
| 5.13-16 | 227, 242 | 18.23-35 | 237 |
| 5.14 | 227, 232 | 18.26-27 | 210 |
| 5.15ff | 63 | 19.1-12 | 75 |
| 5.17 | 62, 255 | 19.4-5 | 75 |
| 5.17-48 | 252 | 19,8 | 75 |

| | | | |
|---|---|---|---|
| 19.17 | 256 | *Mark/Mk* | |
| 19.28 | 73 | 1.1 | 194 |
| 20.28 | 64 | 1.2-8 | 245 |
| 21.14-16 | 228 | 1.9-11 | 198 |
| 21.18ff. | 70 | 1.9-11,12-13 | 198 |
| 21.19 | 70 | 1.12-13 | 198 |
| 21.23-27 | 69 | 1.14-15 | 194 |
| 21.28-32 | 70 | 2.7 | 256 |
| 21.33-46 | 70 | 2.10 | 197 |
| 21.34ff. | 71 | 2.10,28 | 197 |
| 21.40 | 70 | 2.13-17 | 229 |
| 21.41 | 70 | 2.27 | 206 |
| 21.43 | 228 | 2.27-28 | 257 |
| 21.44 | 71 | 2.28 | 197 |
| 22.1-14 | 70 | 3.15 | 198 |
| 22.7 | 71 | 3.23-27 | 226 |
| 22.8-10 | 71 | 3.31-35 | 229 |
| 22.11-12 | 72 | 6.7 | 198 |
| 22.37 | 256 | 7 | 73 |
| 23.8 | 257 | 7.37 | 206 |
| 23.9 | 256, 257 | 8.29-30,31-38 | 194 |
| 23.10 | 257 | 8.31 | 89, 197 |
| 23.23 | 218 | 8.34-38 | 197 |
| 23.37-39 | 71 | 8.37 | 194 |
| 24.3 | 75 | 8.38 | 197 |
| 24.1-2 | 71 | 9 | 89 |
| 24.9,14 | 71 | 9.9,31 | 89 |
| 24.14 | 75 | 9.10 | 197 |
| 24.14 | 195 | 9.31 | 197 |
| 24.15 | 188 | 9.47 | 226 |
| 25 | 207 | 10.1-12 | 75 |
| 25.10-12 | 226 | 10.6-9 | 75 |
| 25.11,24-30,31-46 | 72 | 10.15 | 226 |
| 25.31-46 | 201 | 10.17-22 | 237 |
| 25.40,45 | 206 | 10.18 | 218, 256 |
| 25.32 | 71 | 10,21 | 229 |
| 25.34-40 | 203 | 10.29 | 194 |
| 25.44 | 201, 202 | 10.30 | 229 |
| 26.13 | 75 | 10.32-34 | 197 |
| 26.28 | 64 | 10.34 | 89 |
| 26.45,49 | 67 | 10.41-45 | 231 |
| 26.63 | 68 | 10.45 | 197, 198, 199, 202 |
| 26.64 | 73 | | |
| 27.25 | 75 | 11.1-11,27-12.12,35-37 | 192 |
| 27.43 | 68 | 11.15-17 | 192 |
| 27.51-54 | 73 | 11.17 | 227 |
| 27.54 | 67, 73 | 12.10-11 | 192, 198 |
| 28.15 | 71 | 12.14 | 250 |
| 28.16-20 | 66, 73 | 12.28-34 | 207, 250 |
| 28.18-20 | 68, 71 | 12.29,32 | 256 |
| 28.20 | 5, 73, 75 | 12.30 | 265 |
| | | 12.31 | 265 |

| | | | |
|---|---|---|---|
| 12.35-37 | 192, 257 | 14.62b | 197 |
| 12.38-40 | 218 | 15.38 | 192 |
| 12.41-44 | 229 | 16.6 | 89 |
| 13 | 8, 180, 183, 187, 188, 189, 192, 198 | *Luke/Lk* | |
| | | 1.3 | 91 |
| 13,2 | 187 | 1.4 | 84 |
| 13.3-4 | 187, 188 | 1.7 | 90 |
| 13.4 | 189, 190, 191 | 1.27 | 87 |
| 13.4b | 189, 190 | 1.32,35 | 87 |
| 13.5-6 | 191, 192 | 1.32,69 | 87 |
| 13.5-8 | 190 | 1.32,54,67,69 | 86 |
| 13.5-23 | 195 | 1.46-54 | 90 |
| 13.5-37 | 187 | 1.47 | 87, 88, 89 |
| 13.6 | 191 | 1.47,69,77 | 90 |
| 13.7 | 192 | 1.54 | 86 |
| 13.7-8 | 194 | 1.54,69 | 86 |
| 13.7-8,14-20 | 195 | 1.69 | 90 |
| 13.7-8,14-20,24-27 | 188 | 1.69,71,77 | 90 |
| 13.9 | 67, 194 | 1.70 | 111 |
| 13.9-11 | 193 | 2.1-3 | 82 |
| 13.9-13 | 193, 195, 196 | 2.4 | 86, 87 |
| 13.10 | 194, 195 | 2.4,11,14 | 87 |
| 13.11 | 194 | 2.10f. | 90 |
| 13.13 | 195 | 2.11 | 87, 90 |
| 13.14 | 188, 190, 191, 196 | 2.11,26 | 87 |
| | | 2.11,30-32 | 90 |
| 13.14a | 190 | 2.14 | 90 |
| 13.14-20 | 195 | 2.21 | 87 |
| 13.14-20(21-23) | 195 | 2.22-24 | 87 |
| 13.14-23 | 190, 196 | 2.26 | 86 |
| 13.18-20 | 196 | 2.30 | 88, 89 |
| 13.21-22 | 191 | 2.36 | 86 |
| 13.21-23 | 191, 192 | 2.43 | 86 |
| 13.23b | 191 | 2.41-52 | 87 |
| 13.24 | 196 | 3.1-2 | 82 |
| 13.24-25 | 195, 196 | 3.4ff. | 83 |
| 13.24-27 | 190, 195, 197 | 3.6 | 88, 89 |
| 13.26 | 188, 197 | 3.15 | 83, 86 |
| 13.26-27 | 198 | 3.21-22 | 87 |
| 13.28-37 | 196 | 3.23-28 | 87 |
| 13.29 | 196 | 3.31 | 87 |
| 13.32 | 196 | 4 | 234, 235, 237 |
| 13.33-37 | 196, 197 | 4.16-30 | 233, 234, |
| 13.34 | 198 | 4.18 | 86, 229, 236 |
| 14.3-9 | 237 | 4.18f. | 90 |
| 14.21,41 | 197 | 4.18ff. | 83 |
| 14.22-24 | 199 | 5.21ff. | 90 |
| 14.24 | 198 | 6.9 | 90 |
| 14.25 | 226 | 6.20-23 | 229 |
| 14.62 | 197 | 6.36 | 210, 218, 250 |
| 14.62a | 197 | 7.20ff.,47ff. | 90 |

| | | | |
|---|---|---|---|
| 7.22 | 236 | 23.35 | 86 |
| 7.22-23 | 229 | 24.3 | 87 |
| 7.26ff. | 83 | 24.7,46 | 88 |
| 7.35 | 153, 168 | 24.24-26 | 86 |
| 7.36-50 | 229, 237 | 24.25ff.,44ff. | 83 |
| 7.47ff. | 90 | 24.25,45 | 67 |
| 7.50 | 90 | 24.26 | 84 |
| 8.1-3 | 229 | 24.26ff.,44ff. | 88 |
| 8.48,50 | 90 | 24.26,46 | 83 |
| 9.8,19 | 86 | 24.26,46f | 84 |
| 9.20 | 86 | 24.27 | 245 |
| 9.22 | 88 | 24.34 | 88 |
| 9.45 | 67 | 24.46f. | 90 |
| 9.51 | 89 | 24.47 | 90 |
| 10.16 | 248 | 24.51 | 89 |
| 10.25ff. | 90 | 25.51 | 68 |
| 10.30-37 | 229 | | |
| 11.36 | 164 | *John/Joh* | |
| 11.49-51 | 153 | 1 | 97 |
| 13.28-29 | 227 | 1.1 | 153 |
| 13.33 | 90 | 1.1-2 | 7, 150 |
| 13.34-35 | 153 | 1.1,18 | 152 |
| 14 | 236, 237 | 1.3 | 156, 159, 165 |
| 14.12-14 | 203, 236 | 1.3-5 | 7, 150 |
| 14.13-14 | 229 | 1.3,10 | 110, 207 |
| 14.13,21 | 236 | 1.4 | 159, 164 |
| 14.16-24 | 236 | 1.4b | 159 |
| 15.1-2 | 229 | 1.5 | 96, 162, 164, 165 |
| 15.11-32 | 70 | | |
| 16.1-8 | 237 | 1.6-8 | 163 |
| 16.16 | 65 | 1.9 | 163, 165 |
| 16.17 | 80 | 1.9-12 | 7, 150, 163 |
| 16.19-31 | 229 | 1.10 | 165, 166 |
| 17.11-19 | 229 | 1.11 | 105, 166, 167 |
| 17.25 | 90 | 1.12 | 168, 169 |
| 18.19 | 256 | 1.12a | 167, 168 |
| 18.31ff. | 83, 88 | 1.12ab | 167 |
| 18.31,33 | 83, | 1.12b | 169 |
| 18.33 | 81, 88 | 1.12-13 | 100 |
| 18.34 | 67 | 1.14 | 4, 11, 150, 153, 161, 162, 175 |
| 18.38f. | 86, 87 | | |
| 19.1-10 | 237 | | |
| 19.9 | 90 | 1.14a | 149 |
| 19.9f. | 90 | 1.14,16 | 7 |
| 19.38 | 87 | 1.16 | 150, 169 |
| 19.38,42 | 90 | 1.18 | 152 |
| 20.41 | 86 | 2.22 | 245 |
| 20.44 | 87 | 1.16 | 150, 169 |
| 21.22 | 84 | 1.18 | 152 |
| 22.19f.,37 | 90 | 2.22 | 155 |
| 22.69 | 89 | 3.1-21 | 169 |
| 23.2,3,37,38 | 87 | 3.8 | 163 |

| | | | |
|---|---|---|---|
| 3.15-16 | 152 | 12.35-50 | 96 |
| 3.16 | 100 | 12.35,46 | 162 |
| 3.16-21,31-36 | 94 | 12.37-40 | 96 |
| 3.19 | 162 | 12.40 | 95, 96, 97 |
| 3.19-20 | 101 | 12.41 | 104 |
| 4.1-42 | 229 | 12.42 | 96 |
| 4.22 | 6, 103 | 12.44 | 248 |
| 4.22-24 | 9 | 13.20 | 207 |
| 4.27 | 229 | 13.33,36 | 97 |
| 4.41 | 155 | 12.38 | 97 |
| 4.50 | 155 | 12.44-50 | 94 |
| 5.1-9 | 263 | 12.48 | 155 |
| 5.14 | 152 | 13.34 | 98 |
| 5.17 | 206, 207 | 14.4,5 | 97 |
| 5.24 | 155 | 14.6 | 160, 164 |
| 5.30,38 | 248 | 14.9 | 4, 11 |
| 5.38 | 155 | 14.23-24 | 155 |
| 5.39-40 | 106 | 15 | 134 |
| 6.29 | 248 | 15.12 | 98 |
| 7 | 105 | 15.27 | 97 |
| 7.7 | 101 | 16.5 | 97 |
| 7.8 | 93 | 17.6 | 155 |
| 7.28 | 248 | 17.10 | 152 |
| 7.33-36 | 94 | 17.14 | 155 |
| 7.49 | 73 | 19.28-30 | 104 |
| 8 | 100, 104, 106 | 20.9 | 89 |
| 8.12 | 97, 98, 162, 164 | 20,28 | 152, 153 |
| | | 20.31 | 97 |
| 8.16,29 | 248 | | |
| 8.21 | 97 | *Acts/Apg* | |
| 8.21-27 | 94 | 1.1 | 88 |
| 8.39-41 | 100, 101 | 1.2,9,11 | 89 |
| 8.40 | 100 | 1.6 | 87 |
| 8.41 | 100 | 1.9-11 | 68 |
| 8.44 | 6, 103, 105 | 1.16 | 86 |
| 8.48 | 100 | 1.16f.,20 | 84 |
| 8.51 | 155 | 1.20 | 81 |
| 8.55 | 155 | 1.20ff. | 84 |
| 8.59 | 100 | 2.9-11 | 245 |
| 9 | 103 | 2.17ff. | 84 |
| 9.4-5 | 96 | 2.19-21 | 90 |
| 9.39 | 96 | 2.21 | 90 |
| 10 | 139 | 2.22f. | 85 |
| 10.11-12 | 139 | 2.22,32 | 88 |
| 10.30 | 152 | 2.24ff.,30ff. | 88 |
| 10.34-35 | 103 | 2.25ff. | 81 |
| 11.9 | 97 | 2.25ff.,26 | 87 |
| 11.52 | 100 | 2.25ff.,30 | 83 |
| 12 | 98 | 2.25ff.,38 | 90 |
| 12.16 | 245 | 2.27 | 85 |
| 12.26 | 202 | 2.29 | 86 |
| 12.35 | 96 | 2.29-36 | 87 |

# INDEX OF PASSAGES

| | | | |
|---|---|---|---|
| 2.31 | 86 | 10.41 | 88 |
| 2.33 | 89 | 10.43 | 84, 88, 90 |
| 2.36 | 87 | 10.47 | 90 |
| 2.36-41 | 90 | 11.9 | 249 |
| 2.38 | 90 | 11.17 | 87 |
| 2.44-45 | 233 | 11.19-26 | 248 |
| 3.13 | 90 | 11.28 | 82 |
| 3.13-15 | 89 | 11.33-34 | 249 |
| 3.13,24 | 83 | 13.14ff. | 82 |
| 3.13,26 | 86 | 13.16-25 | 83 |
| 3.14 | 85 | 13.17-25 | 83 |
| 3.15 | 86, 88 | 13.22-23 | 83, 90 |
| 3,15,19,26 | 90 | 13.23 | 83, 87, 88, 90 |
| 3.17 | 69 | 13.23,36 | 90 |
| 3.18 | 86, 90, 111 | 13.27 | 81, 85 |
| 3.18ff. | 88 | 13.28-30,33 | 90 |
| 3.18,21 | 81 | 13.29 | 88 |
| 3.18,24 | 83, 88 | 13.30,37 | 262 |
| 3.21 | 84 | 13.32ff. | 81 |
| 3.22 | 83, 86, 89 | 13.32,34-37 | 87 |
| 3.23 | 84 | 13.33 | 81 |
| 3.26 | 88 | 13.33ff. | 83, 88 |
| 4.9 | 90 | 13.33,34 | 88 |
| 4.10 | 88, 262 | 13.34 | 86 |
| 4.10ff. | 88 | 13.34-35 | 85 |
| 4.12 | 90 | 13.37ff. | 90 |
| 4.24 | 86 | 13.41 | 84 |
| 4.25 | 81, 86 | 13.46 | 69 |
| 4.25ff. | 83, 84 | 13.47 | 84 |
| 4.25,27,30 | 86 | 14.1ff. | 82 |
| 4.26 | 86, 87 | 14.9 | 90 |
| 4.27 | 86 | 14.11-18 | 247 |
| 4.35 | 233 | 14.14ff. | 82 |
| 5.20 | 90 | 14.16 | 90 |
| 5.30 | 88, 89, 90, 262 | 15.2 | 87 |
| 5.31 | 86, 87, 89, 90 | 15.8 | 90 |
| 7.2-53 | 83 | 15.15 | 81 |
| 7.37 | 83, 88 | 15,15-18 | 87 |
| 7.37f. | 86 | 15.15ff. | 84 |
| 7.42 | 81 | 15.16 | 86 |
| 7.52 | 85 | 15.21 | 84 |
| 7.56 | 89 | 16.13ff. | 82 |
| 8.32ff. | 83 | 16.14 | 82 |
| 8.37 | 85 | 17.1ff.,10ff.,17 | 82 |
| 9.20 | 85, | 17.38 | 3, 84, 86, 88, 90 |
| 10 | 73 | | |
| 10.3-6,22,29b-33 | 249 | 17.7 | 87 |
| 10.15 | 249 | 17.21ff. | 88 |
| 10.34-43 | 248 | 17.26ff. | 82 |
| 10.35 | 248 | 17.29-30 | 246 |
| 10.36ff. | 85 | 17.31 | 88 |
| 10,38 | 86, 90 | 18.2,12 | 82 |

| | | | |
|---|---|---|---|
| 18.4 | 82 | 2.9,16 | 251 |
| 18.28 | 83 | 2.11 | 250, 251 |
| 19.2ff. | 90 | 2.12-13 | 252 |
| 19.8 | 82 | 2.14-15 | 251 |
| 20.27 | 88 | 2.17-24 | 251 |
| 20.28 | 90 | 2.18 | 251 |
| 21.21 | 24 | 2.20 | 251 |
| 22.14 | 85 | 2.21-22 | 252 |
| 22.16 | 90 | 2.25-29 | 251 |
| 24.14 | 87 | 3.4,28 | 251 |
| 25.11 | 82 | 3.8 | 38 |
| 26.6f. | 81 | 3.21 | 17, 19, 37, 38 |
| 26.18 | 90 | 3.21-26 | 51 |
| 26.22 | 83, 84 | 3.21-31 | 51, 53 |
| 26.22f. | 83, 84, 88 | 3.22 | 252 |
| 26.23 | 86, 90 | 3.23 | 20, 21, 209, 252 |
| 26.28 | 90 | 3.25 | 4, 12 |
| 27.1 | 82 | 3.28 | 258 |
| 28.20 | 81 | 3.30 | 257, 258, 265 |
| 28.25-28 | 96 | 3.31 | 255 |
| 28.26ff. | 84 | 4 | 4, 48, 52, 53 |
| 28.26-27 | 74 | 4.1 | 52 |
| 28.28 | 88, 89 | 4.1-25 | 258 |
| | | 4.3 | 51 |
| *Rom/Röm* | | 4.5 | 29, 263 |
| 1.1-2 | 49 | 4.6 | 51, 251 |
| 1.1-4 | 49 | 4.9-12 | 256 |
| 1.1-7,8-17 | 48 | 4.11 | 55 |
| 1.2 | 53, 111 | 4.14 | 52 |
| 1.3-4 | 49, 153 | 4.16 | 52 |
| 1.14 | 253 | 4.16-22 | 262 |
| 1.16 | 51 | 4.17 | 29, 30, 51, 262 |
| 1.16-17 | 17, 18, 50, 53 | 4.17b | 51 |
| 1.17 | 18, 19, 51, 55 | 4.17-21 | 30 |
| 1.18,23 | 251 | 4.23-24 | 48, 52 |
| 1.18,25 | 251 | 4.23-25 | 5 |
| 1.18-32 | 251 | 4.24 | 41, 214, 262 |
| 1.18-3.9 | 21 | 5.6-8 | 257, 265 |
| 1.18-3.20,21-31 | 250 | 5-8 | 53, 265 |
| 1.19 | 251 | 5.12c | 252 |
| 1.22-23 | 252 | 5.12,18-19 | 251 |
| 1.23 | 209, 247 | 5.12-19 | 252, 258 |
| 1.25 | 250 | 5.15 | 252 |
| 2 | 250 | 6.2 | 35 |
| 2.1 | 52, 250 | 6.4 | 209 |
| 2.1-5,29 | 251 | 6.4-7,11 | 263 |
| 2.3 | 250 | 6.21 | 37 |
| 2.4 | 210 | 6.22 | 37 |
| 2.5-11 | 203 | 7.4 | 263 |
| 2.6-8 | 252 | 7.7-24 | 29, 252 |
| 2.8,20 | 251 | 7.24 | 251 |
| 2.9-10 | 251 | 8 | 22, 39, 253 |

| | | | |
|---|---|---|---|
| 8.4 | 38, 255 | 11.11-36 | 33 |
| 8.11 | 214, 262 | 11.13 | 202 |
| 8.19-22 | 263 | 11.22 | 210 |
| 8.21 | 252 | 11.25 | 33, 34 |
| 8.29 | 209 | 11.25-26 | 54 |
| 8.32 | 30 | 11.25-32 | 54 |
| 8.34 | 263 | 11.26 | 33, 34, 54, 55 |
| 9 | 33, 37, 53, 54, 55 | 11.26-27 | 56 |
| | | 11.27 | 56 |
| 9.1-5 | 33, 53, 54 | 11.28 | 55 |
| 9.4 | 29 | 11.29 | 33, 34 |
| 9.4-5 | 34, 75 | 11.30-32 | 56 |
| 9.6 | 33, 54 | 11,33-36 | 39 |
| 9.6-29 | 33, 54 | 11.36 | 156, 157 |
| 9.8 | 33 | 12.1 | 210 |
| 9.12 | 248 | 12.2 | 251 |
| 9.14-16 | 56 | 12.17-18 | 253 |
| 9.16-23 | 39 | 12.18 | 251 |
| 9.20-21 | 204 | 12.21 | 229 |
| 9.22 | 210 | 13.8-10 | 253 |
| 9.29 | 33 | 13.9 | 252, 264, 265 |
| 9.30 | 37 | 13.10 | 255 |
| 9.30-33 | 37 | 13.14 | 253 |
| 9.30-31 | 37 | 14.1-23 | 253 |
| 9.30-10,21 | 54 | 14.14 | 249 |
| 9.30-11,10 | 55 | 14.15 | 107 |
| 9.31 | 38, 54 | 15.1-13 | 263 |
| 9.31-32 | 53 | 15.3-4,8-9 | 253 |
| 9.33 | 36 | 15.4 | 5, 41, 48, 64 |
| 9-11 | 27, 32, 53, 54, 55, 252, 253 | 15.6 | 259 |
| | | 15.6,7 | 252 |
| 10 | 37, 54, 56 | 15.24 | 253 |
| 10.1 | 37 | 16.27 | 256 |
| 10.2-3 | 37 | | |
| 10.3 | 54 | *1 Cor/1 Kor* | |
| 10.4 | 36, 37 | 1.26-31 | 231 |
| 10.4-13 | 37 | 3.5 | 202 |
| 10.5 | 35, 36, 37, 39 | 5.7 | 138 |
| 10.5-8 | 28, 35 | 6.14 | 262 |
| 10.6 | 37 | 8.1 | 257 |
| 10.6-8 | 36, 37 | 8.1-3 | 258 |
| 10.8-12 | 253 | 8.1-11.1 | 258 |
| 10.9 | 262 | 8.3 | 258 |
| 10.12 | 250 | 8.6 | 110, 146, 157, 207, 257, 258, 259 |
| 10.18 | 245 | | |
| 11 | 33, 54, 56 | | |
| 11.2,28-29 | 253 | 8.8 | 249 |
| 11.7,26 | 55 | 8.11-12 | 207, 258 |
| 11.8 | 36, 55 | 9.1 | 4 |
| 11.9-10 | 55 | 9.9-10 | 48 |
| 11.11 | 54 | 9.10 | 41 |
| 11.11-16 | 55 | 9.19-23 | 258 |

| | | | |
|---|---|---|---|
| 10.1-11 | 263 | 3.29 | 256 |
| 10.11 | 30, 31, 41, 48, 53 | 3-4 | 33 |
| | | 4.1-11 | 247 |
| 11.1 | 258 | 4.8-9 | 247 |
| 12.2 | 247 | 5.1 | 237 |
| 12.26 | 242 | 5.8 | 248 |
| 13.9 | 10 | 6.14-15 | 252 |
| 15.15 | 262 | | |
| 15.22-25 | 74 | *Eph* | |
| 15.28 | 259 | 1.18 | 164 |
| 15.49 | 209 | 1.20 | 262 |
| 15,51 | 55 | 2.7 | 210 |
| | | 2.11-18 | 241 |
| *2 Cor/2 Kor* | | 4.24 | 210 |
| 1.3 | 210 | 4.25-32 | 210 |
| 1.9 | 262, 262 | 4.28 | 210 |
| 1.20 | 29 | 4.32 | 210 |
| 3 | 22, 28 | 5.1-2 | 210-211 |
| 3.12-18 | 42 | 5.21-6.9 | 265 |
| 3.15 | 36 | 6.9 | 250 |
| 3.15-16 | 60 | | |
| 3.16-17 | 34 | *Phil* | |
| 3.18 | 17, 20, 21, 22 | 1.27 | 246 |
| 4.6 | 259 | 2.1,8 | 210 |
| 4.14 | 214, 262 | 2.6 | 110, 153 |
| 5.10 | 203 | 2.6-11 | 153, 253 |
| 5.14-19 | 252 | 2.11 | 257 |
| 5.15 | 263 | 3.20 | 246 |
| 5.17 | 209 | 3.21 | 209 |
| 5.17-19 | 263 | 4.8 | 265 |
| 9.6-10 | 217 | | |
| 10.1 | 210 | *Col/Kol* | |
| 11.2-3 | 99 | 1.15 | 153 |
| 11.24 | 27 | 1.16 | 110, 157 |
| | | 1.16-17 | 207 |
| *Gal* | | 2.8-23 | 247 |
| 1.1 | 214, 262 | 2.12 | 214, 262 |
| 1.1,11-12,15-16 | 257 | 2.16-3.11 | 249 |
| 1.6 (15) | 248 | 3.4 | 23 |
| 2.6 | 250 | 3.10 | 209 |
| 2.16 | 258 | 3.12,14 | 210 |
| 2.20 | 4, 22 | 3.25 | 250 |
| 3.6-9 | 257, 262 | | |
| 3.8 | 30 | *1 Thess* | |
| 3.13 | 36 | 1.4 | 253 |
| 3.15-18 | 257 | 1.9 | 247 |
| 3.16 | 257 | 1.10 | 263 |
| 3.19 | 256 | 2.3-6 | 250 |
| 3.19-22 | 257 | 2.14-16 | 27, 33, 53 |
| 3,20 | 256 | 4.9 | 265 |
| 3.20a | 256, 257 | 4.14 | 89 |
| 3.21-22 | 257 | 5.24 | 248 |

| | | | |
|---|---|---|---|
| 6.17-19 | 217 | 2.5 | 115 |
| | | 2.5-9 | 125 |
| *1 Tim* | | 2.5-18 | 111, 121 |
| 1.17 | 256 | 2.6 | 115 |
| 2.5 | 256 | 2.6-8 | 113 |
| 3.16 | 153 | 2.6-9 | 112, 114, 115 |
| 6.15-16 | 253 | 2.9 | 115 |
| | | 2.9a | 115 |
| *2 Tim* | | 2.9b | 115 |
| 2.8 | 263 | 2.11 | 121 |
| | | 2.12 | 112 |
| *Titus/Tit* | | 2.13 | 112 |
| 3.4 | 210 | 2.17 | 121 |
| | | 3.1-5 | 111 |
| *Heb/Hebr* | | 3.3 | 6 |
| 1.1 | 108, 109, 111, 124 | 3.6 | 110 |
| | | 3.7-4.13 | 112, 118, 122 |
| 1.1-2 | 110 | 3.7-4.11 | 118 |
| 1.1-4 | 108 | 3.11-19 | 263 |
| 1.1-6 | 109 | 4.1-2 | 122 |
| 1.1-12 | 109 | 4.7 | 111 |
| 1.1-14 | 109 | 4.14 | 110 |
| 1.2 | 157 | 5.5 | 110, 112, 113 |
| 1.2a | 108, 109, 110, 111, 112, 124 | 5.1 | 116 |
| | | 5.1-3 | 119 |
| 1,2β | 110 | 5.2-3 | 121 |
| 1.2bα | 114 | 5.5-10 | 111 |
| 1.2bβ | 110, 114 | 5.6 | 112, 113 |
| 1.3a | 109, 110, 115 | 5.6b | 115 |
| 1.3a.b | 121 | 5.7-10 | 121 |
| 1.3b | 110 | 5.8 | 110 |
| 1.3c | 118, 121 | 5.9 | 121 |
| 1.3d | 115, 116 | 5.10 | 115 |
| 1.3d,4 | 116 | 6.4 | 164 |
| 1.5 | 110 | 6.6 | 110 |
| 1.5a | 112, 113 | 6.12,13-20 | 118 |
| 1.5b | 112, 113, 124 | 6.20 | 110 |
| 1.6 | 112 | 7.1-3 | 116 |
| 1.6b | 117 | 7.3,11,15 | 115 |
| 1.7 | 112, 117 | 7.3,28 | 110 |
| 1.8 | 110 | 7.4 | 111 |
| 1.8a | 115 | 7.5,12,16,18-19,28 | 119 |
| 1.8-9 | 112, 113, 115 | 7.8.23,28 | 116 |
| 1.9b | 115 | 7.11 | 118, 121 |
| 1.10 | 110, 114 | 7.11-28 | 122 |
| 1.10-12 | 112, 117 | 7.11,19 | 119 |
| 1.13 | 112, 113 | 7.12 | 122 |
| 1.13a | 116 | 7.15-17,23-25 | 116 |
| 1.13b | 115 | 7.16 | 116 |
| 2.1-4 | 122 | 7.17,21 | 112, 113, 115 |
| 2.2 | 111 | 7.18 | 119, 122 |
| 2.3 | 109, 122 | 7.19 | 121 |

| | | | |
|---|---|---|---|
| 7.22 | 123 | 10.3 | 120 |
| 7.24 | 116 | 10.4 | 120, 123 |
| 7.25 | 116, 121 | 10.5a | 123 |
| 7.26-27 | 121 | 10.5-8 | 112 |
| 7.27 | 121 | 10.5-10 | 111, 123 |
| 7.27-28 | 118, 121 | 10.7 | 112 |
| 7.28 | 110, 122 | 10.8 | 123 |
| 8.1 | 115 | 10.9 | 123 |
| 8.1-2 | 116 | 10.9-10 | 123 |
| 8.1-2,5 | 118 | 10.9b,18 | 122 |
| 8.1-10,18 | 121 | 10.10 | 121 |
| 8.4 | 119 | 10.10-12 | 123 |
| 8.6 | 256 | 10.10,14,29 | 121 |
| 8.7 | 119, 123 | 10.11 | 119 |
| 8.7-13 | 118, 122 | 10.11-18 | 122 |
| 8.7,13 | 118 | 10.12 | 121 |
| 8.8-12 | 112 | 10.12-13 | 115 |
| 8.8,13 | 123 | 10.14 | 121 |
| 8.12 | 121 | 10.15-17 | 112 |
| 8.13 | 122 | 10.16-17 | 122 |
| 9,1,18 | 118 | 10.16,29 | 123 |
| 9.2-5 | 119 | 10.17 | 121 |
| 9.6-10 | 119 | 10.18 | 121 |
| 9.7 | 121 | 10.19-25 | 121 |
| 9.8-9 | 120, 121 | 10.22 | 120, 121 |
| 9.9 | 120 | 10.26-31 | 122 |
| 9.9-10 | 119 | 10.28 | 111, 119 |
| 9.11-12,24 | 118 | 10.29 | 110 |
| 9.11-12,24-25 | 121 | 10.32 | 164 |
| 9.11-15 | 120 | 10.35-39 | 122 |
| 9.12 | 121 | 10.37-38 | 112 |
| 9.14 | 118, 121 | 11 | 83 |
| 9.14.25-26,28 | 121 | 11.2 | 109 |
| 9.15 | 118, 121, 123, 256 | 11.8-16,39-40 | 118 |
| | | 11.32 | 111 |
| 9.15,23-28 | 120 | 12.22-23 | 118 |
| 9.19 | 111, 121 | 12.2 | 115, 116 |
| 9.19-20,22 | 119 | 12.14 | 118 |
| 9.20 | 118 | 12.24 | 123, 256 |
| 9.22 | 120 | 12.25 | 109, 111 |
| 9.22b | 118 | 12.25-29 | 122 |
| 9.25 | 119 | 13.11 | 119 |
| 9.26 | 112, 121 | 13.12 | 121 |
| 9.28 | 121 | 13.20 | 123 |
| 10.1 | 6, 109, 119, 121, 124 | *Jas/Jak* | |
| 10.1-2 | 120 | 2.1,9 | 250 |
| 10.1-2,4 | 119 | 2.26 | 72 |
| 10.1-4 | 123 | 3.9 | 204 |
| 10.1,8 | 118 | | |
| 10.4 | 123, 125 | *1 Pet/1 Petr* | |
| 10.1,11 | 119 | 1.15 | 248 |

| | | | |
|---|---|---|---|
| 1.16 | 217 | *Did* | |
| 1.17 | 246, 250 | 4.3,10 | 250 |
| 1.21 | 262 | | |
| 2.9 | 248 | *1 Clem* | |
| 2.11 | 246 | 4.1-7 | 101 |
| 3.20 | 210 | | |
| | | *Ign Magn* | |
| *2 Pet/2 Petr* | | 8.2 | 247 |
| 1.3 | 248 | | |
| | | *Barn* | |
| *1 John/1 Joh* | | 19.4,7 | 250 |
| 1.6,10 | 101 | | |
| 2.4,21-22,27 | 101 | *Pol Phil* | |
| 2.8 | 162 | 6.1 | 250 |
| 2.10 | 96 | | |
| 2.10-11 | 98 | *Justin* | |
| 2.11 | 96 | Dial 11.1 | 263 |
| 3 | 101, 102 | | |
| 3.7 | 99 | *Melito* | |
| 3.8 | 99 | Peri Pascha 1-45 | 263 |
| 3.8-9 | 99 | | |
| 3.8,12,18 | 101 | *Irenæus* | |
| 3.9 | 100, 101 | Adv haer | |
| 3.10, | 99 | 4.15.2 | 76 |
| 3.11-12 | 98 | 4.30,4 | 263 |
| 3.12 | 101 | | |
| 3.13 | 101 | *Tertullian* | |
| 3.15 | 98 | Adv Iud 7 | 245 |
| 3.22 | 98 | | |
| 4.10 | 265 | *Tatian* | |
| 4.19 | 218 | Or Graec 15.11 | 115 |
| 4.20 | 101 | | |
| 5.10 | 101 | *Hippolyt* | |
| 5.13 | 97 | V 8.5 | 158 |
| | | | |
| *2.John/2 Joh* | | *Ad Diognet* | |
| 11 | 101 | 1.1 | 245-246 |
| | | 2 | 246 |
| *Rev/Offb* | | 3 | 246 |
| 7 | 128 | 5 | 246 |
| 7.14 | 126, 139 | | |
| 7.14-17 | 126 | *Theophilus, Ad Autolycum* | |
| 7.14,17 | 7 | 1.2,14 | 246 |
| 7.17 | 126 | | |
| 14.7 | 136 | *Clemens* | |
| 22.14 | 140 | Strom VI 5.39-41 | 246 |
| | | Exc Theod 41.4 | 164 |
| | | | |
| | | *Origenes* | |
| D.PATRISTIC TEXTS | | In Joh II.14 | 158 |
| | | XIII,7 | 246 |
| | | C Cel 5.6 | 247 |

E. GNOSTIC TEXTS

*EvPhil*
61.6-10      99

*NHC* II/ 5,145,24-146,11
           151
*NHC* VIII/2    168
   136.12-13    166
*NHC* XIII
   35.12-13    161
   36.16,23-26    168
   36.33-37.1    158
   37.18-20    168
   38.11-12    158
   39.13-40.4    158
   40.4-19    158
   40.29-41.2    161
   41.1,16    161
   46.31-33    165
   47.28-29    161
   47.28-34    161
   47.31-34    158

*BG*
63.18-64.1    161

*CHerm*
I.32    168


F. RABBINICAL TEXTS

*Ab*
3.18    261

*Ber*
1,4-5    261

*Tamid*
5.1    261

*mSan*
4.5    101

*Pes*
54a    151

*Mek Exod*
12.41    261
15.11    257
20.16    264

*Pirke R. Elizer*
21 and 22    99

*Sifre Lev*
19.18    264

*Sifre Num*
§ 84    261

*Sifre Deut*
45    100

*Gen R*
1.1    261
34    264
49.10    257

*Num R*
11.2    260